Korea's
Kyongju

Cultural Spirit of Silla in Korea

Text and Photos
by
Edward B. Adams

Seoul International Tourist Publishing Company
33-16 Nonhyon-dong, Kangnam-ku, Seoul, Korea Tel. 542-9308

Copyright ©1983 by Seoul International Tourist Publishing Company
First published January 1979
Second printing: June, 1983
Printed and bound by Samhwa Printing Co., Ltd., Seoul, Korea

Author's address: c/o Seoul International School
                       4-1 Hwayang-dong, Songdong-ku, Seoul, Korea

Publisher's address: 33-16 Nonhyun-dong, Kangnam-ku, Seoul, Korea
                       Tel: 542-9308
                       Registration No. 14-9

Price: ₩10,000

Korea's
Kyongju

Cultural Spiritof Silla in Korea
By Edward B. Adams
Seoul Int'l Tourist Publishing Co.

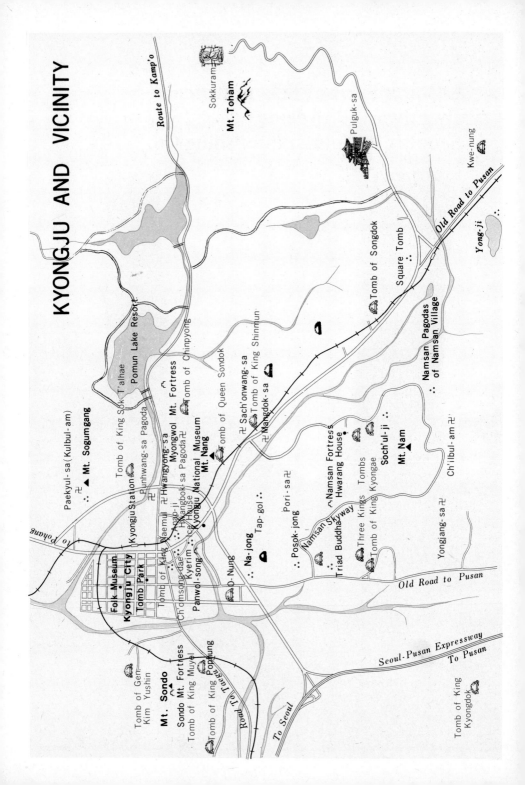

TABLE OF CONTENTS

CHAPTER IV

HISTORIC SITES BETWEEN KYONGJU, PULGUK-SA AND BEYOND

CHAPTER V

THE MANY VALLEYS OF SACRED SOUTH MOUNTAIN

CHAPTER VI

MAJOR ATTRACTIONS WEST OF KYONGJU CITY

CHAPTER VII

HISTORIC SITES FROM KYONGJU TO THE EASTERN COAST

CHAPTER VIII

PLACES OF INTEREST NORTH OF KYONGJU

CHAPTER IX

FURTHER BEYOND THE SILLA CAPITAL

APPENDIX & INDEX

Distance on all maps is shown in kilometers (kilos).

INTRODUCTION

Kyongju has always held for me an aura of mystery and fascination. I first visited Kyongju in 1966 shortly after my arrival to Korea. Since then I have visited this ancient capital of the Silla Dynasty no less than eighty times, wandering up wooded valleys and over rocky mountain slopes in search of hidden Buddhist remains still to be found. Ten years ago Kyongju City was a rural little town of 80,000 citizens and not many foreigners frequented the area.

However, changes have taken place as this hub of Silla art, where marvelous sculptural remnants have stood for over a millennium, is becoming known to the Western world. Though there has been a growing wealth of information in print concerning Korea there has been little research accomplished outside of the museums concerning the "Golden Age" of arts of ancient Korea found throughout the countryside.

Recently the Korean government has given impetus to a growing concern and pride in their own cultural heritage. Kyongju has been designated as the most valuable of the five major tourist centers in Korea. With the help of foreign loans Korea National Tourist Corporation is developing the Pomun Lake Resort, 2570 acres (1040 hectares) of land on the outskirts of Kyongju. Many of the major tourist attractions have been reconstructed with the purpose in mind of making them more available to foreign visitors.

However, *Kyongju Guide* is much more than a tourist handbook. An attempt has been made to present by photography a cultural heritage, which is becoming more difficult to see with each passing year in this rapidly developing nation. In some of the nooks of hidden valleys life in an earlier Korea can still be observed and enjoyed without the commercialism of a folk culture village.

The apparent emphasis of *Kyongju Guide* is to portray the incredible skill of the artisans of ancient Silla but the ultimate intent is to depict photographic glimpses of the spirit of a creative people and an art culture which in many respects rivaled that of early China. In one aspect the researched information in *Kyongju Guide* is comprehensive for students of Korean studies yet it is also suitable for casually interested tourists who are only visiting Korea for a few days.

A total of 350 color photographs, many in full page spreads, and 296 black and white prints offer a unique visual impression to *Kyongju Guide.* For the average tourist or foreign resident in Korea the cultural heritage of this country is what they wish to see and study. Using the many photographs, an attempt is made to follow a loose pictorial thread of visual beauty found in the Korean countryside, while observing traditional customs which illustrate a marvelous heritage inherited by the Koreans.

Recently there has been an upsurge of pride demonstrated by the government in promoting the heritage of Korea's past tradition. Koreans are now proud of their rich cultural legacy which is unparalleled in Asia. The Pomun Lake Development Project near Kyongju is certainly one example of Korea's effort to promote its unique culture to the world.

Through the eyes of one foreigner who has lived in Korea for many years a glimpse can be taken of an artistic legacy, which lasted for almost one thousand years. This tradition representing a "Golden Age" of religious devotion, is still relatively unknown to the Western world. Buddhism and Confucian thought blending with shamanism is a dominant cultural link flowing through the lives of the people. The historical remnants in the Kyongju vicinity express this religious theme which dominated the Silla period.

The first few chapters of *Kyongju Guide* describe the most popular tourist attractions for those with minimal time. The Kyongju National Museum should not be missed as well as Pulguk Temple. Later chapters are arranged according to geographic areas near Kyongju City. For the avid hiker the numerous valleys of Nam-san are highly recommended. Though there is one rough road over this mountainous area, most historic sites can only be reached by walking (from ten minutes to 1½ hours). *Kyongju Guide* concludes with a Tourist Directory which will give useful information for the tourist in Seoul or Kyongju, where to stay, where to eat and agencies helpful to tourists.

To render the many Korean names and words into the Roman alphabet a modified form of the McCune-Reischauer system of romanization is used without the diacritical marks. Some deviation was made from this system because of personal preference and the belief that the change would further aid the foreign reader, who is unfamiliar with the system, to more accurately pronounce Korean words.

One should be aware that there is also a very different system of romanization which was developed by the Ministry of Education (MOE) which is presently in use on many maps and signs throughout the country. The southern province of Cholla-pukto becomes Jeonra-bugdo and Kyongju becomes Gyeongju while personal names of Kim and Pak (Park) become Gim and Bag. The most well-known Sokkuram grotto becomes Seoggulam. To avoid the many problems inherent in the different romanization systems the newcomer should try to learn the Korean phonetic han'gul alphabet which is one of the easiest in the world.

Many portions of *Kyongju Guide* have already appeared as articles in the Korea Herald or Korea Times over the past seven years. It was in 1971 that I began in earnest to prepare for this publication. Over fourteen maps are included which give road distances in kilometers (kilos). Hiking trails have very few signs but one should not become discouraged as it is virtually impossible to become lost in the mountains.

In the publication of any book there are always many who assist and greatly contribute to the material. Probably my greatest indebtedness is to Jung Pyung-jo, Coordinator for Public Relations at Dongguk University. I first became acquainted with him in 1971 at Youngnam University in Taegu. Together we have traveled unbelievable miles of trails in our search for treasures. His depth of understanding in the realm of Buddhist thought belie the age of this young scholar who is now a leading authority in the field of Buddhism.

Others who have served as advisors for portions of the manuscript were Hwang Su-young, Dean of the Graduate School, Director of the museum at Dongguk University and former Director of the National Museum; Rhi Ki-yong, professor of Dongguk University and Dean of Academic Research for Korean Studies; Kang Woo-bang, Research Director of the Kyongju National Museum; and Ha Hyo-gil of the Cultural Preservation Office, Kyongju. Also in Kyongju the assistance rendered by the family of Choe Nam-ju was truly appreciated. Without the assistance of Kang Woo-bang and Choe Nam-ju many of the more remote and difficult sites would have been almost impossible to locate.

My appreciation goes also to members of the Ministry of Culture and Information. Permission to photograph the Sokkuram was essential to the publication of this book. It is unfortunate that now visitors are not permitted to enter the grotto and hopefully this situation will be rectified in the near future. Also the cooperation and assistance rendered by the officials of KNTC is appreciated as this publication is helping to give impetus to the tourist promotion prior to the 1979 PATA conference in Korea.

My appreciation is also extended to Kim Jin-sam and Ahn Dae-ung of the Samhwa staff who dilegently supervised the typesetting, color separation, printing and binding of *Kyongju Guide*. Choi Dong-ho served as map designer and accomplished an outstanding job of rendering my many sketches into readable road maps for the *Kyongju Guide.*

James Wade, who is well known to friends of Korea, served as an excellent proof-reader where my limitations in literary accomplishments began to show. My indebtedness is great for Kim Hyung-shik who served long hours for the promotion of the *Kyongju Guide* in the Korean community. His assistance for the arrangement of the Japanese translation which resulted in a Japanese edition is truly appreciated.

Also a large share of my appreciations goes to the staff of Seoul International Tourist Publishing Company and my wife who worked long hours in the final preparation for this publication. The difficult chore of layout, checking and rechecking proofs and a multitude of legwork necessary before the publication reaches the public is only an aspect that someone involved in publications can really appreciate.

E.B. Adams

Korea's Kyongju
Cultural Spirit
of Silla

Festival Time in Kyongju

The Whirl of the Farmer's Dance

At Work in the Countryside

HISTORIC OVERVIEW OF SILLA

The legends, history and pageantry of ancient Silla have echoed down the years leaving a legacy of beauty and mystery across the Kyongju valley where in a capital city of one million people, kings and queens once reigned supreme for almost a millennium. The vibrant achievements of Silla culture, carried to unprecedented heights, can still be felt in today's society. Visits to the many ruins give the tourist some idea of the city's magnificent scale, height of cultural attainment and great superiority in arts and learning during Korea's "golden age."

From 57 BC through the next millennium of Silla Dynasty rule geographic isolation was an important factor which somewhat delayed the kingdom's cultural growth but without a doubt saved the kingdom from China's predatory advances. The brave young *hwarang* warriors were equal to the task of military defense while the rulers knew the advantages of strategic alliances.

In the seventh century Silla turned to defeat the other two Korean kingdoms in a coalition with T'ang China. Paekche fell in 660 and Koguryo in 668. Because China was unable to subjugate Silla she soon left all the territorial peninsula south of the Taedong River to Silla. Unified Silla came to a peaceful end in the tenth century leaving undamaged scores of valuable remains for study by scholars in the twentieth century.

left: *Silla tiles excavated from a kiln site north of Kyongju.* below: *A scholar's villa rests on the slopes of Soak-san.* next page: *The moon rises over Kyongju's largest tomb mound. (HS-39)*

Dawn of History

It is not exactly known when the Old Stone Age began in Korea. The recent discoveries of palaeolithic remains near Kongju suggest that Korea developed a palaeolithic culture tens of thousands of years ago. The New Stone Age developed possibly 8000 BC when neolithic people of Altaic ancestry inhabited regions along the riversides and coastal areas. Stone implements gradually gave way to bronze tools during the eighth century before Christ.

Though there were many tribal states on the Korean peninsula, the Kingdom of Choson is believed to have been the most powerful. Ancient countries often trace their origin to a legend and this is the case with Korea. Korea's earliest records tell of Ung, a god who visited earth in the regions of the Paektu-san (Ever-White Mountain) at the head waters of the Yalu River, and who transformed a bear into a woman. Their offspring was Tan-gun who assumed leadership and called his kingdom *Choson* which denotes "morning freshness and calm." His capital was established at Pyong-yang in 2333 BC. This event is honored by Korean Foundation Day (Tan-gun Day), a National Holiday which comes in the autumn of each year.

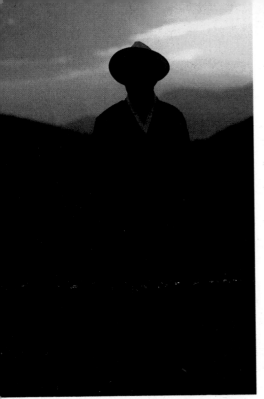

the dynasty's capital until 936 AD.

The rise of the Three Kingdoms in Korea coincided with the decline of the Han Dynasty in China which finally fell in 220 AD. During the next four hundred years the Three Kingdoms were left free to develop without Chinese political interference. An uneasy balance of power existed among the Three Kingdoms until well into the seventh century and might have continued had not events in China intervened.

In 618 the T'ang Dynasty replaced the Sui and the new rulers were to preside over one of the most brilliant eras in Chinese history which also reached a peak of influence over neighboring countries. Wishing to dominate the Korean peninsula, the T'ang court decided to take advantage of the hostilities between the Three Kingdoms and play one off against the other.

Joining forces with Silla the Chinese T'ang troops first attacked Paekche and the kingdom fell in 660. The Silla troops were led by the famed General Kim Yu-shin, a remarkable military leader whose exploits are celebrated

Three Kingdoms Period (57BC-668AD):

In the first century BC the many tribal states were consolidated through wars into three powerful kingdoms, Silla, Koguryo and Paekche. Located close to China, Koguryo was most influenced by Chinese culture including the introduction of Buddhism. Initially Koguryo emerged as the most powerful and advanced of the three kingdoms and founded its capital in Pyongyang (now northern Korea's capital). Paekche in southwest Korea had its capitals in Kongju and finally Puyo.

Though established before Koguryo or Paekche, in 57 BC, Silla was the last to develop as a dominant nation and was more aristocratic and less war-like. At first the Silla monarchy rotated among the Pak, Sok and Kim clans. In the mid-fourth century the kingdom became permanently hereditary in the Kim Clan. Kyongju valley, the cradle of Silla culture, was

The end of a day as darkness settles over the valleys.

in Korea today. Defeating the fierce and proud Asian warriors of the north was no easy matter but because of dissension in the Koguryo court the dynasty fell in 668.

Claiming Paekche and Koguryo territory, T'ang China fully intended to occupy Silla as well. However, revolts within the territories were supported rather than suppressed by Silla leaders. When T'ang armies were dispatched to suppress the revolts, the Silla forces defeated them in a conclusive battle. After bickering and face-saving, a treaty was made under which China recognized Silla as an independent state ruling all the area south of the Taedong River near Pyongyang. The Korean peninsula for the first time achieved unification.

During the pre-unification period of Silla several important leaders rose to prominence. In 424 Buddhism was informally introduced by Priest A-do (or the "black monk" Muk-ho-ja, but they may have been the same person). Priest A-do's missionary zeal was doomed to failure as the Silla people were unwilling to accept the new religion, unlike their neighbors Paekche and Koguryo.

After the martyrdom of the court official Yi Ch'a-don in 527, who prophesied that his own blood would run white as milk after his death to illustrate the truth of Buddhism, the faith prospered throughout Silla. This event occurred during the reign of Pob-hung (23rd king) who later stepped down from the throne to become a Buddhist priest, while his queen became a nun.

In 503 Confucianism was introduced and at the same time certain practices, such as the live burial of attendants with deceased members of the royal families, were discontinued by edict. Chin-hung (24th king), one of Silla's stronger rulers, expanded the kingdom and set up four boundary stones which remain to this day. One tablet is now located in the corridors of the Kyongbok Palace of Seoul but once stood on a peak behind the capital city, two are still to be found in north Korea and one can be seen in Changyong Town in southwest Kyongsang-namdo.

From 632 to 654 two queens inherited the

throne in their own right which indicated a significant difference between ancient Silla practices and the male dominated hierarchy of China. Queen Son-dok quickly established good relations with T'ang China and introduced many foreign customs which included Chinese fashions in court dress, improvement in technological fields and cultural innovations which were in vogue in China. She sent students to Chinese universities, built temples and schools, astutely patronizing Confucianism and shamanism as well as the state religion of Buddhism. One of her passionate interests was astronomy and she built for the court a "star gazing tower" called *chomsong-dae* which can still be seen. This observatory is considered one of the oldest structures left from the Silla period.

Queen Son-dok personally sponsored and supported a military-religious school for young men selected to be trained in a chivalrous code called *hwarang-do*. Had it not been for these accomplished men, the ablest of whom was General Kim Yu-shin, Silla might have been conquered by China in the succeeding years. Under Queen Son-dok's nephew Mu-yol and later King Mu-yol's son Mun-mu (30th king) Silla finally achieved unification.

The Unified Silla Period (668-936):

From 676 for two and a half centuries Silla reached a peak of prosperity and influence unequalled in most parts of the world. Freed from local and foreign wars, this era was marked by peace and great cultural advances in all the arts. Foreign visitors, including some Arabian merchants, appeared in Korea attracted by Silla's reputation. The capital city which is the present site of Kyongju City reached a population of over one million people, ten times the size of the present city.

Buddhism continued to spread and prosper as new sects were introduced from T'ang China and quickly took root. Buddhist learning as well as art continued to flourish in the capital and also in the far provinces. Today some of Korea's outstanding treasured relics come from the creative genius and religious fervor of the artisans of this period. Broken images, carved reliefs and pagoda fragments are now scattered in great number about the vicinity of Kyongju making this valley a country-side museum.

Korea's most remarkable temple, Pulguk-sa, situated a few miles from Kyongju City, was recently renovated by the government. A stone cave behind Pulguk-sa, the Sokkuram grotto, was created during the reign of Kyong-dok (35th king) and is estimated by world scholars as the most unique and classically beautiful piece of Buddhist sculpture in the Far East.

Confucian political ideas were also put into practice as Chinese family names became more common among the lettered classes. Korean scholars who were stimulated by Confucian Chinese literature developed an indigenous literture consisting of native poetry, memoirs and history. This Korean literary development was made possible by the invention of *idu* by the scholar Sol Ch'ong who was the illegitimate son of the famed Priest Won-hyo.

The *idu* was an outcry against the difficulty other peoples had when using Chinese characters and a plea for literary development. The most far-reaching result that we have today

left: Buddhist remnants found in Kyongju's National Museum. right: The twin pagodas of Namsan Village are silhouetted against the early evening sky. (T-124)

was the development of the *hyangga* which were folk songs composed by people who had little education in the Chinese letters. Developed by the Silla people with the use of *idu*, the *hyangga* is truly unique to Korea and many of these compositions remain today.

By the end of the ninth century Korea was able to produce many of its own outstanding scholars. Ch'oe Ch'i-won sometimes called the "father of Korean literature" was considered the most renowned. Though a prolific writer, few of his works are extant.

In this same era the political ties between Korea and China were strong and Silla was carefully watched by the T'ang administration which was interested in keeping the Korean peninsula a model border area. Economically, ties with China were also strong and important for both countries. Koreans were usually in control of shipment throughout the Yellow Sea and even Japanese travelers had to contract passage on Korean vessels. Commodities for export were silks, horses, ginseng, furs and rice paper. Korean paper even in ancient days was highly prized in China for documents, calligraphy and painting.

The increase of trade and travel stimulated the people to broader intellectual achievements. While absorbing the fully matured culture of T'ang, the Silla people nurtured and developed a cultural individuality of their own. Their success in achieving this may be gauged in part by their art, enough of which remains to show that Silla at its best closely rivaled some of the brilliance of T'ang.

The chief channel of foreign importation was through Buddhism and the first institution to grow under its guidance was the religious, military and chivalric organization called the *hwarang-do*, or the way of the knighthood (literally translated as "flower youths"). This "way" included a code of personal conduct, and philosophy of service. Through the *hwarang-do* schooling, an elite corps of public officials was recruited and trained over a ten year period to be later employed by the state. The martial arts were stressed as well as the Buddhist ideals of self sacrifice and compassion for the weak. The *hwarang* corps led the fighting forces of the king and owed personal loyalty to him. Largely through this system Silla was able to weather many crises, both domestic and foreign.

After the 8th century Silla began a gradual decline, stemming partly from the contradictions involved in applying the Confucian Chinese system to an aristocratic society. The battle for power between the many factional parties was one principal reason for Silla decline. Weak and immoral rulers further caused rebellions to persist. Finally in 927 the capital was sacked and the king who was reveling unconcernedly at Posok-jong was killed. A few years later his successor abdicated and General Wang-gon established the kingdom of Koryo. Thus the great dynasty of Silla which lasted almost a full millennium came to an end in 936.

From this time the capital of Silla came to be known as Kyongju. The new Koryo capital was established in Songdo (Kaesong), a city north of Seoul and presently just across the DMZ. Kyong-sun, the last Silla king, moved to the Koryo capital and lived out his days in honorable dignity. Kyong-sun died in 978.

below: *The* hwarang *warrior greets visitors at the expressway entrance.* right: *Kyongju has one hundred thousand inhabitants.*

Korea's Culture City Today:

Royal tombs, temple sites with weathered stone pagodas and Buddhist reliefs, as well as fortress ruins are scattered around the vicinity of this ancient Silla capital. Many of ancient Korea's most unique sculptured art objects of this early Buddhist heritage can often be found well off the beaten trails and tourist haunts. Recently the government has been developing the Kyongju region into an outdoor museum for tourists. Many of the more popular sites can be visited with ease over paved roads.

Kyongju is Korea's "culture city" and for anyone truly interested in delving further into Korean antiquities a visit to the many sites near this ancient capital is essential. Between 1973—76 several Silla tombs were completely excavated by government decree. Many gold objects and other treasures were brought to light and are found in the museums of Kyongju and Seoul. A "white horse" painting delicately designed on a birch bark saddle guard was discovered in nearly perfect condition in a sixth century tomb. In 1976 the "Heavenly Horse Tomb" was opened to the public as a result of the Tomb Park development.

The new Kyongju Museum was dedicated in 1975 on the outskirts of the city. It is one of the finest museums of the country because an abundant amount of art objects are tastefully displayed both within the buildings and scattered over the grounds. The focus of attention as one enters through the main gate is the giant Emillie Bell famous for its legend as well as craftsmanship. The museum was constructed on a Silla palace building site which was accidentally found during the course of ground preparation. Behind the museum are replicas of the famed Tabo-t'ap and Sokka-t'ap located at Pulguk-sa. Another large stone pagoda was moved from the site of Koson-sa near Kyongju and is listed as a National Treasure.

A full day is needed to see the highlights of Kyongju's marvelous culture but two or three days are really recommended. For the serious student of Silla culture two months in this vicinity of Kyongju is not enough time to visit all the known historic sites and see the stone remains still found far from the beaten paths.

Chapter I
Some Major Attractions of Kyongju Vicinity

1. O-Nung: *Foundation Legend of Early Silla*
(Historic Site No. 172)

In a shady grove of regal pines are five mounds which are considered the traditional tombs for the first, second, third and fifth kings as well as the kingdom's first queen. The fourth ruler Sok T'al-hae was buried north of Kyongju City near Paegyul-sa, at the foot of Sogumgang Mountain.

In 4 AD Pak Hyok-ko-se (1st king) died and was buried. After seven days his queen also passed away and was buried next to him. It was said that they were inseparable. Because of the other three kings also buried within the tomb enclosure this tomb complex is referred to as O-nung (Five Tombs).

A legend is told that after the queen died the people tried to bury her in the same tomb as King Hyok-ko-se but could not because a large reptile kept appearing to disturb the workmen. As a result the royal remains were divided into five parts and buried in five separate mounds. Even today these five tombs are sometimes referred to as Sa-nung (Reptile Tomb). As visitors gaze at the wild gyrations of the pine trunks in this grove of trees they are reminded of this legend and ponder if this reptile could still be lurking about.

Before the birth of Silla six village chiefs held a council on the slopes of Nam-san (South Mountain) and agreed to merge their territories into one kingdom. They named their country *sorabol*. (It is now interesting to note that the name of Korea's present capital of Seoul was probably derived from this word *sorabol* which means capital.)

This popular legend further tells that, while these six village chieftains were gathered to contemplate who should be their new king, a great ball of light suddenly fell near a well called Na-jong in the valley below. At this place a shining white horse was seen.

As they approached, the white steed rose through a rainbow in the sky and disappeared, leaving behind a large egg-like gourd called *pagaji* on a rock near the well. The gourd was broken and within was found a small boy whose noble face shone like the sun. This youth at the age of 13 became Hyok-ko-se (Bright Ruler), first king of Silla, in the year 57 BC.

North of this memorial shrine near the traditional tomb site of Hyok-ko-se is another well called Aryong-jong with another legend. Deep inside this well lived a she-dragon and

left: A pleasing serenity is found in a mountain stream of Nam-san. below: Floats in a festival depict the six village chieftains who discovered Pak Hyok-ko-se in a gourd. He was to be appointed as Silla's first king.

from the rib of this dragon a girl appeared who was called Ar-yong. The village elders raised these two children. They gave the boy the name of *pak*, the first symbol of the native word for the gourd (*pagaji*) within which he was found. Even today this is a common family name in Korea. At age sixteen the young king married Princess Ar-yong.

The memorial shrine Sungdok-jon for the first king of Silla is large and complex. The largest tablet within a walled pavilion gives the history of this shrine. Sungdok-jon was erected during the late Yi Dynasty reign of Yong-jo (21st Yi king) in 1759. It is believed by the local people that even though the rock is protected by a roofed pavilion, when it rains this tablet also becomes moist.

Within the first compound behind the main gate is a gnarled cyprus tree, the trunk of which is carefully bound by straw rope. Superstitious belief has endured over the years that if a barren woman would drink tea boiled with the bark, she would readily conceive and bear children. Because the tree was endangered through complete loss of bark the local authorities wrapped the trunk of this unique cyprus with protective straw rope.

Scenes at O-nung portray the five tomb mounds and memorial shrine of Sungdok-jon. (HS-172)

2. Posok-jong: *The Great Tragedy in the Declining Years of Silla (Historic Site No. 1)*

The summer pavilion of Posok-jong (Abalone Stone Pavilion) in closely linked to the final days of Silla. All that can now be seen are the irregular stone channels (15'×19') through which at one time a cool stream of water was directed during royal banquets.

As the later kings of Silla, who often forgot their royal duties, spent most of their time with women and wine, these pleasure houses became increasingly popular and were frequently seen in the countryside. However, Posok-jong is undoubtedly the most famous. Gaily painted banquet halls were erected in this area while the kings of Silla used these rock channels for their favorite recreation.

A cup of wine was set afloat and a specified guest was challenged to compose some verse before the cup reached a turn in the channel. The slow-witted poets were continually drunk because to fail in this sport meant to consume the wine from the cup as it floated past. Posok-jong's fame reached its pinnacle when one Silla king lost his life here as he ignored the warning of messengers who had reported the approach of the enemy.

Stand for a moment beside these rippling stones and reflect on this tragic episode which happened on the 3rd day of August 927. You too may be inspired to compose a poem under the Chinese elms which still shade this arbor.

Sweet wine in floating cups
will soon appear,
Raise your cup and toast while
before you I bow
If you drink this wine for a
kingly treasure,
Long life you'll enjoy and all
love's pleasure.
Lift your cup, I pray! Give a
poem, I say!
Take a cup of this wine of
perpetual bliss.
Sweet wine will give mind's
clarity to think

Silla kings into gold cups their
woes they sank,
And if you down the cup to
drown the sorrow,
You'll write a poem to last
ten thousand years.

The exact date of construction is unknown but we do know that the 49th king of Silla, Hon-gang, used Posok-jong as a pleasure palace. Traditionally it was built when a *shinson* (Spirit Being) from South Mountain appeared and danced before the king. During this period the years of Silla were numbered.

In the reign of King Hon-gang the famous general called Kyun-hwun was born. It was traditionally said that as a small child while his mother was leaving him unattended a tigress nursed him. This accounted for Kyun-hwun's wild and fierce temperment. He rose in the ranks of the Silla military but because of the corruption prevalent throughout the kingdom, he threw off Silla allegiance and gathered about him a band of malcontents.

Kyun-hwun continued to harrass both Silla and Koryo, though he was more successful with Silla. In 920 during the reign of Kyong-myong (54th king) Silla first recognized Koryo and sent an envoy to the courts of Songdo. Four years later the king died without heir so a younger brother became Kyong-ae (55th king). Both kings were from the Pak family rather than the Kim Clan. The once powerful Silla was now so weak that the records mentioned that kings had nothing left but their genealogy.

Kyun-hwun in the south and Koryo in the north were the dominant powers surrounding Silla. Kyun-hwun was keeping up a double fight against Koryo on one hand, and weakened Silla on the other. He burned and pillaged right to the gates of Kyongju. Kyun-hwun who been christened with the title of "King of Paekche" easily entered the Silla capital.

The king and his family were entertaining themselves at the summer pavilion of Posok-jong. It is believed that King Kyong-ae could have prepared for this invasion yet not taking heed fled at the last minute from his merry-making. The king was caught and murdered while the queen and many palace women were ravished by Kyun-hwun and his soldiers.

While Kyongju was being looted Kyun-hwun appointed Kyong-sun, who was a sixth generation descendant of Mun-song (46th king), to succeed the murdered king. King Kyong-sun was the last of 56 kings of Silla.

King Kyong-sun though placed on the throne by Kyun-hwun pledged his loyalty to the Koryo King Wang-gon. Kyun-hwun was now having difficulties in his own household as he had many wives and over ten sons. Kyun-hwun's favorite son was murdered and his eldest son seized his father and imprisoned him at the temple of Kumsan in Cholla Province.

But the wily old wolf managed to get his priestly guards uproarously drunk and escaped. With colossal impudence he wrote a letter to Wang-gon asking for asylum in Koryo against his own sons. This was granted and the battle-scarred veteran was received as a guest and given a house with servants near the Koryo capital.

In 936 King Kyong-sun of Silla was really determined to abdicate and hand over his kingdom to Wang-gon. After 993 years the tottering kingdom of Silla ceased to exist and from that day the capital city of Silla was called Kyongju.

There are very few cases in history which show greater generosity, leniency and mercy for the enemy than can be seen in the life of Wang-gon, the first king of Koryo. To provide a comfortable home of refuge for his life-long enemy, the old rogue Kyun-hwun, and to give protection to the despairing retired king of Silla, treating him as a guest, certainly points to a man with noble intent and purpose for his people and nation.

Gaiety and tragedy have been interlaced among the stones of Posok-jong, shaped as a huge abalone shell on the western slopes of Nam-san. The elms, large in trunk and gnarled with age, may have witnessed the fleeting years during the final tragic scenes of this drama. Listening closely one can almost hear the shrill laughter of the palace girls. . . smell the aroma of food mixed with the pungent sweet odor of wine. One can only envision the rollicking games that must have been played here many years ago. The cool waters flowing through the winding stone channels have long since ceased and now only the imagination holds a visitor who might pause to ponder.

3. Panwol-song: *Earliest Known Silla Palace*
(Historic Site No. 16)

This small artificial soil fortress is located near the center of Kyongju City and has become a popular park and recreation area for the town people of Kyongju and tourists. Panwol-song (Half Moon Fortress) was the heart of the Silla capital for here was located the palace. Anap-ji nearby was part of this palace complex but during the Japanese occupation a road was constructed which now bisects this historic palace site.

The fortress circumference is about 800 meters and of course as the name implies is shaped like a half moon. On the south side of the fortress flows the South Stream where the remains of two bridges Iljong (Sun Spirit) and Woljong (Moon Spirit) can still be seen.

Traditionally there were eight fortress gates and within the walls there were 21 buildings. Panwol-song was used as the site for the royal palace for nearly the entire dynasty period. The spacious gardens at Anap-ji were the site of Silla's surrender in 936, almost one thousand years later. Now large trees have grown along the earthen banks and little remains to typify the refinement of Silla royalty.

While resting on the banks above the South Stream we can push back the foggy centuries to Silla's beginning and see what was taking place in the heart of the kingdom. Nam-hae (2nd king) was on the throne. Into the capital walked a boy who legends claim was born from an egg heralded by magpies.

After some time he found a half moon shaped hill which contained a fine house belonging to a nobleman. The youth decided that this land should be his. He directed a friend to bury pieces of iron and some charcoal dust by the entrance of the nobleman's house.

left: *The stone channels of Posok-jong have become one of Kyongju's most popular attractions. (HS-1)* below: *A float in the Kyongju festival illustrates the birth of Sok T'al-hae, fourth ruler of Silla.*

The next day the youth called on the master of this house on half moon hill and stated that actually the residence belonged to his forefathers. Of course the nobleman denied this and after a violent quarrel a suit was brought before the king. "Can you prove that this house is yours?" demanded the king of the youth.

"Of course I can," he replied, "My grandfather was a blacksmith by trade. During the summer he went to visit a relative in a distant village and upon returning found this man in his house. He has been illegally occupying it ever since. Let the ground be dug up and the evidence will be found."

The king nodded to his servants and they went to dig up the area in front of the house. Of course they soon found pieces of iron and charcoal dust, the typical remains of a blacksmith at his trade. In this manner the youth gained the house. The king was impressed with the boy's wisdom (evidently not suspecting any dishonesty) and offered hi daughter in marriage.

King Nam-hae died in 24 AD and his son became King Yu-ri, ruling for thirty-three years. Upon the death of Yu-ri, this youth who had tricked the nobleman out of his home on half moon hill became King T'al-hae at age sixty-two. He was first of the Sok Clan to rule.

One belief is that the name of Sok was used because it means "old" referring to the fact that he regained his old homestead on half moon hill. However, the character for *sok* also means magpie, the bird that announced his arrival to the kingdom in the legend of his birth.

In the southern part of the fortress area is the shrine of Sungshin-jon (Respecting Spirit) which was built in 1906 to honor King T'al-hae.

Around the grounds in front is evidence of Silla stonework. Along with several foundation stones of unusually large size is a lotus petal base stone used for the well and a tablet base stone which is sixty inches square. A tablet and pavilion are seen to the right of the shrine. The caretaker is a member of the Sok Clan.

A sacred rooster and hen are kept in the shrine for Kim Al-chi, the progenitor of the ruling Kim Clan.

The Japanese authorities took an unusual liking for this particular king as legends state he came from islands beyond the eastern seas and he later was the first to promote relations with Japan as well as the outside world. More likely he was not from the Japanese Islands though, as his size would indicate; Sok T'al-hae according to tradition was over six feet six inches tall.

4. Sokping-go: *Ice Storehouse of Half Moon Fortress (Treasure No. 66)*

Near the east fortress wall toward Anap-ji is a fairly well preserved rock ice storage house. One can only look in through the doorway. The *Samguk Sagi* (History of the Three Kingdoms) mentions that Chi-jung (22nd king) in November of the sixth year of his reign instructed that a stone ice house be built on the palace grounds for the storage of ice over the summer months.

The cave is covered with sod and a stone ventilation hole is seen on the roof. Over one thousand stones were used in the construction. Arches were used in the ceiling's architectural design. The interior is 56 feet long, 20 feet wide and 18 feet high. Though it was probably reconstructed many times it is recorded that the final renovation was undertaken in 1741 during the reign of Yong-jo (21st Yi king).

5. Kyerim: *Legendary Origin of the Kim Family*
(Historic Site No. 19)

A white cock crowed at night near Panwol-song (Half Moon Fortress) and ushered into Silla during the reign of Sok T'al-hae (4th king) the first Kim of Korea. The legend of Kim Al-chi is as well known to every school age child of this country as the Pecos Bill tales are known to students in America. In 65 AD on the eighth month and fourth day a strange light illuminated a forest near Half Moon Fortress. The night mist hung in pallid stillness from heaven to earth.

In the early morning hours King T'al-hae was awakened in his palace by the strange raucous crowing of a rooster in the nearby woods. Early Westerners in Korea quickly learned to respect the Korean rooster. Dr. James S. Gale, pioneer, Canadian missionary who was a scholar and prolific writer, states in his *History of the Korean People* (1927):

"Cockcrowing is one of the characteristic sounds of this gentle nation. Practised through a long series of years, the Korean rooster is a perfect marvel as to crowing. Brass lungs with steam attachment can hardly express it. To have him break forth at 2 a.m. from the rafter point just over your

cottage window, injects into your peaceful sleep a splitting sense of uproar beyond words."

King T'al-hae hearing this earth-shattering, earsplitting sound of Korea's ancestral rooster and probably realizing that this was no ordinary bird sent out a servant to investigate fully this particular disturbance. A gold box was found dangling from a tree and was emanating a strange eery light. Nearby perched a white cock in regal splendor, poised and prepared to herald again this treasure with a vociferous cry.

The messenger immediately reported this mysterious incident to King T'al-hae who went out personally to open the box. Inside was found a beautiful baby boy. He was carried back to the palace while according to the legend birds and beasts followed him singing joyful melodies.

Now the third and greatest of the family clans who were to rule Silla came into existence. King T'al-hae chose an auspicious day and then formally named him Al-chi. He declared the boy would be crown prince and his son. He was given the family name of Kim which is written with the same Chinese character as *kum* (金) meaning gold, as the boy had been found in a gold box. The grove of trees where Kim Al-chi was discovered was named Kyerim (Chicken Forest) to honor the noisy rooster. Later during the reign of Mi-ch'u (13th king), the kingdom was called Kyerim (In 307 the name of Silla was formally used).

Kyerim may not seem a stately and lofty name for a country but perhaps well suited the personality of a people who were not the strongest on the peninsula in terms of military prowess. It is an interesting fact that the three family clans of Pak, Sok and Kim who ruled Silla for almost one thousand years all came

A festival float depicts the birth of Kim Al-chi in Kyerim, a forest grove near Panwol-song. The birth was heralded by a crowing rooster.

miraculously from a gourd, egg or were heralded by a chicken. In fact in those days the outside world referred to the citizens of Silla as the "chicken people."

The legends of the origins of the three royal families who ruled the Silla nation for almost a thousand years seem to lack luster and awesome strength to the Westerner familiar with chivalry and knighthood. To call a nation the "chicken people" might bring smiles. But we can be reminded of the teachings that to live by the sword is to die by the sword.

Known as a peaceful nation the Silla people's gentle spirit and their early rulers did well in laying the foundation for a dynasty which permitted Korea to develop to a high level of culture, art and intellect. How many other kingdoms of the East can boast a millennium of existence? Legends of course are difficult to believe but they do typify the thoughts and dreams of people enjoying a relatively quiet existence with minimal interference from more warlike neighbors.

Silla is the dynasty which gave to Korea its highest level of cultural achievement which some scholars believe even surpassed that of China. Without the help of T'ang China, Silla would never have survived the encroachment of her northern and western enemies. Thus she reached a golden peak during the seventh and eighth centuries attested to by the treasures now on display in the country's museums and located about the countryside near Kyongju.

When King T'al-hae died in 80 AD Kim Al-chi yielded his claim to the crown to King T'al-hae's son P'a-sa, a member of the Pak family, who it was felt had more legitimate claim to the throne. After 180 years a seventh generation descendant of Kim Al-chi became the first king from the Kim family and was called Mi-ch'u (13th king). Of the fifty-six kings of the Silla Dynasty thirty-eight were members of the Kim Clan.

Situated within this grove of Chinese elms is a walled compound. Inside this compound is an octagonal pavilion covering a six foot tablet. This memorial monument was erected in 1803 during the reign of Sun-jo (23rd Yi king). Half a mile away in front of the tomb of King Mi-ch'u a memorial shrine can be seen which was erected and dedicated to the departed spirit of Kim Al-chi.

6. Ch'omsong- dae: *Queen Son-dok's Astronomical Observatory (National Treasure No. 31)*

This stone astronomical observatory is without question the most important structural remains in Korea and dates to the Silla period prior to unification. A bottle-shaped and unique structure, it is considered the oldest existing observatory in the Far East. Having become symbolic of Korea itself, Ch'omsong-dae (Nearer the Stars Place) is frequently pictured on travel posters, in guides and even stamped on Korean coins.

Designated by the government as National Treasure No. 31 this 29 foot stone observatory is mounted on a 17 foot square foundation. It is cylindrical in shape and resembles the upper portion of a glass bottle. Half way up on the south side a square window is visible. It is believed that a ladder was used to reach this entrance as worn marks on the stone can be observed.

The space inside is now filled with dirt to the level of the window sill. From this window level still another ladder or staircase was very likely placed inside the observatory so that the top of this structure could be reached. On the lip of the bottle-shaped circular stones rest eight rectangular stones (8'6") positioned to form a double square.

Within the structure of the upper half of the observatory are two sets of stone bars arranged parallel to each other. One set is positioned directly above the window opening and the other near the top. The ends of these parallel supporting stones can be seen jutting out several inches from the circular surface of the observatory. These stone bars might have served as a type of support for a staircase to reach the top.

Ch'omsong-dae was constructed during the reign of Queen Son-dok, 27th ruler of Silla. Chin-p'yong (26th king) had no sons so upon his death after a fifty year rule his eldest daughter became the first queen to rule on the peninsula. During the early 7th century this wise queen ordered Ch'omsong-dae to be built. It is now the oldest secular structure in Korea.

It is certainly appropriate that this stone observatory has become a national symbol of Korea for it is known that from Korea's early history there has been a preoccupation with the stars. Views of the universe and life itself has been largely dictated by the stars and their movements.

Inherited from China, this belief that the heavenly bodies determine the course of men's lives permeated and dominated most aspects of Korean society. Often what was believed to be astrology regarding the heavens turned out to be scientific discovery. This continuing desire to observe the stars and their relationship with each other often resulted in certain predictable events.

For well over two thousand years the movements of the stars and known planets were carefully studied and charted. Sun and moon eclipses were predicted as well as the course of comets which came within view of the Silla astronomers. When the court astrologers reported and interpreted their findings, the king would then proceed to act according to their predictions. Waging of wars, restrictions, agricultural developments, celebrations and just about every known aspect of royal policy making was governed according to the study and interpretation of the stars.

The exact time of birth for every Korean is closely governed by the heavens. A particular year, month, day, hour and even minute will link the new baby to certain unchangeable influences and patterns of living which are

The gnarled elms of Kyerim (HS-19) frame the tomb of King Nae-mul (HS-188) a short distance away. In Kyerim a gold box was discovered which contained the infant boy Kim Al-chi during the reign of Sok T'al-hae (4th king).

historically developed astronomic combinations. A small child's life pattern is already set. These thousands upon thousands of astrological calculations have been recorded in Korean astrology manuals which today are extensively used by the fortunetellers in a rather lucrative business in modern Korea.

Viewing this unique observatory structure pompously situated within the City of Kyongju, a once proud capital of one million people, one is reminded of structural symbolism which might have been deliberately included by the builders who consulted the geomancer. The total number of stones used was 365, the exact number of days in a calendar year.

There are twelve rectangular base stones positioned in a square, three to each side, representing the twelve months of the year and four seasons. There are twelve tiers of stones to the sill stones of the window entrance and twelve tiers above the window opening. The window space is within three stone tiers which makes a total height of the observatory 27 tiers. Queen Son-dok was the 27th ruler of Silla and this observatory was built during her third year of reign in 634. The use of the twelve tiers above and below the window opening might symbolize the zodiac or possibly the months of the year. The mystery of Ch'omsong-dae still baffles the scholars.

left: Declared as one of Korea's most important relics this stone observatory (NT-31) was constructed during the reign of Queen Son-dok in the 7th century. Exactly how it was used is still a mystery.

The splash of color with flowers, water fowls and exotic plants in the gardens of Anap-ji makes one ponder over the beauty no longer seen.

7. Anap-ji and Imae-jon: *Silla's Palace Gardens*
(Historic Site No. 18)

Anap-ji (Duck and Geese Lake) has become a popular resort area for tourist though little of historical nature is left to be seen. The pond was first developed in February of 674 during the reign of Mun-mu (30th king) who was considered the greatest of Silla kings. His father King Mu-yol and the famed General Kim Yu-shin also were key participants in the unification wars which finally saw the fall of Paekche in 660 and Koguryo eight years later.

Unusual trees and plants were brought from all over the known world and placed in this exotic garden teeming with rare animals and birds. Lake and hills were simulated to represent the twelve peaks of China's most beautiful Mu-san. The botanical gardens became the pride of the Orient as the T'ang emissaries would be lavishly entertained among the lush vegetation with exquisite landscaping while casually watching the myriad species of waterfowl lazily swimming about the pond.

The largest porch was Imhae-jon (Beside the Sea Pavilion) which according to the records could seat over one thousand people. The present pavilion was built during the Japanese occupation and is about one fourth the size of the original structure.

Anap-ji became the center of Silla diplomacy as many decisions of state were decided within these garden grounds. It was here in these gardens of Anap-ji and probably in the pavilion of Imhae-jon that the final surrender of Silla to Koryo took place in 936.

The reign of Hon-gang (49th king) saw the birth of three great rebel generals who were instrumental in the final collapse of Silla. King Hon-gang's son by a young concubine was ordered destroyed because he had been born on an inauspicious day. However, he was saved by a nursemaid as the two fled into obscurity. The boy grew up to be General Kung-gye who established his own kingdom in north Kangwon Province.

Later the more famous General Wang-gon was to serve as a lieutenant in the armies of Kung-gye. When he became general in his own right, Wang-gon was appointed governor of Songdo (Kaesong) which was to later become the new Koryo capital. As was prophesied by the Priest To-son, Wang-gon became the first king of the Koryo Dynasty.

The third great rebel leader born during Hon-gang's reign was General Kyun-hwun who declared himself king of the Second Paekche Dynasty. This was the same general who swung the crippling blow on Silla with the murder of the king and family at Posok-jong. The myth was perpetuated that Kyun-hwun was fathered by an earthworm

Other legends tell that this general had the spirit of a tiger because while a small child he was left unattended in a field and was found by a tigress. As the tigress had recently lost her own cubs she took took pity on the baby and lay down beside him. Hungry and showing no fear the infant began to suckle the mother tiger. This myth helped to futher emphasize the ferocious tiger spirit of General Kyun-hwun.

He quickly rose in rank and soon became general to the queen's personal guards. Queen Chin-song began her ten year rule in 887 during which time the nation fell into utter despair as the queen's morals along with those of her courtiers were completely depraved.

Even the efforts of the great scholar Ch'oe Ch'i-won were of no use so he fled from the Silla capital and withdrew from public office. Many patriots were deeply worried about the affairs of state in Silla. Kyun-hwun finally rose in revolt and many followers rallied about him.

Queen Chin-song appointed a nephew and illegitimate son of former ruler Hon-gang (49th king) to become heir as her adopted son and in 897 abdicated. This son became Hyo-gong (52nd king) while the retired Queen Chin-song died shortly thereafter. King Hyo-gong had no heir so upon his death in 913 a son-in-law of the Pak Clan became Shin-dok (53rd king). King Hyo-gong was the last of an unbroken succession of kings belonging to the Kim family founded by Kim Al-chi in Kyerim and starting with Nae-mul (17th king) in 356.

In 927 during the reign of Kyong-ae (55th king) the tiger-spirited General Kyun-hwun became more bold and sweeping down upon the capital caught the king preoccupied at the pleasure pavilion of Posok-jong. Kyun-hwun set up his headquarters in Panwol-song and permitted his soldiers to plunder and ravish the countryside. He forced King Kyong-ae to fall on his own sword and violated the queen and many of the royal concubines.

After committing many outrageous atrocities General Kyun-hwun appointed Kyong-sun, a fifth generation descendant of Mun-song (46th king), to be ruler and withdrew from Kyongju in triumph, taking with him many noble ladies and aristocrats for slaves, as well as most of the palace treasures.

The king of Koryo, Wang-gon, dispatched a special envoy to Silla to convey condolences and the following year Wang-gon came in person. A welcoming banquet was prepared at Imhae-jon in the lakeside gardens of Anap-ji. With remorse Kyong-sun, the last king, tearfully told King Wang-gon about the atrocities of Kyun-hwun and the dying fortune of Silla. The king of Koryo wept as he listened to the sad words of Kyong-sun.

In desperation King Kyong-sun called for a conference to discuss the surrender terms of Silla to Koryo. Opinions were divided as there was considerable argument. "Silla is now hopeless as we have no strength," said the tired king. "It will be unbearable to see thousands of good people lose their lives over a lost cause. We must surrender peaceably to save out country from a greater catastrophe."

The crown prince bitterly opposing this action fled to the Diamond Mountains and rallied a few of the loyal sons of the *hwarang* to continue the fight against Wang-gon. The king's younger son shaved his head and

becoming a monk lived the rest of his life at Haein-sa.

King Kyong-sun in 936 moved to the Koryo capital of Songdo (Kaesong) accompanied by his military and civil officials. The procession stretched over ten miles with carriages and carts laden with royal treasures. King Wang-gon came to the outskirts of Songdo to meet his royal guest. Wang-gon then presented his own daughter to Kyong-sun in marriage and gave him a high rank in the kingdom. He was also presented with his old territory around the Silla capital and the name was changed to Kyongju.

After 993 years the kingdom of Silla ceased to exist. There are few cases in history where such mercy and generosity have been shown by a king toward his enemies. King Kyong-sun lived out his days in pleasant surroundings, though perhaps not as fine as the gardens of Anap.

Kyong-sun died in 978 during the reign of Kyong-jong (5th Koryo king), who was a grandson of Wang-gon. Records say that King Kyong-jong married one of the daughters of Kyong-sun. There is a temple near Hyongsan Fortress on the way to Pohang, where the spirits of Kyong-sun and his son-in-law, King Kyong-jong, are enshrined.

Though on a smaller scale Imhae-jon is still noted along the shores of Anap-ji. (HS-18)

8. Punhwang-sa: *Oldest Pagoda Remains of Silla*
(National Treasure No. 30)

Punhwang-sa (Famous Emperor Temple) along with Hwangyong-sa was one of the four famed temples of the pre-unification period of Silla. This temple was first constructed in 634 during the reign of the 27th ruler of Silla, Queen Son-dok. Though rebuilt many times it is still being used today and has on its grounds the remains of the oldest datable pagoda in Korea. Punhwang-sa's pagoda (National Treasure No. 30) and the stone observatory (Ch'omsong-dae, NT No. 31) remain the oldest structures from the early Silla era. Though appearing to be brick the materials used for the pagoda were actually cut stones shaped to look like bricks.

This partial pagoda is an imitation of earlier wooden styles. The base is over 40 feet square and height is 30 feet. Originally it had seven or nine stories though now only three remain. In 1915 a relic box was discovered between the second and third stories and in it were found

sari (calcified remains of a cremated priest), gold and stone ornaments, coins, scissors, a belt and needle with case. The relics appeared to belong to a royal lady and even possibly Queen Son-dok herself.

At the base are four rectangular openings with doors which may have been entrances but are now blocked with debris. Ferocious Buddhist guardians called *kumgang-yoksa* (Mighty Diamond Men) are carved in bold relief on each panel. Also on the four corners of the platform guarding this pagoda are stone lions.

Further beyond the pagoda is the main worship hall containing a standing Yaksa Yorae (Buddha of Medicine). Though this image is undoubtedly not the same, it is recorded that Kyong-dok (35th king) had a large bronze image of the Yaksa Yorae cast and placed in Punhwang-sa. These events occurred during the same period that the famed Emillie Bell was being cast.

To the right of the Yaksa Yorae image is the portrait of Priest Won-hyo. Having traveled the length and breadth of this country Won-hyo is one of the most honored priests of Korea. Born as a commoner to the Sol family, he wrote profusely and served the lower classes.

Won-hyo's appreciation for feminine beauty and his taste for good wine and meat apparently did not hinder his activities in the spread of Buddhism throughout the Silla kingdom.

He also walked and talked with royalty and even once became a victim of a plot to wed a king's daughter, Princess Yo-sok. Though legends of Won-hyo are numerous the fact of the matter was that the king's clever plan caused the fair princess, who was deeply in love with this eminent priest, to conceive and bear a child.

The Punhwang-sa pagoda is believed to be the oldest datable pagoda in Silla. (NT-30)

This boy became the famous Sol Ch ong who through his scholarly efforts invented the *idu*, a form of connective endings to aid the Korean reader to understand written Chinese.

In 650 Priest Won-hyo travelled to China. The story is told that while on the Liaotung Peninsula the tired priest slept overnight among some graves because there was no inn nearby. During the night, Won-hyo awoke extremely thirsty. Half asleep, he grovelled around and discovered some old crockery with liquid. Drinking its contents, he was refreshed and went back to sleep.

The next morning when Won-hyo awoke he realized that he had drunk the liquid which had collected in the skull of a tomb's occupant which had washed out of the ground during a recent rain. Won-hyo was known far and wide for his athletic prowess and physique. In Korea the drinking of "tomb water" is believed to guarantee great strength and long life. Older men even in these days have been noted to collect tomb water from graves when sites are moved to other locations.

The spirit of Won-hyo depicted in a portrait and two inwang *guards protect the pagoda of Punhwang-sa.*

The popular Queen Son-dok frequented this temple for worship. A legend is told which illustrates the queen's concern for her subjects. A poor beggar named Chig-ui took his position outside the gates of Punhwang-sa because he felt that here he would receive more alms. As the queen passed, her guards cleared the way for her and beat the beggar back into the crowds.

He shouted, "But I love the queen, if I see her face just once I'll die happy."

The queen realizing what had happened chided the guards for being too cruel. After the ceremony when the queen returned she saw Chig-ui sleeping in the shadows of the pagoda. She stopped and observed his peaceful repose. Taking pity on him the queen took off her gold ring and slipped it on his finger.

Chig-ui opened his eyes and jumping up danced with joy. In his frenzy he burst into flames and was consumed as his spirit entered Nirvana. The flames licked the side of the pagoda and inscribed a memorial to his steadfast gratitude and loyalty for his queen.

Another story of the two monk friends who lived during the reign of Mun-mu (30th king) exemplifies an earthy humor which is often

evident in Korean folklore. This tale must have certainly been a favorite among the celibate and non-celibate priests down through the centuries as the rivalry between the two groups still continues.

Priest Kwang-dok lived in a small hut on the west side of Punhwang-sa. He was married and his wife worked hard weaving straw shoes so that they could earn a living. His close friend Priest Om-jang lived in a small hermitage in another valley.

One evening while the last rays of the sun illuminated the high treetops Priest Om-jang heard a voice from the sky say, "I am on my way to the Lotus Paradise. Be faithful to Buddha and you will see me soon. Farewell."

The priest seeing the bright colors of the rainbow form a bridge from earth to heaven sighed, "My friend has gone before me."

The next morning Priest Om-jang visited the home of Kwang-dok and saw that his friend was indeed dead. He assisted the widow with the funeral arrangements and afterwards came to her home to discuss her future.

"You are now without a husband and must certainly need a man about the house and I too need a helpmate. As your former husband and I were good friends why don't you come and share my house with me?" Priest Om-jang suggested. The good widow replied that she was willing, so they were married.

On the first night the priest began to undress his new wife while discussing with her all the imaginable pleasures they would have in their life of married bliss. The woman blushing in shame said to the passionate priest, "You are a priest seeking paradise with a muddied soul like one who is attempting to catch a fish by

Though appearing to be a brick pagoda this partial structure at Punhwang-sa is made entirely of cut stone shaped to look like bricks. (NT-30)

climbing a tree.''

"I don't understand," objected the priest, "Kwang-dok who has now entered paradise must have often enjoyed you as man and wife. Why can't I?"

"My former husband Kwang-dok," said the woman, "lived with me for more than ten years but we never slept in the same bed. Each night we knelt before the Buddha and recited in unison the Sutra of the Ami'ta and the names of the sixteen gates leading to paradise."

It was now Priest Om-jang's turn to be embarrassed and he apologized to the widow for his lust. He then visited Priest Won-hyo and confessed his desires for this unusual woman. The great monk of Silla then taught Om-jang how he might gain admittance to the Lotus Paradise and Om-jang concentrated on preparing his soul for entry. At long last he succeeded.

The woman then served as a nun at Pun-hwang-sa and later became one of the nineteen Kwanseum (Bodhisattva of Mercy) of the temple.

Located only a few yards east of the highway bypass and west of the silk factory is the site of another large stone pagoda. It is believed that this pagoda was attached to Punhwang-sa during the Silla period. Small pine trees are growing on the site which is uncultivated in a generally cultivated area. There are three guard images about four feet high while two others have been removed to the Kyongju Museum. They are in bold relief and larger than the guardian images at Punhwang-sa. Probably there were originally eight.

Located in a field directly in front of the main gate of Punhwang-sa are two temple banner pillar stones. The pillars are about 20 feet high with a sculptured stone turtle positioned between the pillars at the base. The six holes were used for securing a high pole between the two stone supports. The pole rested on the back of the turtle.

Guarding images from a remnant of an early Silla pagoda lie in the open fields near Pun-hwang-sa on the out skirts of Kyongju.

9. Hwangyong-sa: *Site of the Largest Temple of Silla (Historic Site No. 6)*

After the martyrdom of Yi Ch'a-don in 527 during the reign of Pob-hung (23rd king), Buddhism became the adopted religion of Silla. Yi Ch'a-don, an aristocratic nobleman who was a Buddhist believer, was beheaded to confirm the truth of Buddhism. His blood ran white as milk while the shocked nobles of the court fell on their knees before the priests of this new religion.

The account of the martyrdom of Yi Ch'a-don does not reveal the complete historical reason for the sudden prosperity of Buddhism. By tradition a century earlier Priest A-do brought Buddhism to Silla but failed in this missionary adventure. It was prophesied by his mother, according to legend, that Hwangyong-sa was to be the third of seven principal temples to be erected in Silla.

One of the most important and certainly the largest of the many temples of Silla was Hwangyong-sa (Imperial Dragon Temple) as its construction was a national undertaking to enhance the reputation of the dynasty internationally and protect her from warring neighbors. Other temples such as Sach'on-wang-sa, Mangdok-sa and even Pulguk-sa were also built as edifices to Buddha for a guarantee of protection. However, Hwangyong-sa was considered the "white crane in the pond of frogs."

The dragon, symbol of imperial strength, became significant to the origin of Hwangyong-sa, Silla's largest temple. The stone pillars of Punhwang-sa show sharp contrast in the open fields.

In 554 during the reign of Chin-hung (24th king) the court made preparation to build a new palace east of Panwol-song (Half Moon Fortress). As construction began it was reported that a dragon was observed at the construction site. After looking into this matter the king decided to change the intended palace to a temple, giving it the name of "Imperial Dragon."

Taking 17 years the construction of Hwangyong-sa must have been a monumental undertaking. Many of Hwangyong-sa's foundation stones can still be seen about 150 yards west of Punhwang-sa on the eastern outskirts of Kyongju. The main hall of Hwangyong-sa was colossal as the length was over 155 feet while the width was 55 feet.

Ten large pillars three feet in diameter were used across the front. One can now see three gigantic flat stones which served to support the three Buddha images. Side by side these pedestal stones are over 27 feet long.

One interesting legend tells that at the time of the temple's construction a merchant ship from India arrived. An Indian prince who was aboard the vessel appeared before Chin-hung (24th king) with a letter which read: "I, King Asoka of the Western Buddha Nation, have gathered iron and gold to be used in the casting of three Buddhist images but have always failed. My son had a vision in which he was told that the images must be made in another country so I have commissioned him to search for this country across the seven seas with the prayer that destiny will lead him to the right country."

King Chin-hung graciously received the materials needed to cast the images. The work was begun by Silla sculptors and took five years. The prince returned to India to report to his father who expressed joy and gratitude to Silla.

This central image was believed to weigh over 23 tons. Considering the 8,430 pounds of gold used to cover its surface one can readily imagine the importance of Hwangyong-sa in the eyes of the Silla rulers. Other records indicate that the golden Buddha images were completed during the reign of Chin-p'yong (26th king) who lived closer to the time of King Asoka of India; however, the earlier date seems

Excavation was started in 1978 at the temple site of Hwangyong-sa.

to be more widely accepted.

Another well known legend is told about the famous realist painter Sol-go who was commissioned to paint on the exterior wall of the main hall. He painted a large pine tree and so realistic was it that birds tried to land on its branches. As time and weather eventually faded the painting, it was decided to touch up Sol-go's realistic pine tree picture. This was to be accomplished by the best artist of that period; however, the birds no longer tried to land among the branches.

Later during the reign of Kyong-dok (35th king) the largest bell ever cast in Korea was completed in 754 and hung at Hwangyong-sa.

Its weight, according to the records, was four times that of the famed Emillie Bell now located in the Kyongju National Museum.

The earliest of the great priests of Silla to live and die at Hwangyong-sa was Priest Won-gwang. Won-gwang was born during the reign of Chin-hung (24th king) and by the age of thirteen had become a teacher of Buddhist theology. He was one of the first known Korean priests who journeyed to China to study under the masters.

Priest Won-gwang was the originator of the *hwarang* code used by the "knighthood" during the Silla era. Two men who visited this eminent priest once asked him to give them a guide to their behavior through life.

"For the Buddhist priests there are ten commandments to obey but they are difficult for the lay citizen to follow," spoke Won-gwang. "Therefore, let me give you five secular rules that you can keep."

"First," he explained, "you must serve your king with loyalty. Next, you must always honor your parents, treat your friends with sincerity, and fight the enemy bravely. The fifth and last commandment is that you should not kill indiscriminately."

"These are the five commandments," spoke the aged priest. Both the Buddhist teachings and the Confucian virtues were integrated into this code of conduct called *sesogogye* which was later to be incorperated into the *hwarang* movement.

Some records indicate that Priest Won-gwang lived to be 99 but other sources say that he died at the age of 84. Praised for his talent and wisdom he silently left this world in a meditation pose at Hwangyong-sa.

Legends tell that when his spirit crossed to the other side, the sound of music was heard and sweet fragrance filled the air. At Kumgok-sa (Gold Valley Temple) in Samgi-san the ashes of this great Buddhist master were buried. A *pudo* monument is still to be the seen which traditionally belongs to this eminent priest.

At Hwangyong-sa once stood Silla's largest pagoda which according to the records towered to an unbelievable height of 224 feet. Consisting of nine stories the structure was made entirely of wood. Sixty foundation stones for this wooden pagoda cover an area of 6084 square feet. The base story was at least 78 feet square with eight pillars positioned across one side.

This monumental architectural undertaking was completed after seven years in 643 during the reign of Queen Son-dok (27th ruler) by

Still to be seen are the foundation stones of Korea's largest pagoda which once towered over 224 feet and covered an area of 6084 square feet.

Priest Cha-jang (other sources give the date as 637). This monk was also one of the greatest priests of Silla and was the first to bring the complete set of the *Tripitaka* from China.

Priest Cha-jang, though coming from the ranks of nobility, chose the way of Buddha and isolated himself deep in the mountains. As a young boy his keen mind quickly grasped the rich pleasures of learning. He could have advanced rapidly in court politics.

The king realizing his abilities continued to request that the great priest accept an official position in the court and when threatened with a death penalty for refusing Cha-jang calmly replied, "I would rather die keeping the laws of Buddha for one day than live for one hundred years while breaking them." Seeing the wisdom of this reply the king permitted this noble-born son to continue in the priesthood.

During his studies deep in the mountains of China the Bodhisattva Munsu appeared before him in a dream. "As your country is ruled by a frail woman neighboring nations will take advantage. The dragon spirit of Hwang-yong-sa under the command of Buddha is now protecting Silla. You must go and build a nine-storied pagoda to honor the spirit of this dragon. Your nine neighbors, represented by the nine stories of the pagoda, will surrender and send tribute to Silla."

After receiving the blueprint for the pagoda Cha-jang returned to Silla. He reported his experiences with the Munsu Posal to Queen Son-dok who readily approved the plan for the immediate construction of the nine-storied pagoda. Priest Cha-jang buried before the front pillar of this pagoda many relics including a piece of Buddha's bone he received from heaven while in China.

Five times the giant pagoda succumbed to fire and five times it was rebuilt until the entire temple with its treasures was completely destroyed by the Mongol invaders in 1238 during the reign of Kojong of Koryo.

The center pillar stone of the pagoda was pilfered and a golden *sari* box was stolen in 1964. It was sold to a wealthy art collector in Seoul and fortunately was presented to the National Museum through the efforts of Dr. Hwang Su-young, a former director. It is now on display. The nine hundred characters in the inscription on this *sari* box were deciphered.

In the inscription a formerly unknown story about Cha-jang's reason for conversion to the priesthood came to be known. He had a passion for hunting and frequently took his falcon into the hills. One day he wounded a pheasant and upon reaching it found the bird hovering over its young and crying. The sight was so pitiful that the noble Cha-jang gave up hunting completely and accepted the tenets of Buddhism.

A short distance from the site of Hwangyong-sa toward Anap-ji are the stone remains of another pagoda which is believed to have belonged to this temple. Many foundation stones are nearby and across the road. The main block of the pagoda shows the bold relief of four *sach'onwang* figures on four sides. They are 2.6 feet high and holding swords. One relief figure is holding a small pagoda by one hand. Two roof stones also remain. Nearby is one stone pillar of a former temple banner support.

left: *A pagoda remains and 27-foot pedestal stones are still seen at the Hwangyong-sa site.*
above: *The five- storied wooden pagoda seen today at Popchu-sa was built in the 17th century and is 75 feet high. It is the only wooden pagoda remaining in Korea. (NT-55)*

MAP OF KYONGJU CITY

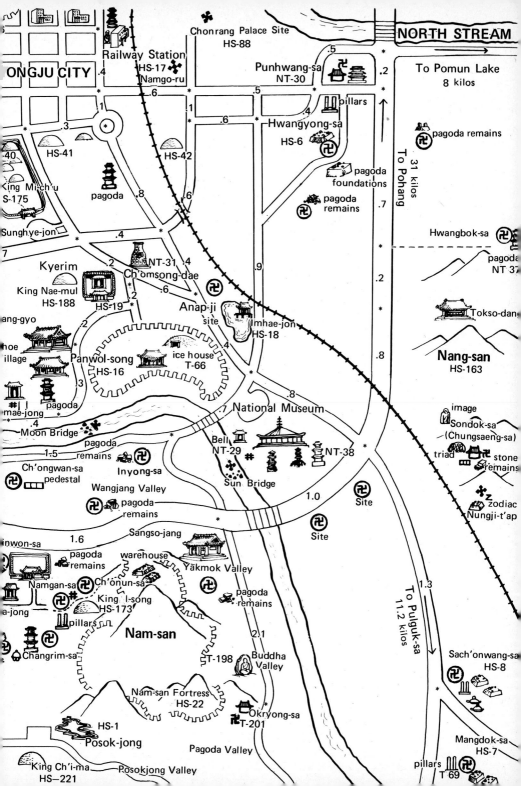

1. Bamboo Tomb of Mi-ch'u: *First Ruler of the Kim Clan (Historic Site No. 175)*

The recent Kyongju Development Program sponsored by the government included the beautification of this site. The area was made into a historical tomb park which included adjacent tombs in downtown Kyongju. Two tombs have been excavated and now the burial pit and remains are exposed in one tomb so that visitors are able to see the core of a Silla tomb. This tomb is the "Heavenly Horse" tomb. The tomb site is near the stone observatory between the center of the city and Panwol-song (Half Moon Fortress).

Mi-ch'u (13th king) was the first ruler of the Kim Clan who began his reign in 262. His reign lasted for 22 years. King Mi-ch'u was a 7th generation descendant of Kim Al-chi who was the founder of the Kim family. Legends claim that Kim Al-chi appeared in 67 AD from a golden box heralded by a chicken in a grove of trees later to be called Kyerim (Chicken Forest).

Thirty-eight descendants of kings followed the rule of Mi-ch'u. Upon his death in 284 this virtuous and much beloved king was buried in a large mound which later became known as the "Bamboo Tomb." Even today the tomb is called Chukhyon-nung (Bamboo Appearing Tomb).

A legend is recorded that during the reign of King Yu-rye, the successor of King Mi-ch'u, Silla was attacked by soldiers from the country of Iso. Though the Silla troops fought bravely they were hopelessly outnumbered. Suddenly a host of strange soldiers with bamboo leaves in their ears appeared on the battlefield to reinforce the Silla army. The enemy was routed.

During the great victory celebration it was discovered that the strange allies had also vanished. They found many bamboo leaves in front of the tomb of King Mi-ch'u. From that day Silla worshipped the spirit of Mi-ch'u as

The tomb of King Mi-ch'u is referred to as the "Bamboo Tomb" because of a legend recorded during the reign of King Yu-rye. (HS-175)

a protector of the kingdom.

Many years after Silla unification Hye-gong (36th king) came to the throne in 765 at the age of 21. He was effeminate and gave little attention to the matters of state. The gradual decline of Silla began with his reign.

A strange incident occurred during the closing years of King Hye-gong's reign. A great storm arose over the hills containing the tomb of General Kim Yu-shin. Above the howling of the wind the clatter of mounted steeds could be heard. As the sound in the sky drew closer to the capital, the shouting of an angry general was unmistakably clear. The galloping sounds thundered over the capital to finally enter the "Bamboo Tomb" of King Mi-ch'u. From inside the tomb the indignant voice of the general was again heard.

"I am your majesty's humble servant who in life assisted the throne by destroying the enemy and unifying our country. In death I became a protective spirit of the kingdom. Now a guiltless descendant of mine was shamefully put to death. It is obvious that the present king and his evil advisors have forgotten my patriotic deeds. I would like to request permission from your majesty to move to another place and cease caring for these ungrateful creatures."

There was a long pause. Finally a stern voice replied, "I command you to continue to display your patriotic spirit. If you and I do not guard this country with our immortal strength what will become of the people?" The general was heard to grumble but the king's spirit continued to argue persuasively. The wind arose once more and soon the voices ceased.

When King Hye-gong heard this account he was greatly distressed. He sent the prime minister to the tomb of General Kim Yu-shin to apologize. If it had not been for the urging spirit of King Mi-ch'u the general's anger may not have been appeased. Many sacrifices were offered and the tomb of King Mi-ch'u was elevated to the country's highest rank, even above that of the founder of Silla.

Historical accounts record that a high official named Kim Yun tried to kill the king and was executed in 771 during the reign of King Hye-gong. Whether this man was in fact a relative of General Kim Yu-shin is not known but it is generally believed that he was not.

This story told in the *Samguk Yusa* has no historical basis but even today the tomb of King Mi-ch'u receives special attention with a fine wall and modern tiled roof gate. The circumference of the tomb mound is 520 feet. Before the mound is a ceremonial stone table with a stone chair. Stone stools to hold the incense are located in front of the table. The tomb of King Mi-ch'u has been designated as Historic Site No. 175.

above: *The dignified portrait of King Mi-ch'u is enshrined in Sunghye-jon.* below: *The tomb of Mi-ch'u is found in Tomb Park of downtown Kyongju.* right: *The Shrine of Sunghye-jon is a memorial to kings Mi-ch'u, Mun-mu and Kyong-sun.*

2. Sunghye-jon: *Ancestral Shrine of the Royal Kim Clan*

Several hundred meters south of the tomb of King Mi-ch'u are two shrines enclosed in a compound wall. The larger shrine is called Sunghye-jon (Respecting the Wisdom). The present buildings of this shrine were erected about two hundred and twenty years ago during the reign of Yong-jo (21st Yi Dynasty king). Before the shrine is a large eight foot tablet within a pavilion while further along the path from the entrance is a small stone marker on which characters are written indicating that this was the place to dismount from one's horse when approaching the shrine.

Two large ginkgo trees, one male and one female, are growing in the front courtyard. Ceremonies are conducted twice a year during both spring and fall equinox. Within the main shrine building are located three *wip'ae* (spirit tablets). In the center is found the spirit tablet of King Mi-ch'u, first ruler of the Kim Clan. On the right is located the *wip'ae* for Mun-mu (30th king) who united ancient Silla with the leadership of General Kim Yu-shin.

The spirit tablet to the left belongs to Kyong-sun (56th king) who ended his nine year rule by abdicating to Koryo in 936. Kyong-sun died forty-two years later in Kaesong, the Koryo capital north of Seoul. On the right side of the main hall can be seen the portrait of Mi-ch'u.

During August of 1972 a painting of King Kyong-sun was discovered in a box hidden beneath this portait. It was believed to have been painted during early Koryo and could possibly be the oldest known painting of a Silla king in existence.

A smaller shrine is located in front of Sunghye-jon to honor Kim Al-chi the ancestral founder of the Kim family. In 65 AD Kim Al-chi was found in a golden box in Kyerim (Chicken Forest) during the reign of Sok T'al-hae (4th king). He received the name of Kim which means "gold." The *wip'ae* of Kim Al-chi is enshrined here. In front of the spirit tablet are the exquisite bronze images of a cock and hen. Over the entrance door is seen a painted chicken which represents the origin of Kim in Kyerim. The name of Silla was not used until later. On the inside walls are painted guards. They are carrying a fan, axe or umbrella to protect the spirit of departed Kim Al-chi. On the outside walls are paintings of deer and cranes, both "goodluck" creatures.

The historic site of Posok-jong is enveloped in tragic tales of the fall of Silla. (HS-1) Stones shaped to the size of bricks remain from the partial pagoda of Punhwang-sa. (NT-30) A memorial shrine and tablet in the forest of Kyerim remind visitors of the appearance of Kim Al-chi. (HS-19) From Kyerim the tomb of Nae-mul is not far away. (HS-188)

3. Tomb of King Nae-mul: *Patriotic Death of Pak Che-sang*
(Historic Site No. 188)

King Nae-mul's tomb is located about 100 meters northwest of Kyerim (Chicken Forest) toward Kyongju City. This king is historically important though the tomb is rather small. When Hul-hae (16th king) died in 356 he had no heir. He was the last of the Pak Clan to reign and King Nae-mul was first of the Kim ancestory to begin a continuous rule of Kim family kings until 913. Nae-mul (17th king) was a nephew of Mi-ch'u (13th king).

Mi-ch'u died in 284 after a 22 year reign. King Nae-mul, the son of Mal-gu (a younger brother of Mi-ch'u), began his reign 72 years later and ruled 46 years. After King Nae-mul's death in 402 a cousin reigned as King Shil-song for fifteen years. In 417 the son of Nae-mul came to the throne and was called Nul-chi (19th king).

Pak Che-sang is thought to have lived during the rules of kings Nae-mul and Nul-chi and his death is one of the most heart-rending tragedies of Korean history. He was Korea's first known patriot.

In 391 a Japanese ruler sent an envoy to Silla to pay homage. An alliance was requested and the envoy suggested that a prince return with them to demonstrate Silla's sincerity. The king's son, a ten-year-old boy, was sent. He was the younger brother of Nul-chi, then crown prince of Silla. Tragically the Japanese ruler did not respect the boy's status as official envoy and held him prisoner.

When Shil-song (18th king) mounted the throne in 402, bitterness grew between the king and Nae-mul's son Nul-chi; King Shil-song, tried to bribe Koguryo to kill Nul-chi; however, because Koguryo admired Nul-chi's wisdom and virtue, they turned instead upon the king. Nul-chi who had earlier married a daughter of Shil-song then became ruler in 417.

Because of Koguryo's assistance in placing Nul-chi on the throne they requested that his brother be sent to the northern capital as an ambassador. This trust was misplaced and

Chang-su (20th Koguryo king), held this other brother as a hostage, as the Japanese ruler had done years before.

The king lamented, "My father King Nae-mul sent his son to Japan and then died without the joy of seeing him again. I sent my own younger brother to the Koguryo courts but now he too cannot return." The courtiers could say nothing for they knew this was true.

"Though I hold absolute power in my kingdom, I worry that I will never see my two brothers again. If only they could return so we could apologize before the grave of my father, I would be content,"the king groaned. He asked "Who would be willing to bring my brothers back to Silla?"

The magistrate Pak Che-sang stepped forward, "When the king is grief stricken the subjects are disgraced," murmured Pak Che-sang, "The subjects of a disgraced king will die. If your subjects only do what is easy and never attempt the difficult, they are disloyal to the throne and if they think only of their own lives they are cowards," he continued. "I will faithfully attempt to do what you ask if you will permit me."

King Nul-chi, unable to control his emotion for this faithful vassal, drank with him and bade him fond farewell. Pak Che-sang in disguise traveled into Koguryo.The rescue was effected, but when the king's brother fled soldiers were ordered to pursue him. However, this prince of Silla was respected and beloved by the Koguryo people and so was permitted to escape. The two arrived safely at the courts of Silla.

When King Nul-chi met his brother he embraced him and shed tears of both sorrow and happiness. "I have gained one arm of my body and can see from only one of my eyes, but I am still sad without the other," he lamented.

Pak Che-sang replied, "I will go to bring your other brother from the island kingdom of the dwarf people." He took leave of his king and traveled directly to the coast. When he reached the islands of Japan he was received by the king.

"Who are you and why do you come?" demanded the ruler. "I was a noble magistrate from the kingdom of Kyerim," Pak Che-sang replied. "My entire family was murdered without reason and I only escaped. Since I have drifted to your shores I wish to seek asylum."

"I know the king of Kyerim is evil," chuckled the ruler. "I will give you a comfortable house and position in this land." Pak Che-sang soon made contact with King Nul-chi's younger brother who was now a middle-aged man of forty. Every morning the two men would go fishing along the coast and upon returning would present their catch to the king as a token of respect. Eventually an opportunity came when one morning a dense fog covered the seacoast. Pak Che-sang told the prince that this was the time to escape.

"The Japanese may discover our attempt soon. I must stay behind to prevent them from pursuing you," cautioned Pak Che-sang.

The prince was greatly distressed. "How can I leave you behind as I look up to you as my own father?"

If I can save your life and in this way comfort my king I will be content," replied the loyal Pak Che-sang.

Pak Che-sang returned secretly to the prince's home and stayed with the door shut until the following day. He told them the prince had become ill and could not be disturbed. Finally this ruse could last no longer but by this time the prince was well across the sea. The king had Pak Che-sang arrested and brought before him.

"Why did you send the prince home?" demanded the ruler. "I am not your subject," calmly replied Pak Che-sang. "My allegiance is to the king of Kyerim."

"You asked to become my vassal and now say you're not. What insolence is this?" screamed the ruler. "You deserve the five penalties but even now if you will become my subject I will give you rank and position." (Originating in early China the punishment of the five penalties was in this order: cutting off the nose, both feet, the genitals, and finally the head).

"I would rather be a pig in Kyerim than a nobleman in this kingdom," he retorted.

The king could not control his wrath. "Peel off his skin from thigh to ankles," he ordered. After this torture the island ruler again asked Pak Che-sang, "Now bold Kyerim pig, of what kingdom are you a subject?"

Though barely able to speak the loyal patriot whispered, "I would rather be whipped as a dog in Kyerim than receive honor here."

The ruler knew he was beaten. "You are straight and unbending; however, you can be of no service to me. Hang him," he ordered. So on Kishima Pak Che-sang was hung and burned.

Meanwhile the prince arrived safely at the shores of Silla. There was great rejoicing in the palace and a festival was given. The title of *Kuktae Puin* (National Wife) was bestowed on the wife of Pak Che-sang and the prince married one of his daughters. Pak Che-sang's deed of unswerving loyalty was praised from one end of the kingdom to the other.

The faithful wife never overcame her grief. On the river's edge at Mangdok-sa she wept bitterly. One account states that she drowned herself in this river. Other records relate that Pak Che-sang's wife took her daughters to Ch'isul (Kite Pass) where she lived out her days sorrowfully looking toward the sea.

Here on this mountain pass a monolithic stone called *mangbusok* (Yearning for the Husband Stone) marks the site of her vigil. Once a shrine was erected nearby but now only the foundation stones are seen.

Though Pak is traditionally the accepted family name of Pak Che-sang, the *Samguk Yusa* (Legends of the Three Kingdoms) gives the family name as Kim. The *Samguk Sagi* says that Pak Che-sang was a fifth generation descendant of P'a-sa (5th king). If Che-sang was from the Pak Clan descended from Pak Hyok-ko-se, his loyalty to King Nae-mul and King Nul-chi, members of the Kim family, is quite phenomenal to say the least, when we compare later dynasties and the loyalty of nobility to the family clan member.

Here is Korea's inner man, brave, unselfish and steadfast. Of the many known heroic men the world over, Korea's hero, Pak Che-sang, surely stands the tallest....a man who had within his heart ideals greater than life itself.

4. Early Excavated Tombs of Kyongju City

Silla tombs can be found in many regional areas beyond the capital city of Kyongju, such as Andong, Taegu, Songju, Ch'angnyong, Koryong, Sonsan and Haman. Officially in Kyongju City there have been only four major tomb excavations during the Japanese occupation. The four sites are still marked though difficult to find. They are located within easy walking distance of each other between the large tomb mounds designated as Historic Sites No. 38 and No. 39.

Silla tombs basically are categorized into two types according to the burial structure and unless they are excavated this category is often uncertain. The outward appearances of Silla tombs are similar except for their size. In the wooden-chamber type a wooden coffin is placed into an earth pit while large boulders are placed over it before the mound is prepared. This type is characteristic of earlier tombs.

However, the stone-chamber type tomb was more popular in later Silla. The chamber or pit is lined with decorated cobblestones or rock slabs while larger stones were placed over the chamber to form a ceiling. The coffin and numerous burial gifts were either lowered from the top or carried in through a temporary passage. This difference is often referred to as a "shaft type" or "tunnel type."

In Kyongju City archeologists have been fortunate in finding many Silla tombs intact with original burial gifts. Often the wooden chambers have collapsed over the years causing the falling stones to crush most of the breakable burial gifts; however, many of the personal ornaments of the rulers have been preserved.

The tomb now called Kumgwan-ch'ong (Gold Crown Tomb)was accidentally discovered in 1921 during the building of a private home. The large tomb mound over the years had actually disappeared. Though not scientifically excavated the entire find was saved in time and is now on display in the museums of Seoul and Kyongju. The site of Kumgwanch'ong is located across the street from tomb Ponghwang-dae (Historic Site No. 38), the largest mound in Kyongju City.

The elaborate crown from which the tomb takes its name was wrought from pure gold. Also found were earrings, bracelets and rings for every finger, including the toes. Belts, pendants as well as weapons and riding gear were also discovered among many pottery pieces. The gold crown and girdle have been designated by the Korean government as National Treasures No. 87 and No. 88.

Three years later in 1924 another tomb called

left: *The Gold Crown Tomb,* middle: *Gold Bell Tomb,* right: *and Lucky Phoenix Tomb were all excavated during the 1920s.*

the Kumryong-ch'ong (Gold Bell Tomb) was discovered and excavated. The site which can now be seen has been left as a deserted plot of ground across the street and a short distance from the Gold Crown Tomb. The gold crown (Treasure No. 338) which was discovered here was considerably smaller. It is believed that the tomb belonged to a young prince. Also found were gold belts, bracelets and other jewelery as well as a gold bell from which the tomb received its name. From among the many thousands of Silla pottery remains, two of the most unusual vessels to be discovered were pottery pieces of mounted horsemen which were taken from this tomb.

The third tomb to be excavated was the Subong-ch'ong (Lucky Phoenix Tomb). During the excavation of this tomb in 1926 a third gold crown was unearthed which has been designated Treasure No. 339. It has a domed frame made from two arched bands crossing at right angles. It was undoubtedly worn with an inner cap though this is missing. Three phoenix-type birds are designed as silhouettes against a flame pattern peak of the crown.

The Lucky Phoenix Tomb site has been better preserved and can be seen behind the Gold Crown Tomb. King Adolf Gustaf II. who was Prince of Sweden and an eminent archeologist during his younger days, came to Korea to assist in the excavation. To honor the Prince of Sweden the name of *su* which is the first sound of Sweden and also means good fortune was attached to the word phoenix which is portrayed on the gold crown.

The tomb mound was once thirty-six feet high. Also from this tomb came many other treasures including earrings, necklaces and golden belts. A bronze cup with a rabbit design indicating the zodiac year of burial was also excavated. It is believed that this tomb was initially constructed during the first part of the sixth century.

Another tomb of a minor Silla official was excavated by Kim Che-won, then director of the National Museum. in 1946 and strangely yielded one of the finest examples of Koguryo work to be found in today's museums. The Hou-ch'ong site is now an empty lot with no marker. A small alley south of the Gold Crown

Tomb can be taken west at a slight angle for half a block.

Tombs of Koguryo were traditionally more often robbed of their contents than tombs of Silla and Paekche possibly because of the easier access to the burial chambers. Therefore, fewer remains from Koguryo tombs are to be found in Korea's museums. The best known piece is the covered bronze washbowl with the date of 415. The bowl was for burial in the tomb of Kwang-gae-to (19th king of Koguryo).

This vessel somehow came into the hands of a Silla nobleman. During this era there were many Silla men in the Koguryo capital both as hostages and as official emissaries of the Silla king. This burial souvenir of this king was somehow brought to Silla and remains today as one of the most valuable examples of Koguryo metal work.

The tomb site called Hou-ch'ong yielded a rare example of a Koguryo metal bowl in 1946.

5. Ancient Tomb Mounds in Center of City

(Historic Site Nos. 38, 39, 40, 41 and 42)

From the earliest times in Korea men buried the dead in underground chambers covered by an earthen mound. During the Silla Dynasty the tomb building system had undergone change, not so much in the underground burial chamber as in the outward shape of the tombs. Hundreds of pre-unification Silla tombs can be found within the Kyongju City vicinity as well as throughout the province. They are noted for their size, and only just recently has the government taken measures to systematically excavate some of these large tombs.

Five tombs have been designated by the government as Historic Sites numbered 38 through 42. The largest of the five tombs has several gnarled trees growing from the slope. The distance over the mound is three hundred and twenty feet. This tomb (HS No. 38) is over seventy-two feet high. The occupant of this tomb is unknown but it is often referred to as Ponghwang-dae (Imperial Phoenix Place).

The legend is told that when Paekche was attempting to defeat Silla the monarch sent a

Silla's largest known tomb in downtown Kyongju is called Ponghwang-dae. (HS-38) It dates to the pre-unification era.

fortuneteller to spy out Silla's weakness. The man entered the court and soon won the confidence of the king and nobles. This spy continued to study military maps to determine the weakness of Silla's fortifications. Finally he discovered that as Silla was shaped like a boat if a heavy weight were placed on one end it would sink like a ship.

The fortuneteller waited for his chance and when an epidemic struck the capital he advised the king that the royal phoenix had flown from the kingdom thus causing the illness. If a huge mound were to be built with trees on top the pheonix would be enticed to return. The king decided to follow his advice.

When the mound was completed the spy sent a message to the Paekche king stating that the signs were right for the attack. However, Paekche was unsuccessful and Silla did not collapse. One wonders if the weight of this giant mound was not great enough to sink the kingdom. This tomb with trees growing from the side continues to loom above the roofs of Kyongju City.

Directly to the west of the tomb called Pong-hwang-dae is a cluster of mounds which is nearly as large, designated as Historic Site No. 39. Tombs designated as Historic Sites No. 40 and No.41 are next to the road and east-ward of the cultural preservation office. It is within this vicinity that the 1973–74 excava-tions were conducted by the government and private archeological teams. This entire area of tombs between the road and tomb of King Mi-ch'u has been developed into a tourist Tomb Park.

Historic Site No. 42 is difficult to find. The distance over the mound is only ninety-six feet. The tomb mound is considerably smaller and one even wonders as to the justification of the designation. The designation of historical sites was first accomplished under the Japanese colonial rule. A major regrouping of the national treasures was accomplished in 1960 but the listing of historic sites has largely remained the same except for a few additions in recent years.

Silla tombs are concentrated in Tomb Park;
HS-39; HS-40; HS-41; HS-42.(top to bottom)

6. Hungnyun-sa: *Priest A-do Introduces Buddhism to Silla (Historic Site No. 15)*

Hungnyun-sa (Flourishing Wheel Temple) is considered the first Silla temple built on the site where Buddhism was established in the kingdom. *Nyun* refers to the wheel of dharma which symbolizes the cycle of reincarnation for Buddhism. The exact introductory date of Buddhism to Silla is difficult to determine; however, most scholars agree that Priest A-do brought the first teachings from Koguryo to Silla in the early fifth century. The officially accepted date for the arrival of Buddhism in Koguryo is 372.

Buddhism's appearance in Silla did not come about with royal sanction as it did in the other two kingdoms. The historical accounts of this event are difficult to determine. The two priests, Muk-ho-ja and A-do, are often confused. Muk-ho-ja, which means "Black Barbarian" might very well be a pseudonym for Priest A-do. There is one theory that this priest might have been a dark-skinned Indian.

Buddhist histories had a way of stretching events in a careless fashion so that often dates were frequently inaccurate. Yet most scholars seem to accept the fact that Buddhism did arrive in Silla prior to 424 through the efforts of either Muk-ho-ja or A-do.

Priest A-do was probably born in Koguryo.

The temple site of Hungnyun-sa is where Buddhism was traditionally first introduced to Silla by Priest A-do. (HS-15)

74

A Chinese envoy who had come to Koguryo had fallen in love and married a Korean girl She bore him a son whom she named A-do. At the age of sixteen he went to China to continue his Buddhist education. His mother prophetically spoke to her son saying, "Three thousands months from now a wise king will appear in Kyerim who will lead his people into accepting the faith."

Deeply moved by his mother's words Priest A-do set out on his journey to Kyerim (Silla). The courtiers were suspicious of the man's strange appearance and his petition was denied. An angry mob would have killed the poor priest if he had not been saved by a kindly villager named Mo-rye. (If A-do was indeed Muk-ho-ja who was believed to be of black skin it might be easy to imagine the suspicion created by a strange foreigner with dark skin and alien teachings.)

King Nul-chi's daughter was stricken with a strange illness which none of the court physicians could cure. The king remembering the words of Priest A-do summoned him to the palace. Burning imported incense Priest A-do conducted a Buddhist ceremony and chanted a strange litany. Soon the princess rose from her bed completely restored.

King Nul-chi of course was overjoyed, "My good monk, whatever is your wish you shall have it," he said.

'I wish nothing for myself," the humble priest replied, "I wish only that His Majesty would erect a temple in which I may continually pray to Buddha to send down blessing upon your kingdom."

The king agreed and erected the temple of Hungnyun-sa; however, there were not many converts. The people mistrusting him tried to kill A-do believing him to be an evil sorcerer. The good priest evidently discouraged with his efforts in a mundane life dug his own tomb, entered it and sealed the door tightly shut.

Apparently during the following years Buddhism died out. In 527 Yi Ch'a-don was martyred for the teaching of Buddhism and the faith rapidly spread throughout the king-

dom. King Pob-hung stepped down from the throne and put on the robes of a Buddhist priest at Aegong-sa while his queen became a nun.

Though the small temple requested by A-do was initially built at the site of Hungnyun-sa evidently after A-do's death it was deserted and abandoned. Probably one of the most engaging romantic legends of Silla relates to Hungnyun-sa, the site of which can be seen near the tombs of O-nung. During the late eighth century there lived a young man by the name of Kim Hyon. Though of a noble family his parents were extremely poor.

Rather than wasting time lamenting his misfortune he vowed he would bring back honor and riches to his parents. There was then a superstitious belief that if anyone prayed all night from the 8th to the 15th of February while circling the pagoda of Hungnyun-sa their desires would be granted.

Kim Hyon decided he would test Buddha and began his prayer-trek around the pagoda. (Even in this day this custom is seen at pagodas on special festival days and is referred to as

The legend of Kim Hyon and the tiger lady is well known in Korean folklore.

t'ap-tori.) While Kim Hyon was deep in t'ap-tori meditation he heard a faint rustle and turning was surprised to see a graceful maiden following him.

The moonlight shone across the girl's elegant features revealing a worried expression. Shyly she approached and spoke hesitantly, "I also have come here with a great desire in my heart but since it is night I am frightened and lonely. Please allow me to follow in your footsteps," she asked. Kim Hyon was so charmed by her radiant beauty that he nodded his head in quick agreement.

They continued to walk one behind the other. Sensing her presence behind him Kim Hyon felt enamored by her feminine warmth. Embarrased by these feelings of affection which stimulated him, he walked faster about the pagoda hoping to keep his mind on the purpose of his worship. The glowing attraction slowly overwhelmed him and soon the couple knew they were in love.

When the final evening of their t'ap-tori arrived they knew they would be forced to part. Taking the girl by the hand he accompanied

her to her home and found it to be deep in the forest.

An old woman hobbled out of the low thatched-roof hut. She quickly turned to the girl, "Who is this that is so brave and impetuous as to keep you company?" she snapped.

The girl explained what had happened at the pagoda of Hungnyun-sa. "This is unfortunate," she grumbled, "But since he is here we must hide him before your three brothers return."

Hardly had she spoken when a thunderous roar broke the silence of the night. As Kim Hyon stood trembling the young maid reached for his hand. He was hidden in the far corner of the hut. Soon three large tigers flung open the door. "Is that the aromic smell of human flesh?" asked the first tiger.

"Nonsense," shouted the old woman in an angry voice, "Now you have brought upon us a real calamity. A prophecy has come from heaven telling us that since you have killed so many humans you will be punished." The tigers paled with fear.

The young girl interceded, "My brothers,you have now broken your promises so often, that Buddha can't condone and must punish you. I have been to the temple to pray for you. If you are willing to truly repent I can redeem your sins and suffer the heavenly punishment myself." Hanging their heads in shame the three tigers agreed to keep the promise and in a moment they were gone.

As Kim Hyon had fainted from fright, the girl woke him and whispered "I cannot forget your tenderness but I must end my own life for the evil deeds of my brothers." Kim Hyon saw before him the stunning girl he desperately loved and could not understand her words.

"It will make me happy," the girl continued. "If I could die by your hand. Tomorrow I will run wild in the streets of Kyongju terrorizing the citizens. King Won-song will offer a reward for my death. Have no fear but follow me into the forest where I will be awaiting the stroke of your sword."

"How can I kill the one I love for gold or fame?" he lamented. He gently chided her for wanting him to commit such an inhuman act.

"Please do as I say," she cried. "My death is heaven's will. After my death you must build a temple for me. Someday we may be joined in another life."

As he embraced his lovely mistress, the youth pleaded but to no avail. Tears streamed down his cheeks as he kissed her farewell.

The following day a large tigress leaped into the marketplace. The king ordered a tiger hunt and offered the rank second to the king as an award. But nobody was brave enough to try. Eventually Kim Hyon came and swore to free the people from this tiger. The king was so grateful that he conferred the title on Kim Hyon in advance.

Taking his sword he ran swiftly into the forest by the North Stream. The girl seeing him ran to her love. Taking his hands in her own hands she pressed them to her breast saying, "My heart is overflowing with joy in that I can meet you again and share one last embrace. Now I can die in peace."

Without hesitation she snatched Kim Hyon's sword and plunged it into her own throat. Kim Hyon stood in shocked disbelief over her crumpled body. As the tears cleared from his eyes he saw no longer the body of a slender girl but a beautiful tigress.

Soon the crowds gathered. The pleased ruler presented additional rewards of gold and silver. Though Kim Hyon now had honor and riches he could not forget the girl he had lost

and the true happiness she had brought him. Near the North Stream he built a temple at the place she had died. This temple was called Howon-sa, the Temple of Tiger Desire.

Even from ancient times the stories of tigers in Korea showed a marked difference from the tales of tigers from other countries. The Korean tiger is more kindhearted and benevolent. It might be conjectured that in this legend the tigress was able to redeem the sins of all tigers for now we can see the Korean tiger in the light of humor, not fright.

The smiling Korean tiger is often depicted talking to other animals or people and even smoking a long stemmed pipe. Often in the shrines of the *sanshin* (Mountain Spirit) the tiger is a friendly, amiable kitten-like animal. To the Korean people the tiger is apparently more friend than foe.

The original location of Hungnyun-sa is designated Historic Site No. 15 and can still be seen in a grove of persimmon trees. The area is adjacent to the new entry highway into Kyongju north of O-nung and the South Stream by several hundred meters. Recently the land was purchased by a nunnery and a new temple will be constructed on the site 1550 years after the period when it was used as the grounds for the first temple of Silla.

A face on a Silla tile discovered at Hungnyun-sa is a rare example. It is seen in the Kyongju Museum. Excavation of Tumulus 98 began in July 1973.

7. Tomb Park in Kyongju City

Several hundred meters north of the stone observatory (*ch'omsong-dae*) is the entrance to Kyongju's Tomb Park, 152,000 square meters of landscaping, containing numerous tomb mounds and tomb sites. Restoration by the Korean government of this area began in 1973 and was completed in 1975.

As a result in the course of excavation many new treasures were revealed. East of Mi-ch'u's tomb numerous buildings were torn down and a new road was constructed as part of the Kyongju Redevelopment Plan. During this construction tomb sites were discovered which were formerly unknown as the burial mounds had long since disappeared.

Archeologists believed that these tombs date between the 1st and 4th centuries. As the tombs vary in style it is believed that this valley during this period was inhabited by a number of different groups of people with differing habits. Among the most notable discoveries were cremation ash-containing jars, a burial mode which previously was believed not to exist in pre-unification Silla.

On the same strata tombs were also found with a simple mode as well as subterranean chambers of irregular shapes made from stone or clay. It is conjectured that these styles preceded the mounded graves with a wooden chamber covered with stone and earth. These earlier tombs to the east of King Mi-ch'u's tomb yielded numerous rare artifacts including a cart-shaped ceramic vessel, weapons with Persian influence, a small gold crown with simple design and many jars and goblets.

As one enters the tomb compound and follows the west trail, the entrance to the tomb of Mi-ch'u is noticed. The gate is usually locked and this tomb can only be seen from outside the fence. With signs indicating the way, the "Heavenly Horse Tomb" is reached at the far northwest corner of the compound. The tomb is designated as Tumulus No. 155.

Before 1973 this tomb with many others was squeezed between many small homes within a populous portion of Kyongju City. The diameter

Ch'onma-cn ong or Heavenly Horse Tomb is an open museum and major attraction of Kyongju.

of the mound is 27 meters while the height is 12.7 meters. Excavation officially started on April 6, 1973.

After 35,000 man days of digging and removing 3,200 cubic meters of dirt the coffin was reached on June 4. About 100 days later treasures began to appear starting with gold earrings.

On July 15 many artifacts began to appear including golden jewelery, beads, a sword, pottery, and gold belt as well as a silver belt and bronze shoes. The gold belt or royal girdle was a major archeological find (length 125 cm.). It is ornamented with arabesque design and heartshaped loops. Thirteen pendants with dangling charms differing in length hang from the belt. These charms include miniature knives, fish, capsules and comma-shaped jade. This most ornate belt to be unearthed in the Orient was believed to have been worn by the king as part of his official costume.

Also found was a heavy corroded silver belt. With adequate treatment at Korea University's laboratory most of the corrosion was removed. The dragon and motif on this silver belt truly demonstrate the superb craftsmenship of the artisans of pre-unification Silla.

Also on July 15 a unique unglazed stoneware vessel with a dragon head and turtle body was unearthed. It has a long narrow spout on the breast and funnel on the rump. Six pendants dangle from the body. The vessel (17.5 cm. long and 14 cm. high) is probably a lamp and the wick was once held in the long spout. In technique this pot is similar to the warrior on horseback found in the 1924 excavation of the Golden Bell Tomb nearby. However, this dragon pot is much more sophisticated in sculptural detail.

On July 26 a gold crown was uncovered and President Park visited the site to encourage the excavation. Of the ten crowns of Silla thus far discovered this is the most elaborate (32 cm. high and 23 cm. dia.) with 58 carved jade pieces. Though the occupant is unknown the estimated date is between the 5th and 6th century.

Within the coffin space a 90 cm. long sword was unearthed. A wooden treasure chest which contained many personal items of the ruler was considered the most valuable find in terms of its content. On 23 August a painting of a galloping or flying white horse was discovered on a birch-

The excavation of twin Tumulus 98 verified that both a king and queen were buried during the pre-unification period of Silla. Tumulus 155 or Ch'onma-ch'ong is reflected in a small pond.

bark saddle guard (75 cm. long and 52 cm. wide). This painting found in the treasure chest was to become this tomb's greatest discovery because of its historical significance.

The galloping horse is a favorite motif of the ancient tribes of northern Asia. The artistic rendering of this horse demonstrated profound mastery of the medium similar to the murals found in Koguryo tombs of northern Korea (37 BC-668 AD). This was the first time for a Silla painting to be found from a pre-unification period. Its discovery caused an immediate sensation and gave this tomb the name of *ch'on-ma* meaning Heavenly Horse.

Three other paintings also unearthed from this tomb provided major documentation to hitherto unknown development of Silla art. Facsimiles of these paintings are exhibited at the tomb's museum.

Two of the paintings are ring-shaped. One portrays a phoenix, a symbol of immortality popular during China's Han Dynasty. The bird with outstretched feathers is outlined in black and painted with yellow and vermillion red on six different attached birchbark panels. Each pose is different. The lines are supple and soft. Stylized lotus petals border each panel. The other ring-shaped painting depicts a man on horseback on each panel.

Among the outstanding examples of the unglazed vessels found was a large jar which contained small nude frolicsome images around the shoulder of the vessel. One pregnant woman is playing a six-stringed *kayagum*

The strong appeal of shamanism is quite evident. Other erotic behavior demonstrates a prelude to sensual love making. Turtles and fish are portrayed on this jar which is ornamented with incised geometric lines. This jar (34.2 cm. high and 22.4 cm. dia.) is now on display in the Kyongju National Museum.

During the excavation of Tumulus No. 155 over ten thousand items were uncovered. Many of them are on display at the national museums of both Seoul and Kyongju. This tomb is now open to the public. The entire project cost over $340,000.

The interior has been reshaped into a domed hall with an entrance corridor. The original river stones were used to refill the grave. A replica of the burial chamber is seen through glass showing how the important artifacts

In August 23, 1973 a rare flying horse painting on a birchbark saddle guard was discovered in Tumulus 155 giving this tomb its name of ch'ongma *(Heavenly Horse).*

were found originally during the excavation. The actual tomb site is directly behind the back wall of the casket room. Facsimiles of over 140 important items taken from the tomb are on display within the semicircular tomb room.

Adjacent to Tumulus No. 155 (Heavenly Horse Tomb) is Tumulus No. 98 which is a twin mound tomb 23 meters high. Excavation started on this larger tomb in July 1973. The base of this tomb is oval with a diameter length of 120 meters and width of 80 meters. The southern mound was excavated first. The work took almost 16 months as this mound is one of the largest tombs in the Kyongju area. (The largest is 25 meters high and designated as Historic Site No. 38, called Ponghwang-dae and several hundred meters away.)

In December of 1974 the northern mound was identified as belonging to a queen of Silla. An inscription in Chinese characters on a silver girdle discovered in the tomb was noticed in the course of chemical cleaning. This was the first time so far that an inscription was found on any object unearthed from any Silla tomb. This absence or lack of inscriptions on previously excavated items hampered the historical study of the Three Kingdoms period of Silla. Now

Tumulus No. 98 has been reconstructed to its original form.

above: *A prelude to sensual love making is depicted on a Silla pot.* below: *Visitors stroll through Tomb Park. The gold crown taken from Ch'onma-ch'ong is considered the finest of the many crowns so far discovered.*

8. The Divine Emillie and Its Tragic Legend
(National Treasure No. 29)

Looking at the Buddhist art achievement of Silla with its many sacred images we are awed by their exquisite development yet rivaling these accomplishments is the superb artistic beauty of the Korean bells.

Some of the oldest metal objects ever found in Korea have been bronze bells for animals which were discovered in the earliest known tombs. However, the technique of bronze bell casting reached a peak of perfection during eighth century Silla never to be duplicated again during the dynasties of Koryo and Yi.

According to records the largest bell ever cast hung at Hwangyong-sa with a weight four times that of the Emillie Bell (National Treasure No. 29) now in the Kyongju National Museum. Four hundred and ninety thousand *kun* of metal was used compared to one hundred and twenty thousand *kun* used in the Emillie bell. However, according to the same historical records this largest bell was one foot higher than the Emillie Bell thus making it difficult to believe that it could have weighed four times more than the smaller bell.

According to museum authorities the Emillie Bell actually weighs about twenty tons. It is also an established fact that the measurement of a *kun* was not the same weight as in earlier periods, both Koryo and Silla.

Of the Silla bells completely intact in Korea today there are only three, with the most recent bell found in 1970 and now on display in the Kongju National Museum. This small 37.5 inch bell has no inscription but was probably cast during the 9th century; therefore, it is not as old as the other two remaining Silla bells. It was

The Emillie Bell (NT-29) is Korea's largest bell from the Silla Dynasty.

accidentally found near the river bank at Chongju City by a construction crew. The bell has two relief devas on the surface.

The other two bells of Silla are registered national treasures. The Emillie Bell (NT No. 29) is largest. The other Silla bell though smaller is the oldest known bell of Korea (NT No. 36). It was originally placed in Andong City, north of Kyongju. In 1459 during the reign of Ye-jong (8th Yi Dynasty king) this bell was moved to Sangwon-sa in Kangwon Province. The 5.5 foot bell of Sangwon-sa was cast in 725 during the reign of Song-dok (33rd king).

Sonrim-sa. There was on the surface of the bell an inscription containing one hundred and fifty characters which gave the date of casting as 804 during the reign of Ae-jang (40th king). The bell was moved to Woljong-sa rather than Seoul as this large temple had no bell.

When the Korean War began two years later the temple was burned by retreating south Korean troops. This superb Silla treasure melted in the tragic fire. After the war Dr. Hwang Su-young, Director of the Dongguk University Museum, brought thirty pieces of this bell to Seoul where they are now kept at the National

left: *Two devas are cast in bronze on the surface of Korea's oldest bell at Sangwon-sa. (NT-36)*
right: *A rubbing was taken from a Silla bell cast in 804. This bell was destroyed during the Korean War at Woljong-sa.*

Another early bell located at Yongju-sa near Suwon City has been listed by the government as National Treasure No. 120. It is accepted by most scholars that this bell was cast in the late tenth century. The inscription on the bell is a fake and was done by temple priests during this century. This 4.8 foot bell, nevertheless, is one of the finer bells of early Korea and is considered one of the earliest of Koryo.

In 1948 near Mich'on Village in the Yangyang district of Kangwon Province an unbroken Silla bell was discovered at the temple site of

Museum.

In 1967 another Silla bell though broken was discovered buried at Shilsang-sa near Namwon in North Cholla Province by Dr. Hwang Su-young. This bell also portrays the intricate design of the deva and is now displayed at the Dongguk University Museum.

Over the centuries many bells were taken from Korea and even now most of the ancient bells of Korea are to be found in Japan. Bells were pirated out of Korea as early as the Koryo period. A large number of bells were taken to

Japan during the Hideyoshi Invasion of 1592. Actually very few bells were taken and none of Silla origin during the Japanese occupation of this century.

Though it is difficult to determine accurately there are now apparently ten to twelve large bells in South Korea of Koryo origin while in Japan over fifty larger Koryo bells can be found at various temples and Shinto shrines throughout the country. One small Silla bell with an inscription is located at the Shinto shrine of Usa on Kyushu. Another Silla bell is located at the Jogu Shrine in the northern port town of

The quality and artistic development of Korean bell making has been recognized worldwide and must be ranked among the proudest examples of Korea's cultural achievements. The apex of this development was reached during Silla with the most perfect example seen in the bell of Emillie.

The Emillie is ten feet high and seven and a half feet in diameter. (Often the dragon hook is measured which gives an additional foot.) Now the largest in the world is the twenty foot Moscow bell, but the Emillie bell is one thousand years older, more beautiful and

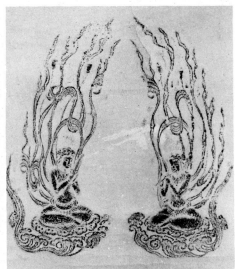

left: *A bell located at Yongju-sa in Suwon dates to the early Koryo Period. (NT-120)* right: *An ink rubbing was made from a broken Silla bell found at Shilsang-sa in 1976.*

Tsuruga. Four or five other Silla bells are also found in Japan.

There are known to be several Koryo bells existing in north Korea with the most famous being the bell of Kaesong (capital city of the Koryo Dynasty) which has a legend similar to the child sacrifice associated with the Emillie Bell. Within the last fifteen years many bells of Koryo origin have been recovered from temple sites through the use of electronic detectors. These smaller bells total almost fifty according to government authorities and can be found in both museums and private collections.

infinitely more graceful. The strong solemn tone reputedly can be heard as far as forty miles on a clear crisp night.

Buddhist temple bells of old Korea which are generally not geometrically stylized are different from either Chinese or Japanese bells in shape and design. One characteristic of Chinese bells was retained: the arrangement of nipples within an arabesque border. A hollow tube extends from the top and during earlier periods one dragon was used to form a hook for hanging. Later during the Yi Dynasty two dragons emerged to form artistic effects. The quality of the bells during Koryo and Yi periods was inferior to that of Silla.

The body of the bell has two ornamental bands of arabesque patterns circling the top and the rim. Below the shoulder are four square areas bordered by arabesque bands. Within each area are nine nipples arranged in rows of three. There are usually devas or flying angels depicted in prayer or playing instruments. Occasionally Bodhisattva or Buddha images are cast in relief on the side of the bell.

The purpose of the hollow tube protruding from the top is to amplify the tone. Korean bells can be heard at unusually long distances. It is believed that initially large clay vessels were buried beneath the bells. Korean bells have no clappers. When the bell was struck on the side with a wooden log on a chain the sound would echo from the clay vessel. From this echo chamber the sound would be transmitted through the tube at the top.

The Emillie Bell embodies the characteristics of the ancient Korean bronze bells. There is a lengthy inscription carved into both sides as well as four relief devas facing each other and depicted separately in a kneeling posture on a lotus flower. Wisps of floating garments swirl into heavenly clouds. This magnificent bell has no defect; therefore, it is matchless in the Orient.

Though now called the Emillie Bell of Pongdok-sa, the actual name is engraved on its surface. "Song-dok Tae-wang Shin-jong" (Divine Bell for Great King Song-dok) is the name inscribed though people still refer to this bell as *emillie.*

Kyong-dok (35th king) commissioned his artisans to cast a bell to honor the spirit of his deceased father Song-dok (33rd king) who died in 737. However, King Kyong-dok died before its completion in 770. King Hye-gong, grandson of Song-dok, had the bell hung in Pongdok-sa.

The question is often raised as to how these gigantic bells could be cast with such artistic beauty of design. Apparently the complete technique is now lost. We must certainly stand

When the giant eleven-foot Emillie Bell was moved to the new National Museum Buddhist ceremonies and pageantry honored this day.

in awe before the master bell artisans of Silla for their accomplishments are unequalled and unmatched throughout the world.

It appears that the ranking bell technicians who served the court in casting early Silla bells were from the Pak Clan and were held in high repute. Today the term for one who holds a doctoral degree is *paksa,* a possible reference to the degree holders of the Pak Clan. These technicians who were skilled in the casting of bronze bells were recognized as the trained degree holders of that day.

One theory is mentioned that wax was used in the casting of Korean bells. A clay mold would be made in a large pit while lime might have been used to harden the clay. Then a thick layer of wax would be placed over the entire mold to the desired thickness of the bell. Relief devas and other decorative patterns would be formed on the surface with wax. The entire pit would than be filled in with additional clay and lime so that only the top of the wax mold would be visible.

As the molten metal (copper and tin) was poured between the clay molds the wax would melt out through the bottom into the ground. This pouring of the metal would be completed during the continual beating of temple drums with fervent prayers by the priests.

The legends of Silla are more numerous than the seeds of a pomegranate and yet most are virtually unknown. But among all the myths of this ancient Buddhist civilization the strange unrecorded account of the Emillie Bell has

travelled to the furthest corners of the world. It is a tale held close in the hearts of the Korean people.

The strange fact of the matter is that nowhere in Korea's early annals is this legend recorded. Apparently it has survived by word of mouth, from father to son. This is the legend that gives the Emillie its name yet the source, and there must have been an origin, has remained lost. . . . an unresolved mystery. Some point to the Middle Kingdom as the origin as certain bells of China were known to have similar tales of human sacrifice.

The great temple of Pongdok-sa had been dedicated by the royal family. Hyo-song (34th king) had arrived in person to mingle with the thousands of pilgrims and priests from every corner of the kingdom. In the great central hall sat the gold Amit'abul, arousing the human soul to aspire to the perfect bliss of paradise. All worshipped the Buddha in solemn ceremony.

Yet something was missing, a bell could not be heard calling those who desired peace to come and worship. But the money had all been spent from the royal treasury, so the king suggested that donations come from Buddhist believers throughout the country. The monks of Pongdok-sa went from door to door and the people gladly donated what they could for the bell.

The giant bell was then cast but strange to say it would not ring. King Hye-gong was completely dumbfounded and wondered if this was an ill omen. Again and again they tried

but always with the same results while the bell technicians shook their heads in disbelief.

One night the chief priest of Pongdok-sa had a strange dream of an old *shinson* (Supernatural Being, or Spirit) who accosted him. His long silvery beard and tousled hair above bushy eyebrows comprised an alarming vision in the mind of the sleeping priest. "Who are you?" he stammered.

The lips of the ancient hermit moved slowly, "You may call me the deity of your silent bell. Complete submission to the will of Buddha has not been accomplished. My bell will remain mute unless you follow my directions." There was a long pause as the awed priest gazed into the dark flashing eyes of the spirit.

Finally the priest nodded and the *shinson* continued, "When your monks were collecting donations they came upon one poor widow who offered to the temple her baby daughter. This child was born in the year, month, day and hour of the dragon and the treasured bell will only ring when it is possessed with the fire-spirit of the dragon. You must recast this bell and offer this child to the fiery metal."

The priest gasped, "Surely the merciful Buddha would not. . . ." and his voice trailed to a whisper. "A noble and glorious way for a child to enter paradise, and isn't it far better to sacrifice one for the souls of many? The only course for your mute bell. . . ." The vision faded and the dazed priest awoke to the melodious tones of a temple bell echoing through the still night from a bleak hillside where there was no temple.

The chief priest then called the other monks together and asked if they could remember a widow who had offered her daughter to the temple. One monk came forward and said that a girl had been offered but he thought the mother had been jesting when she offered her daughter as she had nothing else to offer. "Do you think you can find the place?" asked the priest. The young monk nodded but wondered as he tried to remember which part of the city he had travelled.

Groping to recall he wandered for several days until he finally found the woman and child, a small girl of about three. "What can I say?" thought the shy monk as he pretended to beg alms. "I have nothing to give!" shouted

Why do you return?'' she asked.

''. . . to accept your offer for the casting of the bell,'' he whispered in a low voice. The woman started as fear clouded her eyes.

''I don't understand,'' she stammered. ''The bell has been cast and rumors are that it is mute. Why do you need my daughter?'' For a moment the eyes of the priest wavered. Then in a trembling voice he told of the strange vision received by the chief priest of Pongdok-sa.

The mother almost fainted as she pulled her child closer to her. ''How can the merciful Buddha expect this of me?'' she wailed. ''An innocent baby, and mine, why mine?'' The monk too felt like weeping but could say nothing and politely gave his farewell to the distraught mother. He repeatedly came to call upon the woman over the weeks and months, using every persuasive argument that he knew to convince her.

Finally one day the mother brought her daughter to the temple. The mute bell was again melted down. As prayers for the soul of this

the woman but the priest continued to chant while thinking what approach he might use. ''Is this your beautiful daughter?'' he inquired. ''She must be four or five.''

''Actually she is only three,'' the good woman replied. ''You see it was ill fortune but she was born in the year, month, day and even hour of the dragon. Unfortunately she will be difficult to marry,'' the mother lamented, ''though you can see she is attractive.''

The monk had a friendly face and pleasant nature so the two continued to chatter in the courtyard. ''Several months ago another priest came to my humble dwelling to inquire about donations.'' the widow mentioned. ''Do you know if this bell was completed? I only wish I was not so poor,'' she sighed. ''All I have is my daughter and I offered her, thinking that possibly she could be of service to the Buddha. The priest refused my offer and went away empty handed.''

The young priest cleared his throat, ''My good woman, I am that priest. . . do you not remember?'' The woman peered intently into the monk's face ''Yes, you do resemble him.

The Emillie Bell cast in 770 once hung in Pong-dok-sa to honor King Song-dok. Kneeling devas on the side of this bell are matchless in design.

small virgin were lifted up to the lotus paradise the infant child was thrown into the molten metal. The sound of her tiny voice was heard echoing.... "Emi! Emi! (Momma, Momma)."

On the day the bell was to be tested the monks gathered about while the chief priest prepared to strike. As the wooden log struck and the pealing notes sounded out loud and clear there was a gasp of astonishment as eyes dimmed with tears. The heartrending peal sounded like the infant calling for its mother. "Emi.... Emi.... llie...." low as if to sigh yet sometimes strong and clear but always sad.... a mournful tone resounding over the Silla countryside. The dragon spirit was enshrined indeed in the bell while the legend of sacrifice continued to be told over the centuries and reminded by the mournful tolling of the bell.... Emillie.... Emillie.

This legend is difficult to reconcile with the compassion of Buddhism and many feel that the story is unfair to the tenets of this religion. The inscription on the side of this

above: *The tragic unrecorded account of the casting of the Emillie Bell is known far and wide.* below: *The pealing of this bell can be heard for forty miles. The twin-headed turtle tablet base came from Sungbok-sa site.*

bell leaves a far more noble thought as it reads: "True religion lies beyond the realm of visible things while its course is nowhere seen. As a sound heard through the sky without a clue to its origin, so is religion. We hang this great bell that it may awaken our need for the Sokkamoni. A fitting place to inscribe the virtues of Great King Song-dok whose deeds are eternal as the hills while his glory is like the sun. The noble and true he called to aid him in his rule. Proper ceremonies always accompanied him. He encouraged farmers to enjoy their toil and merchants to exercise honesty. He had little use for gold and jewels while education and skills of talent were considered treasures beyond compare. His great aim was to conduct his life in a noble manner and for this reason people came from distant regions to seek his counsel. All revered him."

The bell of Emillie with its melodious and mystic peal fills a historic niche in the annals of Buddhist art. Through the centuries its tone has echoed through the valleys of Korea, sweet yet sad. And hearing the Emillie Bell one can not forget.

The truth of this tragic legend we will never know yet one will always wonder. During this period of achievement and devotion to the Buddha even kings and queens were as nothing. Through the years the many known records of the scholars were lost and now little remains but what is briefly carved in stone or molded on the smooth bronze surface of a temple bell, the Emillie Bell, a living record with a sad legend, unforgotten.

9. Kyongju National Museum

In addition to the National Museum of Seoul, Kyongju National Museum has the most excellent exhibits, especially relating to Silla culture. Though the entire Kyongju valley can accurately be called an open air museum, the concentration of art objects both from temple sites and ancient tombs makes this particular museum most intriquing and beneficial for any tourist with limited time to spend in the Kyongju area.

Whatever else is seen the Kyongju National Museum should not be missed. It is open during the weekend and closed on Monday as well as major Korean holidays. Unfortunately the descriptive designations of the various displays are extremely limited both in English and Korean for any student of Koreanology. Brochures give little information.

However, as the museum is relatively new eventually it is to be expected that additional comprehensive materials giving more detailed information on artifacts on display will be forthcoming. Even government listed treasures are unidentified in the museum yet they are well marked with permanent stone tablets in the surrounding countryside.

Many large stone objects are placed on the picturesque grounds of the museum. As one walks through the entrance a gigantic stone lantern first catches your eye. Considered the largest of Silla lanterns its original location is unknown. Eight *p'albujung* relief images are seen about the base.

Nearby is a 9th century twin-headed turtle base stone from Sungbok-sa site south of Kyongju. It is believed that the lost stele was engraved by the famous scholar Ch'oe Ch'i-won. Both heads are badly damaged. This is one of three two-headed turtle bases in the

Kyongju area. Nearby is the head from one of the pre-unification turtle bases still located at the site of Sach'onwang-sa. Only four turtle bases remain from this early 7th century Silla period. Again the tablet has been lost.

To the west is the 20 ton Emillie Bell (3.75 meters high and 2.27 meters in diameter) the largest of Silla bells remaining in the world. Another chapter is devoted to this bell.

Along the west side of the museum grounds are eight 4' desciple images carved in relief on four pieces of stone from a pagoda remains. Next to this are five 2' high zodiac relief images which came from several 9th century stone pagodas. Other carved stone image remnants from pagodas are displayed.

On a long base stone are depicted 12 dancing zodiac figures. This unique carving came from a pagoda base at Kamsan-sa site. Six larger zodiac stone relief carvings came from other temple sites as well as tomb sites. One image of a zodiac horse was taken from Nungji-t'ap, the site of which can be seen at Nang-san (east of the road to Pulguk-sa). This was the cremation site of Mun-mu (30th king) in 681.

A tablet base stone with lion reliefs, a lantern pillar also with lion reliefs and various other 8th century carved stones with peacocks, deva guardians *(inwang)*, etc. are displayed. The lion is important as the protector of Buddhist law and scripture.

On the south side are numerous stone cisterns, well rimstones, various types of pedestal stones, and roof parts coming from stone pagodas. Two pagoda replicas of the Tabo-t'ap and Sokka-t'ap at Pulguk-sa are displayed in the center of the southern yard. The original structures are listed as National

At the Kyongju National Museum stone remains from Silla are pleasingly displayed on the grounds. The zodiac horse relief is from a 9th century pagoda. A lion relief decorates a pedestal. The standing Buddha with broken mandala came from Changhang-sa site.

Buddhist images are displayed. On the north side are *inwang* (good king) images from a 9th century pagoda found near Ha-dong.

The large standing Buddha which has been pieced together comes from the temple site of Changhang Village east of Kyongju. On this site are seen two five-storied pagodas with excellent *inwang* guardian relief images. Nearby is the pedestal where this Buddha once stood with a lion relief on the side. Note the excellent mandala behind the image which has small Buddha relief figures interlaced within the design.

Nearby is a seated Piroch'ana image which came from Changrim-sa site on western Nam-san. A large reconstructed pagoda and two head turtle tablet base are still seen at this site. Many of the headless images came from the temple of Punhwang-sa, a short distance from the museum.

The large head came from Chŏlwa Valley

The Yaksa Yorae on a lotus pedestal once stood in Yongjang Valley of west Nam-san. A deva guard is noted in relief on the side of a pagoda.

Treasures No. 20 and 21. Note that the four stone lions are placed as guards on this replica while at the original Tabo-t'ap three are missing, presumably taken to Japan during the early days of the occupation.

The large three-storied stone pagoda at the corner of the museum grounds came from the temple site of Koson-sa east of Kyongju. This pagoda is considered Korea's largest three-storied pagoda along with the pagodas of Kamun-sa. A turtle and lantern base stone were also moved to the museum. The pagoda was relocated to make way for the Pomun Lake Development Plan sponsored by the government. The pagoda base is 17 feet square and has an estimated height of 30 feet. This temple site was made famous by Priest Won-hyo. Fragments of a tablet found in 1915 and 1966 are now in Kyongbok Palace and Dongguk University Museum.

Along the east side of the grounds are stone and pottery jars used for coffins during the Silla era. Pagoda deva guards carved in relief as well as four-sided granite blocks with on east Nam-san behind the Unification Hall. This is the largest head thus far discovered in the Kyongju area. Several other Buddha heads are displayed from unknown temple sites. The 8th century Yaksa Yorae on a pedestal with a mandala comes from Yongjang Valley on the western side of Nam-san. The three-storied 8th century pagoda near the entrance came from Sungso Valley of Nam-san on the way to Ch'ilbul-am.

Inside the museum building the displays begin first with some of the earliest artifacts that have been found in the Kyongju vicinity prior to the Three Kingdoms period. Simple pottery, stone knives, swords and chipping instruments once used by a primitive society are displayed. Iron and bronze implements including unglazed pottery from the Three Kingdoms period are followed by many more sophisticated objects.

The influence of Buddhism is not apparent

Korea's largest three-storied 30 foot pagoda was moved to the National Museum from Koson Temple site a few years ago.

during this early period. However, shamanism had a strong effect on the people. Items found from 4th and 5th century tombs are exhibited. The abundance of silver and gold will catch the eye of all visitors.

The fourth room is devoted to tile and clay sculpturing. The famous feet portion of the *sach'onwang* images are seen crushing the evil spirits of Buddhism. These came from the temple site of Sach'onwang not far away. Various tile patterns reflect Buddhist and shaman influence with the lotus, pheonix, dragon, turtle and also the *tokkebi* (devil chasing spirit) face. This tile came from Hungnyun-sa where the first temple of Silla was constructed by Priest A-do in the 4th century.

Next are displayed stone sculpturing which has special historic significance. The standing zodiac image of the monkey which came from the tomb of Song-dok (33rd king) is notable. Badly damaged figures of the eleven other images are still seen at the tomb site on the way to Pulguk-sa. Also the eight-sided pillar monument dedicated to Yi Ch'a-don who was martyrd for the cause of Buddhism in 527 shows this official in relief without a head and spurting what the legend says is white blood.

The pre-unification triad which came from Samhwa-ryong on the slopes of Nam-san as well as the standing Yaksa Yorae image (National Treasure No. 28) from Paegyul-sa are also important cultural remains. Several *sari* containers are displayed. The many remains which were recovered in 1915 from the pagoda of Punhwang-sa dating to 634 are exhibited. A mysterious crystal glass, the exact purpose of which is unknown, has been placed with these early artifacts.

An adjacent building is used exclusively for objects unearthed from tomb excavations. Here one can see heavily beaded necklaces which have been reconstructed to show how they were originally discovered as the tomb mound was uncovered. Many of the current items seen here came from the more recently excavated Tumuli No. 98 and No. 155.

As one leaves the National Museum of Kyongju a salute of respect is justified for the early artisans of Silla. They were without doubt masters of their trade whether it was bell making on a massive scale like the Emillie Bell or the intricate arabesque design which was frequently employed in royal gold belts and crowns. The impression one has is bewildering as the realization focuses on the incredible skill that was achieved during the peak years of golden prosperity of Silla's pomp and wealth in the 8th century.

Silla achievement certainly belies Korean progress during the last few centuries of the Yi Dynasty as most artistic skills were somehow completely forgotten. Even today the technique of bell and imagery craft is impossible to duplicate. If one only compares

the Emillie Bell with the massive Friendship Bell of 1976 in Los Angeles, presented by Korea as a gift for the U.S. Bicentennial, the difference is realized.

One can also understand that Korea is only beginning to tap the surface of a vast wealth of archeological discoveries in this country. Certainly more is yet to come as the Koreans are now enthusiastically interested in their past and are willing to pursue active programs of archeological effort. The pride that they now have in their heritage has come to the forefront as the survival and reconstruction period after the Korean War grows dim.

above left: *Many broken images came from Punhwang-sa.* middle left: *Dancing zodiac figures came from a pagoda at Kamsan-sa.* lower left: *A turtle head came from the temple site of Sach'onwang.* above middle: *Small Buddhist reliefs are found on a mandala.* above right: *This pagoda came from Sungso Valley of east Nam-san.* next page: *At the Kyongju National Museum are replicas of the Tabo-t'ap and Sokka-t'ap.*

10. Other Historic Sites in Kyongju City from South Stream to North Stream

Inwang-sa Pagoda Remains:

Several scattered fragments of a broken three-storied pagoda are still seen about forty meters south of the road opposite the South Stream at Panwol-song. When the fields are bare of crops it is easy to notice the granite pieces piled by the side of the field. Inwang means 'Virtuous King'' and refers to the deities which guard Buddhist truth and are often depicted at entrance gates.

There is some speculation that this temple site might actually be Inyong-sa (Virtuous Face Temple) mentioned in the death of Kim In-mun, who was returning from China. Others believe that the Inyong-sa site was nearer the National Museum and east of South Stream.

Good Son Tablet of Hyoja Village (Treasure No. 68):

The small 6'4'' stone tablet is located west of Tomb Park and 30 meters back from the main road. Nearby is the Hwangnam Primary School. The tablet was erected in 1122 during the reign of Myong-jong (19th Koryo king) to honor Son Shi-yang. The tale comes from the *Tongguk Yoji Sungram* compiled during the Yi Dynasty. Son spent three full years living by the tomb site of each parent after their death eating only vegetables and keeping incense burning with food offerings on the altar before the graves. The governor of Kyongju, Ch'oe Chong, requested that the tablet be erected to honor this filial devotion.

Stone Pillars of Samnang-sa (Treasure No. 127):

Located west of Kyongju Station and near the West Stream is the temple site of Samnang-sa marked by two stone banner pillars eleven feet high and 6'6" in girth. The pillars are relocated within a fence and positioned 3'6" apart. Samnang-sa (Three Youths Temple) was built in 597 as one of Silla's earliest temples. Many unusual myths are associated with Samnang-sa. Priest Kyong-hung was one of the more famous monks who came from here.

Ch'on'gwan Temple Site:

This temple was dedicated to the girl who was Kim Yu-shin's first love, an attractive daughter of a *kisaeng*. She never married but became a Buddhist nun. After her death this temple was built to honor her. Though there are few remains one unusual octagonal stone measures five feet across. It has a center hole and is broken through the middle. It is thought to be a pedestal stone. The site is located about 150 meters from the entrance of O-nung eastward toward the hills and 40 meters west of the culvert. The stone is on the edge of a field and difficult to find when crops are growing.

Wangjong Valley Temple Pagoda Remains:

The temple site is about 200 meters north of the main road coming off the expressway at the pass beyond O-nung. Park the car just over the pass on the east side and follow the fields along the eastern slopes. The valley is called Wangjong (King's Well) and the temple's name is unknown. Two large roof stones (5 feet across) and several foundation stones are found in the fields.

Iljong (Sun Spirit Bridge):

Stone remains are still seen directly below the National Museum on the South Stream. This bridge was believed to be the entry bridge to Inyong-sa made famous by the return of Kim In-mun from China during the reign of King Mun-mu.

Moon Spirit Bridge of the Good and Bad Sons:

A few stone remains can be seen in the South Stream near the southwest corner of Panwol-song. Many traditional Korean homes are nearby. The bridge became a pilgrimage point for young maidens wishing to succeed in marriage. Because of the nightly visits and nearness to the fortress it received the name of Woljong (Moon Spirit).

Traditions say that sevens sons of a widow wishing for their mother's happiness secretly built the bridge so that she might be able to visit her lover at night without the discomfort of wading the icy stream. However, the sons demonstrated a lack of filial respect for the spirit of the dead father, which was bad. Thus the name was also used, "Good and Bad Sons Bridge."

Site of General Kim Yu-shin's Ancestral Home:

The site is marked by a tablet house and an ancient stone well several hundred meters west of Panwol-song along the north bank of the South Stream. The stone well is about 20 feet deep and still being used. The well stone measures 3'6" square. In the same compound behind the well is a tablet in a small pavilion erected in 1870 to honor Korea's greatest military leader. The well is now called *chaemae-jong* (Profit Making Well).

Ch'oe Village:

Near the area west of Panwol-song are the largest number of traditional style Korean homes. One home has been turned into an elaborate restaurant. Many stone images and pagodas as well as pedestal stones, pillar foundation stones and cisterns have been moved into the courtyards of these well-to-do homes.

Hyang-gyo (Village School):

Located near King Nae-mul's tomb and Kyerim the buildings and grounds of this Yi Dynasty Confucian school are open to the public. The structure was rebuilt 340 years ago using stone material from Panwol-song. Reconstruction was done in 1971.

Tablet and Stone Image:

North of the bus terminal by the side of the road is a small tablet erected during the Yi Dynasty. About 100 meters south from the tablet and 50 meters east of the stream is a headless four foot standing image.

Yongmyo-sa Site:

The site is near the West Stream and north of the railway track. Only one foundation stone remains. Yongmyo-sa (Spirit Shrine Temple)

(1) Inyong-sa pagoda remains; (2) Good son tablet, (T-68); (3) Pillars of Samnang-sa (T-127); (4) Pedestal stone of Ch'on'gwan-sa; (5) Site of Iljong Bridge; (6) Site of Moon Spirit Bridge; (7) Wangjong Valley temple pagoda remains; (8) Well at the ancestral home of General Kim Yu-shin

left: *Near South Stream is the traditional home site of General Kim Yu-shin.* right: *Hyanggyo is an early Yi Dynasty Confucian school.*

(9) Stone tablet near bus terminal; (10) broken image; (11) remains of Kyongju City fortress (HS-96); (12) Image from Saja-sa at Kyongju Station; (13) Ancient forge

(14)

Railroad Station is a three-storied pagoda which was moved from the site of Saja-sa (Lion Temple) during the Japanese occupation. The site was near Ich'a-sa site on the way to Pulguk-sa. Now there are no remains left at the original temple site. The proportions of this pagoda are somewhat poor. Nearby is a lotus design pedestal with other carved remains. A stone guardian image was also brought from Saja-sa but unfortunately it is badly damaged.

Namgo-ru (Historic Site No. 17):

About one kilometer from the Railroad Station toward Punhwang-sa is the historic Koryo site of Namgo-ru (South Old Pavilion). Little can be seen except the marker indicating the site. The pavilion was once connected to the canal and flood control system for the city but the actual architectural design is not completely understood.

Chonrang Palace Site (Historic Site No. 88):

This area is located north of Namgo-ru toward the North Stream. Sixteen foundation stones are found over 16,000 square meters of land. This area is also thought to be the site of Pongdok-sa.

was famous for the pond called Okmun-ji (Jade Gate Pond) which became associated with a legend during the reign of Queen Son-dok. (see story of Woman Valley) Also the talented artist Priest Yang-ji painted and sculptured images for this temple. In one project he modeled over 3000 Buddha images in bricks for the construction of a pagoda.

Kyongju City Fortress (Historic Site No. 96):

Two blocks from the Railroad Station one can see portions of the old city wall which was constructed in 1012 during the reign of Hyon-jong(8th Koryo king). In 1378 the wall was renovated. The final repair took place in 1746 during the reign of Yong-jo (21st Yi king). Now the remaining wall is surrounded by city homes and large elm trees grow from the site.

Ancient Forge:

The stone remains of a possible forge are seen west of the Kyongju Girls' High School. It may have been used for casting coins. The entrance is seven feet wide. The structure is eight feet high, 17 feet wide and 22 feet long The stone surface inside is quite black.

Saja-sa Pagoda and Remains:

Located directly in front of the Kyongju

(14) Saja-sa pagoda at Kyongju Station; (15) Namgo-ru (HS-17); (16) Stone ice house in Panwol-song (T-66)

(15)

(16)

Chapter III
Apex of Silla Temple Architecture

Built on a series of stone terraces ten miles from Kyongju City in the foothills of Toham-san the recently renovated Pulguk-sa (Buddhist Country Temple) probably attracts more visitors than any other temple in Korea today. If we accept the legends concerning this temple, which were written during the Yi Dynasty, we will assume that Pulguk-sa is one of the oldest surviving temples in Korea.

A smaller temple called Hwaom-popnyu-sa was constructed about 535 during the reign of Pob-hung (23rd king). Pob-hung had this temple built for his queen so that she might pray for peace and prosperity for the kingdom. This first temple was small in comparison with the structure designed by Kim Tae-song who lived during the reign of Kyong-dok (35th king) two hundred years later.

The legends surrounding Kim Tae-song are numerous and fascinating. He first lived with his widowed mother. He was an odd looking boy with a big head and flat forehead; thus, he was teased with the name of *taesong* meaning "Big Wall." Though extremely poor, he was

1. Pulguk-sa: *Korea's Best Known Temple*

honest and faithful to Buddhsim. The boy died and was reincarnated into the family of the Prime Minister, Kim Mun-yang.

The lad's rebirth had been prophesied by a mysterious voice from heaven and when the prime minister's wife gave birth to a baby boy they found in his palm the characters of *taesong* written in gold. As the boy grew to manhood his heart was moved by divine inspiration and he designed this marvelous memorial. Pulguk Temple honors the prime minister and his wife, the parents of his second life. The Sokkuram behind this temple was built to honor the parents of his first existence.

As we ponder the legends of Kim Tae-song, the reincarnated man credited with building this graceful structure which epitomizes the spirit and soul of Silla, we may smile but we must also stand in awe before Korea's most remarkable achievement. Pulguk-sa and its annex hermitage, the Sokkuram, symbolize the apex of architectural artistry.

When we contemplate the achievements of Silla artists we cannot but admit that they bear witness to a refined aesthetic taste. Restraint and classical beauty are Korea's unmistakable characteristics of true artistic development. The architectural design of Pulguk-sa is one of constrained dignity and peaceful harmony.

Large stones loosely fitted together without mortar of any kind have somehow outlasted the earthquakes and wars of the last twelve hundred years. Including the recent renovation completed in 1973 there have been 23 reconstructions. The final renovation during the Yi Dynasty was in 1549 during the reign of Hyo-jong (17th king). Now the temple is one tenth the size of the original Silla temple.

Pulguk-sa was not one of the more important temples of Silla as it is mentioned infrequently in all the histories. We can well imagine the size of some leading temples like Hwangyong-sa. However, the balance and symmetry of its former glory are still seen in the walls, bridges, pillars and stone pagodas.

It is no exaggeration to say that the Silla Dynasty was responsible for the most beautiful classical works of art in the Far East, differing both from the ornate and often distorted works of China, and from the frequently pattern-ridden and sentimental arts of Japan.

This Buddhist temple still remains one of the most remarkable achievements of the ancient Far East. At Pulguk-sa we can view six national treasures and one second rank treasure. These include two stone bridges, two gilt bronze Buddha images, two pagodas and one *sari-pudo*.

Sokkye-mun (National Treasures No. 22 and No. 23)

The stone staircases and gates called Sokkye-mun are the traditional two entrances to the temple grounds. These two double-level bridges permit the worshipper to rise and enter over the one hundred meter stone wall. These bridges have been successfully restored with most of the original stone blocks. In its architecture we find simplicity harmonizing with a strong artistic sense of symmetry and proportion.

The larger bridge stairway (NT No. 23) has thirty-three stone steps terminating at the

The twin pagodas called Tabo-t'ap and Sokka-t'ap blend into the architectural harmony.

gate of Chaha-mun. The lower portion of this stairway is called Ch'ongun-kyo (Blue Cloud Bridge) while the upper stairway is called Paegun-kyo (White Cloud Bridge). Down the center of each staired section is one long single piece of granite. The width of the bridge is nineteen feet. The lower arch is eight feet wide and twelve feet high. There are thirteen stones used in spanning this larger arch.

Under Ch ongun-kyo was once a small fish pond. This pond represented the pure land of Buddha or the Western Paradise of the Amit'a world. As a pilgrim mounts these steps to cross the "blue cloud" bridge, he symbolically leaves the world of suffering behind to enter "Buddha's Country" or *pulguk*.

The second bridge stairway (NT No. 22) is smaller in size and consists of only seventeen steps terminating at the gate of Anyang-mun. The lower flight of steps is called Yonhwa-kyo (Lotus Flower Bridge) while the upper stairway is called Ch'ilbo-kyo (Seven Treasures Bridge). The width of this bridge is thirteen

A visitor drinks from an ancient stone cistern near the entrance of Pulguk-sa.

feet. The arch of Yonhwa-kyo is four feet wide and seven feet high.

Since the renovation of 1973 neither one of these two bridges is used by visitors. A trail up the hillside to the right is used to enter the courtyard containing the main hall.

In the area in front of the stone arched bridges are two pairs of temple banner pillar supports, both rising about twelve feet. Nearby is a stone tub (8 X 4 feet). On the right another stone tub is presently in use as water is piped in through the center. The temple well which is still in use is also located nearby.

Haengnang, Kyong-ru and Chong-ru

On either side of Chaha-mun and Anyang-mun, roofed corridors extend out and around the Taeung-jon and Kuknak-jon. Until the 1973 reconstruction only some of the base stones used for these corridors could be seen. Haengnang (Walking Corridor) is completely restored. These corridors are now open to the courtyards but are walled on the outside. One hundred and thirty pillars were used on the upper terrace while seventy-three pillars were used on the lower courtyard.

Chong-ru (Bell Pavilion) is located in the corner of the wall between the two entrance gates. In this pavilion a large drum resting on the back of a turtle is seen. Projecting out over the retaining wall Chong-ru rises high and impressive against the green of the mountain slopes and blue skies. Two wooden pillars are supported by a series of foundation stones beneath the floor. Under this floor there is a passageway.

The Kyong-ru was earlier destroyed but has been reconstructed. This corner pavilion to the east of Chaha-mun contains a large wooden carp and elaborately designed gong.

Tabo-t'ap and Sokka-t'ap (National Treasures No. 20 and No. 21)

On the terraced courtyard before the great hall of the Taeung-jon are two great pagodas of Silla, one simple in construction and the other complex, complementing each other and symbolic of Buddhism's contemplation and detachment from the world.

The legendary designer and architect was the master craftsman, Asa-dal who possibly

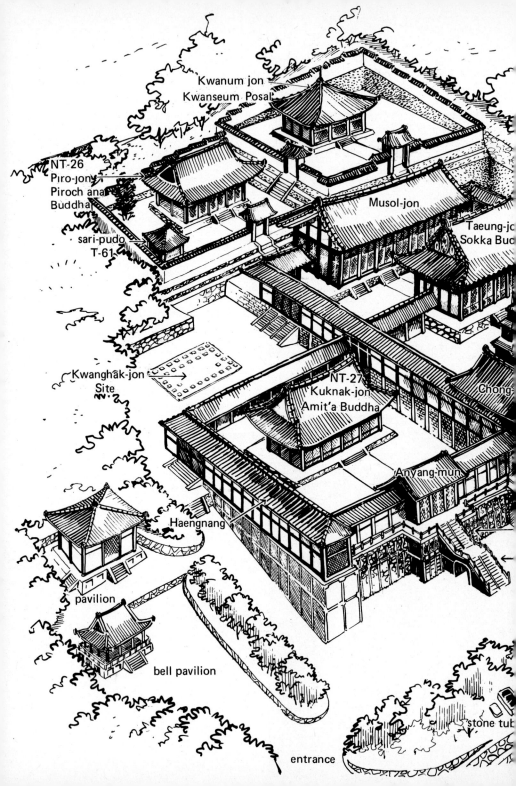

Kwanum jon
Kwanseum Posal

NT-26
Piro-jon
Piroch ana
Buddha

Musol-jon

Taeung-jo
Sokka Bud

sari-pudo
T-61

Kwanghak-jon
Site

NT-27
Kuknak-jon
Amit'a Buddha

Chong

Anyang-mun

Haengnang

pavilion

bell pavilion

stone tub

entrance

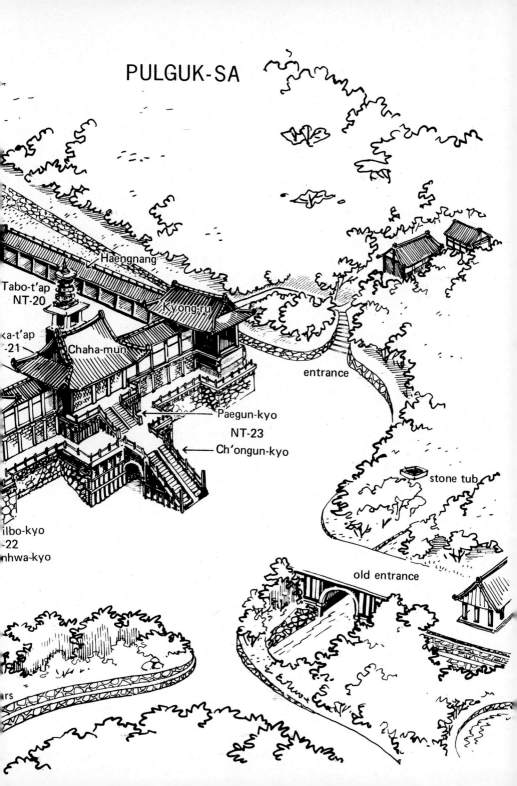

PULGUK-SA

Haengnang

Tabo-t'ap
NT-20

Kyong-ru

a-t'ap
-21

Chaha-mun

entrance

Paegun-kyo
NT-23

Ch'ongun-kyo

stone tub

ilbo-kyo
-22
nhwa-kyo

old entrance

ars

came from Paekche or even as far away as T'ang China. Asa-dal who lost his wife Asa-nyo near Pulguk-sa is the subject of one of the saddest stories of Silla. He sculptured a stone image of a seated Buddha at the place of Asa-nyo's death and slipped back to his own country to never return. (see story of Yong-ji)

From this legend the two pagodas have received the folk names of Yong-t'ap (Shadow Pagoda) and Muyong-t'ap (No Shadow Pagoda). Asa-nyo in attempting to see the image of her husband reflected in Shadow Pond saw only the shadow of the Tabo-t'ap and not the Sokka-t'ap where her husband was then working.

The genius of Asa-dal's craftsmanship is characterized by the calm simplicity of lines,

the elegance of proportion which here avoids exaggeration and the loftiness of expression in the representation of the Sokka Pagoda (NT No. 21) named for the historic Buddha absorbed in transcendent peace.

The complexity of the Tabo Pagoda (NT No. 20) symbolizes the Tabo Yorae's (Buddha of Many Treasures) manifestation in a diversified universe. There are few stone monuments in the Far East which, without a trace of mortar, are pieced together so tastefully and with such rich variation as the Tabo-t'ap.

As the Buddhist pilgrim enters the Chahamun to journey between these two pagodas he will readily realize that as he enters Nirvana he is leaving behind the forces of human existence characterized from the time of creation by

opposites.

The twenty-seven foot Sokka three-storied pagoda with its stair-stepped eaves and low sloping roofs constitutes the basic formula for Korean pagodas. Ornaments and sculptured reliefs are not used. Around the fourteen foot square base are eight circular lotus-shaped stones, 30'' in diameter, connected by long rectangular stones.

In the Sutra of the *Lotus of True Law* it mentions that as the Sokkamoni came at the time that the Tabo Yorae was preaching, eight large lotus blossoms fell from heaven. These eight lotus-shaped stones possibly represent this event in the life of the Tabo Buddha. It is the opinion of some scholars that these eight stones once served as possible foundation stones for pillars in a stone fence structure about the Sokka-t'ap.

In the last reconstruction of this pagoda several items of value were discovered including sutra, wood blocks, a *sari* box and silver sutra plates. These items are now in the National Museum. The pagoda's pillar crown of plate and ball sequence was replaced. Unfortunately one original stone of the Sokka-t'ap was badly damaged during the reconstruction work.

The Tabo-t'ap is unique to Korea and for that matter in the entire East. Also designed according to legend by Asa-dal, this pagoda

The stone staircases and gates called Sokkye-mun are the two traditional entrances to the temple grounds. (NT-22 and 23)

is the best known in all Korea and is depicted on tourist travel posters around the world.

The Tabo-t'ap is named for the Tabo Yorae (Many Treasure Buddha). During the life of Buddha, Tabo was one of the Sokkamoni's disciples. On one occasion after Buddha finished preaching on the subject of the *Lotus of True Law* Tabo replied that every time he heard this sermon he envisioned rising from the ground as a Tabo-t'ap (Pagoda of Many Treasures).

He requested that when he departed this world his cremated remains and *sari* be enshrined within the Tabo Pagoda. After his death he became a *yorae* (Buddha) living in one of the thirty-three Buddhist heavenly realms. The first historical record of the building of a Tabo-t'ap in China was in 732. Less than

twenty years later the Tabo Pagoda was also constructed by Asa-dal in Korea.

While this elaborate thirty-four foot stone structure reveals supreme beauty, the pagoda has also been held up as an example of the versatile genius of Korean artisans. Four stone stairways of nine steps flank the four sides of the pagoda's base. On the six and a half foot base four heavy square corner pillars hewn from single blocks of granite and a fifth central pillar serve as a base support for a considerably more decorative structure of a four-sided and eight-sided story each surrounded by a stone veranda railing.

It is the opinion of archeologists that the unenclosed chamber of the first story may have sheltered a Buddhist image in the past. The roof is supported by spoke-like stones. The

pillars in the octagonal-shaped story are unique in that they were carved to represent bamboo stalks complete with nodes carved realistically. This motif can be found on lanterns in Korea as well as at Horyu-ji a temple near Nara, Japan, which was strongly influenced by Korean artisans.

The pillars are fifteen inches in thickness. If they were actually bamboo the pillars would be capable of supporting the enormous weight. The artist's concept was true to nature.

The crown of the eight-sided roof flares out with a flower design while from the center rises a pillar of plate and ball sequence. At the top of the west side stairway a stone lion sits on its haunches with its head badly damaged. It is believed that once there were four. The lion in Korea is often associated with the Bodhisattva

Munsu, an attendant to the Sokkamoni. Here at the Tabo-t'ap the lion serves as a guardian spirit. Stone lions can also be seen at the pagoda (NT No. 30) of Punhwang-sa and at several tomb sites near Kyongju.

Located between the two pagodas in front of the Taeung-jon is a stone Silla lantern, simple and pleasing in design yet typical of this early period. In front of the pagoda is a *paesok* (Prayer Stone) once used by the many pilgrims.

On the terraced courtyard before the grand hall called Taeung-jon are the two great pagodas of Silla. Calm simplicity of lines characterizes the three-storied Sokka-t'ap (left) while the noted complexity of the Tabo-t'ap (right) reveals unsurpassed beauty and is an example of Korean artisans' versatility. (NT-21 and 20)

above left: *A stone lion sits on a lotus pedestal to guard the Tabo-t'ap.* above right: *The Tabo-t'ap and Sokka-t'ap are silhouetted against the sky.* below left: *This ancient Buddhist symbol represents the unity of cosmic forces within the universe.* center: *Visitors crowd before the Tae-ung-jon* below right: *The connecting eight lotus blossom stones encircle the Sokka-t'ap.*

Taeung-jon (Housing the Sokkamoni)

The dimensions of the main hall which houses the Sokkamoni (Historic Buddha) are 53 by 47 feet. To the right of the main image is the Miruk Posal (Bodhisattva of the Future) while on the left is the Bodhisattva called Chyehwagara Posal. These two attendants of the Sokkamoni are not so common in Korea as the Munsu Posal and Pohyon Posal. In addition to the central three images are two standing figures depicting two of the ten disciples of Buddha.

As you face the images Kasop is on the extreme right and on the far left is Ananda. Kasop is considered the wisest of Buddha's followers and was selected as the first of the twenty-eight Patriarchs of Buddhism.

Ananda was a cousin to the Buddha and served the Buddha as secretary. In later years as scriptures were being prepared Ananda had the best knowledge as to the actual words spoken by Buddha. He was extremely handsome and thus popular among the women followers. Because of his convincing argument to the Buddha, women were permitted to enter the priesthood to become nuns..

On the right wall of the Taeung-jon are sixteen *nahan* (disciples of Buddha) figures sitting in deep meditation. The *nahan* are not associated with the ten first disciples but were followers who lived during later periods. In the center of this group is the Sokkamoni and his two attendants, Munsu Posal and Pohyon Posal.

110

Musol-jon (Meditation Hall)

Musol-jon with nine pillars is considered the largest building at Pulguk-sa. The platform foundation is 112 feet long. Musol-jon was used as a meditation hall. Until the 1973 reconstruction only the foundation stones were evident but now Musol-jon has been completely reconstructed and is located directly behind the Taeung-jon.

According to one record during the reign of Mun-mu (30th king), Musol-jon had thirty-two rooms. If this was a portion of a temple established prior to Kim Tae-song's master plan for Pulguk-sa in 751 then this is a positive indication that Musol-jon is the oldest known building site of Pulguk-sa. The Haengnang (Walking Corridor) which encircles the area terminates at Musol-jon. Behind Musol-jon stone steps take the visitors to upper levels where the Piro-jon and Kwanum-jon are now located. These buildings have been rebuilt.

Kuknak-jon and the Amit'a Buddha (National Treasure No. 27)

When passing through Anyang Gate after climbing the stone steps of Ch'ilbo-Yonhwa Bridge (NT No. 23) the courtyard of the Kuknak-jon is entered. In front of the Kuknak-jon is another Silla stone lantern with prayer stone. The Kuknak-jon (43' × 35') houses the gilt bronze image of the Amit'abul (Buddha of Western Paradise). The Amit'abul presides over *kuknak* or Pure Land located far west of this world and known as Western Paradise.

This image is one of the three bronze statues extant in Kyongju which were believed to have been produced at the same time as the stone image of Sokkuram behind this temple. From an artistic standpoint this image is now recognized as a classical masterpiece of Buddhist sculpturing. The curved lines and classical symmetry of the figure's anatomy are apparent in spite of the new paint.

The Amit'a Buddha (left) *and the Piroch'ana Buddha* (right) *represent masterpieces of Oriental Buddhist sculpturing during 8th century Silla. (NT-26 and 27)*

Piro-jon and the Piroch'ana Buddha (National Treasure No. 26)

The building housing the Piroch'ana Buddha is located on the high terrace behind the Musol-jon. The Piroch'ana is the Buddha Body of Truth which became fully developed during Silla with the popularity of the Hwaom Sutra. According to the Hwaom Sutra it is from the Piroch'ana that other Buddhas have emanated, including the historic Buddha of India, the Sokkamoni. The Hwaom Sutra stresses the three bodies of Buddha. The Body of Truth is Piroch'ana while the Historic Body is the Sokkamoni. The third body is spiritual and is called Hwashin or Nosana.

Unfortunately the original pedestal has been lost. The hand positions of the Piroch'ana are easy to recognize in that one hand is clasping the raised forefinger of the other hand, symbolizing unity of spirit and matter, also the finite and the infinite. Whereas, the Amit'a Buddha is symbolized by the setting sun, the Piroch'ana Buddha with its "creating gesture" is symbolized by the sun at midday.

Similar to National Treasure No. 27 (Amit'a) the sitting Piroch'ana Buddha is the same in height (6.5 feet) and style. Only the hand positions (mudra) are different. These two images, marked by imposing appearance, forceful body lines and balanced symmetry, are masterpieces of gilt bronze sculpturing. They excel in technique and style the many other gilt bronze Buddhist images of Silla existing.

This image is the oldest gilt bronze statue of the Piroch'ana extant today. One can note the elongated ears which to the Buddhist symbolizes the fact that the Buddha obeyed the higher voice and that every earthly pilgrim must give ear to the eternal laws. The

The recently reconstructed open corridors of Pulguk-sa encircle the Tabo-t'ap. (NT-20)

Piroch'ana's robe is draped simply about the image falling from the arms with unsurpassing grace.

Until 1973 only the foundation stones of Piro-jon remained. The image was also kept in the Kuknak-jon but following the renovation period, the Piroch'ana was moved to its own new building on the original site.

Kwanum-jon

The pavilion enshrining the Kwanseum Posal (Bodhisattva of Mercy) is located on the highest terrace to the right of the Piro-jon. Its roof rises to a central point in the center and the image within is new. During the recent reconstruction, attempts were also made to imitate the traditional style of temple flooring. On each side of this hall small square tiles are used. The circular foundation stones upon which the building pillars rest date to the Silla era of the eighth century.

above: *The Kwanum-jon housing the Goddess of Mercy was recently reconstructed.* below: *The walls and roofed corridors surrounding Pulguk-sa present a formidable defense.* below right: *Architectural skills are once again demonstrated in the reconstruction of Pulguk-sa in 1973.*

Kwanghak-dang, Other Buildings and Points of Interest

During the 1973 reconstruction twenty-two foundation stones were placed within a fenced area behind the Kuknak-jon and next to the living area of the priests. As the name Kwang-hak-dang implies light and study, evidently this former building was used as a study hall. by the priest.

Within the walled area of the Piro-jon is a *sari-pudo* listed as Treasure No. 61. Resting on a highly decorated octagonal base this monument is lantern shaped. The waist portion has a dragon and wave design. The center roof has a turned-down leaf motif. The top portion is a sphere having three *ma-aebul* (Buddhist relief) images deeply carved and bordered by spiral arches. A heavy stone roof projects out as far as the base giving a rather unaesthetic appearance. Due to this broad roof the *sari-pudo* has weathered the

storms of time. This eight foot monument was found on the premises of Pulguk-sa and it is believed to have been constructed during the Koryo period or possibly late Silla. It was originally located in front of the Piro-jon and was taken away by the Japanese but returned in 1934.

Who was enshrined in this relic monument is unknown. However, there is some belief that it may have been a nun by the name of Kwang-hak, who was a royal daughter of Hon-gang (49th king). This assumption was made because the name on the *sari-pudo* is the same as this king's daughter who became a member of the priesthood during the closing years of Silla.

Directly in front of this exhibition hall is a bell pavilion containing a good imitation of the Emillie Bell. It was cast by a famous bell-making company of modern Korea. The buildings to the far west are living quarters for the priests.

114

above: *Early photos were taken at the turn of the century before any major reconstruction. The top photos face east and the bottom photos face west.* below: *Early photo of the Sokkuram was taken at the turn of the century. The Sokkuram was rebuilt during the Japanese era.*

2. Sokkuram: *The World Famous Stone Grotto (National Treasure No. 24)*

The Sokkuram (Stone Cave Hermitage) should be placed in a unique achievement category of its own. To only list it as National Treasure No. 24 does not give due emphasis to its importance in Oriental culture. It is without exaggeration the most remarkable and unequalled art treasure accomplished by Far Eastern civilization.

Other Buddhist cave remains in China are not as artistically complete and unified as the arrangement in the Sokkuram. The Sokkuram, located high on the ridges of Toham-san, about an hour's climb behind Pulguk-sa, (Also a road can be use by bus or taxi), was constructed during the mid-eighth century by the famed Minister Kim Tae-song who is also credited with building Pulguk-sa in 751.

Legend Versus History

History's single reference to this stone grotto called Sokbul-sa (Stone Buddha Temple) is found in the *Samguk Yusa* (Legends of the Three Kingdoms). This legend mentions that while Kim Tae-song was carving the circular dome ceiling rock it suddenly broke into three pieces. The artisan wept bitterly and fell into a trance.

He dreamed that celestial beings descended and repaired this crucial ceiling stone. Kim Tae-song awoke and immediately saw that the stone was restored and in position; however, the three cracks can still be seen. Gratefully he went out and burned incense to honor these good devas.

Legends tell that Kim Tae-song built the Sokkuram for the parents of his previous life when he lived in Moryang Village, as a son of a poor widow. Pulguk-sa was built for the parents of his second life. This is one of the most intriguing stories of reincarnation found among the legends of Silla. Born into the royal family, Kim Tae-song later became minister and while serving Kyong-dok (35th king),

Today the Sokkuram is housed in an artificial grotto behind a roofed pavilion on Toham-san above Pulguk-sa.

116

was the chief architect of Pulguk-sa and the Sokkuram.

The styling of the Sokkuram was greatly influenced by the Chinese and the cave temples of India; however, some of the Sokkuram characteristics such as the orderly spacing arrangement of the various figures, their proportions and contrasts of earthly-divine representations are strikingly unique. Scholars are in agreement that the figures are akin to the great works of China and India. but without a doubt they have a character all their own which is uniquely Korean, unparalleled in the Far East

Astonishment soon swells to curiosity. From where did Korea derive this touch of excellence and who was the master craftsman ? The few examples one can point to in the East are not sufficient evidence to account for the artistic perfection of the Sokkuram images, the soft-loose effect of garments, and stone faces with aesthetically worn or ceremonially stern expressions. In brief the monumental skill developed in this artistic achievement sculptured in stone has yet to be equalled.

It is strange that over the centuries this culmination of artistic achievement emanating from religious piety which made startling contributions in 8th century Silla was to become relatively unknown.

During the Yi Dynasty Buddhism fell into disfavor and this nation's greatest sculptural masterpiece was virtually forgotten and lost from the general public as both Pulguk-sa and the Sokkuram were almost deserted.

Though the Sokkuram may have been known to some local Korean inhabitants the accounts from Japanese sources claim that the location of the Sokkuram was completely forgotten and accidently rediscovered. The Japanese prior to the annexation learned of its existence through the postal authorities. As a

Designated as National Treasure No. 24 the Sokkuram (Stone Cave Hermitage) is the most remarkable and unequalled art treasure accomplished by Far Eastern civilization. The artistically complete cave arrangement is unique for the Buddhist art world and at the Sokkuram can be seen the most classical example.

result the tale of a postman on a mountain trail has received popular acclaim. This story goes thus.

In 1909 a lone postman traveling over the wilderness ridges of Toham-san suddenly had to seek shelter when a thunderstorm descended upon him. He saw an opening to what appeared to be a small cave, so crept inside. As his eyes grew accustomed to the dark ·he found himself standing in awe and wonder before the stone image of a gigantic Buddha, with a serene expression of harmonious peace. Surrounding him stood stern guards and attendants leering at this inquisitive face. This spontaneous outburst of an early artist's sensitive heart and hands again became known through the eyes of a simple postman.

Initially the Japanese Governor Terauchi wished to have the Sokkuram moved to Seoul (at least so he said). He directed a road to be built to Kamp'o so that ships could transport the granite blocks to Inchon. Fortunately this task wasn't achieved. Local Korean authorities declined to cooperate with headquarters in Seoul. And of course no one but the Governor General himself could be certain that the ships would proceed to Inchon rather than the coast of Japan with their precious cargo of stone.

In 1913 the occupation government of Japan spent two years in repairing the grotto. When the workers dismantled the carved relief rock slabs they found a complicated super-structure of larger stones beneath. As a result of the inadequacy of the original reconstruction planning these base rocks forming the super-structure surrounding the Sokkuram were completely destroyed. Cement and iron were used in their place.

By using cement which caused inadequate ventilation the stones began to sweat. Soon water leaks developed over the dome. In 1920

the earth was removed from the dome which was then waterproofed with asphalt and tar. The soil was then replaced. Following World War II there were no programs underway to renovate the Sokkuram until 1961 when Dr. Plenderleith arrived from Italy under the auspices of UNESCO to survey and evaluate the cost of reconstruction. The Korean government then commenced massive renovation which was completed in 1964. Air conditioning and heating were installed to keep temperatures more constant.

In 1973 a toll road was constructed to the Sokkuram. Still though, the one hour climb up the forested slopes behind Pulguk-sa is most rewarding especially in the early morning. To the east the pilgrim is greeted magnificently by a view of the Sea of Japan while far below is seen the coast of Kamp'o and Taewang-am, the underwater tomb of Mun-mu (30th king) who unified Silla.

left and center: *A priest begins his prayers in the Sokkuram as the sun rises from the Eastern Sea.* above right: *From the Sokkuram the Eastern Sea is seen in the distance.* center right: *Cracks on the roof stone remind visitors of the legend and dream of Kim Tae-song.* below right: *Lotus patterns are in relief on the floor.*

Questionable Identity of the Buddha

Because of the water tomb of King Mun-mu and the legendary account that the Sokkuram was built for Kim Tae-song s parents of his first life, it is speculated by some scholars that the Buddha image could be the Amit'abul (Buddha of Western Paradise) rather than the Sokkamoni. The Amit'abul rules over the Paradise World after life. The "dragon spirit" of the tomb of King Mun-mu faces west to Toham-san and the Sokkuram. As Taewang-am was recently discovered in 1967 by Dr. Hwang Su-young this theory concerning the identity of the Sokkuram Buddha is extremely current.

There is additional written proof which comes from sources prior to the Japanese occupation period stating that the Buddha of the grotto is the Amit'abul rather than Sokkamoni. In the writings of the eminent Japanese Buddhist theologian Dr. Ono Gen-myo.the Sokkuram is listed as one of the three Buddhist masterpieces of the Far East.

Dr. Ono mentions that he read in the temple records of the Sokkuram which were kept at the hermitage site that there was a wooden plaque hanging before the Sukwang-jon (Life and Light Hall). Unfortunately these records have since been lost. This building was built below and in front of the Sokkuram. He states that on this plaque were the Chinese characters meaning "Amit'a Cave".

This wooden signboard was made by Cho Sung-sang in the last decade of the 19th century. Cho was assigned as the regional governor of Ulsan. One night while travelling to Kyongju he had a vision that there was a cave image on the slopes of Toham Mountain. In his dream the Buddha was crying out in desperation.

He awoke next morning and asked local villagers if there was a *sokkuram* high on

(left to right) *The four* p'albujung *guardian images are positioned on the southern wall.* next page: (left to right) *four other* p'albujung *images are seen on the northern wall.*

the mountain slopes. He was told there was, so he searched for the cave and discovered it to be identical to the cave image in his dream. He knew then that he had been commissioned by divine messengers to repair and reconstruct the Sokkuram. This he did. He than made a wooden plaque with his signature and left a notation in the historical records.

In 1964 a small piece of this plaque was discovered by Dr. Hwang Su-young, former director of the National Museum. Regrettably both ends of the sign board had been cut making it smaller than its original size. The board was being used in the temple's repair behind the living quarters. This plaque is now preserved at the Dongguk University Museum.

The Japanese initially designated the Sokkuram Buddha as the Sokkamoni with little authoritative proof. The hand positions were rarely seen in Japan but common to the Korean Sokkamoni, Amit'abul, Yaksa Yorae and many other *yorae* (Buddha). Stone was the common media in Korea but relatively unused in Japan where good granite was scarce.

Some Korean Buddhist scholars and historians have even presented the idea that possibly the Sokkuram image is the Piroch'ana Buddha. Traditionally Munsu Posal and Pohyon Posal as well as Chyesok Ch'onwang and Taebom Ch'onwang are attendants to the Piroch'ana according to the *Hwaom Kyong Sutra* of Avatamsaka. Originally the Piroch'ana did not always have the typical hand position that we commonly see today.

The group arrangement of the many figures also points toward the possibility that this

Buddha is the Piroch'ana. Pulguk-sa became one of the larger Hwaom Buddhist temples built throughout the country during the popular rise of the Hwaom sect in the 7th century. There are many scholars seriously wondering today about the true identity of the Buddha of the Sokkuram.

Purpose of the Sokkuram

The recorded purpose for Kim Tae-song to build the Sokkuram for his first mother is difficult to accept and scholars are searching for more logical reasons. The newly discovered tomb of Mun-mu (30th king) at Taewang-am is presented as one reason because of its importance and location near the Sokkuram. Was the Sokkuram built to honor this great king of Silla unification?

Also we can accept the fact that Toham-san served as a natural eastern boundary barrier facing the Sea of Japan. The *Samguk Sagi*

(History of the Three Kingdoms) states that Toham-san was the eastern mountain of the five traditional sacred mountains protecting Silla. The Sokkuram was constructed to protect the eastern coast from Japanese invasion.

Furthermore, we know that King Mun-mu requested that he be buried in the Eastern Sea so that his "dragon spirit" could serve Silla in protecting the kingdom from eastern intrusion. It seems reasonable to accept the idea that the Sokkuram served as an example of the deep religious piety of a people and their faith in Buddha's protective power. Eternally the Sokkuram Buddha watches the Eastern Sea in unity with the "dragon spirit" of the great King Mun-mu.

The name of Pulguk-sa (Buddhist Country Temple) certainly implies that this temple and the Sokkuram were built for more lofty reasons than a memorial to parents. According to the *Samguk Sagi* the prime minister, during the early reigning years of King Kyong-dok was Kim Tae-jong. He resigned as prime minister in the ninth year of King Kyong-dok. The following year construction commenced on Pulguk Temple and the Sokkuram.

The theory has been presented that Kim Tae-jong and Kim Tae-song were actually the same person and the historical recording in the *Samguk Yusa* errored in the last character of the name. There are many cases where lack of careful recording has resulted in inaccuracies with personal names. Prime Minister Kim Tae-jong resigned his position to become the king's chief architect. It is believed that he died before its completion; however, records indicate that the temple was completed by the nation, which implies a national concern for this temple's construction.

Other kings beside King Mun-mu were cremated and buried in the Eastern Sea so it is reasonable to consider that the Sokkuram is a memorial for the ancestral parents of Silla kings rather than the parents of the Minister Kim Tae-song.

Guardian Deities in the Foyer

The entrance foyer (14 × 21 feet) to the Sokkuram is now enclosed by a building. Numerous tiles were found during the initial reconstruction, leading some scholars to think that a wooden structure with a tile roof was used over the foyer. However, others believe that tile rather than dirt was initially used over the artificial cave itself while the entrance foyer was open to the sky.

On side walls of the foyer are eight relief figures of the *p'albujung* (Eight Congregated Devas) who serve as guardians. These seven foot images are carved on a single slab of granite. Originally the two first images on either side of the entrance were positioned facing toward the Buddha; however, during the last reconstruction these two stone images were moved. Now all eight devas face each other across the aisle of the foyer.

Though some are dressed in armor and hold weapons, their general countenances appear congenial compared to the *inwang* (Wise King). The third figure on the south wall has an especially knightly appearance with head slightly turned and feet set apart. Its armor is conventional and amazingly realistic. The hands are expressively raised in salutation.

As the corridor narrows to eleven feet, two

ominously threatening guards protect each side of the entrance. These scowling *inwang (kumgang-yoksa)* with one fist raised to strike are facing toward the entrance. Their bare chests elegantly illustrate the skill of the artist as muscle lines are flexed with super power.

Their waist garments are swept violently and dramatically to one side. The left hand of the northern *inwang* warrior is broken. The southern *inwang* has an open mouth while the northern guard has a closed mouth, meaning the beginning and the end, the first and the last.

At the western end of the ten foot vestibule are two octagonal pillars supported by a lotus design base and encircled by lotus wreaths halfway from the floor. Near the roof over a distance of 6'6" the pillars are connected by an arched lintel stone.

On the vestibule walls before reaching the pillars one sees the relief images of the *sach'onwang* (Four Heavenly Kings). These four Deva Kings are often referred to as the directional guards and are most frequently found positioned in entrance gates to the more famous temples of Korea.

On the north wall is the east king Chiguk Ch'onwang (Protecting the Country Heavenly King) followed by the north king Tamun Ch'onwang (Many Hearing Heavenly King) while on the south wall are the south king Chungjang Ch'onwang (Increasing Prosperity Heavenly King) and Kwangmok Ch'onwang (Wide Vision Heavenly King). This last west king's head has been broken and replaced.

These kings in elaborate armor are crushing demons beneath their feet. Instead of holding such objects as a stringed instrument, pagoda, sword or dragon as usual in today's temples, three of these *sach'onwang* are holding only swords.

The east and south kings are both holding their swords across the body with both hands while facing the entrance. The west king is holding his sword with his left hand while the blade is resting on the left shoulder. This king has an unusual stance as his left foot crosses his right while holding down a crouching

demon. The other kings have their feet spread apart. The north king is holding a pagoda.

During the Japanese reconstruction this stone slab was set in place with the upper left corner of the stone missing. Recently a pagoda relief was found buried near the Sokkuram which turned out to be the pagoda once held in the raised right hand of this *sach'onwang*. It has now been replaced.

Note the sandals worn by the four kings. The leg lacing is similar to the Roman centurion with a thong passing between the big toe and second toe of the foot. This style of footwear can now only be found in Japan but for many centuries was typical on the China mainland.

The first known reconstruction of the Sokkuram took place in 1913 during the Japanese occupation. At this time the stone superstructure was completely destroyed.

At the entrance to the Sokkuram corridor are two ominously threatening inwang *guards.*

The sach'onwang *(Four Heavenly Kings) are on the vestibule walls before reaching the pillars and rotunda. The two guards on the left are on the southern wall while the two guards on the right are on the northern wall. Devilish imps are being crushed beneath their feet. An early photo of the North King shows the pagoda missing from the right hand.*

Central Buddha Image

Slightly off center within the 30 foot domed rotunda is a sculptured octagonal lotus shaped pedestal with eight pillars supporting the Buddha cut from a single piece of granite.The pedestal is 5.5 feet high and 29 feet in circumference. The image including the pedestal is 17 feet high. The left hand is resting palm up on the lap while the right hand, fingers extended and palm downward, is placed gently over the knee of the right leg which is crossed over the left leg.

The gesture symbolizes the call to witness or surrendering of evil and this mudra (position of the hands) is especially popular among Korean Buddhists. This mudra symbolize Buddhism's peace and tranquility while stressing Buddha's involvement in the world of strife and his response to evil forces who question his right to enlighten and save the world.

The Buddha image is sculptured in perfect proportion with stark simplicity while the garments were accomplished by shallow cuts. Curled knots of the head and the sacred jeweled spot on the forehead are evident but not conspicuous. The face is full and round with a comparatively small nose and clearly defined mouth. The eyes are half closed under long arching eyebrows while there is no hint of a smile.

The appeal which cannot be denied is

The universal appeal of the massive stone image in the rotunda of the Sokkuram cannot be denied. below: *An annex shrine at the Sokkuram is dedicated to the shaman spirits.*

universal whether it be religious or artistic. The image seems almost alive in spite of the cold hard stone. .... a superb example of the idealistic naturalism achieved by Silla artists.

Bodhisattva and Disciple Images on Rotunda Wall

The entire rotunda is walled with 15 granite panels each carved with a seven foot relief image. Excluding the entrance the walled surface of the rotunda covers a distance of 62 feet. On either side within the eleven foot vestibule are two devas called Taebom Ch'onwang and Chyesok Ch'onwang. Both are very feminine in appearance and each has an ornately elongated mandala behind its head.

The former is holding a bottle in the left hand and a spirit whisk in the right while the latter is holding a spirit whisk in the right hand and a thunderbolt in the left. As a result of borrowing from other religions these deities, which were originally the Hindu gods of Brahma and Indra, now belong to Buddhism.

During the closing years of Silla the legend is told that the Bodhisattva Chyesok Ch'on-wang descended and sat for ten days in the main hall of Hungnyun-sa, the first temple to be built in Silla. Fragrant five-colored clouds covered the temple premises. This unusual event caused the temple to be immediately reconstructed to its former grandeur and beauty.

In the rotunda next to the Taebom Ch'on-wang is the figure of Pohyon Posal while across the aisle next to Chyesok Ch'onwang is the relief image of the Munsu Posal. The Munsu Posal is holding a treasure cup in the right hand while the waist is thrust slightly forward. These figures frozen in stone appear ready to step from the wall with rustling fabrics. Though feminine in form the serene faces and lithe bodies give these sacred images an aura of dignity and compelling spiritual beauty.

Following the two Bodhisattvas are the ten historic disciples of Buddha. These disciples are monks with lean gaunt faces and long noses typical of the Indo-European. There are five on either side of the rotunda. Their heads are

turned toward each other as if in conversation. The face of each disciple shows individual character as well as racial differences which emphasizes the fact that the Buddha's original ten followers were from many racial origins.

The sculptural appearance representing humility on the faces of these religious personalities seem strangely out of place with the usual characterization of Chinese T'ang prevalent during this century of Silla. Their appearance is earthly as if they truly belong to mankind.

The historical names of the ten disciples are well known but the exact identification of these disciples on the rotunda wall of the Sokkuram is uncertain. The suggested order now posted on the tourist diagram at the Sokkuram site is by no means conclusive.

According to the Buddhist Research Institute in Seoul the correct order of the ten disciples should be thus: (south side) Mognyon, Kajonyon, Subori, Upari and Ananda; (north side) Saribul, Kasop, Puruna, Anayul and Rahura.

The first disciple (next to Pohyon Posal) is Mognyon who was a miracle worker and best friend of Saribul (across the aisle next to Munsu

above: *Four Bodhisattvas are on either side of the pillars directly inside the rotunda. These eleven foot images are from left to right Taebom Ch'onwang, Pohyon Posal, Munsu Posal, and Chyesok Ch'onwang.* below: *The following disciples from left to right on the southern wall are Mognyon, Kajonyon, Subori, Upari and Ananda.*

The last five disciples from left to right on the northern wall are Rahura, Anayul, Puruna, Kasop and Saribul.

Posal). Mognyon demonstrated filial devotion and interceded to rescue his mother from the torments of hell which she had earned through her evil life on earth.

The second disciple Kajonyon was the best debater. His thoughtful pose illustrates a firm persuasiveness which would enhance the spread of the Buddhist doctrine.

Subori was the exponent of the Buddhist doctrine of emptiness. His right hand shows the circle symbol representing emptiness or nothing.

The fourth disciple is Upari who was the legal advisor for the ten disciples. By earlier profession he was a barber so his responsibility was to shave the heads of those who took the vows. He is holding in his left hand the begging bowl illustrating complete compliance to Buddha's desire that all disciples rely on others for sustenance.

The fifth disciple on the south wall next to the Kwanseum Posal is Ananda. His hands are quietly folded in meditation. Ananda was a cousin to the Buddha and second in importance among the disciples. As Ananda was the official secretary for the group his memory was best concerning the exact wording of the sermons which were later recorded in Sutras.

The disciple next to Munsu Posal on the north wall is Saribul who was considered the wisest of all the disciples but who unfortunately died before the death of Buddha. Saribul was the Buddha's closest friend.

The second image represents the famed Kasop who was considered the most important of Buddha's disciples. After Buddha's death Kasop was selected to succeed him and he became the first of 23 Patriarchs of Buddhism. His hand is raised as if to request alms. The wandering Buddhist monks who now beg throughout the countryside look to Kasop as their patriarchal protector.

The next image which holds a bottle in the right hand is Puruna who was considered the most accomplished preacher of the entire ten disciples. It is interesting· to note that his birthday was the same as Buddha's.

The fourth image represents blind Anayul.

He is holding in his hands a small stick-like object. The story is told that while Buddha was preaching Anayul fell asleep and afterwards the Buddha chastised him. Vowing he would never close his eyes again he continued to meditate for many days and nights until finally his exhausted eyes became blind. His other senses became acutely sensitive, Anayul could through his other senses actually visualize things beyond the range of normal vision.

The last disciple on the north wall is Rahura. His face is not lean like the others but has a Grecian appearance, kind and princely. Rahura was the only son of Prince Siddharta (Buddha) who referred to him as his worldly obstacle. Rahura's name means obstacle. Buddha felt that a family hindered his mission to go out and preach. Rahura became the first child priest and was diligent in his studies.

Goddess of Mercy (Symbolism of the Eleven-Faced Kwanseum)

On the rear wall of the rotunda directly behind Buddha and between the disciples Ananda and Rahura is the eleven-faced image of the Kwanseum Posal. Representing the compassion of Buddha, the Kwanseum (or Kwanum) is the best-known Bodhisattva in Korea and is commonly referred to as the "Goddess of Mercy." Historically in Asia the Bodhisattva is neither male nor female. But the feminine form is usually used to denote compassion.

This image is considered by many scholars as the most beautifully sculptured figure in all Korean art as it is tall, slender and elegantly dressed in astonishingly fluent and realistic garments with tassels and jewelry arranged in loops. Crossed folds and knots are gracefully tied to enhance the supple feminine form beneath while emphasizing the thinness of the fabrics.

The flatness of the body does not detract from the overall gracefulness which seems to radiate a spiritual dignity rather than physical

On the rear wall of the rotunda directly behind the central Buddha is the most unusual eleven-headed Goddess of Mercy (Kwanseum). The other ten heads are located in the crown.

Upon careful scrutiny it is still difficult to determine the expressions on the ten small faces. Some theories have been presented in this respect.

One opinion is that the three heads on the right side (south) of the crown portray angry expressions while the three heads on the left side (north) represent expressions of true compassion. Three heads on top and in front appear to have laughing countenances while the remaining head on the peak of the crown is roaring with laughter. These expressions of the Kwanseum represent four personalities of this Bodhisattva as it views the struggles of all mankind.

Some people never obey the laws of Buddha thus making the Kwanseum angry. Man will then turn from his evil ways and do good so the expression changes to one of compassion. However, humans tend to err and though trying to follow Buddha's laws occasionally slip, so the Kwanseum watches these attempts with humor. This third personality of the Kwanseum is one of smiling laughter.

Finally as the Kwanseum looks upon the whole world attempting to do right and helpless in its plight as it never reaches the ultimate goal of perfection, the Bodhisattva laughs aloud and in this respect the miseries of the world tend to grow lighter. This roaring laughter represents the ultimate of Buddha's wisdom, broad-mindedness and understanding as all are loved, the good and bad.

The ten heads of the Bodhisattva of Mercy are artistically portrayed in the crown with little aesthetic offense on the rear wall of the Sokkuram rotunda.

beauty. The Kwanseum is standing on a simple lotus pedestal and holding in its left hand a lotus flower in a bottle containing the "dew of divinity," to be given to those suffering and in torment.

Though this eleven-headed concept is often difficult to portray artistically, in this image symbolism is notably well achieved with little aesthetic offense. Ten heads are symmetrically arranged in an ornate crown while in the center a standing image represents Buddha's wisdom.

Another aspect of symbolism which causes one to ponder is that the angry faces (south side) represent the military word *mu* while the three faces of mercy (north side) represent the word *mun* for civilian officials. The scholar and the military are drawn together to form the name *mun-mu* which is also the posthumous title for the 30th king of Silla whose water tomb the Sokkuram faces at Taewang-am.

There are many legends concerning the Kwanseum in Korea but the ones that tell about the eleven-faced Kwanseum are few. From the records of old Silla comes this story. The Emperor of China had a court favorite whose beauty was unparalleled and wishing always to look upon her beauty in the bloom of youth he decided to have her portrait painted. A young eminent artist was commissioned to paint a faithful likeness of this Asian beauty.

However, when he was adding the finishing touches to his portrait, he was so dazzled by the exquisite charm of his subject that his hand trembled and his brush slipped, making a mole-like mark just below the girl's navel. The artist tried to paint it out but could not. Knowing that he had no time to cover up this flaw, he worried because he well realized that women are ashamed of any imperfections even in paintings.

As the portrait was brought, the Emperor after close inspection became livid with rage. "This painting is too realistic! How could you have known that she had a mole under her navel?" screamed the jealous Emperor, who was certain that the artist had taken liberties with his favorite concubine.

The artist was thrown into prison with the execution set for the following day. Fortunately the prime minister intervened and pleading for the artist's life said, "He is straight like the bamboo and has known no woman but his own wife." The Emperor agreed to give him one more chance and spoke to the artist saying, "Since you were so clever as to paint the mole without seeing it, paint for me the picture of the lovely woman whom I saw in my dreams last night and you shall have your pardon."

The artist then painted the graceful figure of the eleven-faced Kwanseum much to the surprise of all." You are right," exclaimed the astonished Emperor and reluctantly gave the artist his freedom. After this narrow escape the artist no longer wished to live in his own country so crossed the sea to Silla where he painted again the portrait of the merciful Kwanseum which remained as an admired treasure enshrined in Chungsaeng-sa during the years of Silla.

Ten Kamshil on Sokkuram Walls

High on the circular wall of the 30 foot dome of the rotunda are ten niches, eight of which contain small images which even to this day remain a mystery although there has been some speculation as to their identity. The height of the images varies from 28—32 inches and they maintain a variety of poses. These niches are called *kamshil* which is literally translated as a "small room or hut."

In the first two niches directly inside the entrance the images are missing. During the Japanese occupation these two figures were transported to Japan by high ranking officials. It is said that in the forehead of the two stolen images were crystal jewels similar to the original crystal piece once found in the center forehead of the main Buddha.

In the original construction the Sokkuram was built so that the first rays of the morning sun shining through the entrance would cause a rosy-flesh glow on the stone Buddha. The sunlight reflecting from the crystal jewel of the forehead would refract to the jewels of the two *kamshil* images in front of the Buddha. The light would be refracted again from the *kamshil* images over the shoulders of the Buddha to radiate upon the head of the eleven-faced Kwanseum.

Several years ago a piece of the crystal was found (probably belonging to the main Buddha) which was surfaced with gold on the reverse side. The gold evidently increased the capability of the light refraction of the crystal. Directly behind the image there was previously a small five-storied pagoda believed to have been made of white marble. This pagoda was also taken with the two *kamshil* images to Japan. There is now a rumor that these lost treasures have been located and may some day be returned to Korea.

The average visitor will find it difficult to leave the Sokkuram and will only do so with

reluctance. The natural sense of beauty in lines and proportions depicted in baffling simplicity has a strange magnetism on those who come for the first time. Within the Sokkuram we see one distinctive quality of Korean art. . . . a certain earnestness matched with dignity and grandeur, classic and idealistic naturalism yet simple with modest and unobtrusive interpretation of form—which is seen in the classic art of Greece.

Korea in her position between China and Japan maintained the role of assimilating and passing on to Japan the arts of China. During this period of T'ang assimilation she improved upon it in accordance with her national characteristics and raised it to the highest classical plateau in the Far East. Korea not only accepted the tradition of her teacher but in many cases ennobled it. In the Buddhist art of cave temple tradition, Korea has produced the most classical example.

above right: *High on the rotunda wall in the Sokkuram are eight* kamshil *images. There are ten niches but two remain empty due to theft in the early days of the Japanese occupation.* **below:** *Sunlight from the entrance silhouettes the Buddha's head on the mandala above the Kwanseum.*

above left: *Beyond the stone pillars in the vestibule is the Sokkuram entrance.* above right: *A priest at prayer stands before the masterpiece of Buddhist art.* below: *The identity of most of the eight* kamshil *images, located in wall niches, is unknown.*

Chapter IV
Historic Sites Between Kyongju, Pulguk-sa and Beyond

1. Sach'onwang-sa Site: *Guardian Temple of Four Heavenly Kings (Historic Site No. 8)*

Sach'onwang-sa built south of Nang-san (Wolf Mountain) during the early years of unification is considered one of the more important temples of Silla. The site is located about two kilos from the Kyongju National Museum on the left side of the highway to Pulguk-sa. The 8.5 foot banner pillar supports marking the entrance of this great temple are positioned just off the road on the left among a cluster of homes.

Sach'onwang refers to the Four Heavenly Kings or Devas who legendarily honor the Buddha and guard the heavenly peaks of Sumi-san. These images are often seen today in the entrance gates of the larger temples of Korea. Originally these Devas were rulers of kingdoms located in the four corners of the universe. Small dwarfs representing the enemies of Buddha are usually seen being crushed beneath the feet of the *sach'onwang*.

As the ferocious *sach'onwang* protect Buddhism, so this temple was built in 669 during the reign of Mun-mu (30th king) to protect Silla against the mighty T'ang armies of China. When the celestial armies turned upon Silla after the defeat of Paekche and Koguryo, King Mun-mu ordered his troops to fight them. The Emperor of T'ang was indignant over these events and had the Silla envoy Kim In-mun, the brother of King Mun-mu, thrown into prison, and prepared for an invasion of Silla

The king sought the advice of the mysterious Buddhist monk Myong-nang who had studied supernatural arts. Priest Myong-nang suggested that Sach'onwang-sa be erected south of Nang-san and be used as a military training camp.

The temple of Sach'onwang was one of the most important early temples of Silla. (HS-8) The peaks of Nam-san rise in the distance in front of this temple site.

Priest Myong-nang and his disciples bowed before the images of Sach'onwang-sa calling upon the spirits of heaven and sea. A typhoon arose and swallowed the Chinese vessels before they reached Silla shores. The following year the exasperated T'ang Emperor sent fifty thousand men on a second expedition and they met the same fate. The Emperor summoned the Korean envoys who were in prison and asked, "What is this magic art that you have in Silla?"

The envoys cleverly answered, "We heard that the Silla king erected the Sach'onwang Temple on Nang-san to pray for the long life of the Emperor in gratitude for the help of his armies in unifying Silla."

This delighted the Emperor and he sent an envoy to Silla to inspect this mysterious temple dedicated for his welfare. King Mun-mu politely demurred that the honored T'ang envoy should wait for a month as the temple was now being repaired. Pleasures and entertainment were provided for this special envoy. The king then ordered workmen immediately to construct a replica of Sach'onwang-sa in front of the present temple. The T'ang envoy was then taken to this new temple but the ruse did not work.

The envoy was given a luxurious feast served by a bevy of the most beautiful maidens in the land. After being presented with large sums of money he returned to report to the Chinese Emperor that the people of Silla prayed for the Emperor's long life in a new temple.

At this temple site were found four broken images of the sach'onwang. The upper portion of their bodies was missing. These carvings are considered masterpieces and are now to be seen in the Kyongju National Museum.

On the site the foundation stones for two large wooden pagodas remain. The wooden pagoda predates the stone and the foundations of a few wooden pagodas can be seen at several temple sites within the Kyongju area. The base size of the east and the west pagodas of Sach'onwang-sa are 28 feet square.

We can only guess about the number of

Stone pillars are seen at the entrance of Sach'onwang Temple site near the modern paved highway to Pulguk-sa.

stories and actual height. The large rock in the center which held the central support pillar is almost four feet square. Behind the foundation stones of the two pagodas are additional foundation stones for the main hall.

In front of the temple site and next to the highway are two stone turtles with their heads missing. The severed head of the north turtle can now be seen in the Kyongju National Museum. Both stone turtles are six by seven feet in size. Their dimensions are somewhat smaller than the turtle tablet base for Kim In-mun (Treasure No. 70).

The sculpturing skill of these two stone turtles is similar to the exquisite monument stele at the tomb of King Mu-yol (National Treasure No. 25) and tomb of Kim In-mun. The shell appears natural and life-like with hexagonal relief designs covering the back. These turtle monuments are two of the four earliest carved stone turtles of the Silla period.

2. Mangdok-sa Site: *An Unsuccessful Ruse*
(Treasure No. 123 and Historic Site No. 7)

The site of the temple of Mangdok (Yearning for Virtue) is located directly across from Sach'onwang Temple site beside the main highway to Pulguk-sa. The temple banner pole supports are seen near a grove of pines. These support pillars have been listed as Treasure No. 123.

Mangdok-sa was built in 670 following the construction of Sach'onwang-sa during the reign of Mun-mu (30th king). As mentioned previously Mangdok Temple was hurriedly constructed upon the order of Mun-mu to protect and conceal the Sach'onwang Temple from the suspicious envoy of T'ang China. It

was completed in one month.

Mangdok-sa also had two wooden pagodas and it is claimed that both were 13 stories high. All 16 foundation stones of the east pagoda still exist. The stone staircase entrance is intact and faces south. The pagoda's foundation stones are positioned in an area 25 feet square which made these pagodas slightly smaller than their counterparts at Sach'onwang-sa.

It was in front of this temple along the sandy river that the bereaved wife of Pak Che-sang prostrated herself in mourning for her patriotic husband who was killed while loyally serving the country. People even today call this area Changsa (Longing Sand) for the widow could not long endure the yearning of her heart for a husband who would never return.

She later took her three daughters to Ch'isul Pass and there mourned in sorrow until her death. She was faithful and never remarried. A rock formation called *mangbusok* (Yearning for Husband Stone) can still be seen high in the mountains but is difficult to reach without a guide.

Though Mangdok-sa was built as a ruse in tricking the Chinese into believing that the name of "Yearning for Virtue" was meant to honor the T'ang Emperor, it also seems to have interesting implications for the wife of Pak Che-sang.

During one ceremony held at Mangdok-sa, Hyo-so (32nd king) attended in person and while worshipping was strangely attracted to a ragged priest standing nearby. Bent with age and dressed in course gray cloth he looked out of place among other temple monks dressed in rich and gaudy ceremonial attire.

The bedraggeled fellow asked if he might worship with the others and as the king was in

above: *The pillars of Mangdok-sa site still stand in the fields. (T-123)* below: *A turtle tablet base stone lies at Sach'onwang-sa site.*

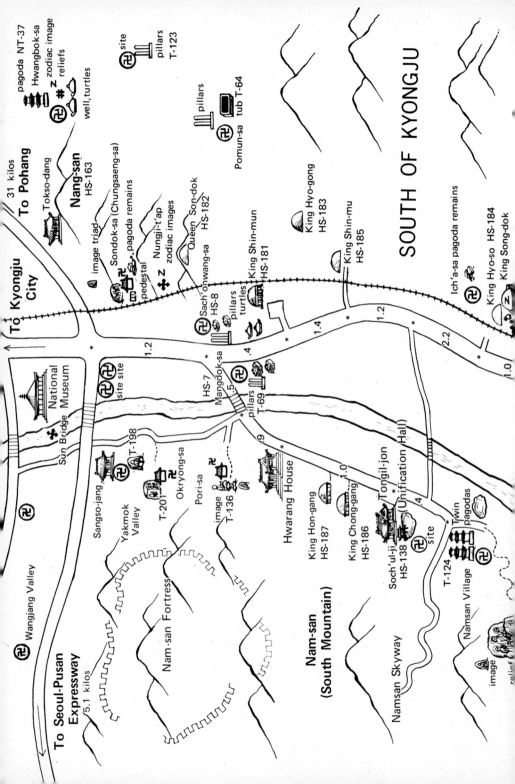

SOUTH OF KYONGJU

To Kyongju City

To Pohang
31 kilos

To Seoul-Pusan Expressway
5.1 kilos

pagoda NT-37
Hwangbok-sa
z zodiac image
reliefs
well, turtles

site
pillars T-123

pillars
tub T-64
Pomun-sa

Tokso-dang
Nang-san
HS-163

Sondok-sa (Chungsaeng-sa)
pagoda remains
Nungji-t'ap zodiac images
Queen Son-dok HS-182
image triad
pedestal
z
Sach'onwang-sa HS-8
pillars turtles
King Shin-mun HS-181

King Hyo-gong HS-183

King Shin-mu HS-185

Ich'a-sa pagoda remains
King Hyo-so HS-184
King Song-dok

National Museum

Sun Bridge

Wangjang Valley

site site

Mangdok-sa
pillars T-69

1.2

.4
.5

1.4

1.2

2.2

1.0

HS-7

T-198
Sangso-jang
Yakmok Valley
Okryong-sa
T-201
Pori-sa
image T-136

Hwarang House

King Hon-gang HS-187

King Chong-gang HS-186

Tongil-jon (Unification Hall)

Soch'ul-ji HS-138
site
T-124
Twin pagodas
Namsan Village

Nam-san (South Mountain)

Nam-san Fortress

Namsan Skyway

image
relief

.9

1.0

.4

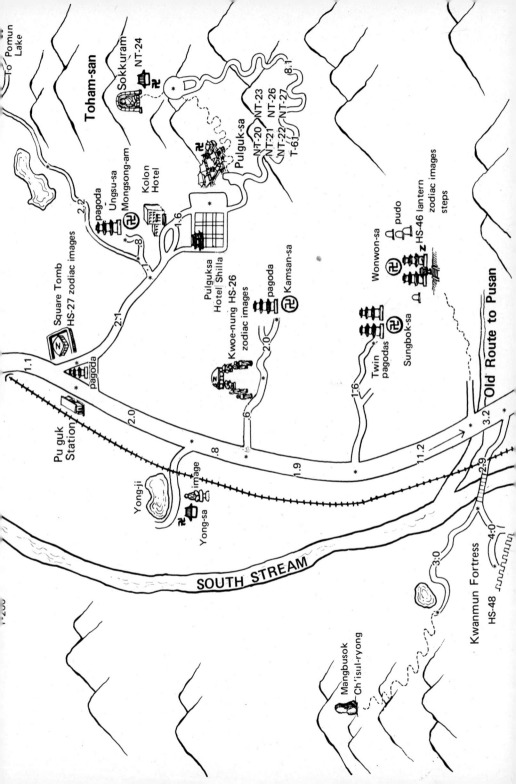

d good mood he consented. Following the ceremony King Hyo-so asked the poor priest where he lived. "I come from Pip'a-am on South Mountain," the priest replied.

Jokingly the king laughed, "When you return to your temple you must not mention the fact that you offered sacrifices to the great Buddha in the presence of the king."

The startled monk smiled in a tolerant way and replied, "My good king, you also must not mention when you return to the palace that you worshipped in the company of the Sokka Buddha." And with these words he rose into the air and disappeared toward the south.

Realizing with shame that the Buddha had actually attended this ceremony, he sent court attendants to follow the flying monk. However, they only found his staff and wooden bowl at the place he disappeared.

above: *Sculptured stones are scattered about the temple site of Mangdok. (HS-7)* right: *The tomb of Shin-mun is located a few feet from the highway leading to Pulguk-sa. (HS-181)*

3. Tomb of King Shin-mun: *Son of Great King Mun-mu* *(Historic Site No. 181)*

The tomb of Shin-mun (31st king) is located beside the highway a short distance from the temple site of Sach'onwang. This tomb is considered transitional in style. The tomb of King Mu-yol, the grandfather of Shin-mun, does not have a retaining wall. However, three decades later King Shin-mun's tomb was more firmly designed by adding cut stone beneath the mound which is supported by 44 triangular buttresses.

The meaning of four is unlucky as the number represents death. It is interesting to observe that here at Shin-mun's tomb the four is doubled (forty-four) for the number of bracing buttress stones. One wonders if this was accidental or planned for the original construction of the tomb.

In only three known tombs are triangular buttresses like this found. This tomb is the largest. The circumference is 303 feet while

the distance over the mound is 117 feet. The other tombs traditionally belong to Song-dok (33rd king) and Min-ae (44th king).

Following the death of Mun-mu (30th king) in 681 his eldest son Shin-mun became king and ruled for eleven years. King Shin-mun had two sons who later became 32nd and 33rd kings of Silla. Probably the most far-reaching and important event occurring during Shin-mun's reign was the invention of *idu*, a form of phrase endings used in the margins of Chinese texts to aid the Korean reader. In these early days reading was as rare an accomplishment as it was in England during the days of Chaucer. Clerks were hired to write.

This difficulty was so great that Sol Ch'ong, the illegitimate son of the king's favorite Priest Won-hyo, attempted to find a solution to this problem. Sol Ch'ong's invention was the first outcry against the difficult primitiveness of the Chinese ideography. The *idu* remained through the centuries and was commonly used until the invention of *han'gul* in the mid-fifteenth century.

Its invention marked a new era in the literary growth of the Korean people. Probably one of the most important outgrowths of *idu* was the *hyangga* (folk song) which was a true Korean folk song developed by the Silla people. About 25 *hyangga* remain today of the many that were written. Usually the *hyangga* illustrated some moral or in many cases contained political overtones in much the same way that nursery rhymes of England were satires against the throne. However, the *hyangga* was meant to be sung or at best chanted.

The legend of the "Flute which Calmed Ten Thousand Waves" took place in the reign of King Shin-mun. During the rule of his father the construction of Kamun-sa was begun on the east coast. The purpose of this construction was to secure divine aid against the Japanese pirates. Many temples were built as a protective influence against the enemies. To name only a few, Hwangyong-sa, Sach'onwang-sa and Mangdok-sa can be cited.

But unfortunately before Kamun-sa was completed King Mun-mu died and was buried at sea near the temple site. Legends tell that his spirit became a sea dragon to live in the eastern seas and protect the kingdom. In the second year of King Shin-mun's reign Kamun-sa was dedicated.

One day a small island floated near shore off Kamun-sa and when it was reported to the king he summoned his astrologers. They advised him that the sea spirits of the General Kim Yu-shin and his own father, King Mun-mu, had come to present invaluable treasures to the kingdom.

King Shin-mun journeyed immediately to the coast. At a place along the shores the king received a piece of bamboo and a jade belt. Legends tell that within the many jeweled ornaments of the belt lived a dragon who would assist in the protection of the kingdom. After King Shin-mun's return to the palace a flute was made from the bamboo piece and was stored in a vault at Panwol-song.

It was believed that when this flute was played the enemies of Silla would flee, plagues would disappear, rain would come during droughts, and on the sea the wind would become mild and the waters calm; so the flute was prized as a national treasure and given the title of "Flute to Calm Ten Thousand Waves."

No one is certain as to what eventually happened to the flute. There are some rumors that the scholar Ch'oe Ch'i-won took the flute with him into exile in the Kaya Mountains near Haein-sa.

left: *Song-dok's tomb is one of six royal tombs now known where the zodiac figures are evident. This tomb* (also right photo) *is the only example where the images are not in relief but are statues. (HS-28)* center: *The tomb of King Song-dok's brother Hyo-so is nearby. (HS-184)*

4. Tombs of King Song-dok and His Brother: *During Peace and Prosperity of the Kingdom.* (*Historic Sites No. 28 and No. 184*)

Hyo-so (32nd king) was the eldest son of Shin-mun (31st king) who began his rule at age sixteen and reigned for ten years beginning in 692. Song-dok (33rd king), his younger brother, is buried nearby in the same grove of pines, however, King Song-dok's tomb is considerably more elaborate. The traditional tomb of King Hyo-so consists of a simple small mound, 206 feet in circumference. There is no stonework. It is listed as Historic Site No. 184.

The reputation of Silla and respect for its kings in the courts of T'ang was exceptionally high. It is mentioned that the palace gates of the capital of China were closed for two days when King Hyo-so died. A special envoy was also sent to be present at King Hyo-so's funeral.

In appreciation for this unusual respect King Song-dok returned gifts of fine horses, bolts of silk, seal garments and two of Silla's loveliest princesses.

It is said that the Emperor of T'ang, who was by no means a recluse, was so deeply moved at the sight of these lovely maidens exiled from their native land that he returned them under safe escort. He stated that they were of royal blood of the honorable house of Silla and he felt that it was morally wrong to accept them.

The tomb (Historic Site No. 28) for King Song-dok is unique from tombs of other Silla kings in that the zodiac figures surrounding it are statues rather than relief carvings. There are now eleven zodiac images remaining and

all have been badly damaged. The heads are of animals while the bodies are in human form dressed in warrior's armor.

The one zodiac figure best preserved is the monkey which is now on display in the Kyongju National Museum. These stone figures are about 3.5 feet high. There is a four foot retaining wall of stone with a rock apron. Thirty triangular stone braces or buttresses are used against the retaining wall and the granite zodiac statues are placed in spaces between. The mound is 150 feet in circumference. In tomb construction for rulers of Silla there are left only six examples where the zodiacs are used. Though they are not exactly identified these tombs traditionally belong to rulers Chin-dok, Song-dok, Kyong-dok, Won-song, Hon-dok, and Hung-dok. At Kim Yu-shin's tomb and the square tomb, which is still a mystery, we have further examples of the zodiac. They were also evidently used on some pagodas.

In front of the tomb is one eight foot stone civil official. Only the head and shoulders of the other official are seen nearby. Three of the four lions are presently guarding this tomb. Out in the fields in front of this grove of pines is the remains of a large nine foot stone turtle base. Its head is missing and other parts of the body are badly damaged.

As King Song-dok's tomb is located on the way to Pulguk-sa and only a minute's walk east from the road it is worth a stop to see this unique tomb.

Eighth century Silla opened with the reign of King Song-dok who mounted the throne at the age of 22. Following the rule of his brother he was destined to hold the throne for 35 years. During this era of King Song-dok, relations with China were probably better than they had ever been before. Song-dok's first son died in infancy but his second and third sons later became ruling kings Hyo-song and Kyong-dok respectively while his daughter's son became the ruler Son-dok (37th king) as well as another grandson, Hye-gong (36th king).

King Song-dok erected the temple of Pong-dok in memory of his great-grandfather Mu-yol (29th king). After several years his son then commissioned the construction of the bell which we now call the Emillie. This great bell hangs in the National Museum of Kyongju and has been designated as National Treasure No. 29. This divine bell with the dragon spirit from the soul of a child according to the legend has on its surface an inscription bearing witness to the religious worth of Buddhism and the noble character of great King Song-dok.

During this period of King Song-dok's reign comes one of the more intriguing *affaire d'amour* legends illustrating historically the appreciation of the physical beauty of women. During Silla there apparently was a greater freedom between the sexes which did not exist during the rigid Confucianism of the Yi Dynasty. Many stories both from legends and historical accounts fully amplify this theory.

Lady Su-ro was the graceful wife of Sun-jong, a county magistrate of Kangnung. Young and rosy cheeked, her radiant loveliness seem to affect all those around her. Even the elderly men would gaze with appreciative eyes upon the elegant figure of Lady Su-ro. One day while relaxing on the east coast beaches she saw high on a rocky cliff a cluster of blooming azaleas tossing their colored heads about in the ocean breezes. She expressed her desire to have some of the blossoms but was warned that the overhanging rocks were too dangerous.

But an old man who was hobbling along the road with his cow overheard this conversation and quickly climbed the cliff to pick some of the azaleas which he then offered to Lady Su-ro. Many scholars believe that the old man was a supernatural being referred to in Korean simply as *shinson*.

When the *shinson* presented the azaleas to Lady Su-ro he sang a song which has been left to us as one of the few *hyangga*. Now only 25 remain in two historical books. This lyric of the *shinson* to Su-ro Pujin is considered the finest of the sensuous *hyangga* and well known to most Koreans because of its rich subtle suggestiveness.

> Beside the scarlet cliffs I climb
> Letting go my cow's tether.
> And if you do not blush at me
> I'll pick azalea blossoms for you.

Evidently Lady Su-ro's difficulties because of her great beauty did not end for it seems that wherever she travelled she would be seized by admiring spirits and dragons according to the legends.

5. Square Tomb: *Traditional Grave of Kim Tae-song*
(Historic Site No. 27)

This unusual tomb is located a few meters from the intersection branching to Pulguk-sa, the station and old highway to Ulsan and Pusan. The rotary has a reconstructed pagoda in the center.

Traditionally this tomb is believed to belong to Kim Tae-song. This distinguished minister and architect is credited with building the historic Pulguk-sa and the magnificent Sokkuram. It is one of eight within the Kyongju vicinity containing the zodiac images; however it is the only tomb that is square in shape. Each wall is approximately 30 feet. (The west and east side seem to be several inches shorter than the north and south.) The retaining walls contain three zodiac images per side.

The figures are 2.5 feet high with several of the zodiac images having broken faces making them unrecognizable. (The order is the same on all the tombs as each of the twelve zodiacs have fixed direction.) Immediately to the right of the horse image is the chamber entrance

Three stone lions and portions of stone guards are still found near the tomb of King Song-dok. Stone statues of zodiac figures are guarding this tomb.

which is ten feet deep. The size of the tomb chamber is 9 × 7.5 feet while the height of the room is 5'8'' and within this burial chamber is a stone coffin (6'4'' × 2'8'' × 1'5'').

As this tomb has been designated as Historic Site No. 27, the Kyongju Development Plan enlarged this site area so now visitors can easily enter the grounds to view the tomb through a southern entrance gate.

Kim Tae-song was undoubtedly a historic person and we have every reason to believe that during the early reigning years of Kyong-dok (35th king) in 751 the construction of the temple of Pulguk was begun. On December 2, 774 Kim Tae-song died at the age of 73 before the fulfillment of his dream. The history of this period, with an abundance of legends and myths enveloping this eminent minister, is well known to Koreans.

below left: *The three-storied pagoda in the center of the rotary near Pulguk Station was moved from a former temple site during the Japanese occupation.* above and center: *The horse zodiac, one of twelve, is found on the south side of the Square Tomb near the Pul-guk Station rotary. (HS-27)*

6. Ungsu-sa Site Pagoda: *The Bear Legend*

On the road to Pulguk-sa and 2.3 kilos from the triangular intersection at Pulguk Station a small road leads east from the intersection road to Pomun Lake. The distance is not far as the pagoda can actually be seen from the main road behind the Kolon Hotel.

It is well known that Kim Tae-song built the magnificent Pulguk Temple and cave grotto hermitage called Sokkuram. However, the fact is not well known that he also built another temple during his younger years. The temple's legend is most interesting because in it we find one of Korea's few myths concerning bears. It is recalled that the legendary founder of Korea was Tan-gun who was born of a woman who had previously been a bear.

In this story of Kim Tae-song the bear also takes on human characteristics which might indicate a continuing practice of totemism in the Silla period. In view of the mythological origin of the Korean people it is strange that for the most part bear legends in Korean mythology are conspicuous for their absence.

Kim Tae-song had a compelling desire to hunt as a young man. One day as he was hunting on the wild slopes of Toham he tracked and killed a large bear. As night was quickly descending he decided to sleep in a village at the foot of this mountain. While sleeping he had a vision, dreaming that the ghost of the dead bear was chasing him across the slopes of the mountain and Kim Tae-song had no weapon. Knocking him to the ground the huge beast was ready to devour him. "Why must you kill me?" Kim Tae-song screamed.

right: *A three-storied pagoda is located at the site of Ungsu Temple traditionally built by Kim Tae-song to honor a bear who saved his life in a dream.*

148

"Today you killed me for no reason and in revenge I will now take your life!" growled the angry beast.

Trembling with fear Kim Tae-song pleaded for his life. "How can you say this? I love the sport of hunting and I was only testing my courage and strength against yours. I risked my life in a fair fight," he pursuasively reasoned. "You lost and now the hunt is over. If I have offended you I will gladly apologize if the wrongdoing was mine."

"Will you build a magnificent temple to honor my spirit?" the bear demanded, "And perhaps I will spare you."

"I swear that I will do as you ask," Kim Tae-song replied. He awoke with a loud cry. His bed was damp with sweat.

True to his promise Kim Tae-song built a temple and gave up the sport of hunting. This temple he called Ungsu-sa (Honoring Bear Temple). Today a three-storied pagoda is seen on this site. The name of the new temple

Ungsu-sa pagoda reveals a unique myth of Silla relating to a bear. In 1978 a clay bear image was excavated for the first time.

nearby is Mongsong-am (Dream Achieving Hermitage) which also refers to Kim Tae-song's vision.

On April 20, 1978 a clay image of a bear's head was excavated at a Silla kiln site north of Kyongju. This was the first known excavation of a bear image.

7. Yong-ji and Yongji-am: *The Sad Legend of Shadow Pond*

Located only a few miles from Pulguk-sa this small pond is the scene of one of the tragic love legends of ancient Silla. In the reign of Kyong-dok (35th king) construction of Pulguk Temple was begun in 751 under the supervision of Prime Minister Kim Tae-song. Skilled stone masons from all over Korea and even as far away as the T'ang Kingdom of China were invited to come to Silla.

One of the most renowned was Asa-dal from the Paekche region of Korea (though other sources say he came from T'ang) who was commissioned to design and build the twin pagodas in front of the main hall of Pulguk-sa. His young and lovely wife whom he had recently married was left at home.

Asa-dal worked long hours and eventually completed the Tabo-t'ap (Pagoda of Many Treasures) and began work on the Sokka-t'ap (Pagoda of the Sokkamoni). Though working day and night the stonecutters took longer to complete this second pagoda. One night a vision of his lonely and patient wife loomed before his eyes. She was standing forlornly by a pond below Pulguk Temple anticipating his return.

Unknown to Asa-dal his lovely wife Asa-nyo had made the difficult trek from her home to be near her husband. It had been many years and she had heard no word from him. The gatekeeper of Pulguk-sa refused to permit her entry. As women were thought to be unclean she was told that she could not see her husband while he was working on the great pagodas.

The clever gatekeeper finally told Asa-nyo that if she went to the Shadow Pond she would see the reflection of the great pagodas and her husband. When the work is finished he will be free to join you, she was told. With a heavy

Shadows on a temple pond recall for visitors the sad legend of Asa-dal who designed the Tabo-t'ap and Sokka-t'ap of Pulguk-sa.

heart she went to the pond and gazed intently upon the surface of the water.

She saw the reflection of the Pagoda of Many Treasures (Tabo-t'ap) but could not see the Sokka-t'ap and her husband. In grief and sorrow she waited and watched in vain. Finally thinking that her husband would never return she plunged into the waters calling his name near the shadow of the Tabo-t'ap.

Asa-dal after his vision ran from the temple grounds but arrived too late. "Asa-nyo, Asa-nyo," he cried but there was no answer except the quiet lapping along the lake shore and murmuring wind sighing among the pines. After mourning there for many weeks, he thought he saw Asa-nyo on the opposite shore flitting through the trees. He ran to the spot shouting her name but found only a large stone strangely resembling a person.

In despair he stood motionless before the rock as it appeared to change into the form of the merciful Buddha. Soon Asa-dal began to carve this stone into a Buddha image which he dedicated to the spirit of his departed wife. Later a temple was erected to enshrine this image beside Yong-ji (Shadow Pond).

The Buddha image is still located on the eastern side of this pond among the pines. In sad remembrance of this event the village people began to call the Sokka-t'ap, the Muyong-t'ap (No Shadow Pagoda) and the Tabo-t'ap, the Yong-t'ap (Shadow Pagoda).

Now a new small shrine called Yongji-am (Shadow Pond Hermitage) stands next to the 13 foot Buddha image which is on a pedestal five feet high. The image is badly damaged about the face.

Though this lake is near the main road few people come. Often on a bright sunny day picturesque shadows of the peaks of Toham-san float on the surface reminding the visitor of the love story of Asa-dal and Asa-nyo. No one knows what happened to this master stonecutter who eventually left this place of grief to return to his homeland.

above: *Near the small temple of Yongji-am is a Buddhist image traditionally sculptured by Asa-dal to memorialize his lost wife.* below: *A stone civilian official silently guards the tomb called Kwoe-nung.*

8. Kwoe-nung: *Guarded by Zodiac Images Carved in Stone (Historic Site No. 26)*

This royal tomb is one of the easiest to reach and one of the most elaborate. One must follow the old Pusan Highway past Pulguk Station Intersection about 14.5 kilos from downtown Kyongju City. The entrance is to the left of the main road. There is an entrance fee.

Kwoe-nung meaning "Suspended Tomb" was traditionally a pond. It is believed that this tomb was constructed over this pond. For many years it was considered to be the traditional tomb for Mun-mu (30th king) who was the unifier of Silla, however, in recent years the actual water tomb of King Mun-mu was discovered near Kamp'o. Thus Kwoe-nung is now believed to belong to Won-song (38th king) who ruled during the last fourteen years of the 8th century.

Of the hundreds of Silla tombs about the Kyongju area very few can be accurately identified. Though we cannot be certain that Kwoe-nung is the tomb of King Won-song we can be reasonably positive that it does belong to a ruler of the post unification period. This tomb features the twelve zodiac figures on the retaining wall. In the case of royalty they are represented in military dress and armor with the heads of the animals. The zodiac images at tombs are always positioned according to the 12 points of the compass.

In the customary order of the zodiac cycle the rat comes first representing due north and is located at the rear of the tomb. This direction represents the midnight hours and the winter months, the passive, feminine and negative form of the *um*(yin) in the cosmic influences of the universe. Proceeding clockwise the ox, tiger and rabbit come next. The rabbit always faces east and represents a balanced portion of the *um-yang* influence. Following comes the dragon and snake while the horse is in the

At Kwoe-nung (HS-26) stand two nine-foot military guards with clenched fists to protect the tomb from evil intrusion.

position to represent the noon daylight hours and warm summer months.

The horse faces due south and represents the active, masculine and positive form of the *yang*. Continuing westward are the sheep, monkey and chicken. The chicken always faces due west and is equally influenced by both the *yang* and *um*. The dog and pig are positioned nearer to the rat. The cycle is now complete.

Adopted from China these twelve zodiac positions still control universal time from the years to the minutes as well as directional and seasonal aspects. With the zodiac encircling the tomb, the king's spirit within is protected throughout all time and space.

The tomb itself is 230 feet in circumference. A stone apron flares out five feet from the 4.5 foot retaining wall. Also surrounding the tomb are 42 pillars about six feet high and 4.5 feet in girth. These were used as supporting pillars for a stone fence about the tomb mound. Besides the twelve zodiac images the tomb contains four lions, military and civilian guards, as well as entrance pillars referred to as *mang-jusok*. This tomb and the tomb of Hung-dok (42nd king) located near Angang Town are the only two sites where the stone guard officials are still preserved completely.

At the entrance of the tomb about one hundred meters away are two stone pillars almost nine feet high. The origin of these *mangjusok* (Yearning Pillar Stones) is shrouded in mystery but strangely enough even today at common grave sites these stone pillars are usually seen. Representing filial yearning for the spirits of those departed, the two pillars are positioned on either side of the grave to remind the living to respect the departed.

There is some belief that the *mangjusok* has phallic symbolism though this idea is held by only a few scholars, while others say that it represents a candle to light symbolically the spirit's way through the dark land of the dead. The shape of the *mangjusok* has changed very little over the centuries.

One tale originating during early Silla tells the sad story of a fisherman who sailed out to

sea and was lost in a storm. His wife faithfully waited for his return. Each night she would climb a small hill to watch and wait. This touched the hearts of the villagers, so after her death she was buried on this same hill while two pillars were erected to remind others of this woman's faithfulness.

Called *mangjusok*, which implies the longing of this woman for her husband, these pillars became the symbol of all those living who yearned for the relatives of the departed.

On each side of the tomb walkway is a nine foot military stone guard with one hand raised in a clenched fist while the other holds a sword with the blade pointed toward the ground.

At Sungbok-sa near Hwoe-nung the remnants of a Buddhist legacy are still evident in nearby fields south of Kyongju.

Nearer the tomb mound are positioned two civil officials with hands folded under their long gowns. These figures are slightly smaller in size. Also situated along the entrance way are four stone lions.

The story is told that there was once a young man by the name of Kim Kyong-shin who had held the position of state minister and was a member of the royal family. One night he had a strange and foreboding dream. He dreamed that he lost his official hat but found in its place a white hat. While wearing this white hat he entered the well of Ch'ongwan-sa.

This was the temple dedicated to the pretty young maid named Ch'on-gwan who had been romantically involved with the famous young General Kim Yu-shin. She was of low birth so could not marry him but instead became a Buddhist nun. The temple site which honored her can still be seen on the northwestern slopes of Nam-san. Inside the well of Ch'ongwan-sa Kim Kyong-shin dreamed that he was holding a twelve-stringed harp. When he awoke he went immediately to consult a fortuneteller.

"This omen is unfortunate." he ominously stated. "The lost hat means losing your position while the entering of the well means prison." The fortuneteller then took his fees reluctantly given and departed.

The worried Kim Kyong-shin never left his

154

house for fear the prophecy would come true. One day a close friend came to visit.

"I can see by your face that you are facing grave trouble," the friend consoled. "Perhaps if you will tell me your problem I can help you." Kim Kyong-shin then related his dream and the interpretation by the fortuneteller.

"But I don't understand," said the friend. "Actually you had a very good dream. If you promise not to forget me when you become king I will interpret this dream for you." Of course the grateful Kim Kyong-shin promised. "The loss of your hat," said his friend, "means that there will be no man above you and you will wear the royal crown." Thoughtfully he continued, "The entering of the well is symbolic of your happy entrance into the palace."

Not long after the king died. The Silla court proclaimed Kim Chu-won successor to the throne and a body of court officials went out to announce the matter. Suddenly a heavy rain fell and the emissaries could not cross the North Stream to the home of Kim Chu-won. As they stood waiting in vain Kim Kyong-shin put on his court dress and entered the palace amid the cheers of his followers.

The court then decided that the will of heaven had intervened and pronounced Kim Kyong-shin king, known by his posthumous title of Won-song. Unfortunately his friend who had prophesied his good fortune had also died. But remembering his promise he summoned his friend's children and conferred titles and official positions on them. This was in the year 785.

above: *A stone lion, one of four, guards the tomb called Kwoe-nung.* below: *Kwoe-nung is one of the most picturesque and elaborate of all Silla tombs.*

9. Wonwon-sa Site: *Twin Zodiac Pagodas (Historic Site No. 46)*

Wonwon-sa (Remote Aspiration Temple) was built following the unification wars of Silla in 668 and dedicated to the spirits of the war dead. It is believed that Wonwon-sa was founded by the powerful Priest Myong-nang who possessed magical and mystic talents. Myong-nang was a nephew of Priest Cha-jang on his mother's side. He was the youngest of three sons all of whom became monks.

In 632 Myong-nang was sent to China for study and three years later returned. Legends tell that during his return sea voyage he was invited to the palace of the Sea Dragon King. Later during the reign of Mun-mu (30th king), Myong-nang was called upon to use his mystic powers to stop the Chinese attack. He recommended the building of Sach'onwang-sa (Four Heavenly Kings Temple) to forestall the Chinese attack on Silla. He was so successful that Myong-nang was honored by the entire nation.

Some sources claim that it was really the disciple of Myong-nang, Priest An-hye, who was instrumental in establishing Wonwon-sa. Priest An-hye and the other disciples are now buried at the top of the eastern mountain near Wonwon-sa.

To reach Wonwon-sa take the road from the Pulguk-sa rotary toward Pusan for 13 kilos. At the bridge the car must be parked. Walk east taking the north side dike trail. A path on the same side of the river leads into the foothills. The hike will take about 45 minutes. The trail is wide and gradual.

The area around this temple site is picturesque and one can easily spend an entire afternoon under the shade of stately pines watching the late sun glitter from the rice fields in the valley below while the wrinkled shadows of the twin pagodas stretch far to the east. Because of its importance the temple area is now designated as Historic Site No. 46. The original stone steps dating to the Silla Period are unique to this temple site. Behind the stairs are the twin pagodas and lantern.

These two pagodas probably date to the early 9th century and are in themselves worth the trip. Except for the Tabo-t'ap at Pulguk-sa these three-storied zodiac pagodas are the most

The twin pagodas of Wonwon-sa are the only ones near Kyongju where the twelve zodiac images are found in relief. (HS-46)

unusual and fascinating of any within the area. They were restored during the Japanese occupation. These are the only pagodas using the twelve zodiac images in the Kyongju vicinity outside of the Kyongju National Museum.

Each pagoda is identical and approximately 22 feet high. Along the eight foot walls of the square base are twelve zodiac figures. Four of the figures have been completely destroyed but most are recognizable. Between these two pagodas is a 5.5 foot stone lantern with the middle stone portion missing. After finding your bearings the zodiac images can be identified as follows: south center is the horse; to the left and around are sheep, monkey, cock (west center), dog, pig, rat (north center), cow, tiger,

rabbit (east center), dragon and snake. These zodiac figures are almost two feet tall.

The first story stone was made from a single 3.5 foot block cube. Each side depicts the *sach'onwang* (Four Heavenly Kings). The second story is 14 inches high and 2'10'' square. The third story is smaller and the pagoda's crown is a lotus blossom cap.

Behind the pagodas are seen the foundation stones of the main worship hall. Also at the foot of the stone steps are additional remnants which include a portion of the stone brace for the temple banner pole. In the valley vicinity are four *pudo* monuments which were recently discovered. Little information is known about them.

left: *The* sach'onwang *and zodiac images are carved on the two pagodas of Wonwon-sa.* right: *The pagodas of Wonwon-sa exemplify the architectural style of the late Silla Period.*

10. Other Historic Sites South of Kyongju

Two Unknown Temple Sites West of Nang-san:

Located 50 meters behind the service station at the junction for Pohang and Pulguk-sa are pagoda remains. A roof stone and base stones are near a bamboo grove. South of the road to the expressway and before the bridge is another temple site with several base pillar stones and a considerable amount of tile.

Tomb of King Hyo-gong (Historic Site No. 183):

This 52nd ruler of Silla is supposedly buried near the tomb of Shin-mun (31st king) across the railroad tracks. He died in 913 and had no heir. The circumference of the tomb is 232 feet while the distance across the mound is 82 feet.

Tomb of King Shin-mu (Historic Site No. 185):

King Shin-mu ruled only four months in 839 as 45th king of Silla. The tomb site is 200 meters from the main road and 1.4 kilometers from King Shin-mun's tomb. The circumference of the tomb is 160 feet while the distance across the mound is 78 feet.

Pagoda Remains of Ich'a-sa Site:

After a fifteen minute walk northeast from the tombs of Song-dok and his brother the temple site of Ich'a-sa can be seen in a field near a village. Cut stones are piled together. Some of these pagoda stones were taken to be used in the pagoda now seen at the Pulguk Station Rotary.

Pagoda of Kamsan-sa Site:

About 1.5 kilometers past the tomb called Kwoe-nung is the temple site of Kamsan. Now a reconstructed three-storied pagoda can be seen (several stones are missing). The base stone is six feet square. Also on the site is a floral design lantern base. Kamsan-sa was established in 719 by Kim Chi-song.

A large Miruk Posal and Amit'a Buddha were discovered on this site and taken to the Seoul National Museum in 1915. They are listed as National Treasures No. 81 and No. 82. Also found at the Kyongju National Museum are 12 stone dancing zodiac figures which once decorated the base of a pagoda.

Twin Pagodas of Sungbok-sa Site:

After following the main highway 1.9 kilometers beyond the entrance to Kwoe-nung a road to the left leads to a village about 2 kilometers away. A ten minute walk is needed to reach the site. The temple was built to honor the departed spirit of Won-song (38th king).

Both three-storied pagodas contain relief images of the *p'albujung* (Eight Congregated Devas). The relief figures are 2'6" high. The pagoda base is 6'6" wide and 3'7" high. The two headed turtle base stone now relocated to the Kyongju National Museum was found at

this temple site. It is thought that the tablet which has now disappeared was engraved by the famous scholar Ch'oe Ch'i-won. Both heads of this turtle are unbroken.

Kwanmun Fortress Wall (Historic Site No. 48):

About 32 kilometers south of Kyongju on the old Pusan highway is the boundary fort and wall built by Song-dok (33rd king) in 722. Near Mohwa Village a small road should be taken west to Rok-dong (Deer Village). At Songju Village Kwanmun-song (Main Gate Fortress) can best be seen. Supposedly it once reached the Sea of Japan and was Silla's longest line of defense. At this point in the wall once stood the main gate (Main Gate Village is just beyond).

Yearning for Husband Rock in the Tale of Pak Che-sang:

The legend of *mangbusok* (Yearning for Husband Rock) is well known in Korean folklore; however, the exact location is somewhat of a disappointment after an arduous climb of two hours. This sad tale is told in another chapter. The rock can be seen from the Deer Village where the climb must start. The trail may be your own but get your bearings before starting. Near the summit are three clusters of stone. The *mangbusok* is the large rock on the left slope about 100 feet from the summit.

The perpendicular stone face is over 46 feet high. At the foot of the rock is a small cave about four feet deep which could provide some shelter for Pak Che-sang's wife during her vigil. At the summit is a small crater which might have been a foundation for a shrine building. It is claimed that on a clear day the islands of Japan can be seen on the horizon from this point. A wife's faithfulness to her husband's unswerving loyalty has served as a shining example for Korean women over the centuries.

(1) Pagoda remains on site of Ich'a-sa: (2) The p'albujung *reliefs on pagoda remains at Sungbok-sa; (3) Kwanmun Fortress wall (HS-48); (4) Author sitting above the rock called* mangbusok; *(5) Pagoda on Kamsan-sa site;* next page: *Occasionally the "topknot" is still worn by the elders. During the Yi Dynasty it was an indication that he was married, otherwise, his hair would be kept in a braid.*

Chapter V
The Many Valleys of Sacred South Mountain

1. The Valleys and Slopes of Nam-san and Fortress
(Historic Site No. 22)

The rock-strewn mountain of Nam-san (South Mountain) was undoubtedly the most sacred of peaks during the Silla period. The Silla capital was surrounded by many rugged peaks which helped to form a natural defense perimeter. Nam-san is no exception with a fortress remnant (Historic Site No. 22) that can still be seen winding its way among the northwestern slopes. Foundation stones of two large Silla warehouses still exist. Carbonized rice found at the sites is valued for medicinal purposes.

Nam-san (often called Kumo Mountain) became a religious sanctuary in a country completely dominated by Buddhism. The highest peak is 1,535 feet and the seventeen major valleys abound in legends. Over fifty temples were believed to have existed on these slopes but of this number only a few sites are known today.

Over the years more than sixty Buddhist stone figures and forty remains of pagodas or *pudo* (containers for relic remains of priests) have been located along the valleys. Even to this day new discoveries are being made of images found in hidden rocky niches lost over the centuries. Interested archaeologists and historians trudge over the rock-strewn hillsides looking for worn lines carved in stone.

The people during this "golden era" prayed for peace and prosperity for the kingdom by building temples in the valleys and carving Buddhist images on the cliffs behind. From these temple sites, scattered pagodas and Buddhist images have remained in Nam-san from the Silla period to the present day.

It was from Nam-san that the six village chieftains of the Yi, Ch'ong, Son, Ch'oe, Pae and Sol clans witnessed the miraculous arrival of Pak Hyok-ko-se, the founding king of Silla. On the lower slopes of the western hills one can still see the site of his arrival in the grove of trees called Na-jong.

Shamanism and Buddhist tradition have been existing side by side over the centuries in the many valleys of Nam-san near Kyongju City.

2. Na-jong: *The Appearance of King Pak Hyok-ko-se*

Near O-Nung is Na-jong, a small walled compound (21' × 45') in a grove of pines. Inside the enclosure a Yi Dynasty tablet is housed in a pavilion. The tablet was erected in 1803 during the reign of Sun-jo (23rd Yi king). Behind this tablet within the compound is a rock slab marking the exact site where the gourd was found which contained the boy, who became first king of Silla, Pak Hyok-ko-se.

Nearby is a newly constructed shrine built in memory of the six tribal chiefs who saw the spectacular ball of fire descend from heaven heralding this first ruler of Silla. A memorial celebration is held here once a year on August 17th of the lunar calendar.

Standing within this rather small and insignificant grove of pines at the site where the beginnings of Silla occurred, the feeling of antiquity is overwhelming as the visitor reflects in time, back two thousand years.

3. Sangso-jang: *Legends of the Lone Cloud Scholar*

This humble shrine is located on the right side of the exit from the expressway and immediately before crossing the South Stream, along the northern slopes of Nam-san.

Ch'oe Ch'i-won is considered the "Father of Korean Literature" and certainly is ranked as the leading Confucian scholar of the late Silla period though he was fundamentally a Buddhist. Born in 857 and receiving the highest academic degree in the Chinese T'ang court, he continued to serve the Emperor for a period of sixteen years. Though he wrote voluminously, very little has survived.

Ch'oe was born in the troubled era of Silla decline during the reign of Hon-an (47th king). As a young boy of twelve he went to China and

above left: Na-jong is the site of Hyok-ko-se's appearance. below: *Sangso-jang is the site of Ch'oe Ch'i-won's home .*

at eighteen he completed his doctoral degree. While in China he served the Emperor with distinction both in war and peace. He was honored with the rank of ambassador and was not yet thirty when he returned to his native land in 886.

He believed that the prestige of his achievements in China and the imperial authority he possessed would enable him to institute the needed reforms for Silla. He was doomed to disappointment. Hon-gang (49th king) was inclined to be more interested in his court favorites while his influential sister, who later became Queen Chin-song, led the royalty to new depths of moral depravity. Driven by royal indifference Ch'oe Ch'i-won assumed a voluntary exile and gave himself up to literary pursuits.

By tradition Sangso-jang is the site of Ch'oe Ch'i-won's home and in 1874 a tablet was

erected to honor him. It is also traditionally believed that from here Ch'oe Ch'i-won wrote a letter to the popular new general of Koryo praising him for his deeds and declaring that he would be the salvation of failing Silla. This general was Wang-gon who in later years was to become the first king of the Koryo Dynasty.

Though Ch'oe Ch'i-won did frequently correspond with Wang-gon, however, one poetic stanza which came from the brush of this most eminent scholar is well known.

"The leaves at Kyerim are brown and yellow,
While the pines on Snow Goose pass are fresh and green."

Kyerim was the early name for Silla while Snow Goose Pass was the ancestral home of Wang-gon.

Ch'oe Ch'i-won's penname was "Lone Cloud" which is certainly appropriate when we consider his lack of rapport with the court of Silla. From his diary came a strange story of romance, a tale which will tug at the heart-strings because of its tragedy. While in China he found pleasure in accompanying a group of friends into the countryside for a picnic. Near the area were the tombs of twin sisters.

Ch'oe Ch'i-won's mind like a lone cloud drifted along as he wondered who these sisters might be and the circumstance surrounding their deaths. No one seemed to know. After returning home he continued to ponder sadly about the twin sisters who had evidently died tragically. In the early morning hours the words for a lyric came to mind and picking up his brush he began to compose.

"From where did these maidens come
Who lie in this lonely tomb?
Spring now comes and goes,
But its blossoms no longer cheer you.
Imagining your bright young faces,
I ask you, are you the moon?
I call to you with pretty names,
Yet I hear no echo from your tomb.
My yearning heart leaps out
And chases you through my dreams.
In this long and weary night,
Your beauty cruelly stings my heart.
If I could see you in my lonely bed,
We'd pour our love as rain drenching clouds."

On the following day Ch'oe showed his lyric verse to a poet-friend Chang Su who read it intently and then with a twinkle in his eye teased, "Well, my dear friend, it appears that Lone Cloud has fallen in love with two feminine spirits." The young Ch'oe Ch'i-won looked embarrassed and said nothing.

Several days later his closest friend Chen came to visit. He had heard the poem from Chang Su and was worried about his Korean friend, far from home, who seemed to be so preoccupied with the dead. Chen knew the tragic story about the tomb. The beautiful twin daughters were forced to marry rich salt merchants whom they did not love. In anger over what was inevitable they decided to take their own lives rather than live an intolerable existence.

Chen invited Ch'oe to his magnificent home. Upon his arrival Ch'oe wondered where the other guests were. "Today I wish to drink only with you," Chen demurred. After hours of pleasure Chen suggested they walk in the gardens. After passing a lotus pond and several arbors they came to a small pavilion. "This is my summer house," Chen said, "Let's enter." Again a table had been spread with several bottles of wine and numerous dishes of food.

After more pleasantries and drinking Chen suddenly rose and went to the veranda. He returned shortly with a young maiden beside him wearing a dazzling white dress. She smiled in a shy manner, her face framed with flowing black hair. Ch'oe couldn't remember when he had seen such a vision of loveliness. She made a low bow before the dazed poet.

"This is Lone Cloud, the greatest scholar of Silla," Chen said to her. Then turning to Ch'oe she was introduced as his cousin. "When my uncle died she came to me to be raised," he explained, "Her name is Soo."

Turning to this young girl of eighteen Chen asked that she serve a cup of wine for their distinguished guest. Ch'oe Ch'i-won's heart missed several beats and his hands trembled noticeably as he took the cup of wine from Soo.

"My cousin is quite talented," Chen smiled, "Recite a verse for Lone Cloud." Soo lowered her eyes and blushed deeply until Chen again requested that Soo recite for Ch'oe Ch'i-won. In a high clear voice, sweet and refreshing as the song of the oriole, Soo sang Ch'oe's lyric of the Tomb of the Twin Sisters.

As his eyes were fixed on her lips the poet appeared to be in a trance. Suddenly the voice of Chen broke the spell. "How did she do?" he asked. "I imagine she did not do justice to your fine lyric?"

"She has truly sweetened a bitter taste," Ch'oe replied. "Her angelic voice has in fact ennobled my wordly effort." Chen laughed and urged more wine for his friend and bade him to offer a cup to his lovely cousin. Soo would not drink but only held the wine cup in her hands.

"Drink, Soo, drink the wine and be merry this evening, as you must leave everything to me." With shy eyes lowered she brought the wine cup to her lips and emptied it cautiously. "Good! Now let's see you dance for my friend Lone Cloud," he cheerfully commanded. Then to an adjoining room he shouted, "Yoo, will you now play on your harp?"

The bewildered Ch'oe Ch'i-won was startled speechless as he heard the soft melodious notes of the stringed instrument behind the closed doors "Who was Yoo? Why had the musician not been called in but ordered to play in the other room?" Ch'oe wondered with growing curiosity.

As the music began Soo began slowly to move with dégagé grace much as a white wisp of smoke wends its way through a dense dark forest. So lovely and elegant was this radiant vision to the eternal senses that Ch'oe Ch'i-won in a rapture of joy elegantly whispered. "When your face is hidden behind the mist and clouds, I wonder if you will hear my cries! How long will you only smile and sail past me while I mourn and sigh?"

As the dance finished Ch'oe pointed to the adjoining room and asked who the harp player might be. However, Chen only nodded to Soo and the person behind the door and told them it was time to leave. Turning to Ch'oe he asked, "Well, my dear Lone Cloud, what do you think of my cousin?"

"Her beauty is beyond the stars," Ch'oe replied.

"Do you love her?" he bluntly questioned. "Why do you ask when I have only met her tonight?" Ch'oe stammered.

"If you love I will give her to you, and even if you do not I would wish you to have her. But I must tell you truthfully she is against marriage and if you were to marry her without her consent, she would hang herself." Chen continued, "She was strongly attracted to your lyric when she heard the verse from me and I thought maybe she was beginning to fall in love with you."

With these words of encouragement Ch'oe Ch'i-won began frequently to visit Chen's home to see the lovely Soo. Eventually a warm relationship grew and Ch'oe took courage to ask her to come and live with him. Slowly she shook her head and firmly said, "No, you must let me go!"

"It is impossible to marry as I am a girl who may die at any moment." Her eyes filling with sadness sent a chill of defeat through the young poet's heart. With a heavy sigh she spoke, "You'll never know the yearning I've had for you since I heard your lyric. Oh, if only I were free to catch your love...."

Suddenly Soo burst into uncontrollable tears. Ch'oe could not understand the deep

The legends and tales of ancient Silla are told and retold by the village elders.

sorrow that engulfed the young girl. Pointing to the adjoining room she sobbed, "Even now my sister is there for she is the one who played the harp on the very first night we met. She and I are twins and we were both extremely pretty in our childhood. But everyone seemed to agree that my sister was more beautiful than I and often told us, so that frequently my pride was hurt and I became unreasonably jealous. I grew to hate her.

"One night when all was quiet in our room I lifted a tea pot from a red-hot brazier and poured a few drops of boiling water into my sister's left eye as she lay asleep. She awoke screaming in agony and I wished that I were dead because of my evil action. But it was too late and my sister became blind in one eye."

Ch'oe Ch'i-won listened quietly as Soo continued her tragic story. "Strange as it may seem, my sister instead of hating me loved me more than ever and this kindness strengthened my new-found love for her."

"About one year later when my sister was alone she ran a gimlet through her right eye and became totally blind. I was shocked in disbelief that she would do such a thing! She calmly stated that she was sadder when looking into the mirror with only one eye. Now she had peace of mind as she could see nothing. Numerous times I have attempted to kill myself but always failed.

"One day when we were alone she pleaded with me that I not consider the old saying that twin sisters must be married together to find true happiness. I understood her meaning. In my love for my sister I told her I would never marry for I knew that to find a good match for her was impossible. I promised not to leave her until death separated us. We cried with each other until we fell asleep."

"Yes," she sighed, "many young men in enviable positions have asked for my hand in marriage. If I were forced to marry I would take my life. If it were not for my cousin Chen's sympathy and deep understanding I would have been dead long ago. Even now my dear sister Yoo is sitting in the next room for I have promised that I would meet no male in her absence."

Ch'oe Ch'i-won heaved a heavy sigh, realizing the hopelessness of their love. A few days later Chen sent an urgent message to Ch'oe and when the Korean scholar came his friend received him tearfully with the news that the twins had committed suicide.

Ch'oe Ch'i-won could not believe his ears. Evidently when the blind sister heard Soo tell of her sorrow, she reasoned that she was only standing in the way of Soo's happiness with the one she really loved. "If I were dead," she thought, "Soo would be free to marry the Korean scholar." So Yoo sacrificed her life by hanging herself.

When Soo saw what Yoo had done, she also hanged herself on another bough of the tree beside her blind sister. Chen handed Ch'oe a note found in her room.

Lone Cloud, my dearest,
I am sorry but I must leave this world with my poor blind sister.
If I am born again as a girl who can enjoy her freedom
I vow that I will be your bride when you join me
....for our unfinished love!

Thus we find in the late 9th century a Korean youth who from the hills of Silla came to walk in the courts of T'ang with the power of his word to sway the destiny of millions. Honors were heaped upon him. One wonders why he returned to Silla, but Ch'oe Ch'i-won was determined, though the Emperor requested that he remain. If the sad tale of the twin sisters was true, possibly this tragedy influenced his decision to leave China.

He was a man before his time. Retiring somewhere in the Kaya Mountains he began the period of his greatest literary activity. He was a poet, essayist and historian of the highest caliber and yet today we do not know his tomb site. What we know of the writings that have survived has ranked him as the greatest literary scholar of Silla. His best known surviving work is "Pen Scratching in a Cinnamon Tree Garden."

The career of this romantic and mysterious scholar came to an end more with legends than history. The spirit of Ch'oe Ch'i-won still flows through the deep valleys of the Kaya Mountains where the Father of Korean Literature lived out his final days recalling the dreams of the past and discouraged over the future of his nation.

4. Pori- sa: *Sokkamoni of Miruk Valley (Treasure No. 136)*

Pori-sa can be reached after a five minute walk behind the bamboo farm situated on the way to the Hwarang House of Nam-san. Take the paved road right at the site of Sach'onwang-sa from the main road to Pulguk-sa. Again one must turn right after crossing the bridge for Pori-sa, T'ap Valley and Pul Valley.

Pori-sa (Enlightened Awakening Temple) is a small nunnery in Miruk Valley of East Nam-san. The original temple built in 886 was located west of the present temple.

The principal attraction of this small nunnery is the sculptured image of the sitting Sokkamoni on a pedestal with a large boat-shaped mandala. It has been designated as Treasure No. 136. The pedestal consists of the traditional circular lotus design wheel on the top and bottom of an eight-sided column.

The mudra of the image portrays the call to witness. The robes appear heavy and are draped over both shoulders. The delicately sculptured mandala was broken near the peak but has been repaired. On this mandala seven small Buddhist images were carved in relief, two on each side and three in a triangular pattern behind the head of the Sokkamoni.

On the back side of this mandala is a relief image of the Yaksa Yorae (Buddha of Medicine) which was popular during the more turbulent final years of Silla. The remains of a stone pagoda can be seen with two relief carvings.

After a three minute walk south of the temple along the slope one can find a four foot relief image carved deeply in the rock. The style indicated a possible post unification period and the image seems to be laughing. Though its exact identity is unknown the elaborate crown probably makes it a Bodhisattva.

left: The Yaksa Yorae relief is found behind the mandala of the main Sokkamoni image of Pori-sa. right: On eastern Nam-san a relief image is seen near Pori-sa.

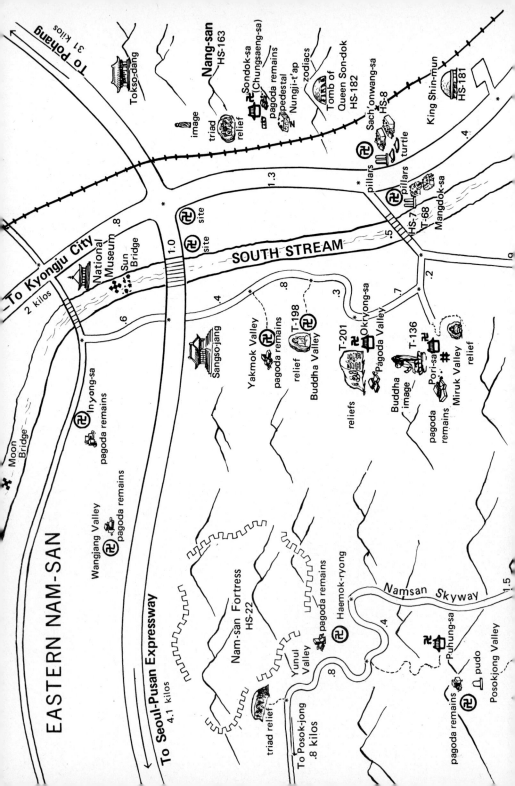

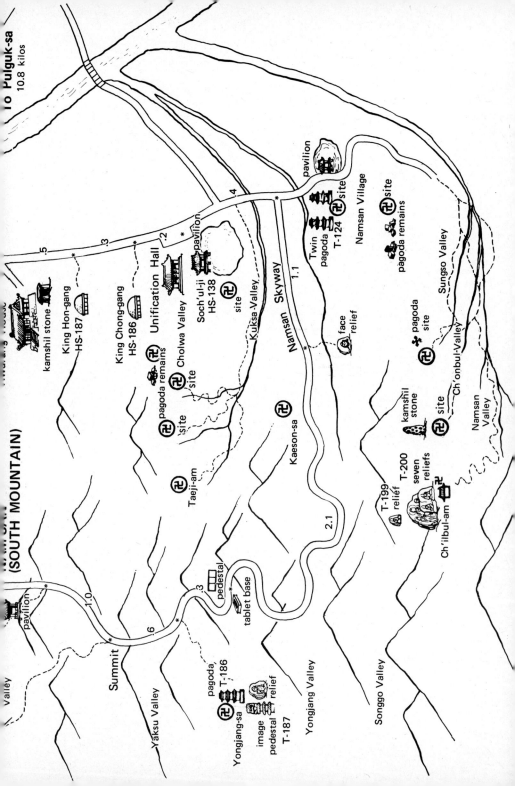

To Pulguk-sa
10.8 kilos

NAMSAN
(SOUTH MOUNTAIN)

Yaksu Valley

pavilion

Summit
.6

.10

pagoda
T-186
Yongjang-sa

image
pedestal relief
T-187

pedestal

tablet base

.3

Yongjang Valley

Songgo Valley

Kaeson-sa

2.1

T-199
relief

seven
reliefs
Ch'ilbul-am
T-200

kamshil
stone
site

Namsan
Valley

Ch'onbul-Valley

pagoda
site

Sungso Valley

pagoda remains

site

Namsan Village

Twin
pagoda
T-124

site

face
relief

Namsan Skyway

1.1

Kuksa Valley

Kaeson-sa

site

pavilion

Soch'ul-ji
HS-138

Cholwa Valley
site

Unification Hall

pagoda remains
site

Taeji-am

site

King Chong-gang
HS-186

King Hon-gang
HS-187

kamshil stone

.5
.3
.2
.4

pavilion

valley

5. Okryong-am: *Varied Reliefs of T'ap Valley*
(Treasure No. 201)

Pagoda Valley is on the eastern slopes of Nam-san. One can drive down the road from Pori-sa one kilometer to a small cluster of houses and take a sharp left up the valley for several hundred meters. It is a five minute walk to the temple.

T'apkol (Pagoda Valley) is unique in many ways. The greatest cluster of relief carvings found anywhere in Korea is concentrated here on one large rock. Situated in a densely wooded valley is the recently constructed temple of Okryong-am (Jewelled Dragon Hermitage). Previously the temple was called Yongam-sa (Dragon Rock Temple) but when the buildings burned the name was changed. Dedicated to the Amita Buddha, the main hall is Kuknak-jon.

Many of the relief images on the thirty foot rock behind the temple are most difficult to distinguish. On the high ground and south side are the remains of a broken pagoda. A seven foot Bodhisattva carved from a single rock is easily seen. The face and mandala of the image are badly damaged.

Directly behind is a three-foot relief image of a possible disciple. Carved in deep relief are two four foot relief images constructed during the same period. Another five foot image is facing to the side while two other relief carvings are quite faint. On a low rock in front is a side view of a 2.5 foot relief figure of a disciple. In total there are eight images on the south side.

On the east face of this same rock are twelve more relief figures. Some of these carvings are considerably worn by age and almost not distinguishable. In the center of the cluster is a triad with the Bodhisattva on the right quite indistinct. Across the top of the rock wall are four *sach'onwang* (Four Heavenly Kings)

prior page: This Sokka Buddha on a pedestal with a boat-shaped mandala is the principal attraction of the small nunnery of Pori-sa in Miruk Valley. (T-136) left: *Relief carving of a Buddhist disciple is one of many sculptured pieces in T'ap Valley.* right: *An ink rubbing of the same carving shows it is holding an incense burner.*

known as protectors of Buddhism.

High above is an additional figure which is presumably a deva. Across to the left is a faint relief of a sitting Buddha and what appears to be Bodhi trees on both sides. Further left another standing figure is almost impossible to see. At the foot of the rock is a small relief of a Buddhist disciple.

On the north wall are to be found the most interesting of all the reliefs. In the center is a five foot sitting Sokkamoni under a canopy while on both sides are two relief carvings of stylized pagodas. The left pagoda is nine-storied while the right pagoda appears to be only seven-storied. The larger pagoda is seven feet tall and above it is a flying deva.

The structure seems to have been patterned after earlier wooden pagodas of Silla. The pagodas are wide with tiers closely spaced. Under the corners of each roof hang the *pung-gyong* (fish bell). Three center support pillars are seen from top to bottom. There are few sites where relief pagoda carvings are found in the Kyongju area.

Under each pagoda appears an animal in relief which is probably a guardian lion. They are facing each other. The lions are almost four feet long and 2.5 feet high. One forepaw is raised. Lions traditionally guard pagodas; however, among the scholars there seems to be disagreement as to their real identity as they actually do not resemble lions because of their bushy three-pronged tail and wings.

One theory is that they are *yongma* (Dragon Horse) and represent the dragon for which the temple was dedicated. In fact it appears more logical that they are a type of dragon as both the former and present names of this temple allude to this creature. There are six relief carvings on this east wall.

On the west wall are faintly seen three images making a grand total of 29. The center sitting Buddha image is clearer and there appears to be a Bodhisattva on the Buddha's left. Though very faint there is a flying deva above the head of the Buddha image.

Though none of these images is really a skilled work of art, the 29 carvings represent an unusual cross section of Buddhist art from the late Silla period. This boulder with all these reliefs is designated as Treasure No. 201.

above: *Two pagoda reliefs with sitting image above and twin flying horse-like creatures below decorate the north wall of a large rock in T'ap Valley. (T-201)* center: *On the east wall are found twelve relief figures.* below: *A sketch has been done of the east wall of the treasure rock in T'ap Valley.* next page: *In Buddha Valley of Nam-san is an image sculptured into a three-foot deep niche. (T-198)*

6. Sitting Buddhist Image of Buddha Valley

(*Treasure No. 198*)

From T'ap Valley 200 meters north is Buddha Valley. Near a culvert a trail can be used west into the foothills. This trail follows the right slope until terraced fields are reached. Up the steep bank about fifty feet to the right a large rock contains a niche and Buddha image.

This seated Sokkamoni of Buddha Valley has been designated as Treasure No. 198. It is most unique in that it was sculptured into a deep three foot niche. The rock chosen for this accomplishment is only eight feet high.

The head of this five foot image appears to be covered with a wrap and is bent slightly. The mouth seems to have a faint smile. The hands are hidden behind a thick robe which falls below the feet, concealing the pedestal. The cuts in folds of the robe represent a pre-unification style but it is presumed that this image was carved after the unification period. Although this niche is not really deep enough

to be called a cave, it does suggest that the concept of cave temples had already begun during the unified Silla era. This idea of cave temples or *sokkuram* (rock cave hermitage) was introduced to Korea from China, and not only large cave temples were constructed but many miniature crevices or overhangs were used as sanctuaries for the Buddhist images.

7. Kings Chong-gang and Hon-gang
Tombs of Ruling Brothers (Historic Sites No. 186 and No. 187)

These tombs on the east slopes of Nam-san are easy to reach. They are very near each other and not far from the road just beyond the Hwarang House 6.5 kilometers from Kyongju City.

The first of the two tombs, located about 200 meters from the road traditionally belongs to Hon-gang (49th king). The tomb mound circumference is 157 feet and it has a four foot retaining wall consisting of four tiers of cut stone. This tomb has been designated as Historic Site No. 187.

The second tomb located south and 150 meter from the road belongs to the younger brother, King Chong-gang. The tomb mound is approximately the same size as Hon-gang's tomb as the circumference is 161 feet. The

retaining wall is only two feet high consisting of two tiers of cut stone. The government has designated this tomb as Historic Site No. 186.

Hon-gang began his reign in 876 upon the death of his father Kyong-mun (48th king). His reign was considered one of the best during this period of Silla decline. During King Hon-gang's rule the population of capital rose to over one million people, comparable to the city of Taegu today.

Following King Hon-gang's death his younger brother became Chong-gang (50th king) and ruled for only one year. In 886 a sister came to the throne to rule for ten years as King Chong-gang had no heir and the son of Hon-gang was too young. However,

174

Queen Chin-song's reign was choked with immorality.

One day King Hon-gang with his attendants spent a few days at the beaches near Ulsan. As he was preparing to leave a dense fog covered the land making travel impossible. The king was informed that the Sea Dragon was frollicking nearby and that he should give due respect in order to avoid its anger. Mang-hae-sa was erected to honor the Sea Dragon which so pleased him that he personally appeared with his seven sons to praise the king's virtues.

One of these seven sons accompanied the king to the capital and became a vassal. King Hong-gang named him Ch'o-yong. The fact that he was exceptionally mild tempered leads one to believe that he was foreign.

The following folk tale which is popular in Korea illustrates the complete lack of anger in Ch'o-yong. When Ch'o-yong became of age he was offered by the king a wife from among the most attractive maidens of Silla. Her beauty drew such attention that even the mountain spirit took notice. One particular Plague Spirit fell desperately in love and taking the form of a handsome youth he secretly met her to try and seduce her.

The Plague Spirit knowing when Ch'o-yong was away from home frequently visited his lovely wife. However, on one occasion Ch'o-yong returned home unexpectedly early and upon entering his bedroom was surprised to see four feet protruding from the blankets. Chuckling over the humor of this situation he composed a lyric which he sang as he danced before the two caught in adultery.

Fortunately this song, in the form of a *hyang-ga*, remains. This form of verse which was meant to be sung is unique to Korea.

"Under the moon of the Eastern Capital
I reveled far into the night.
Then coming home I entered my room
And saw four legs.
Two legs belonged to me but to whom
Do the other two belong?
The person below belongs to me but whose
body is raping her?"

"What shall I do?" he sang as he finished his lyric and dance in front of the Plague Spirit and his seduced wife. The Plague Spirit rose from the bed and fell on his knees before Ch'o-yong pleading for forgiveness.

"I was captivated by the bewitching beauty of your wife. I could not control my passion for her and now I have despoiled her. But I am dumbfounded with admiration for you," he said, "because you are not enraged over my sensuous pleasures with her."

Bowing in humble repentance the Plague Spirit continued, "I realize that my acts can not be forgiven but this I can do to show my sincerity. Hereafter, when I see your portrait on any doorway I will not enter the house." The Plague Spirit suddenly disappeared leaving Ch'o-yong amazed and his wife crying with humiliation.

For many centuries the Korean people would hang a portraits of Ch'o-yang beside their gates as protection against lurking spirits of disease. None of these pictures of Ch'o-yong are known to exist though it is possible that one might be discovered in a remote village.

above: *King Hon-gang's tomb is located on the eastern slopes of Nam-san. (HS-187)* below: *The tomb of Chong-gang, a younger brother of Hon-gang, is located nearby. (HS-186)* next page: *Soch'ul-ji appears in winter fantasy under a light snow. (HS-138)*

8. Soch'ul Pond: *Letter Appearing Prophecy*
(Historic Site No. 138)

Soch'ul Pond with a Yi Dynasty pavilion is located on the eastern slope of Nam-san about 4.5 miles from Kyongju City. One must take the road to Namsan Village passing the tombs of kings Hon-gang and Chong-gang.

The present pavilion was built by the Im family about three hundred years ago and is called Iyo-dang. Lantern and pillar stones are seen lying about among the broken tile. The pavilion has been recently repaired. The cyprus and crape myrtle along the pond's banks are beautifully gnarled with age.

About forty meters from Soch'ul-ji in the compound of an old Korean villa are many stone remains from an unknown temple site. Some of the rocks have been used in the foundation of this home while others from the site are still lying in the courtyard.

A tale concerning this pond is most intriguing and is one of the well known legends concerning this era. One spring day in 489 So-ji (21st king) was enjoying a royal outing in the Namsan vicinity. He mildly pondered the very strange reason that his queen refused to come. She had suddenly become ill and he had left her sleeping in her room.

The palace priest of this new religion called Buddhism had promised to fetch the court physician. Soon his mind was on the gaiety of the picnic. While eating some sweetmeats he noticed not far away some rats and crows making a noisy commotion.

Suddenly one large gray rat leaped forward and bowing low before King So-ji squeaked, "Follow that crow when it flies."

The surprised king quickly commanded a mounted officer to follow the black crow as it flew away to the eastern slopes of Nam-san. In a small village the warrior was distracted by two fighting pigs and when he looked again the crow was gone.

He walked on pondering what to do and

finally reached this small pond. While gazing at the reflection of his frowning face in the placid pool an old hermit appeared and gave him a sealed letter. Written on the envelope were the words, "Unopened one will die; opened two will die."

King So-ji after reading the ominous note felt it was far better not to open the envelope. However, the royal astrologer stated that the one person was the king himself and he should by all means open the envelope. Nodding his approval the king read the message inside. "Shoot an arrow through the garment closet of the queen's chamber."

Though puzzled the king hurried back to the palace. The queen stirring from her own pretended rest quickly gathered some loose garments and greeted her husband. She was wild-eyed with fright by the king's unexpected return.

Ignoring her questioning eyes he shot an arrow into the closet standing by the wall.

There was a muffled cry and as the door was opened the partially clad body of the court priest fell forward with the broken arrow in his shoulder. This priest had gained the love and confidence of the queen, as the two of them had been plotting to kill the king. The queen cried her innocence but to no avail. The monk was taken out and strangled together with the guilty queen.

From this event it became the custom for people to stay indoors on the new year's first day of the pig, rat, and horse. Also on the 15th day of the first lunar month glutinous rice was presented in ceremonial offering to the black bird that saved the king's life and brought death to the adulterous queen and her partner.

This day is called Ogi-il (Crow Day). On this day the village people would eat only wheat or corn but no rice. King So-ji renamed this pond Soch'ul (Letter Appearing) and today the government has designated this scenic area as Historic Site No. 138.

Though Soch'ul-ji pavilion dates to the Yi Dynasty, the pond's historic legends date to early Silla with the tale of the strange appearing letter.

9. Ch'ilbul-am: *Controversies of the Seven Buddha Reliefs (Treasures No. 199 and No. 200)*

Namsan Village can be reached after taking a paved road off the main highway to Pulguk-sa at a junction near the Sach'onwang-sa site. Follow the paved road southward along the eastern slope of South Mountain, passing the Hwarang House and Soch'ul-ji, 9 kilos from Kyongju City. It is best to park at this village (near the two pagodas). From here it will take 1.5 hours to walk to Ch'ilbul-am.

In the village are the ruined remains of another set of stone pagodas. At the junction by the reconstructed pagodas is a road which traverses Nam-san to the west side and Posok-jong. It is unpaved and a difficult road to use.

Ch'ilbul-am (Seven Buddha Hermitage) is considered the most delightful and scenic of sites within the entire Nam-san (South Mountain) region. Excluding the famous Sokkuram behind Pulguk-sa these relief carvings are considered the best within the Kyongju vicinity.

After leaving the village follow a trail through pine woods. The calm serenity broken only by the chatter of a small brook will delight the infrequent visitor. The air is freshly scented with the odor of pine and moss. During the last twenty minutes of the hike the gorge narrows and the path becomes quite steep. Finally a small thatched hut is seen beside a clear spring.

The small hermitage of Ch'ilbul is relatively new. Upon reaching the courtyard the visitor

The many relief images of Ch'ilbul-am provide the most unusual historic site in the entire Kyongju area of Nam-san. (T-200)

The most popular shaman deity today is the sanshin *or Mountain Spirit similar to this portrait at Ch'ilbul-am.*

is suddenly awed by the first glimpse of the seven bold relief images (Treasure No. 200). Over the many centuries these seven *ma-aebul* (Buddha relief) images have survived well.

Today these figures stand unique, continuing to baffle the Buddhist scholars, and still there is little agreement. On the rear cliff wall are two eight foot attendants standing in relief on either side of the main sitting image. It is certain that the left attendant (holding a bottle) is the Kwanseum Posal (Bodhisattva of Mercy) while the right attendant is Taesaji Posal (Bodhisattva of Power). Traditionally the center eleven foot image should be the Amit'abul (Buddha of Western Paradise). However, it is facing east rather than west so might be considered the Sokkamoni (Historic Buddha). Korean scholars are in doubt.

In front of this triad *ma-aebul* is a large cube-shaped stone which continually baffles the Buddhist scholars. Comparisons are made with the square stone of Kulbul-sa (Excavated Buddha Temple) site at Paegyul-sa (Chestnut Curd Temple) near Kyongju and a similar rock on display at Horyu-ji, a Japanese temple near the city of Nara. This temple was designed to imitate Korean architectural design, as Buddhist influeneces had recently arrived from Korea.

It is certain that the front five foot image is the Yaksa Yorae (Buddha of Medicine). However, this is as far as agreement is reached. Many Buddhist scholars will argue that because

left: *Buddhist relief on a cliff above Ch'ilbul-am is probably the Kwanseum Posal. (T-199)*
right: *The triad is located on the stone wall.* below: *The identity of the images baffle scholars.*

of Horyu-ji, the northern image is the Sok-kamoni while the southern image is the Miruk (Buddha of the Future). Possibly the image behind the Yaksa Yorae is the Amit'abul as it is facing the traditional western direction. This position is also similar to Kulbul-sa with the Amit'abul in front (west) and the Yaksa Yorae behind (east) on the cubed rock.

When the Hwaom sect was brought into Korea from China by Priest Ui-sang, there was mention of the four directional Yorae (Buddha) and their definite positions. The Yaksa Yorae is positioned in the east while the Amit'abul is positioned in the west. The Posunjang Yorae (Widely Victorious and Magnificent Buddha) is found in the south and the Pudongjon Yorae

(Unmovable Buddha) is positioned in the north. If one follows the Hwaom sect this may be the image identification of the cubical rock

A small spirit shrine is found to one side. Portrayed are the three spirits of Sanshin, Ch'ilsong and Toksong. The Mountain Spirit (*sanshin*) is most unique and colorful. The topknot is seen under the scholar's hat. The old gentleman is wearing a long flowing red robe and yellow *paji* (trousers). The tiger messenger at his side has both spots and stripes typical of the early folk humor in the crossbreeding of leopards and tigers.

After a ten minute walk up the steep hillside behind Ch'ilbul-am another *ma'aebul* image is seen on the cliff wall. From here the view over the entire valley and ancient Silla capital is excellent. This Buddhist carving has been designated as Treasure No. 199. It is probably the Kwanseum Posal (Bodhisattva of Mercy) but again there is little agreement as some scholars feel that it represents th Miruk Posal (Bodhisattva of the Future). I s face is stern and hard which is not typical of the more compassionate features of the Kwanseum.

below: *The Yaksa Yorae relief in front and Kwanseum on the rear wall can be accurately identified.(T-200)*above: *At Ch'ilbul-am Toham Mountain can be seen in the distance. (T-199)*

10. Twin Three Storied Pagodas of Namsan Village
(*Treasure No. 124*)

These two pagodas located 75 feet apart accent the twilight days of a once flourishing temple in this quiet valley of South Mountain. The name of this temple is unknown. At first glance the pagodas seem similar; however, on careful scrutiny they are quite different. The foundation of the east pagoda is simple and plain while the foundation stones of the west pagoda contain the carved images of the *p'albujung* (Eight Congregated Devas) in bold relief.

The east pagoda is one of the few examples of a stone pagoda built to imitate the style of brick. The brick pagoda was a transitional concept in Korea between wood and stone though they did not really flourish. It seems that brick attracted the curiosity of the artists who were more accustomed to using stone. Occasionally stone pagodas were built in the style of brick pagodas during late Silla.

The characteristic effect of this pagoda is inevitable if the pagoda is to be built with small bricks; thus we can safely assume that the architect intentionally wished to imitate the brick style with the use of stone.

The west 16.5 foot paogda is typical of the style of stone pagodas that emerged during the United Silla period. There is a gentle roof line slope with the stair-step formation only under the eaves. Also the pillar relief on the corner of each story as well as the base is conspicuous.

The pagodas of Namsan Village are a popular attraction for this rural village. (T-124)

11. Namsan Skyway and Yongjang Temple Site
(Treasures No. 186 and No. 187)

In recent years a dirt road was constructed between the eastern valley near the Namsan Village twin pagodas and the western valley of Posok-jong. The pavilion conspicuously seen along the ridge of the mountain was also built at this time and is located beside this road as it meanders over the upper ridges. The road is rough, steep and difficult to use.

About 8 kilos from the pagodas is a Buddha face relief high on a cliff rock to the left across the stream. Some scholars feel that this stone face was once worshipped as a phallic symbol.

About 2.2 kilos further a trail from the road leads to Yongjang-sa site (15 minute walk). From the road the three-storied pagoda is easily seen along the ridge. Only .5 kilos further is the summit. From here one can hike into Yaksu Valley where the largest relief Buddha for the Kyongju area is located. Also from the summit a trail can be taken along the ridges to Samnung Valley and Sangson-am.

The large pavilion to the west is overlooking Posokjong Valley. Several temple sites with pagoda remains can be seen by walking down into this valley from the pavilion. One site is only 100 meters below the pavilion while the other is reached after a fifteen minute walk. Puhung-sa, a newly built temple, is located further beyond. From the pavilion the road descends rapidly into the western valleys.

1.6 kilo down from the pavilion the road passes the remains of Nam-san Fortress(Historic Site No. 22) on the right. This fortress was built in 591 during the reign of Chin-p'yong (26th

above left: On the hillside of Kuksa Valley of east Nam-san still lie the remnants of a large three-storied pagoda. above right: This excellent relief is seen at Yongjang-sa site near the summit of Nam-san. below left: An incomplete relief is seen near Namsan Village while (below right) the rock itself is worshipped by women because of its phallic characteristics.

king) and was 3,854 feet long. There was a stone tablet erected to commemorate this event. Four pieces of this tablet have been discovered and are located in the Kyongju National Museum. There is very little that can be seen of the original wall. Near the northern end of the fortress the remains of two ware-houses are found where carbonized rice grains can still be discovered even today.

Less than 2 kilometers further, before the road crosses the stream in Yunul Valley, is located a triad *ma-aebul*. The triad is seen on the hillside about 50 meters to the right. Further up the side of the hill are seen more remnants of the fortress wall. The center image is probably the Sokkamoni and both attendants are the Yaksa Yorae (Buddha of Medicine). One kilometer further the road reaches Posok-jong and the tomb of Chi-ma (6th king).

Probably the most unique of all the historic remains that can be seen along the skyway route is that of Yongjang Temple site. Situated on a scenic vantage point sits a typical Silla pagoda and an unusual Buddha image on a circular pagoda-like pedestal. These relics are near the site of Yongjang-sa (Continuous Growing Grass Temple) located directly below in a small clearing. Potsherds and pieces of tile are plentiful.

On a clear day the western mountains are seen surging into the blue haze of the distance while the fertile fields cut by the pride of Korea's modern expressway are vividly viewed in the valley below. Not much is known of Yongjang-sa except that it was first mentioned by Tae-hyon, a priest who lived during the reign of Kyong-dok (25th king) in the mid-eighth century.

The three-storied pagoda, designated as Treasure No. 186, is a typical post unification pagoda. The total height is about 17 feet. Located a short distance below the pagoda is a headless stone image positioned on an unusual pagoda-like pedestal (Treasure No. 187). Three circular wheel-shaped stones are tiered with three alternating smaller wheel-shaped stones placed between. Behind this Buddha image on the cliff wall is a six foot *ma-aebul* (Buddha relief) of the Sokkamoni in a sitting position on a lotus blossom.

A strange legend is told about Priest Tae-hyon who founded this Temple of Yongjang in Nam-san. He was in the regular practice of circumambulating the 16 foot image of the Miruk Posal. It was said that as he went around the image would always turn its head to face the priest. The custom of *t'ap-tori* was commonly practiced in Silla as it is today by walking around a pagoda while fervently praying.

Yongjang-sa was romantically linked to. the famed scholar of the Yi Dynasty, Kim Shi-sup. Though many of his literary works are now lost, the novel of the Myths of Kumo (*Kumoshinhwa*) has survived and is considered Korea's first novel by many historians. While living at this temple, he wrote his epic, an imitation of a Chinese novel relocated to the Korean setting of Nam-san, which was originally called Kumo-san (Gold Crow Mountain).

This 17-foot three-storied pagoda is found at Yongjang Temple site which has a spectacular view over the valleys of Nam-san. (T-186)

Kim Shi-sup was born in 1435 during the reign of Korea's most benevolent ruler, King Se-jong. Twelve years later he graduated with honors and was destined for a high government position. King Se-jong died in 1450 and was succeeded by his son Mun-jong (5th king) who lived only two years more. Mun-jong's son who was only eleven was pushed to the throne thus setting in motion the bizarre tragedies that were to follow as the boy's uncle through blood baths of assassination finally mounted the throne in 1455. The innocent and gentle Tan-jong (6th Yi ruler) was exiled to Yongwol where he was later strangled by orders of King Se-jo, the boy's uncle.

While political entanglements were mounting for many outspoken scholars of that day, the young Kim Shi-sup had fallen desperately in love. As concentration on his studies became increasingly difficult he chose a temple retreat for pursuing his studies with greater intensity. The girl had been promised to him and he knew that the sooner he finished his studies the sooner they could be married.

The news of King Tan-jong's murder completely changed the life of this sensitive young scholar. He burned all his books and shaved his head. His self-imposed exile continued throughout the years of King Se-jo's reign. After the death of King Se-jo, Kim Shi-sup returned to the capital. By chance he met the girl to whom he had been promised in marriage.

Kim Shi-sup, now 45, felt the spark of a former romance from 25 years ago flicker and burst into flames. The girl had never married while waiting over the years. Her love and devotion had remained steadfast though friends had encouraged her to marry another.

So they were married but tragically for only a few years. In their old age a son was born but shortly after his wife died. In abject sorrow he entered the priesthood again and went to live at Yongjang-sa. Here he wrote the *Kumoshinhwa* which today has brought him fame. In 1493 he quietly passed away during one of his travels. Kim Shi-sup was a great scholar who lived with a sense of true honor. Though his life was tragic it was not snuffed out by King Se-jo and today Kim Shi-sup is remembered as one of the six great exiled scholars of this period.

12. Buddha Triad: *Pre-unification Images of Sungbang Valley* *(Treasure No. 63)*

At the entrance of Sungbang (Priest Room) Valley are three stone Buddha images which are considered some of the oldest of Silla, possibly 6th century. The name of this former temple is unknown. At a site a short distance up the valley from where the images now stand, these pre-unification statues were found in 1923. They have been designated as Treasure No. 63.

The height of the central image which is the Amit'a (Buddha of Western Paradise) is 8.5 feet. The two Bodhisattva, the Kwanseum Posal and Taesaji Posal, on either side are slightly smaller. The images are characterized by round plump faces and conspicuous smiles which give these figures a similarity to the sculpture style of Paekche.

This image, on a pagoda-like pedestal, at Yong-jang-sa is unique. (T-187) The stone Kwanseum is seen at Sungbang Valley.

The faces appear far too large for the stocky stone bodies. The central Buddha is carved from of a single piece of granite with a boat-shaped mandala reaching from pedestal to head.

Two newly constructed temples located in front are called Sambul-sa (Three Buddha Temple) and Mangwol-sa (Longing for the Moon Temple). Near Sambul-sa are portions of a Silla pagoda which have recently been reconstructed. It is believed that the stones came from Kiam Valley temple site nearby.

Located approximately 200 meters behind the triad images is another partial image. One must follow the north bank of the stream (10 meters from the stream). This image was also found buried. After 1945 someone broke off and took the stone head. It is also broken across the chest and stands about five feet high.

The small village nearby is called Pae-ri. An interesting story is told about a village man

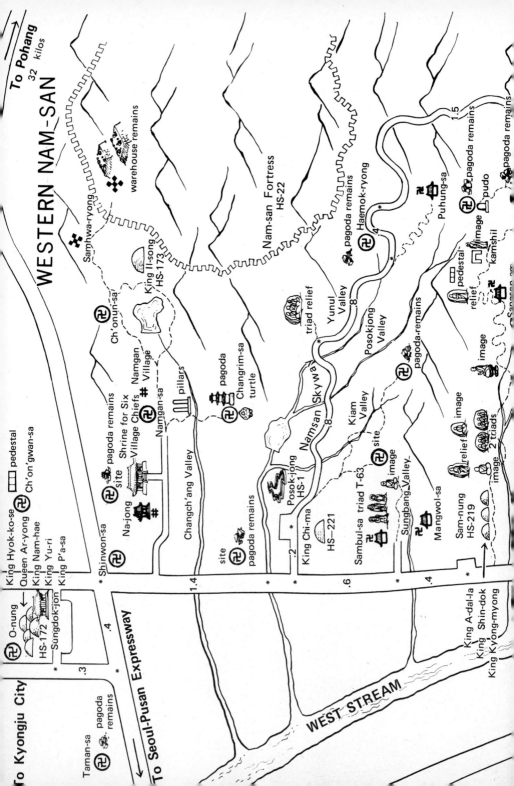

WESTERN NAM-SAN

To Pohang
32 kilos

To Kyongju City

To Seoul-Pusan Expressway

Taman-sa

pagoda remains

O-nung
HS-172
Sungdok-jon

King Hyok-ko-se
Queen Ar-yong
King Nam-hae
King Yu-ri
King P'a-sa

pedestal
Ch'on'gwan-sa

Shinwon-sa

pagoda remains
site

Shrine for Six
Village Chiefs

Na-jong

Namgan-sa

Samhwa-ryong

warehouse remains

Ch'onun-sa

King Il-song
HS-173

Namgan
Village

pillars

Changch'ang Valley

site

pagoda remains

pagoda
Changrim-sa
turtle

Nam-san Fortress
HS-22

triad relief

Posok-jong
HS-1

King Chi-ma

HS-221

Sambul-sa triad T-63

Namsan Skyway

.8

Kiam
Valley

Sungbang Valley

Mangwol-sa

Sam-nung
HS-219

King A-dal-la
King Shin-dok
King Kyong-myong

Yunul
Valley

Posokjong
Valley

pagoda-remains

site
image

image

relief

image
2 triads

Haemok-ryong

pagoda remains

1.5

Puhung-sa

pagoda remains
pudo

image
pedestal

relief

kamshil

image

Sansan-am

WEST STREAM

.4

.3

1.4

.2

.6

.4

.8

named No-sang. One day his elderly father was gathered to his ancestors so the filial son No-sang wanted the best funeral service money could buy for his departed father. He went to a monk who was a friend he could trust and asked him to find the most eminent priest in the country to perform the service. He took No-sang to the house of a famous monk but when he saw the hovel he was shocked. He was introduced to an unkempt and dirty individual in the clothing of a Buddhist priest.

No-sang believed that he had been tricked. He then severely rebuked his friend in the presence of the apparent beggar. He certainly would not hire the services of this dirty old priest. Upon hearing this the old monk reached into his grimy sleeve and pulled out an object which immediately turned into a lion. He then climbed on the lion's back and rode from sight.

No-sang was again dumbfounded as he realized the error of his judgement. In reality he had been in the presence of the Munsu Posal. He quickly knelt at this sacred place and prayed to be forgiven. Whether he eventually found the right monk to perform the ceremonial duties toward his deceased father is unknown; however, from that time on this region has been referred to as Pae-ri (Bowing Village) in honor of the Munsu Bodhisattva.

The triad images of Sungbang Valley are believed to represent the Amit'a Buddha and two attendants. (T-63) below: The Sam-nung tombs traditionally belong to Pak family kings. (HS-219) right: Often the park-forest tomb sites become recreation areas.

13. Sam-nung: *Tombs of the Royal Pak Family*
(Historic Site No. 219)

Sam-nung (Three Tombs) are located on the western slopes of Nam-san (South Mountain). Take the road 3.2 kilos from the crossroad near O-nung southward passing Posok-jong and Sambul-sa. As the road passes through a pine grove three tombs are seen about 100 meters to the east. These tombs also mark the entrance to Samnung Valley.

It is traditionally believed that these tombs belong to three rulers of the Pak Clan. Of the 54 kings of Silla ten of them came from the Pak family whose founder was Pak Hyok-ko-se. All the Pak family tombs, identified according to tradition, strangely are located on the western slopes of Nam-san.

Of the three tombs at Sam-nung (Historic Site No. 219) it is legendarily believed that the first mound belongs to A-dal-la (8th king). He ruled 30 years beginning in 155 AD. As King A-dal-la had no heir, upon his death the crown went to a descendant of the Sok family, grandson of the first Sok family king, T'al-hae

(4th king).

Traditionally the middle tomb belongs to Shin-dok (53rd king). A member of the Pak family, he had married the daughter of Hyo-gong, the previous king. After a four year rule King Shin-dok died and his son became King Kyong-myong in 917 and was buried in the third mound after a seven year rule.

During the reign of King A-dal-la appeared this unusual legend. In a small seaport town near the present city of Pohang lived a simple fisherman and his wife. Yono-rang and Syeo-nyo were completely devoted to each other and lived a perfect life of married bliss. The villagers looked upon them as the bearers of good and continued fortune for their community.

One day when Yono-rang was fishing a storm suddenly descended upon him capsizing his small craft. The poor fisherman struggled for his life but knowing it was hopeless cried for his wife as he sank below the waves. A huge rock (another reference to this story says a great

fish) suddenly floated toward his desperate hands and he clambered from a watery grave. The rock floated eastward and poor Yono-rang completely exhausted fell fast asleep.

When he awoke he found himself on a distant shore of the Japanese Isles. Here a strange people were speaking a language he could not understand. Impressed by his noble qualities the people of this region made him their king.

During this time Syeo-nyo was mourning the apparent drowning of her husband and would search the beaches for his body. One day she saw his straw sandals on a rock and climbed up to fetch them. Suddenly the rock moved and floated out to sea. In the same manner it took her also to the strange land of many islands far to the east

After this event the kingdom of Silla lost its fine weather and became gloomy and chilly. King A-dal-la traveled to the east coast of Silla and offered sacrifices but with little result.

Annoyed, he asked court astrologers the reason for this sudden calamity. He was told that the spirits of the "sun" and "moon" had left for the Eastern Islands. The king sent royal messengers to bring them back.

The happy couple only shook their heads and refused. They pleaded with Yono-rang and Syeo-nyo, telling of the hunger and suffering of the people. Taking pity on the emissaries Yono-rang offered a bolt of fine silk. "Take this," he said, "and offer sacrifices to heaven!"

Though disappointed the messengers took the gift and returned to report to the king. The king immediately climbed Son do -san, west of the capital and offered this silk to the Spirit of Heaven. Before the ceremony ended the clouds scattered and the sun shone from a blue sky. The wonderful silk cloth was made a national treasure and kept at an honored shrine in a detached palace near the eastern sea at a place called Yongil (Welcoming Sun).

The many valleys and streams of Nam-san are a paradise for hikers wishing to spend a day away from the crowded cities.

14. Tok-nung: *Lonely Tomb of a Murdered King*
(Historic Site No. 222)

During the closing years of Silla as the ruling Kim family had lost its ability to hold the throne, three kings from the Pak Clan came to power for a period of 14 years. The first was Shin-dok (53rd king) who was the son-in-law of Hyo-gong (52nd king). As King Hyo-gong had no heir, Shin-dok taking the throne in 913 ruled four years and was succeeded by his son Kyong-myong (54th king). Both kings are buried at Sam-nung.

In 924 a second son of Shin-dok mounted the Silla throne. Three years later Kyong-ae (55th king) became famous by his death in 927. He was last of the Pak family rulers to reign and died tragically at Posok-jong. As King Kyong-ae reveled in his merrymaking at the "Abalone Stone Pavilion" the armies of General Kyun-hwun descended upon the weakened defenses of Silla. Capturing the king and his courtiers, he killed most of them.

Kyong-ae was then buried in the "Lonely Tomb" which has been designated as Historic Site No. 222. Silla, a once proud kingdom faded in the bearded years of old age, but now draws pity and sorrow from today's historians. Tok-nung or the "Lonely Tomb" expresses the feeling of despair as this mighty kingdom of almost a thousand years slowly submerged into a sea of historical records. Tok-nung is located about 100 meters from Sam-nung on the western slope of Nam-san.

Legends claim that General Kyun-hwun was the son of an earthworm though actually he was the first son of a Silla nobleman. The myth was perpetuated that a wealthy landowner had a young daughter who was exceptionally beautiful as well as modest. One day this daughter became unusually thoughtful and silent..

above: *This large Buddhist image of Sam-nung Valley is still worshipped daily.* below: *The tomb of the last king to be buried in Silla is called Tok-nung. (HS-222)*

192

Eventually she confided to her father and revealed that a young man had entered her bedroom over the past several nights. He was so handsome that she couldn't send him away and he taught her the art of lovemaking. "Until now I have been too ashamed to tell you," she cried.

"Will he come again tonight?" queried the shocked father. "I am certain," answered the daughter blushing with embarrassment. "Then thread a needle," her father commanded, "and when he leaves in the morning pin it to his robe."

That night as before the handsome young man slipped into her room clad in a regal robe of purple with a belt of gold. After a night of passionate lovemaking the youth prepared to leave but as he embraced the girl for one last farewell kiss, she reached behind and pinned the threaded needle to the back of his purple robe.

Next morning she followed the trail of thread and it led her to the garden wall where she found her needle piercing the back of a large purple earthworm with a yellow band around the body. She soon gave birth to a son who grew up to become General Kyun-hwun.

King Kyong-ae was the last king to die in Kyongju and to be buried near the Silla capital. His successor who was placed on the throne by General Kyun-hwun was a sixth generation descendant of Mun-song (46th king). Kyong-sun (56th king) after lamenting the weakness of Silla and probably fearful for his own life abdicated in nine years to General Wang-gon and retired to Songdo (Kaesong) the new Koryo capital to the north. He died 42 years later and was buried near Songdo.

The "Lonely Tomb" near Sam-nung marks the end of a near millennium. This tomb mound is one of the smallest in the Kyongju vicinity as its circumference measures 138 feet.

A lonely stone Sokkamoni sits on a pedestal in Samnung Valley.

15. Samnung Valley Treasures and Silla Lore

A hiker must take the trail directly behind the three tombs (Sam-nung) on the west side of Nam-san. After a 15–20 minute walk a large headless Buddha image is seen. Near the ridge above the small temple is a large *ma-aebul* Miruk image which is still worshipped by the people. Near the top of the ridge are other Silla remains including a square base stone, Buddhist niche (1' × 2' × 5'), and headless image (30 inches). Also a spirit altar (Sanshin-dang) is presently in use.

More images are found in Sam-nung Valley than any other valley of South Mountain. However, they are extremely difficult to locate even with maps. You will not miss the large headless Buddha image beside the trail. This rock carving is over six feet high and 5.5 feet wide. Possibly depicting the Sokkamoni, it is considered classically exquisite in beauty and design. The thin robe which hangs over the left shoulder, showing the straps and tassels, is superb and typical of the post unification period.

Fifty meters to the left of the trail and up a steep hillside from the headless image is a boldly carved five foot relief. The flask and headdress typify the Kwanseum (Goddess of Mercy).

Seventy meters further on the trail from the headless Sokkamoni are two triad carvings. Rather than carved in protruding relief the images are deeply incised into the relatively smooth surface of the rock. These six images

left: *A Kwanseum relief guards the entrance of Samnung Valley.* right: *A broken stone image is found near Kat Valley.*

are found north of the stream about forty meters from the trail.

The central Buddha of the left triad is ten feet high and stands on a lotus blossom. Each attendant is kneeling and facing the central image while presenting with both hands an offering of what appears to be a dish of fruit. Approximately 150 meters further up the hillside behind the two triad images is a solitary sitting incised image approximately 11 feet high and carved in the same style.

Deeper into Samnung Valley on a small knoll north of the mountain trail is a stone Sokkamoni statue. This image is impossible to see from the trail until you are well past the area. Higher up one can look down on this solitary figure sitting on a pedestal. The nose and other portions of the lower face were badly mutilated and crudely repaired with cement. making the face quite ugly. However, the carved eyes with delicate lines are beautifully preserved undamaged.

It is not pure coincidence that so many images have broken noses. Because of shaman superstition it is believed that if the stone nose of a Buddhist image is ground to powder and taken with tea certain illnesses can be cured. Also this was a potent remedy for barren mothers. It is small wonder that any Buddhist image's nose survived to this day. The *kwang-bae* (mandala) stone was deliberately broken by hikers about ten years ago. Its pieces are found behind the image.

After another thirty minute walk further up a steep ascent the hermitage of Sangson-am is reached. A married priest lives here with his wife. Behind this hermitage after a ten minute walk the gigantic 20 foot relief image of the Miruk (Bodhisattva of the Future) is viewed facing east so as to catch the first rays of the early morning sun over the slopes of Nam-san. The image's width is 15 feet and the head is protruding from the solid rock.

During the Silla period the Miruk image was extremely popular. This particular Miruk is the second largest image in the Nam-san region. Gazing upon the granite features one can reminisce about the two legendary priests who became incarnate Buddhas.

In the White Moon Mountains lived two men, Pu-duk and Pak-pak, who at the age of twenty

above: *A cluster of triad images are found deeply engraved into the stones of Samnung Valley.* below: *At the entrance of Samnung Valley is found a large headless stone image.*

shaved their heads and exiled themselves into the wilderness where they built two small huts in which to live and worship the Buddha. This event occurred during the reign of Song-dok (33rd king) and as the years passed Pu-duk favored the Miruk Posal while Pak-pak devoted his prayers to the Amit'abul (Buddha of Western Paradise).

On the eve of Buddha's birthday a young attractive maiden appeared at the hermitage of Priest Pak-pak. She was fragrant with the scent of rock orchids while her graceful movements accentuated her elegant beauty. The twilight breeze ruffled her flimsy garments revealing a firm and supple body, and when she spoke her voice rang as music on the mountain air.

"The sun sets soon for travelers in these mountain peaks and the evening mist quickly veils the trail which leads to town. I wish to rest my weary body for the night," she spoke to the startled priest. The willowy beauty fairly melted the lonely heart of the stunned Pak-pak.

However, taking a firm hold on his rising emotions he quickly replied, "A Buddhist temple should be kept undefiled. Please leave quickly lest you further tempt my rising desire."

Blushing with shame at the words of the startled priest, the radiant lady hurried to the cave cell of the other priest, Pu-duk. Again she pleaded for a place to rest from her journey.

"From where have you come on this special day of Buddha's birth?" questioned Pu-duk.

"I have heard your prayers so I have come to help you achieve your desire. Listen to my song and do not ask who I am," the enchantress murmured.

"The sun has set and a thousand mountains are dark, As I travel my lonely heart knows no bounds. Where the bamboo and pine darken the green shadows of the valleys, the fresh spring water sings a sparkling new tune.

"The traveler is weary and needs hospitality tonight, Not because she has gone astray in this world, but because she wants to lead you on a noble path."

Several unique incised images are only found in Samnung Valley of Nam-san. This eleven-foot image is about 150 meters beyond two triad images closer to the valley trail.

Pu-duk's lonely heart cried out in desire, but he calmly replied, "This is a holy place, but Buddha does command that a priests must come to the aid of all creatures." So with trembling hands he unlatched the door. "Come in! My hut is far too bare and humble for a noblewoman such as you!"

Graciously the woman entered and Pu-duk quickly returned to his prayers in order to keep carnal temptation from his mind. At midnight the woman called from her bed, "Please kindly bring a straw mat and a tub of hot water for I am going to give birth to a child."

"Women are most pitiful when giving birth," he thought. "It is strange I did not notice she was with child before." As he started to do what she had requested a loud cry was heard.

"The child was born sooner than I expected," she replied. "Please, I will need the hot tub of water so that I can bathe myself and the baby."

Seeing this young maid endowed with beauty disrobe before him, the humble priest shook with emotion but having pity for her condition he prepared the tub and gently placed her in it

As he tenderly washed her soft white skin with trembling hands, he was astounded to see the water change to a golden liquid. A sweet scent permeated the room. This stunning

196

girl with a warm smile of mercy leaned toward Pu-duk "You also should bathe in this water," she gently commanded.

"Bare my own body before the eyes of this woman? Why must I do this?" he thought to himself. But the girl's eyes were so dramatic and compelling that he obeyed. As the water cleansed his body he felt his mind becoming clean and fresh while his skin became the color of gold. The crockery tub slowly turned into a lotus pedestal.

"My dear monk," whispered the woman. "I am Kwanseum!" And with these words she disappeared.

The next morning Priest Pak-pak, thinking surely that his friend had fallen to the ways of flesh, called to admonish him. Astonished he found Pu-duk sitting as a Miruk radiating light. Bowing respectfully he asked, "Who has made you a Miruk?"

Pu-duk related the episode of the previous night. His friend sighed. "Because I was more fearful that I'd succumb to her ravishing beauty I turned her away and thus lost my chance," he groaned.

"Please do not despair," Pu-duk consoled his friend. "There is still some golden liquid left in which you can also bathe." When Pak-pak emerged from the bath he was transformed into the Amit'abul and took a position facing his friend. For several days these two incarnate Buddhas preached sermons to the people and finally disappeared into the sky riding the clouds.

below: *The forces of nature, the rocks, wind and water have transformed the twenty valleys of Nam-san into regions of natural beauty.* right: *This Tomb of Kyong-dok, one of several in the Kyongju area, displays the twelve zodiac images in relief on the retaining wall. (HS-23)*

16. Tomb of Kyong-dok: *The Ruler Who Argued with God*
(Historic Site No. 23)

Kyong-dok (35th king) began his rule of 23 years in 742. Kyong-dok was the third son of Song-dok (33rd king). His elder brother Hyo-song ruled for five years before him. Pulguk-sa was constructed by Kim Tae-song during King Kyong-dok's reign.

After the reign of King Kyong-dok the kingdom slowly declined. Kyong-dok's son was murdered in 780. A 10th generation descendant of Nae-mul (17th king) was then selected to succeed Hye-gong (36th king). The aristocrats were out of favor with the rulers of Silla and rebellion frequently occurred to further weaken the absolute power of the monarchy.

King Kyong-dok's first queen did not bear children and had to be put aside. Lady Man-wol (Full Moon) was then selected to replace the discarded queen; however, Kyong-dok was taking no chances.

He summoned the famous Priest P'yo-hun and requested that the good monk should go immediately to see the spiritual powers and request that a son be given as heir to the throne. He returned with the news that the king was to be blessed with a daughter but not a son.

"I want a son," snapped the irate king and commanded that the priest return to heaven and ask that this blessing be changed so that

he might have a son.

God was upset and stated that if the king kept his selfish wish the kingdom would fall to ruin. P'yo-hun relayed to Kyong-dok the angry words from heaven. Pondering this ultimatum for a moment he replied that even though his kingdom was endangered he could not be content until he had a son.

A son was soon born to Queen Man-wol but he had a feminine character and behaved like a girl from infancy. As prophesied by Priest P'yo-hun the decline of Silla began with the reign of Hye-gong (36th king), this weak son of King Kyong-dok. Priest P'yo-hun, the most famous disciple of Priest Ui-sang, later became the first head priest of Pulguk-sa.

King Kyong-dok's tomb is one of five royal tombs known to depict the zodiac images. Also the zodiac relief figures are seen on the tomb of Kim Yu-shin, the square tomb, and various pagodas found within the vicinity of Kyongju.

The Oriental zodiacs originated in China before the Christian era and represent the twelve deities of direction and time. They were carved and buried within tombs from the early T'ang period. Their purpose was to protect the dead person's spirit from twelve directions. The zodiac figures at Kyong-dok's tomb are simplified and dignified, bearing cheerful expressions. The figures are almost three feet high.

The retaining wall is four feet high while the tomb circumference is 215 feet. The stone apron projects six feet from the retaining wall. Forty stone pillars are positioned around the mound. They are about 5.5 feet high and over one foot thick. There are now no stone officials near the tomb.

After following the road south along the western slopes of Nam-san for 12 kilos from Kyongju City, take a road to the west, cross the river and go under the expressway. One kilo further park the car and walk toward the hills on the right (15 minutes). The tomb is difficult to see from the road as it is hidden by pine trees on a high ridge.

The zodiac sheep dressed in a military uniform was carved in relief during the 8th century on King Kyong-dok's tomb. Ink rubbings are often seen in the art galleries of Seoul.

17. Other Historic Sites in the Valleys of Nam-san

Yakmok Valley:

Yakmok (Medicine Wood) Valley is located just north of Buddha Valley on the east side of Nam-san. In the last field before the forest begins are pagoda remains, both roof and body stones piled together. Also found are several foundation stones and a possible pedestal stone with a hole in the center. The temple name is unknown.

Kamshil Stone near Hwarang House:

A *kamshil* is a stone niche which will hold an image. This is the largest known in the Kyongju area. The stones have been positioned directly in front of the Hwarang House. Having a lotus shaped pedestal its total height is six feet. Its inner demensions are 4'6" × 3'.

Pagoda Remains of Nam-san Village:

A short distance south of the village from the twin three-storied pagodas (Treasure No. 124) are the remains of additional three-storied twin pagodas (roof 6 feet wide). The numerous cut stones are piled in a heap to one side of the village fields. This temple site is thought to be Kaeson-sa.

Sungso Valley Temple Site:

This temple site is extremely difficult to find. At first the trail is followed to Ch'ilbul-am, however, before crossing the stream a small trail is taken to the right while keeping the stream on your left. As the valley widens the temple site is reached. Though the temple name is unknown the valley name refers to the cremation of a priest.

A five-foot stone wall is first noticed. A pagoda roof stone (2'3" wide) as well as several foundation stones can be found. A stone marker shows the site of a three-storied pagoda which was moved to the Kyongju National Museum in 1931. This pagoda depicts the *sach'onwang* (Four Heavenly Kings).

Ch'onbul Temple Site :

This temple site is almost impossible to find. At first the trail to Ch'ilbul-am must be taken. The central stream must be crossed twice. As the trail goes through a cluster of grave sites with the main stream on the left one must bear right crossing another small stream and follow the valley for about twenty minutes. The site of Ch'onbul (Thousand Buddha) Temple is hidden in a grove of thick pines at the junction of two creekbeds.

There is a five foot stone wall about sixty feet in length. On the temple site is a seven foot stone pillar with a circumference of 7'6''. Nearly one hundred small niches or *kamshil* (7'' high and 3'' deep) are carved in the surface. This unique style of *kamshil* pillar was first discovered by the author in June 1974.

A Stone Face Relief above Namsan Village :

Half a mile up the valley on the Namsan Skyway from the twin pagodas of Namsan Village is a relief carving of a Buddha head. It is seen across the stream and on a large rock 100 meters up the slope to the left. Some scholars believe that it was worshipped as a phallic symbol because as one stands behind the rock the resemblance to a penis is noted.

Kuksa Valley Temple Remains :

Several temple sites can be found in this valley. The area is reached after a thirty minute walk behind Sojul-ji. A woodcutter lives on the site of Taeji-am now called *chiam* (earth rock). In the valley to the east can be seen large temple walls, where pagoda remains and pedestal stone (48'' cir.) are found. Lotus and animal image carvings are seen on the pedestal. The largest pagoda roof stone measures six feet in width. In the National Museum of Kyongju is another pedestal stone from this site with two lion faces carved on the surface. Numerous roof tiles are found in the area. These sites are difficult to locate.

Pedestal Near Yongjang Temple Site:

A few yards from the skyway road at the pass from east to west of Nam-san ridge (.3 km. south of the trail to Yongjang pagoda) is a large 7'6'' circular lotus pedestal carved into a huge rock on the ridge. About 30 meters on the other side of the road at the pass is a tablet base stone. The three foot tablet has long ago disappeared.

Temple Sites of Posokjong Valley :

The newly constructed pavilion near the peak of Nam-san overlooks Posokjong Valley. About 100 meters directly below this pavilion is an unnamed temple site. Roof and block stones of a small three-storied pagoda are scattered about the site. The largest roof width is 3'6''. A four foot temple retaining wall remains. After a 15 minute walk down toward Puhung-sa the remains of a larger granite pagoda are seen. The pagoda base is 4'6'' square. Nearby in a ravine is a square stone *sari-pudo* (2'6'' X 1'6''). The cap is a long rectangular stone with a sloping roof.

Haemok-ryong Valley Temple Site:

Located about 1.5 km. downhill on the skyway road from the pavilion near the summit is the temple site "Crab Ice Hill." Several stone pagoda roofs and square body blocks can still be seen as well as pillar foundation stones. The site is in the fields below the road.

Four Temple Sites Near O-Nung:

Three names are known, Shinwon-sa, Konwon-sa and Tamon-sa. Shinwon-sa was located at the main intersection between O-nung and Posok-jong. The stone remains are now buried under the asphalt. Konwon-sa site is found due west of O-nung near the highway. Stones found here were moved to the Kyongju National Museum. It is believed that Konwon-sa was the temple where the murder of Ui-jong (18th Koryo king) took place in 1173.

Tamon-sa is located nearer the West Stream. There are six stone remnants of a gigantic pagoda with one roof stone measuring seven feet across. Eight large carved images in relief were moved to the Kyongju National Museum. The fourth temple site is found behind the Onung Primary School. Few stones remain from these three-storied pagodas. Also seen is

(1) Yakmok Valley temple site; (2) A kamshil *or stone niche at the Hwarang House; (3) Pagoda remains of Namsan Village; (4) Stone remains from Sungso Valley temple site; (5) The* kamshil *stone discovered by the author in 1974 in Ch'onbul Valley temple site; (6) Face and phallic symbol above Namsan Village; (7) Author next to a stone which once held a Silla tablet near Yongjang-sa site; (8) Lotus pedestal near the site of Yongjang-sa; (9) Ruined pagoda in Kuksa Valley; (10) A* pudo *remains in Posokjong Valley; (11) Stone pagoda roof in Posokjong Valley; (12) Pagoda remains in a field of Haemok-ryong temple site; (13) The triad images of Yunul Valley in western Nam-san; (14) Giant pagoda remains of Tamam Temple site; (15) Silla stone remains near the O-nung Primary School*

a lantern roof and rim stone of a well.

Namgan Village and Temple site :

Located east of Na-jong on the western slopes of Nam-san are Buddhist stone remains from the site of Namgan-sa (South Brook Temple). Stone temple banner pillars twelve feet high are seen in the field (2'6" apart). In the village are found stones that once served as wells, pedestals and pillar foundations.

Changrim Temple Pagoda and Other Remains :

About 500 meters south of the pillars of Namgan-sa is the three-storied pagoda of Changrim-sa (Flourishing Forest Temple). The *Samguk Yusa* recorded that this site was Silla's first palace. A temple was built during the unification period. In 1824 a record was found which indicated that the pagoda was built in 855 during the reign of Mun-song(46th king).This pagoda was reconstructed in 1976 December. Four of the eight *p'albujung* images remain. The base is 14'3" square and 6'6" high. (roof: 8'8"; 1st story: 5'1" × 5'1" × 4'4 ') The three roof stones, 1st story stone and part of the base stones were original.

In 1968 a headless Piroch'ana image was taken from this site to the Kyongju National Museum. Many foundation stones are seen nearby. About 50 meters from the pagoda is a two-headed turtle pedestal. Both heads have been destroyed. This pedestal (5'5" × 5'2") is one of three turtle pedestals with two heads in the Kyongju vicinity. The other two are at the National Museum and Mujang-sa site.

Ch'onun-sa Site :

Beyond Namgan Village and rice fields is the temple site of Ch'onun (Heavenly Gratitude) located in a persimmon orchard. Eight foundation stones were used for construction of a *sowon* (Confucian Study Hall) but it was destroyed about a century ago.

Silla Grain Warehouse and Armory Remains:

It is recorded in the *Samguk Yusa* that Mun-mu (30th king) had warehouses erected on South Mountain near the site of Ch'onun

Temple. The foundations can still be seen. After a fifteen minute climb up the slope east of Ch'onun-sa near some fields the foundations can be found. One warehouse measures 275 feet by 40 feet. Carbonized rice can still be discovered and is highly valued for Korean medicine.

Tomb of King Il-song (Historic Site No. 173) :

Il-song was the seventh Silla king and ruled for twenty years beginning in 135 AD. His tomb is traditionally believed to be behind the reservoir of Namgan Village. The circumference is 153 feet and distance across the mound is 56 feet. Nearby are the crumbling rock walls of Nam-san Fortress built in 591.

Tomb of King Chi-ma (Historic Site No. 221) :

Located about 150 meters from Posok-jong is the tomb of the sixth ruler of Silla. The circumference is 130 feet and distance across the mound is 45 feet.

Kiam Valley Temple Sites :

This temple site can be reached after a 30 minute walk from Posok-jong behind the royal tomb of Chi-ma. A series of three retaining walls are over 15 feet high. Little is known of this temple called Kiam (Chest Rock). The remains of a stone pagoda (roof width is 4'2") are found here. Previously a Piroch'ana Buddha image (2'4" high) with no head was found and taken to the Kyongju National Museum.

Additional Stone Remains of Samnung Valley :

At the hermitage of Sangson-am is the side section of a large stone image. At the summit behind the hermitage (five minute walk from the Miruk) are several stone remains. One is a square stone base (30" × 33") near the bluff. Next to a field 30 meters away is a *kamshil* in a cliff (niche—2' × 5'). Nearby is a 30 inch stone Bodhisattva with its head missing. About fifteen meters away is the inscription *sanshin-dang* (Bearing Spirit Place) where an altar is still used for barren women to come and pray for children.

*(16) Ink p'albujung rubbing taken from Nam-san's largest pagoda at Changrim Temple site;
(17) Temple wall of Kiam site; (18) Stone pillars on the site of Namgan-sa; (19) Ch'onun temple
site foundation stones; (20) Nam-san's largest Miruk relief in Yaksu Valley; (21) Image and
pedestal of Yaksu Valley; (22) Site of two Silla warehouses in Nam-san; (23) Tomb of King
Il-song (HS-173); (24) Pagoda remains of Yolban Valley; (25) Small headless image at summit
of Samnung Valley; (26) Reconstructed pagoda at site of Changrim-sa.*

204

Kat Valley Stone Buddha Image :

Located a short distance from the main road and found in a field behind the village homes of Pae Village is an especially fine sculptured image. Pieces of the pedestal and mandala are broken. It now stands four feet high from the waist. Several small relief images appear on the mandala. The image's head has tight curls and long ear lobes. The robe is draped over both shoulders. The right hand is held up and across the stomach with the index finger pointing out.

Yaksu Valley Relief:

This valley is located behind Kyongju Prison and takes about 45 minutes to reach by hiking. The trail is difficult to follow. The temple site has several stone walls. Near the entrance about five meters to the right of the trail is a headless stone image 3'6'' high in a sitting crosslegged position. Its feet and toes are quite distinct. The left hand is open on the lap while the right hand is positioned over the right knee. Pieces of the pedestal (4' and 2' square) with floral design are found nearby.

On the rock wall behind the temple site is a 30 foot standing relief image of the Buddha of Medicine called Yaksa Yorae. This is the largest image in the Kyongju vicinity. The head, however, is missing. At the top of the cliff is a 2'2'' carved recess where the head was once placed. The shoulders are 12 feet across while the robe at the base is 14 feet across. This relief carving is faint and difficult to see at first.

Sokka-sa Pagoda Remains in Pip'a Valley :

The valley is less than half a kilometer beyond Yaksu entrance. After a twenty minute walk on the right side of the stream the trail crosses to the left bank. After an additional 50 meters one must climb up the steep slope to the left. Among a large cluster of boulders the remains of a three-storied pagoda are seen. There is no path. A roof and two story block remain.

Additional Buddhist Remains of Yongjang and Yolban Valleys:

A complete hike into Yongjang Valley from the road at Yongjang Village will take 1.5 hours.

(27) Yaksa Yorae image located on the lower slopes of Yongjang Valley; (28) Remains of an imitation brick pagoda in Yongjang Valley ; (29) Pagoda remains in Sokka Valley

A side valley of Yolban is taken to the right after a fifteen minute walk following the stream. Behind a small farm the temple site is reached in ten minutes. There are two stone walls about four feet high and 60 feet from each other. The remains of a stone pagoda can be found.

Down near the mainstream at the entrance at Yolban Valley a large image of a headless Yaksa Yorae was discovered and taken to the Kyongju National Museum. In 1965 the missing head was discovered and joined to the body. In 1973 another portion of the mandala was found and also taken to the museum.

Five minutes further up Yongjang Valley is a small ravine left of the trail. Within several minutes one can reach several stone walls of another temple site. The last wall is 15 feet high. Nearby is a headless stone four foot image of the Yaksa Yorae. Its recently discovered head was taken to Seoul's National Museum. A fragment of a pagoda base and another stone image are also seen at this site.

Further into Yongjang Valley the trail bears southward finally reaching a reservoir. At the small lake the trail turns left and soon reaches a temple site (200 meters) where the complete remains of another three-storied imitation brick pagoda are noted. Several pillar foundation stones are seen nearby. The largest roof stone is five feet across.

Ch'onryong-sa Site:

Ch'onryong (Heavenly Dragon) Temple site is located high on the slopes of Koui Mountain south of Nam-san. The trail begins at Yongjang Village and is well used and clear to follow. The walking time is about one hour to the temple site which is located in a cluster of farm houses. One field contains parts of a three-storied pagoda (roof width is 5'8"). A lotus design lantern base stone is nearby. Stone remains are seen everywhere within walls and courtyards.

One pillar stone base was measured at four feet across indicating the size of the building known as the "Golden Hall" referred to in the *Samguk Yusa*. A stone base turtle with floral design hole on its back is seen in one court-yard. The turtle measure 4.5 feet. In a nearby field is a four foot grinding stone and a stone water trough (2'6" × 7'6"). A new temple by

(30) Stone turtle lantern base of Ch'onryong-sa site; (31) Pagoda remains of Ch'onryong-sa site; (32) A stone cistern at Ch'onryong-sa site;

206
the same name was constructed nearby.

Yongmun-sa Buddha Relief Image of Paegun Valley:

Following the western slope of Nam-san to Yongsan Village a small road at the stream leads into Paegun Valley and to Myonggye Village (4 kilometers from the bridge). At Myonggye (Hole Valley) Village is the temple site of Pukmyong (North Hole). A short distance from the primary school are remains of a stone pagoda (roof width is 6'4") and many pillar foundation stones. Several dolmens are seen in the fields.

At the pass between the villages of Myong-gye and Nogok is a trail which leads to Masok Mountain. Yongmun (Dragon Gate) Temple is easily seen from below. The relief image is 15 feet high and six feet wide (30 minute climb).

Five Other Temple Sites and Remains of Paegun Valley:

These temple sites are most difficult to find without a guide as trails are almost nonexistent. Soksu-am (Rock Life Hermitage) of Paegun (White Cloud) Valley is the easiest to reach but less interesting as only a retaining wall is seen (45 minute hike from Nojok Village).

After a 20 minute walk beyond Soksu-am site one can reach Chimshik Valley. Beyond a six foot rock retaining wall is a headless 3'6" Buddha image and circular pedestal (diameter 4 feet). After walking 15 minutes over the south ridge of Chimshik Valley into an adjacent valley a tomb marks the location of another temple site. In a jumbled pile are the stone remains of Nam-san region's largest pagoda (roof width 6'10"). Foundation stones of Yangjae (Nourishing Talent) Hermitage can be seen. Yangjae-am site is at the head of Chulpaui Valley.

After hiking ten minutes down the mountain trail fields on the left contain remains of a Buddhist image, portions of a mandala and pedestal. Two 18 inch devas are carved in relief on the pedestal. After an additional 20 minute walk along the slope the trail turns left and up a steep grade. Retaining walls indicate another temple site.

A Buddha image is found 200 meters behind and right of the trail up this slope. The head was broken from the body after the Korean War. The image is four feet high while the large pedestal is five feet in diameter. Remains of a mandala are found buried hearby. It will take 40 minutes to return to Nojok Village from Chulpaui Valley temple site.

*(33) An image in upper Sungbang Valley;
(34) Fifteen-foot relief image of Masok-san;
(35) Small kamshil at the peak of Samnung
Valley (36) An image of Chimshik Valley;
(37) Pagoda remains at site of Yangjae-am;
(38) Eighteen-inch deva reliefs on pedestal
stone of Chulpaui Valley; (39) Broken Buddha
and pedestal of Chulpaui Valley*

*The young and old in valleys of Nam-
san live within a rich Silla tradition.*

Chapter VI
Major Attractions West of Kyongju City

1. Kim Yu-shin: *Tomb of Silla's Greatest General (Historic Site No. 21)*

With some history and probably as many myths about this famous Silla general Kim Yu-shin, it is difficult to separate fact from fiction. He was certainly the most popular of the Silla generals if not the greatest of all Korean generals. Through his military genius Silla was unified during the reign of Mun-mu (30th king) in 668.

Many years prior in the Kaya Kingdom, which was located on the southern coast of Korea, ruled wise King Su-ro. He needed a queen to provide the country with an heir before he died. One day a foreign ship landed on his coast and a strikingly beautiful young girl debarked with twenty handmaidens.

"I am a princess from the distant country of Ayut'a (possibly India or Thailand) and a daughter of the king," she stated. "I'm now sixteen and my name is Ho Hwang-ok. Weeks ago I had a strange dream. I saw the heavenly Emperor come and command that I set sail for the Kingdom of Kaya. Here I would find an unmarried prince and would be his bride."

"I awoke and told my parents this dream," she continued. "My father, king of Ayut'a, has sent me." The two were married and soon she bore a son. Fourteen generations later Kim Yu-shin was born into the family of Kim So-hyon, a direct descendant of King Su-ro.

Another intriguing legend, concerning the birth of General Kim Yu-shin, records that once there lived a wise soothsayer named Ch'un-am. The evil queen of Koguryo wishing to know more about his powers invited him to court when she heard a strange tale about a river flowing uphill.

When the queen questioned how this could possibly be, Ch'un-am told her that it was so because the queen acted against the natural course of the *yin* (Korean-*um*) and *yang* and that the stream would flow normally only after her death. The evil queen flew into a rage and vowed to kill him instantly. However, the court advisors quickly soothed her temper

and suggested gently that Ch'un-am be given one more chance.

A box was brought and the queen pointing to it demanded to know its contents. Ch'un-am declared that there were seven mice, whereupon, the queen laughed. Convinced that the soothsayer really had no power she then decided to kill him for his impudence.

Ch'un-am calmly said, "I have never been wrong but I warn you that if I am killed I will return to avenge my death by killing you and destroying Koguryo." After the luckless Ch'un-am was dismembered it was discovered that the one mouse within the box had given birth to six mice. The queen trembled as she pondered the fortuneteller's final warning.

After a few months a son was born to the house of Kim So-hyon and named Yu-shin. Po-jang (27th king) of Koguryo also dreamed that the wandering spirit of the unfortunate Ch'un-am had entered the body of Kim So-hyon's wife. King Po-jang commissioned Paek-sok to serve as a spy for the express purpose of killing Kim Yu-shin.

After many years of living in the Silla capital the king came to trust Paek-sok. He was raised eventually to the rank of general though little was known of his origin or family. One day Paek-sok had the opportunity to suggest to General Kim Yu-shin that the two of them should first spy out the enemy's true strength before beginning the campaign. Kim Yu-shin gladly agreed.

They left the capital in disguise and travelled north deep into enemy territory. One evening after camp was made Kim Yu-shin went wandering alone in the deep mountain forest, when suddenly two lively nymphs appeared before him. "Where are you from and why are you here in the deep mountains?" asked the curious Yu-shin who was enthralled by the ravishing sweet beauty of the lovely girls.

"We are from the village beyond," they answered. "Would you care to enjoy some of our sweetcake?'' they asked coyly. Kim Yu-shin was beside himself with joy and love for these three girls. They beckoned shyly, ''Come to the woods with us and there we shall have our pleasures in a forest bed of fragrant flowers, unseen by the rest of the world.''

Unmindful of passing time Kim Yu-shin accompanied the three nymphs among the trees but suddenly they were transformed into noble god-like creatures. ''We are not nymphs of the woods but three goddesses,'' they told the shocked general. ''We have come to warn you of impending death. You are being lured by an enemy spy at this very moment. Be on guard!'' With these words the three deities

This tomb, traditionally belonging to General Kim Yu-shin, is one of Kyongju's most popular tourist sites. (HS-21) Dressed in civilian garb, the zodiac images are the most well preserved of all those remaining.

gracefully rose and disappeared.

Kim Yu-shin returned to the campsite to find Paek-sok fast asleep. The next morning he announced that he had forgotten some very important maps and must return. Suspecting nothing he returned with the general to the capital where Kim Yu-shin immediately had him arrested.

After confronting Paek-sok with his new knowledge, he fully confessed that he had been commissioned by the Koguryo king to kill Kim Yu-shin, who was believed to be the reincarnated spirit of Ch'un-am, the soothsayer. Kim Yu-shin put the Koguryo spy to the sword. Koguryo was soon defeated and both the king and his queen met the fate that was prophesied by the wily fortune teller Ch'un-am.

Kim Yu-shin was born in 595 during the reign of Chin-p'yong (26th king). He had two sisters and a younger brother. A nephew of Queen Son-dok (27th ruler) married the younger sister of General Kim Yu-shin. Later this prince became Mu-yol (29th king) and their first child was a boy who in 661 became Mun-mu (30th king) of Silla. King Mu-yol had seven sons.

One of King Mu-yol's daughters became the wife of Kim Yu-shin who married at the age of forty. He had five sons and four daughters by this wife. He also had another son named Kim Kun-sung by an unknown woman. Since we do not know the mother's name we might assume this may have been a son by the famed *kisaeng* Ch'on-gwan whom Kim Yu-shin loved dearly during his younger days though never married because of his position and reputation.

The Silla tale that is associated with Kim Yu-shin and Ch'on-gwan is without doubt in a special class all its own. Every Korean child knows the sad story of the general's favorite white horse and his youthful romance. The entire spectrum of Silla legends would be incomplete without telling this tale of tragic disappointment and sorrow.

During his youth he frequented the wine houses of the capital and on one occasion met the attractive young daughter of a *kisaeng*

The twelve zodiac relief images at the tomb of Kim Yu-shin are: rat (north), cow, tiger, rabbit (east), dragon, snake, horse (south), sheep, monkey, chicken (west), dog and pig.

(professional entertainer) named Ch'on-gwan.
He was soon staying long hours with her as his
unrestricted passion knew no bounds.

Without doubt she was a faithful girl and
attractive; however, Kim Yu-shin's mother,
realizing that her son's position in life was
being jeopardized and responsibility to his
country disregarded, felt that to marry this girl
would be ill advised. She counseled and gently
chided him over this matter. As Kim Yu-shin
was a dutiful son he promised his mother that
he would never see Ch'on-gwan again.

He then threw himself into his studies and
military training, vowing to keep his promise to
his mother and forget the girl. However, months
later during a warm spring day Kim Yu-shin
was enjoying a festive time with friends on the
banks of the South Stream. Soon the hour was
late and the moon was far into the sky. As he
had drunk too much wine, the young warrior
with difficulty mounted his favorite white horse
and gave him his head for home.

The strong wine had taken its toll and young
Kim Yu-shin was drowsily thinking of the
day's events as his horse plodded through the
streets of the capital. Finally the steed stopped
and Kim Yu-shin thinking he had arrived home
dismounted. The faithful horse remembering
previous days when his master had led a life
of overindulgence with the beautiful Ch'on-
gwan dutifully brought his master to the
house of the *kisaeng* as he had done so many
times before.

The youth tried to turn his horse around but
the tired animal was unwilling to leave as
he believed he was home and the hour was late.
In a drunken rage the young *hwarang* roared,
"My good horse, because of you I have broken
my pledge to my mother." So saying, he drew
his battle sword and with one blow severed his
mount's head. He then sped homeward on foot.

Hearing this commotion Ch'on-gwan rushed
through the gate in time to see through tears
her love disappear in the gathering mist of night.
She had remained faithful to him in the hopes
that someday he might return. Shocked from
seeing the dead horse beneath her feet she fell
in a swoon knowing her earthly despair would
be eternity. Some legends say that she killed
herself, though other sources tell that she cut
her long hair and entered a nunnery for the

remainder of her life.

After her death admirers who knew of her devotion for Kim Yu-shin erected a temple in her memory on the site of her old home. This temple was called Ch'on'gwan-sa, the site of which is now seen a short distance from the site of the ancestral home of General Kim Yu-shin. As one gazes on the stone fragments left in the fields at this temple site, one cannot help but recall this tragically romantic tale of a beauty and her young soldier who later became Silla's greatest general during the period of unification.

Of the many sons of Kim Yu-shin, the one he loved the most was Won-sul, a second son who also became a great general. During a crucial battle against the Chinese armies Silla forces lost heavily but somehow Won-sul managed to survive. The brave Won-sul was about to take his own life but his aide held his sword and told him that his time to die had not yet come.

Kim Yu-shin fully expected that his son had died in battle with honor. When he saw him returning he felt certain that he had fled the battlefield. Because of this suspected dishonor he angrily tried to kill Won-sul. He fled from his home and Kim Yu-shin never saw his son again. Later when he heard that his father was near death he hurried home and begged to see him but his father refused. Shortly after Kim Yu-shin died.

The following year in 674 the last great battle was fought with China near Pyongyang. There were over a million Chinese soldiers on the field. Silla won a great victory and General Won-sul was wounded in the right arm and had to have it amputated. He returned to Silla with fame and honor. Visiting his father's tomb he desperately wished that he could have brought family's glory home while his father was still alive.

Many of the tombs of Silla are in dispute including the tomb of General Kim Yu-shin. Though the general was posthumously awarded the title of king by Hung-dok (42nd king), nevertheless, he was a subject, though a

An imitation brick pagoda with two inwang images is located on the slopes of Sondo-san west of Kyongju. (T-65)

meritorious one, whose tomb could not be so elaborate. Others state that the topography of the region, legends concerning the tomb and articles unearthed from the vicinity confirm that this tomb belongs to General Kim Yu-shin. Until the tomb is officially excavated we may never be certain.

The tomb, listed as Historic Site No. 21, is located on Songhwa Mountain. Overlooking Kyongju City from the entrance to the tomb we see it is a direct line down main street leading to the railroad station. Seven foot military officials and six foot civil officials were once positioned on each side. As the poor craftsmanship was accomplished in the Japanese occupation period they were taken from the site in 1974 during the reconstruction of the tomb and the environment.

An eight foot rock apron extends out from the retaining wall. A stone fence with six foot high pillars was reconstructed in 1974 around

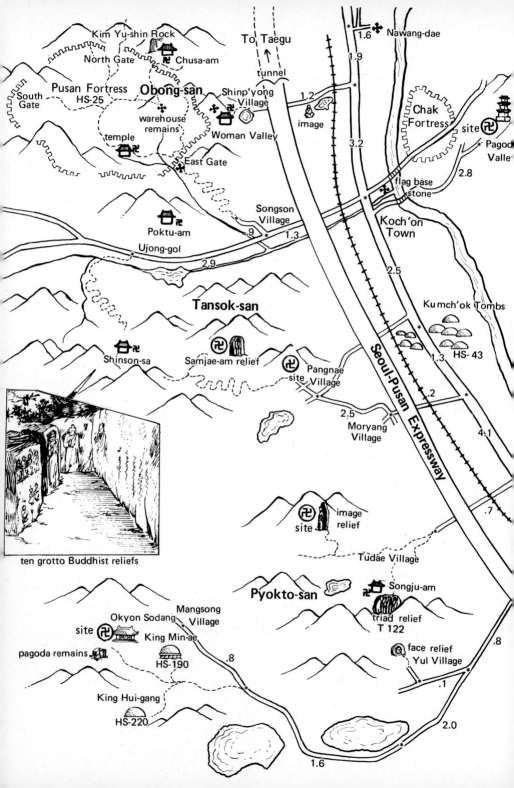

Kim Yu-shin Rock

North Gate

Chusa-am

To Taegu

tunnel

卍 1.6

Nawang-dae

1.9

Pusan Fortress
HS-25

Obong-san

Shinp'yong
Village

1.2

image

3.2

Chak
Fortress

site 卍

South
Gate

warehouse
remains

temple 卍

Woman Valley

Pagod
Valle

East Gate

2.8

flag base
stone

Songson
Village

Koch'on
Town

Poktu-am

.9

1.3

Ujong-gol

2.9

2.5

Tansok-san

Kumch'ok Tombs

1.3

HS-43

Shinson-sa 卍

Samjae-am relief 卍

site 卍

Pangnae
Village

.2

2.5

Moryang
Village

4.1

.7

ten grotto Buddhist reliefs

site 卍

image
relief

Tudae Village

Pyokto-san

Songju-am

site 卍

Okyon Sodang

Mangsong
Village

King Min-ae

triad relief
T 122

pagoda remains

HS-190

.8

face relief

Yul Village

.8

King Hui-gang

.1

HS-220

Seoul-Pusan Expressway

2.0

1.6

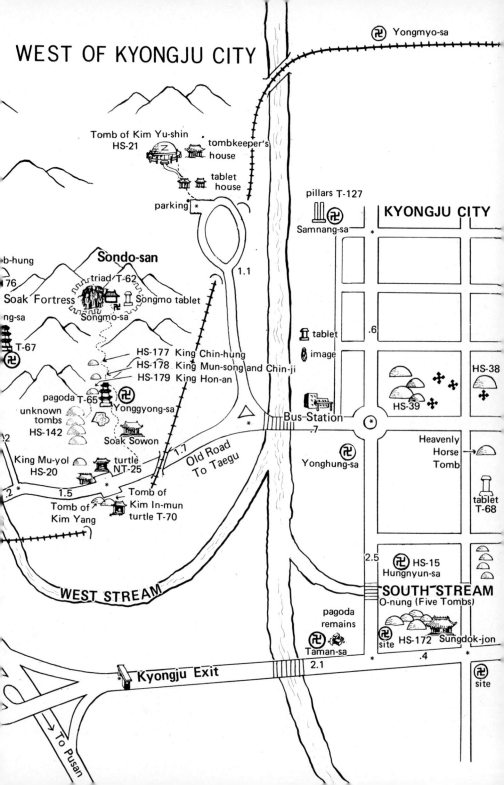

WEST OF KYONGJU CITY

Yongmyo-sa

Tomb of Kim Yu-shin
HS-21

tombkeeper's house

tablet house

parking

pillars T-127

KYONGJU CITY

Samnang-sa

b-hung

76

Soak Fortress

ng-sa

T-67

Sondo-san

triad T-62

Songmo tablet

Songmo-sa

HS-177 King Chin-hung
HS-178 King Mun-song and Chin-ji
HS-179 King Hon-an

tablet

image

.6

pagoda T-65

unknown tombs
HS-142

Yonggyong-sa

Soak Sowon

HS-39

HS-38

Bus-Station

.7

2

King Mu-yol
HS-20

turtle NT-25

1.7

Old Road To Taegu

1.1

Heavenly Horse Tomb

Yonghung-sa

tablet T-68

2

1.5

Tomb of Kim In-mun
turtle T-70

Tomb of Kim Yang

2.5

HS-15

Hungnyun-sa

WEST STREAM

SOUTH STREAM

O-nung (Five Tombs)

pagoda remains

site HS-172

Sungdok-jon

Taman-sa

Kyongju Exit

2.1

.4

site

To Pusan

the mound. The retaining wall is 4.5 feet high with a mound circumference of 164 feet. The truly striking features of this tomb are the zodiac relief figures (1'6'' × 2'9'') seen on the side of the retaining wall. They appear to be the most distinct and best preserved of any of the zodiac images which can now be seen on Silla tombs. The zodiac images are shown dressed in civilian garb.

During T'ang China the zodiac figures were known to have been buried at 12 points of the compass. This evidently was also done in Korea as two small carvings on waxstone about twelve inches high of the rabbit and horse images were discovered accidently near Kim Yu-shin's tomb. They are now on display in the National Museum. The positions are located as follows from due south toward the west, north and east: horse, sheep, monkey, chicken, dog, pig, rat, cow, tiger, rabbit, dragon and snake.

Kim Yu-shin died in 673 at the age of 78, It is strange how such a meritorious historic leader could appear on the Korean scene with an elaborate record of ancestry but also disappear with little mention of later generations. We know that Kim Yu-shin had ten children yet only one historical mention is made of a grandson. Often historical records are frustrating and silent.

2. Tomb and Tablet of King Mu-yol: *Legends of Silla Unification*
(*National Treasure No. 25 and Historic Site No. 20*)

Mu-yol (29th king) is considered one of the greatest of Silla rulers whose reign came during the unification period. His mother was a daughter of Chin-p'yong (26th king), a younger sister of Queen Son-dok who became 27th ruler in 632.

Mu-yol and Kim Yu-shin were boyhood friends and as a result of this friendship Mu-yol met a young sister of Kim Yu-shin and soon they were to be married. The first child to be born was Mun-mu who later became 30th king of Silla and is also considered one of the greatest of this dynasty's rulers.

At the beginning of King Mu-yol's reign in 654 Silla's future looked dark and foreboding. Koguryo and Paekche had formed a league against Silla and may well have crushed this southern kingdom, if it had not been for Chinese intervention. Silla's alliance with the Chinese caused Koguryo to divert its attentions to the northern borders rather than attacking Silla. Fortunately for Silla the Paekche courts were irreconcilably corrupt and the last king was utterly incompetent.

The story told about the marriage of Mu-yol to his wife is one of the most famous and popular folktales of Silla. As a young prince in the courts of Queen Son-dok, his aunt, Mu-yol was an energetic warrior about the same age as Kim Yu-shin.

Yu-shin had two younger sisters. One night the older sister dreamed that she had climbed to the peak of Sondo-san (behind the tomb of Mu-yol) and urinated high on the slope. The stream of fluid tumbled into the valley, flooding the entire capital. The next morning she told her younger sister Mun-hui about her strange dream.

Mun-hui offered to buy it from her. Koreans attribute great significance to dreams and if purchased the blessing in the dream would be transferred. So selling her dream with girlish laughter she flung it to her younger sister Mun-hui who caught it in her skirt.

Several days later while Yu-shin and Prince Mu-yol were playing an active sport, a colorful streamer was accidentally torn from the prince's jacket. "Come to my house," offered Yu-shin, "and we'll have this ribbon sewn back on." Yu-shin called on the older sister to come out and sew the jacket but being shy she mildly complained to her brother that it was improper for her to be seen by a young man.

The younger sister, Mun-hui, was then called. The noble prince was astounded by the radiant beauty of his friend's sister and it was love at first sight. They began to see one another frequently.

Later Kim Yu-shin realized that Mun-hui was pregnant. He was furious and decided to burn her as an example to all immoral women. Preparations were made. On the day of Mun-hui's death Queen Son-dok, who was having a picnic on the slopes of South Mountain, noticed black smoke rising from the home of Kim Yu-shin.

Upon inquiry she learned of the illicit love affair which had resulted in pregnancy. Noticing that her nephew appeared nervous she suspected the young prince and said, "I believe it was you who caused all of this. Go quickly to the house and save this girl," she commanded.

They were then formally married. By Mun-hui King Mu-yol had six sons; thus the dream that was purchased from her older sister was fulfilled in that she flooded the capital with the issue of her body. In addition to her children she helped raise three more boys and five girls born to King Mu-yol by his concubines.

After the death of King Mu-yol in 661 final unification was accomplished by his son Mun-mu (30th king) and General Kim Yu-shin.

From the tablet pavilion the tomb of King Mu-yol is seen in the background. This historic site is one of Kyongju's popular attractions.(HS-20)

218

Koguryo was eventually defeated with the help of T'ang China. This final struggle closed the career of the proudest, hardiest and bravest kingdom of the three upon the peninsula.

Designated as Historic Site No. 20 the mound is 380 feet in circumference. This tomb of Mu-yol's is one of the few tombs of Silla which can positively be indentified as belonging to a particular ruler. Near the base of the mound are nine half buried stones which were possibly used in protecting an underground structure. In front of the mound is a stone table 7 by 10 feet. The grounds have been meticulously kept by attendants. There is an entry charge to the area.

Located in a pavilion at the entrance of the tomb site is the famous turtle base with tablet cap-stone which is considered one of the most important historical remains in Kyongju today and is listed as National Treasure No. 25.

Most tablets (*pisok*) consist of three parts, the base (often turtle-shaped), the stele (tablet) and the cap-stone. One of Korea's earliest tomb epitaphs is inscribed on this tablet but unfortunately the inscription is missing. It is claimed that the calligraphy was done by Kim In-mun, the second son of Mu-yol.

The large turtle-shaped rock squatting on heavy feet is remarkably realistic. Turtle bases for tablets of later periods tend to be more formal and stylized with fierce dragon-shaped heads and sometimes fangs protruding. At the base of the shell are flying cloud patterns while hexagonal relief designs cover the top portion of the turtle.

On the turtle's back rests the cap-stone with three pair of entwined dragons carved in bold relief. A *kusul* (jewel) is held in an inverted position by their feet in the center. The six dragon heads are facing earthward side by side on each end of the cap-stone. The cap-stone has sustained a split through the middle but was repaired by steel wedges.

Below the *kusul* on the front of the cap-stone are the eight Chinese characters which give the title of this tablet as belonging to King Mu-yol. It specifically says, *Tae-jong Wang Nung* (Tomb of King T'ae-jong) the posthumous name of Mu-yol. This turtle base is considered the best example of four among the stone monuments of this earlier period.

below: *This turtle tablet at the tomb of Mu-yol is one of Silla's oldest sculptured stones extant. (NT-25)* next page: *The tomb and tablet base stone of Kim In-mun, son of Mu-yol, is located near the father's tomb. (T-70)*

3. Tablet of Kim In-mun: *Diplomatic Brother of King Mun-mu (Treasure No. 70)*

Located across the street from the entrance of King Mu-yol's tomb are two smaller tomb mounds. The larger tomb traditionally belongs to Kim In-mun the second son of Mu-yol (29th king) and younger brother to King Mun-mu. The smaller mound is believed to belong to Kim Yang who was another statesman and politician of distinction who died in 857. Kim In-mun was originally buried near the tomb of Kim Yu-shin but was later reburied on this site near King Mu-yol's tomb. The tomb circumference is 276 feet.

Also a turtle base stone is located in a small pavilion near Kim In-mun's tomb. This turtle also has five toes and is similar to Mu-yol's tablet. The cloud and lotus petal designs are similar but slightly less skillfully executed. This is the second best stone turtle of this early pre-unification period and has been designated as Treasure No. 70. During this century realism apparently dominated the carvings but later in the eighth century there was more stylization.

Kim In-mun was one of the great Silla statesmen. China had assisted Silla in the overthrow of Paekche and Koguryo with the full intention of controlling the entire peninsula. The poor relations between Silla and China were badly strained as this southern kingdom became a military power of no mean size. Silla was willing to stay friendly with China but on her own terms. Into these smoldering embers of suspicion walked the brilliant Silla envoy.

Kim In-mun quickly won the respect and trust of the Chinese. Evidently this rapport with China was so successful that the ruler offered Kim In-mun the throne of Silla. He of course refused but he was proclaimed king of Silla anyway and was sent with three generals to enforce this claim. This attempt on the part of China failed. When Kim In-mun returned to China he was thrown into prison as the Emperor was in a rage over Silla's disloyalty.

King Mun-mu asked for his brother's release and it was granted. Kim In-mun was then permitted to return to his own country but before arriving he died. He was exonerated from his apparent disloyalty and buried with honors. His patriotic soul was enshrined in the sacred halls of Inyong-sa. (Virtuous Face Temple).

4. Mu-yol's Ancestral Tombs

(Historic Site No. 142)

Located directly behind the tomb of Mu-yol (29th king) are four gigantic grassy mounds which traditionally belong to the ancestors of this ruler. Factual information about these pre-unification tombs is almost nonexistent. The first is the largest as the circumference is 622 feet. The second mound measures 541 feet while the third is 494 feet in circumference. The fourth tomb is separated from the others by a small path. It is 510 feet in circumference.

King Mu-yol's ancestral tombs are located on the slopes of Sondo-san. (HS-142)

5. Four Kings Buried on Mount Sondo's Slopes
(Historic Sites No. 177, No. 178 and No. 179)

Four Silla rulers are traditionally thought to be buried in three mounds which are extremely small behind the tomb compound of King Mu-yol on the slopes of Sondo Mountain. These tombs are in a separate compound near the three-storied pagoda of Yonggyong Temple. Scholars today question the authenticity of these tombs.

The first tomb belongs to Hon-an (47th king) and has been designated as Historic Site No. 179. King Hon-an ruled four years from 857 after the death of his nephew Mun-song (46th king).

During Hon-an's reign there was a noble *hwarang* (Silla knight), by the name of Ung-nyom. When the boy was twenty he was invited to a royal banquet. After the feast the king questioned the young man closely.

"You have visited many regions of my kingdom during your physical and mental training," the king said, "What have you witnessed that has impressed you most?"

The *hwarang* replied with a sparkle in his eyes, "I was more concerned in what I saw in men than in scenic beauty. I saw three men who in the eyes of heaven are saints because of their noble deeds."

"What do you mean?" the surprised king asked.

"First was a man who gave his position to another in order to prevent strife in the nation even though he was more qualified. Another friend I know wears cotton garments to be frugal even though he is rich, as he does not wish to parade his wealth. The third man, though he is noble by birth, does not flaunt his own position."

The king was moved to tears when he heard these words. "You are most certainly a person of highest virtue," he said. "I have two daughters. You may choose the one you wish for your wife."

Upon reaching home he told his parents the good news. They were overjoyed and strongly recommended that he choose the younger sister because she was a well known beauty while the older princess was rather ugly.

When the chief priest of Hungnyun-sa heard of this affair, he hastened to advise the youth. "Beware my boy, beauty is not everything. Take care! If you marry the elder sister I can promise three great fortunes." Ung-nyom heeded these wise words and married the older sister.

Three months later the king became ill and died. Before his death he directed that since he had no heir Ung-nyom, his son-in-law, should be his successor. The priest arrived in court and congratulated the young Kyong-mun (48th king) on his three accomplishments.

He had married the elder daughter first thus making the parents happy; he had inherited the throne; and now as king he could also marry the younger sister and keep her as his favorite. The wise priest was well rewarded.

One day the king awoke to discover that his ears had grown long and furry during the night like those of a donkey. With grave misgivings and consternation he contracted a tailor to design a turban which would cover his ears. He gave strict orders under pain of death that the tailor not breathe a word of this to anyone. The king wore this unusual turban both day and night. However, the tailor was continually tormented with the knowledge that he could not speak about this matter to anyone.

Finally he became ill over this constant worry and went to Torim-sa on the outskirts of the capital to regain his health. After several days of convalescing he took a stroll behind the temple. Noting that he was alone he plunged into a dense bamboo grove and began to shout repeatedly with wild eyes, "My king has the long ears of a donkey!" As his shrill voice echoed among the slender bamboo stalks, the small tailor fell dead from a stroke.

Soon after as the breezes blew gently through the bamboo grove the whispering winds would echo out, "My king has the long ears of a donkey!" This strange phenomena reached the ears of Kyong-mun. "Go cut the bamboo down at Torim-sa!" the king roared. Palm trees were planted instead.

The king died in 875. The bamboo started to grow again from the old roots while the temple was abandoned. People who heard of this tale came and transplanted the young bamboo to their own private gardens. Soon all over the capital the citizens could enjoy the singing bamboo. "My king has the long ears of a donkey!"

The tomb mound behind Hon-an's tomb traditionally belongs to both Mun-song (46th king) and Chin-ji (25th king). Slightly larger, it is 208 feet in circumference. This tomb has been designated as Historic Site No. 178. King Mun-song ruled for 18 years during a period of constant revolts and court intrigues. His father King Shin-mu ruled only four months.

King Chin-ji was an insignificant ruler who reigned for three years between the reigns of Chin-p'yong (26th king) and Chin-hung (24th king), who between them ruled almost ninety years. King Chin-ji was the second son of King Chin-hung.

The historical accounts tell that King Chin-ji was deposed because he was hated by the people for his misgovernment and sensuous overindulgences. There lived near the capital a country girl whose extraordinary beauty was widely known. She was called the Peach Girl. King Chin-ji had her brought to the palace with the intention of making her his concubine.

"You must let me return to my home," she pleaded. "Do you not know that I am already a married woman and cannot accept your love. Though you offer me great honor, even a king should not take away my responsibility for my husband.."

"What are you talking about, you ungrateful wench?" snapped the king, "Don't you realize that everything in the kingdom belongs to me?" The Peach Girl broke into uncontrollable tears as she shook her head in stubborn resolution. "I'll have you killed," shrieked the angry ruler.

"Yes, you may kill me if that's your wish, but I will not submit to becoming your wife," she calmly replied with tearful eyes. Her simple honest beauty shone fresh and bright to the

On the slopes of Sondo-san is the traditional tomb of King Hon-an. (HS-179)

frustrated King Chin-ji.

"If your husband should die would you then come to me?" he whispered. The sobbing girl nodded and murmured that it was possible. Sighing resignedly the king waved the Peach Girl out of his chamber saying, "I hope your husband realizes your loyalty. Go home in peace but I cannot forget you. Your beauty is like the stars....unattainable."

"May you live a hundred years for your kindness," sobbed the girl as she left. However, shortly after the king died. Three years later the Peach Girl also lost her husband. Ten days after the funeral the ghost of King Chin-ji appeared before her late at night. "You made a promise long ago," it whispered, "and now your husband is dead."

After asking her parents, consent, she arrayed herself as a bride and entered her bedchamber. For seven days she stayed in her room with the spirit of Chin-ji. Soon she knew she was pregnant. On the night of her child's birth the earth shook with thunder. The boy was named Pi-hyong.

King Chin-p'yong heard this tale and invited the Peach Girl and her son to come and live in the palace. The boy became a *hwarang*, serving his country well; however, it was noticed that during the night he often disappeared from the palace. The king was curious and directed the captain of the guards to watch where Pi-hyong went and after several days the captain reported his findings. After sunset Pi-hyong was seen flying over Panwol-song (Half Moon Fortress) to the banks of the West Stream where he met a crowd of spirits.

This unusual tomb traditionally belongs to both kings Mun-song and Chin-ji. (HS-178)

Wondering about this the king summoned Pi-hyong who readily admitted that he consorted with ghosts. Evil spirits greatly feared the power of Pi-hyong. It became the custom for the local villagers to hang this song of praise for Pi-hyong on their gate to protect their home from evil spirits.

"Here is the house protected by Pi-hyong,
Strong son of a king's spirit who made love.
All devils must depart for they cannot come,
As they fear the general's spirit and do not stay."

Traditionally the third tomb highest on the slope belongs to Chin-hung (24th king) who ruled for 36 years from 540. He was a nephew of Pob-hung (23rd king) who had no heir. The tomb mound is 198 feet in circumference and has been designated as Historic Site No. 177.

The boy became king at the age of seven while his mother ruled as regent. Chin-hung like his uncle King Pob-hung shaved his head and became a priest while his queen became a nun.

King Chin-hung is credited with founding the *hwarang* movement which began with girls called *wonhwa* (original flowers). Through jealous friction one of the two leaders put the other to death and the *wonhwa* movement came to a sudden end. Shortly after, the movement called *hwarang* (flower youths), which was a chivalrous type of Silla knighthood, was established.

Sol-go, the greatest of Korea's artists, walked across the pages of history during the reign of Chin-hung. Son of a poor farmer who loved to draw pictures on the rocks, he prayed that he might receive the divine gift of painting. The Mountain Spirit presented him a brush from heaven.

The master artist painted a pine tree on the temple wall of Hwangyong-sa and so realistic was it that the birds beat their wings against the wall in their attempt to land among the branches. Sol-go's shadow in history, bearing the touch of brilliance, moves on as we wonder if his reputation was fantasy.

During the 6th century Silla expanded her borders beyond present day Seoul and now we have the stone record of four boundary tablets erected by King Chin-hung in 569 after the completion of his inspection tour. These tablets are the oldest stone monuments of Silla. Two of them are in northern Korea. Of the two in southern Korea the tablet which is best known is now found in the corridors of the main audience hall of Kyongbok Palace.

Until 1971 it stood on the peak of Pi-bong of north Seoul near Sungga-sa. The original site is still marked. The calligraphy is hardly legible but in the 18th century, Kim Chong-hi was able to translate as many of the characters as possible and carved his own translation into the side of the tablet.

He was able to decipher 68 characters of the original 150. Because of its great historical importance this 4.5 foot tablet is designated as National Treasure No. 3. The fourth boundary stone for the southern limits of Silla is located in Changyong Town of South Kyongsang Province and has been designated as National Treasure No. 33.

The last tomb of three in the compound on the slopes of Sondo-san belongs traditionally to Chin-hung. (HS-177)

6. Soak Sowon: *Confucian Hall to Honor Three Leaders*

The Confucian study hall of Soak (West Peak) Sowon is close to the main road near King Mu-yol's tomb. The structure has received renovation repairs in 1978.

Soak Sowon was first erected during the early years of the 16th century to honor three men, Ch'oe Ch'i-won, Sol Ch'ong and Kim Yu-shin. The present buildings are about three hundred years old. Ch'oe Ch'i-won and Sol Ch'ong are known as the Confucian giants from the Silla period and only their names appear today in the main Confucian Shrine of Seoul.

Sol Ch'ong lived earlier and is credited with the invention of *idu,* a system of using Chinese ideographs phonetically in order to represent sounds of the Korean language. The *idu* system was in use until the invention of *han'gul* in the 15th century.

The second man to be honored was Ch'oe Ch'i-won. His influence was as great as Sol Ch'ong's. He travelled to the T'ang Kingdom at the age of 12 and resided in China 16 years. He was born during difficult times as Silla was declining. The year was 859. Met with hatred and jealousy, he was treated with royal indifference and neglected.

He was the most learned and educated scholar of his time. Though he was a prolific writer most of his works are lost to us. Ch'oe Ch'i-won disappeared from the Korean scene almost as a legend. Some say he never died.

The third member to be honored in Soak Sowon is General Kim Yu-shin, the greatest of all Silla generals. Through his efforts and military genius Silla was unified during the reign of Mun-mu (30th king) in 668.

Kim Yu-shin was a fourteenth generation descendant of Su-ro of the Kaya Kingdom so was not a member of the royal Kim Clan of Kyongju. Kim Yu-shin died in 673 at the age of seventy-eight. As a historic figure with an elaborate ancestral record it is strange that there is little mention of his descendants.

The *wip'ae* or spirit tablet of these three men, two scholars and a general, are enshrined in Soak Sowon.

7. Imitation Brick Pagoda of Yonggyong- sa Site
(Treasure No. 65)

This three-storied stone pagoda is located in a field, a ten minute walk directly behind Soak Sowon. It appears to be an imitation of a brick pagoda. The brick pagoda was a transitional style between wood and stone.

Several stone pagodas built to imitate brick are found in the Kyongju region. The one similar to this style is the east pagoda of Nam-san Village. The stairstep effect is found on the upper roof slope as well as the eaves.

This pagoda, however, has two *inwang* relief images . These guards flank the door design on the south side of the first story where the *sari* and relics of an unknown priest were interred at a temple called Yonggyong-sa (Eternal Respect Temple). These two glowering reliefs are two feet high. The total height of this pagoda is 22 feet.

above: *On the picturesque slopes of Sondo-san is the temple site of Yonggyong-sa with a three-storied stone pagoda. (T-65)* below: *Soak Sowon is near the site of Yonggyong-sa.*

above: *The study hall of Soak Sowon has pleasing architectural style and is dedicated to two scholars and a great general.* below left: *The crumbling walls of the fortress of Sondo-san are still seen along the peak.* below right: *A memory tablet for Song-mo still stands overlooking Kyongju City.* next page: *Buddhist remains at Sondo-sa on Sondo peak were reconstructed in 1977.*

8. Sondo-san : *Myths of Sacred Peach Mountain*
(*Treasure No. 62*)

Sondo-san, a 1300 foot mountain, is located due west of Kyongju and can be reached by taking the old Taegu highway. Before reaching Kim Mu-yol's tomb turn right at Soak Sowon. The trail up the mountain begins behind this Confucian study hall and passes to the right of a three-storied pagoda at Yonggyong Temple site. The hike to the peak will take about 1.5 hours.

Soak-song (West Peak Fortress) is also referred to as Sondo Fortress. It is located near the summit of Sondo peak. The date of initial construction is unknown, In 593 during the reign of Chin-p'yong (26th king) it is recorded that this fortress was rebuilt. Eighty years later during King Mun-mu's reign it was again repaired. Traces of this fortress wall can still be seen as a line of rock piles wending its way along the upper slopes.

The name of Sondo has an interesting meaning as *do* refers to a peach while *son* has the meaning of spiritual or supernatural. A legend is told that once a humble villager went fishing in a pond high in the mountains. He took his boat into a cove that he had never seen before.

As he drew close to a cliff wall he noticed along the shore what appeared to be a cave. With a small light he entered the crevice. After walking some distance he suddenly entered a beautiful hidden valley.

He wandered about as if in a trance. He noticed that the valley had peach trees growing in profusion and when he met people he found them to be friendly. He was invited to the village and was ordered peaches to eat. They told him that this valley had never known war or sickness. Truly this was a valley of peace he thought. He enjoyed his new friends so much that he remained for three days.

When the erstwhile fisherman returned he found that the people of his own village were all strangers. Even a strange family was living in his own home. When he spoke of his name a few of the elders of the village vaguely remembered the story of one villager with that name who had disappeared two hundred years before while fishing at a certain lake in the far distant mountains. His widow raised his children.

"One descendant is still living in this village and he could show you the family tombs," the elders told the startled man.

"But I am that man," the old fisherman shouted, blinking with disbelief. "I was only gone three days."

The villagers shook their heads thinking that certainly this old man was crazy. He tried to find the cave entrance again but could not. No one believed the old man's tale but the story of the supernatural peach garden grew and people wondered if maybe this fisherman had entered the eternal world of the *shinson* (Spirit of the Supernatural Being). The peach is believed to be the spirit food of the *shinson*. Song-mo who is the legendary guardian of this mountain is believed to be a *shinson*.

Probably the single most interesting feature is the colossal Buddha triad located near the peak of Sondo Mountain. The center image though badly damaged around the head is a stone carved relief about 25 feet high. For many years the two heads and other body appendages of the two Bodhisattva images remained scattered nearby. Following World War II the Korean government ordered a search for all the missing stone pieces in an attempt to reconstruct the two images on each side of the main relief. The Bodhisattva's head stone alone is three feet high. In 1977 the two Bodhisattva images on either side of the main Buddha were reconstructed with the use of metal bracings. This triad has been designated by the government as Treasure (*pomul*) No. 62.

The present temple of Sondo-sa was built about twenty years ago. At one period there were seven other known temples on the slopes of this peak.

A small shrine to the right of the image is called Songmo-gak (Holy Mother Shrine). Inside the shrine is the *wip'ae* (spirit tablet) of Song-mo, a Chinese princess who appeared mysteriously and left behind many lengends.

Because of a forced impending marriage she fled her country and came to Silla before the 7th century. She resided in Sondo Mountain. Though said to be quite beautiful she chose never to marry. During her lifetime many mysterious episodes occurred and after her death the people of Silla continued to pray to her during periods of distress. It is claimed that Nan-sung who was the boyhood tutor of young General Kim Yu-shin prayed fervently to the spirit of Song-mo asking that Yu-shin be given the power to unify Silla.

Kyong-ae (55th king) was an avid hunter in his youth. He frequently came to the slopes of Sondo-san to hunt and on one occasion lost his favorite falcon. Knowing of Song-mo's reputation he prayed to her spirit. Immediately the bird flew to the king's shoulder. The ruler was amazed as he had spent many hours that morning looking for his pet. A memorial shrine was made in her honor and Song-mo's fame was perpetually etched into Korean folklore.

After taking a trail along the slopes to the right of the temple a pass is reached. On a small knoll east and surrounded by Sondo Fortress is a small tablet within a walled compound. It was constructed to honor the spirit of the Princess Song-mo. From this site one can obtain an excellent panoramic view of Kyongju City.

As you pause to rest you may ponder the legend previously told about the sale of a dream between the two sisters of Kim Yu-shin. This dream took place on this peak and from somewhere near here the older sister flooded the entire city. Down the northern slopes from this tablet one can see many rocks piled in scattered profusion marking the site of the fortress wall.

above: *The triad of Sondo-sa stands behind the shrine dedicated to Song-mo. (T-62)* below: *Painted on the doors of temples are frightening faces for warding off the evil spirits.*

9. Tomb of King Pob-hung: *The Rise of Silla Buddhism (Historic Site No. 176)*

Though Buddhism had entered the Silla Kingdom in the early 5th century, it wasn't until the death of Yi Ch'a-don a hundred years later, during the reign of Pob-hung (23rd king), that Buddhism became popular. This event took place in 527. The death of this court official rocketed the popularity of this religion. King Pob-hung shaved his head and took the vows of a priest while his queen entered the monastery of Yonghung-sa to become a nun.

King Pob-hung had no heir but his daughter married a younger brother. Their son became Chin-hung (24th king) in 540. The dramatic effect of Buddhism was so pronounced that this king also shaved his head and took on the robes of a Buddhist monk.

Pob-hung was the first ruler of Silla to take a posthumous name. A law was made to prohibit the killing of animals on certain days. When Hungnyun-sa (Flourishing Wheel Temple), the first temple of Silla, was constructed King Pob-hung insisted that many of his relatives become priests and servants of Hungnyun-sa. It is believed that he went to live at Aegong-sa (Child of Sorrow Temple) where he died in 540. This temple site is located near the tomb of Pob-hung.

King Pob-hung is traditionally buried in a tomb mound west of Sondo-san within a large grove of pines. The circumference of the tomb is 141 feet.

The martyrdom of Yi Ch'a-don during the reign of King Pob-hung has raised questions by Korean historians. Yi Ch'a-don was not a priest. Historically Yi Ch'a-don must have been a person who was executed by the court but the question is asked, was it really for the sake of Buddhism or was his strange death a political action to strengthen the king's control on his subjects? Certainly Yi Ch'a-don's fame rose by his death.

The uniqueness of this legend creates a certain sense of suspicion especially in an era when only a few years before Buddhism was extremely unpopular. Yi Ch'a-don who was twenty-six at the time of his death, requested that the king kill him for the sake of Buddha.

"In the same manner that the songs of the birds herald the spring, the flow of my blood will herald the full bloom of Buddhism In my death the stubborn people will see a miracle," he exclaimed. King Pob-hung at first refused but Yi Ch'a-don continued to plead.

"Your own life is dear but the eternal lives of many are more precious," he reasoned. "I will vanish like morning dew but the strength of Buddhism will rise with the blazing sun."

The king finally consented and at the death of Yi Ch'a-don blood spurted white as milk. His final words rang in the ears of the shocked court who witnessed the execution. "I die happy for the sake of Buddha. If Buddhism is a true faith let there be a miracle in my death." There is a stone monument honoring Yi Ch'a-don in the Kyongju National Museum. This monument pillar once stood on the slopes of Sogumgang-san where his head traditionally fell after flying off the body.

The traditional tomb of Pob-hung is located in a wooded grove west of Sondo-san. (HS-176)

10. Aegong-sa Site Pagoda

(Treasure No. 67)

This temple site is located a short distance from the tomb of King Pob-hung. Legends claim that King Pob-hung served as a priest at Aegong-sa (Child of Sorrow Temple) prior to his death. Nothing remains at this site except a small three-storied pagoda which has been designated by the government as Treasure No. 67. The total height of the pagoda is 17 feet and there are no image carvings. Located near a village among a few tall pines this site offers tranquil rural beauty.

Pob-hung gave up the throne to become a priest at Aegong-sa, where a pagoda remains. (T-67)

11. Songju-am Triad Buddha Reliefs

(Treasure No. 122)

After driving past King Mu-yol's tomb on the old highway to Taegu 2.3 kilos, a small road to the left crosses the railroad tracks and passes under the expressway. In Tudae Village the road ends. Keeping to the left side of the valley and after a twenty minute ascent into a wooded area the small nunnery of Songju-am is reached on the western slope of Pyokdo-san.

Though this site dates prior to the early 9th century, the present building was dedicated 30 years ago. The *ma-aebul* (relief carving) triad on the stone cliff a few feet behind this small hermitage has been listed as Treasure No. 122.

These Buddhist figures are frequently visited by pilgrims today as well as centuries ago when they were made by an unknown sculptor. The center image of the Amit'abul (Buddha of Western Paradise) is eight feet tall. The stone

Prior page: Shinson-sa in Tansok-san is the origin of many legends concerning Kim Yu-shin. right: *The central image of the Songju-am triad in Tudae-ri is the Amit'a. (T-122)*

of the central figure is quite white as it has apparently been cleaned frequently.

However, the two attendants also carved in relief are difficult to discern. In facing the triad the right attendant is the Kwanseum Posal while the left relief depicts the Taesaji Posal (Boddhisattva of Power). The Kwanseum is holding in its left hand the bottle containing mercy dew, symbolic of its duties to serve as the Bodhisattva of Mercy.

The Taesaji Posal's right hand is held across its breast while the left hand is held at its side with a closed fist representing the power and strength of this Bodhisattva. Both attendants are over six feet in height.

The most unusual set of relief images found in the Kyongju area are at Shinson-sa. Ink rubbings best illustrate the style. above: *Two religious priests carry a willow branch and incense burner.* below: *The four images, 13 feet above the ground, are difficult to identify though the right image is probably the Miruk Bodhisattva sitting in a meditation pose. The other religious saints are paying homage to the Miruk.*

12. Shinson-sa: *Buddhist Reliefs in the Miruk Grotto*

The route to Shinson-sa is one of the most interesting hiking routes in the Kyongju area. One must take the old highway from Kyongju to Taegu and when you reach the town of Konch'on (14 kilos) turn left, cross the railroad tracks and pass under the expressway. Continue on this road passing a reservoir until you reach the village of Ujung-gok 6.5 kilos further. The main road is high on the right side of the valley near a cluster of houses by the side of the road. This village has many pottery kilns.

One should climb down to the stream and hike up through the village, following a trail to the right of the stream through terraced rice fields. Near several rock slides the trail crosses the stream and begins a sharp ascent up the left slope. This path reaches a higher valley to the left of the main valley. Hiking time from the village is somewhat over one hour.

Nestled high in a wooded dale, remote and hidden, Shinson-sa (Spirit of Supernatural Being Temple) gained famed during the period of Silla when Kim Yu-shin used these mountain ridges as his training grounds for the *hwarang* (flower youth).

The *hwarang* have held a fascination for historians in recent years. With historical material concerning the *hwarang* warriors as an institution there is still considerable mystery and speculation as to their function. We know that many Silla generals claimed early training with the *hwarang* movement and probably because of this the *hwarang* has become synonymous with "Korean Silla knighthood."

It is also known that many Buddhist priests including the famed Won-hyo Taesa were also *hwarang* during their youthful years. There was a definite religious emphasis on the *hwarang* movement, especially directed toward the Miruk deity (Future Buddha). However, Silla youth did not remain *hwarang* for life.

The *hwarang* movement appeared to be a type of schooling for the sons of aristocrats of Silla; however, there are cases of sons of low ranking parents belonging to this elite group. The movement was certainly royally supported as kings themselves served as *hwarang* before taking their responsibilities upon the throne.

Today many novels and films have portrayed the *hwarang* as a zealous military strategist whose unflinching goal was the unification of Silla and protection of the kingdom. Now in modern Korea the *hwarang* ideal is continued in terms of unfailing patriotism and military prowess. We can readily perceive how this concept has merit in a divided Korea.

On the mountainside of Tansok-san, with relatively few large rocks, one massive rock formation of rectangular columns is now seen. A legend tells that the young *hwarang* leader Kim Yu-shin dreamed that a bearded mountain spirit appeared and presented him a mystic sword. Picking the sword up he severed the rocks beside him. The mountain was thus named *tansok* (Divided Rock) because of this feat.

Another legend relating to these unusual rock formations indicates that the teacher of Kim Yu-shin, Nan-sung, presented this famous sword to Kim Yu-shin with which he cut the rocks of Tansok. Near the small temple of Shinson-sa is a cluster of columned granite rocks which form what is considered to be the remains of the oldest temple grotto in Korea. The roof has long ago collapsed but many tile pieces can still be found.

The north wall is severed with one rectangular column standing 30 feet high with a fifty foot girth. Between this portion and the main rock is a four foot passageway. The surface is smooth and straight as if cut by a sharp blade. Beyond this passageway several *ma-aebul* (Buddhist relief) images are carved.

This grotto consists of an inner and outer chamber. In the more sacred inner chamber are triad *ma-aebul* images. The outer chamber (west) was reserved for the worshippers. The largest relief image on the north wall is 22 feet high and represents the Miruk (Buddha of the Future).

This Miruk was probably the central image of the triad for this Buddhist cave temple built during the late 6th century. The head in bold relief portrays a face with an archaic smile typical of the earliest period when Buddhism was first introduced. This image is one of the oldest as well as largest examples among the stone Buddhist sculpturing of Silla.

The 22 inch toes of the image were carved directly above the altar. The palms are held out with fingers of the right hand pointing up and fingers of the left hand pointing down.

In front of the Miruk Buddha on the opposite cliff (south wall) is another relief image barely discernible. This image is about 15 feet high with the head more distinct. To the left of this image within reach of the ground is a carved inscription. The name of Shinson-sa is clearly recognized in the inscription. The inscription has twenty lines with each line containing exactly nineteen Chinese characters. It tells of the construction of this temple grotto. Only one fourth of the entire inscription is legible and was translated in 1969.

On the far wall facing down the ten foot wide corridor is another 18 foot relief image of the second Bodhisattva and attendant of the Miruk

A faint inscription found on the grotto wall of Shinson-sa dedicated this sanctuary to the worship of the Miruk and the hwarang *force prior to Silla unification.*

Buddha. Its right hand is holding an object. This third image is also barely discernible.

On the northern cliff surface 13 feet above the ground and along the inside passageway are four additional relief carvings approximately four feet in height. The *ma-aebul* on the far right is the Miruk Posal sitting in a meditation pose. The right foot is resting on the left knee. The right hand is raised to the chin in a thinking pose. This carving in its original setting is the only Miruk in a meditation pose existing from the Silla era.

The second of the four images was carved in a standing position and believed to be a *yorae* (Buddha). Its robe is draped over the left shoulder with voluminous trousers.

The third standing image which is probably a Boddhisattva has caused greater consternation among the scholars as to its identity. The fourth image on the extreme left is the most distinct. The left hand is raised in salutation toward the Miruk image similar to the middle two images. The eyes are large and swollen indicating that the carving is representative of a pre-unification period.

Low to the ground is a smaller relief standing image of another *yorae* (Buddha) which it is

these images represent the *hwarang* priesthood. The two worshipping figures appear to be paying homage to the main Miruk *ma-aebul.* The *hwarang* movement generally followed the worship of the Miruk.

Silla referred to the *hwarang* group as "Yonghwa Hyangdo." Traditionally "Yong-hwa" is a mountain in India where the Miruk lived. We realize now that the terms *"hwa-rang" "Miruk,"* and *"shinson,"* can be used almost interchangeably. The *hwarang* were followers of the Miruk. A reference in the *Sam-guk Yusa* (Legends of the Three Kingdoms) implies that *shinson,* the spirit of a super-natural being, was often called Miruk by the Koreans.

Thus the *hwarang* movement and worship of the Miruk is interwoven into the history and

The unusual style of dress of the priestly figures suggests a strong shaman influence. below: *The straight-cut rock with the Miruk image reminds one of the legend of Tansok.*

believed was carved during the Koryo or possibly the Yi Dynasty period.

However, near the ground are the two most unusual relief images seen anywhere in Korea. The larger figure is four feet high while the smaller one stands 3.5 feet high. They are both wearing high pointed caps which dip forward at the top. The collar and lower hem of the *chogori* (vest) is quite pronounced. Under the *chogori* appears to be a ceremonial apron which reaches well below the waist. The trousers are voluminous, typical of the Korean style *paji.*

The toes of the shoes turn up typical of the wooden shoes of early Korea. The front figure appears to be carrying a long handled incense burner while the second figure in the rear is holding a willow branch used to brush away pesky spirits or for calling on the rain spirits.

Even today shamans use damp willow branches for spattering water in praying for rain. It is interesting to note that the village below Shinson-sa is called Ujung-gok which means "rain center valley."

It is generally believed that these two unusual figures represent persons who founded this temple. Some authorities believe that

legends of Silla. Founded by the *hwarang* centuries ago, the eyes of the Miruk image still gaze as worshippers continue to come to pray and pay homage.

Out from the wooded valley on the bare slope a visitor can imagine the pageantry of the *hwarang* in training, dancing over the hillside with powdered faces and jewelled garb. Far below in the valley the silvery mist permeates the steep slopes while the restless wind rustles the dry leaves under the gnarled oaks. The vaporlike mist reaches the higher slopes while the blue-green mountains on the far horizon beyond appear to lose identity with earth, yet like the *hwarang* long ago, they still belong to this country once called Silla. The spirit of the *hwarang* may still be present in the courage and strength of the Korean people.

The spirit of the hwarang *warrior still seems to haunt the mysterious slopes of Tansok-san, a mountain west of Kyongju.*

13. The Fortress of Pu-san and Chusa- am
(Historic Site No. 25)

It will take the better part of a full day to hike round trip into the fortress area and to Chusa-am. One can start from Songson Village on the east side of Obong-san (Five Peak Mountain) about 2.3 kilos from Koch'on Town. After a 40 minute climb the sites of the east gate and fortress wall are reached. It will take another 1.5 hours to reach Chusa-am, passing the warehouse remains and northwestern portion of the fortress wall.

Pu-san (Rich Mountain) Fortress is said to be about twenty miles in circumference and was utilized as a recreation site for Silla's military. In many places the stones of this ancient fortress wall are clearly seen and even the sites of the four gates are noted.

Where the trail meets the stream the site of the east gate is seen. Here is found a small tablet showing that Pu-san Fortress was designated as Historic Site No. 25. The upper valley soon widens with terraced fields and some houses At a junction the left trail is recommended which ascends steeply over a small hermitage. Soon a higher valley is reached with fields and more farm houses.

Circling to the right the trail reaches a high knoll overlooking the eastern valley far below. This plateau area is quite flat and used for cattle grazing. Here are the sites of at least two large Silla warehouses called Changji (Sword Site) built in 663 during the reign of Mun-mu (30th king).

The size of the smaller warehouse was 35 × 100 feet and about 30 pillar foundation stones are still seen. The other site further back on the ridge is larger as the area measures 100 feet wide and 250 feet long. However, fewer stones of the original foundation remain.

The legend of Hwarang Tugo-sil who was required to serve as the warehouse keeper of Pu-san Fortress is a most interesting tale. Tugo-sil served the noble Hwarang Chuk-jirang faithfully every day so as to receive the best physical and mental training.

But one morning this loyal Silla youth did not report. Chuk-jirang went to Tugo-sil's home and was told by his mother that he had been appointed as warehouse keeper of Pu-san Fortress by order of Ik-son, an army commander from Moryang.

"Tugo-sil is one of my bravest soldiers," Chuk-jirang lamented, "I must go to visit his superior and attempt to bring him back." Taking baskets of cake and wine he departed with his servants and 137 *hwarang* youths.

Arriving at the gate of Pu-san Fortress he inquired as to where he might find Tugo-sil. Chuk-jirang royally entertained Ik-son with cakes and wine. He then requested that Tugo-sil be granted a leave of absence upon which Ik-son flatly refused as Tugo-sil was a good worker and did not grumble over his forced labor. He offered 30 bags of rice to the corrupt Ik-son if he would release Tugo-sil. Only after a saddle and harness were added to the bribe would the stubborn and corrupt Ik-son permit the kidnapped youth to go home.

When the king heard about this greedy behavior of the fortress commander he sent out a company of men to arrest Ik-son only to find that he had gone into hiding. They captured

The remains of the Pu-san Fortress wall are still seen meandering over the hills. (HS-25)

238

his eldest son instead. They forced the son to take a bath in a palace pond to wash away his father's guilt. Unfortunately this cleansing event took place in mid-winter so that the youth froze to death.

When the affair of the son being punished for his father's crime reached the ears of the throne, the king issued a decree that all natives of Moryang, the home town of this corrupt fortress commander, would be expelled from government office. Tugo-sil returned to the services of Chuk-jirang. Chuk-jirang became one of the bravest of all the *hwarang*. Serving with the famed General Kim Yu-shin, he often rendered meritorious service during unification.

Chuk-jirang also became state minister for four rulers, Chin-dok, Mu-yol, Mun-mu and Shin-mun. Fortunately for historians today the devoted Tugo-sil wrote a *hyangga* concerning the virtues of Chuk-jirang. This verse was one of the more popular lyrics of that time.

This particular verse dedicated to Chuk-jirang and composed by Tugo-sil is nostalgically sad as it was written in his later years as he was growing old. Standing on the remains of the warehouse site overlooking the rugged cliffs of the fortress one might begin to perceive how the beauty of friendship developed between these two soldiers.

When I sing of spring memories,
My heart is lonely and sad.
In a twinkling the bloom of youth is gone,
While deep furrows are carved on the brow.
Take cheer, my eternal youthful flower!
For on the autumn road of no earthly cares,
You'll enjoy sleep under the sage-brush roof.

From the warehouse sites it is less than a 20 minute walk to the west gate site of the fortress. A trail should be taken westward and up the right slope. This main trail up the slope will lead to Chusa-am. At one place the trail passes through the fortress wall. After an additional 15 minute walk the hermitage is reached.

Chusa-am (Red Sand Hermitage) was founded by Priest Ui-sang, one of the greatest priests of Silla. Priest Ui-sang prophesied during the fortress construction that if this temple were included within the fortress wall Silla would never be defeated. The temple was left outside yet it took many centuries before Silla finally did meet defeat in the 10th century.

The main hall is the Yongsan-jon which houses the Sokkamoni and sixteen *nahan* (disciples). Behind is the Samsong-gak which portray the three major shaman spirits as well as the Dragon Spirit. A colorful portrait of Priest Ui-sang is also hanging on the side wall of the Samsong-gak.

About 100 yards away is a large flat rock overlooking the west valley of Pu-san Fortress. It was here according to legends that General Kim Yu-shin made wine and held victory celebrations for his men. From this cliff the site of the north gate and remnants of the fortress wall are clearly seen along the western ridge. This rocky butte is a picturesque area for panoramic views of the fortress region and valley below.

The portrait of one of Silla's most famous priests is at Chusa-am. next page: A flat rock overlooking the valley near Pusan-song was used by the soldiers of Kim Yu-shin.

14. The Superstitions of Woman Valley

This valley, located 7.2 kilos from Konch'on Town on the old Taegu highway west of Kyongju, can be reached by a small road which goes under the Expressway after turning left. The center of the valley is reached after a 15 minute walk from Shinp'yong Village. From the expressway this valley is observed 1.3 kilos east of the tunnel.

The name of Woman Valley in Korean is *yogon-gok* which literally means "Woman Genitals Valley." As can well be imagined there are many sensuous legends about this valley. The best known tale concerns the famous Queen Son-dok (27th ruler) who heard white frogs angrily croaking during winter in Okmun (Jade Gate) Pond at the temple of Yongmyo (Spirit Tomb).

The courtiers were all wondering what this sign could possibly mean. The wise queen immediately directed two generals to lead Silla troops to Yogon-gok and capture the enemy they would find hiding in this valley. The court wondered as they had received no reports of invading troops. Upon reaching Woman Valley they found 500 Paekche troops camped in the forest. They were routed and captured.

Court officials were mystified and asked Queen Son-dok how she knew that enemy troops were within her borders. She replied, "white is the feminine color and also means west while a croaking frog means anger and is symbolic of soldiers. The frogs were warning us from Okmun-ji and as we well know Okmun (Jade Gate) is an expression frequently used

to describe the female's genitals." The queen smiled and continued, "When any man enters the 'Jade Gate' of a woman he will lose his strength eventually and die."

During the Yi Dynasty it was a known fact that newly appointed district governors of Kyongju came from Seoul via Angang even though the route was much longer as it was considered an ill omen to view Woman Valley before taking office. Also when young men traveled to Seoul to take government exams it was customary for them to look the other way while passing this valley. To peer at Woman Valley would bring them bad luck and possible failure in the exam.

Beside a large pond before the village is a headless three foot Piroch'ana stone image sitting on a lotus pedestal. The figure is believed to have belonged to a temple relating to Woman Valley.

The village at the end of the road is called Shinp'yong; however, in the vernacular the name for this village is *saeptol* which has no particular meaning but was changed slightly from an extremely vulgar form which meant "Intercourse Field."

In these fields four dolmens can be pointed out by the villagers. One is by the pond while the other three are south of the expressway. At the entrance to Woman Valley is a small temple apparently dedicated to the Sokkamoni. There are five buildings. It is strange that this private temple of only five years has no name. The mountain behind this valley was often referred to as So-san (Genitals Mountain) and initially the temple was called Sosan-sa; later the name was dropped.

Woman Valley is now quite wooded with a small stream, and if one follows this stream several hundred meters from the temple a spring is reached. In the area surrounding this spring, the center of Woman Valley, are many large flowering cherry trees which were planted during the Japanese occupation. In winter when the pine trees on the slopes are green the cherry trees are conspicuously bare.

An interesting tale is told about an ignorant district chief who unwittingly sold Woman Valley to a Kyongju man who wished to cut and sell the trees. After the cutting there was a hue and cry that this would bring many years of bad luck to the country. It is traditionally known in Korean society that any woman without pubic hair will bring misfortune as a marriage partner.

The government immediately apologized for this oversight and new Japanese cherry trees, the national flower of Japan, were planted around the spring area. In early April the entire region turns a pink hue.

If the spring water is touched or defiled it is believed that the young girls in the village below will leave their homes to marry without parental consent.

left: *Woman Valley is noted in the center foothills.* right: *In T'ap Valley a three-storied pagoda blends into a picturesque harvest scene.*

15. Other Historic Sites West of Kyongju

Tomb of King Min-ae (Historic Site No. 190):

One must take the old Taegu highway past King Mu-yol's tomb and after crossing the bridge take a left turn under the expressway. This road leads to Mangsong Village (3.3 kilometer from the main road). After the second reservoir park the car and take a trail left for ten minutes.

At the pass the tomb of Min-ae can be reach within a few minutes by following the ridge to the right. The mound has a 2.5 foot retaining wall with eleven 5-sided buttress stones leaning against the wall. The tomb circumference is 136 feet and the distance across the mound is 50 feet. Min-ae was 44th king of Silla.

Tomb of King Hui-gang (Historic Site No. 220):

Located near King Min-ae's tomb, the ridge to the left at the same pass must be taken for a walk of several minutes. The tomb is quite flat. The circumference is 150 feet while the distance across the mound is 45 feet. Hui-gang was 43rd king of Silla.

Okyon Sodang and an Unknown Temple Site:

From the pass near the tombs of Min-ae and Hui-gang in the next valley is a picturesque study hall called Okyong (Jewel Pond). Stone pieces of a Silla pagoda with several foundation stones are noted within the grounds of this Confucian study hall.

Stone Buddha Face of Chestnut Village:

Taking the same road to Mangsong Village (2 km from the main highway) turn right at the first junction for Yul-dong (Chestnut Village). After a fifteen minute walk behind the village a large chestnut grove is reached. Just before reaching the power lines as the trail leaves the orchard, the carved face can be seen left of the trail on a stone cliff four meters away.

Discovered only in 1974 the carving is 5'10" high and located fifteen feet from the ground. The carving is not relief but etched into the rock surface in the same manner as the triads of Samnung Valley of Nam-san. The carving looks incomplete.

(1) Standing Bodhisattva image near Tudae Village; (2) Relief image of Samjae-am in Tansok Mountain; (3) Tomb of King Min-ae (HS-190);

Standing Stone Bodhisattva Image in Tudae Village:

This small six foot image is located across the valley from Songju-am near Tudae Village. The temple site and image will be almost impossible to find without a guide. It is a 45 minute hike from the village. After passing a reservoir on the left a small trail branches left. After reaching the first cliff a temple wall and level area are noted. Continue 50 meters further past the second cliff and then climb between the rocks to the right. The image is near the crest of this cliff. The boat-shaped mandala is 6'6'' high and 2'4'' wide. The right hand is at the side and left hand is across the waist. The robe covers the shoulders. One eye and nose are slightly damaged.

Kumch'ok Tombs (Historic Site No. 43):

Located 11 km. from Kyongju on the old Taegu highway this cluster of tombs is easy to find beside the road. There are about forty mounds. The name *kumch'ok* means "gold measurement." Legends say that a Silla king owned a golden ruler which gave immortal life. The Chinese Emperor upon hearing this fact wished to have it for himself but the Silla monarch buried the measuring rod in one of the tombs of this area.

Relief Image of Samjae-am in Tansok-san:

Drive from Kyongju City 8.5 kilos on the old Taegu highway and take a road to the left leading to Moryang Village. From Moryang Village one can go 3 kilos. further to Pangnae Village under the slopes of Tansok Mountain. The hike to Samjae-am site will take over 1.5 hours. The trail is steep with little shade and no water most of the way. Just beyond the village is an unnamed temple site. At the pass can be found a spring. A trail follows the slope to the right for 15 minutes. A temple rock wall and tomb are reached.

On the cliff about 30 meters behind the temple site is a 21 foot relief image. The face is most distinct. The right hand is raised to the shoulder while the left hand is broken away. It is believed that the image is a Miruk. The robe drapes over the left shoulder. Though the face is typical of the pre-unification period

the three creases appearing under the chin of the image typify a post unification period.

Chak-song (Magpie Fortress):

Located one kilometer from Konch'on Town (13 km. from Kyongju on the old Taegu highway) is Chak-song. The fortress is difficult to see as the walls were made of earth. It was 2.5 kilos long, had four gates and was first built during Chin-p'yong's reign. The story of the magpie comes from the era of Kim Yu-shin and wars between Silla and Paekche. A daughter of the Paekche king became a magpie to spy out the enemy camp but was discovered by General Kim Yu-shin. In Konch'on Town is a stone (3.5 feet high) which is claimed to be the base for the banner pole of Kim Yu-shin during the war years at Chak-song.

Three-storied Pagoda of T'ap Valley:

Five kilometers north from Konch'on Town is T'ap (Pagoda) Valley. The 20 foot three-storied pagoda is located in a field next to a village. The base is almost 9 feet wide. The area is very rural and picturesque. The name of the temple is unknown.

Nawang-dae (Silla King's Place):

About 22 kilos from Kyongju on the old Taegu highway and one kilometer north of the main road is the site of Nawang-dae. On top of a steep knoll a pleasure pavilion once was used by Silla kings. It was a favorite pavilion for Hon-gang (49th king). All that now remains is a large lotus blossom stone pedestal with the characters *na-wang* written across the top.

(4) Kumch'ok tombs west of Taegu (HS-43); (5) Chak-song (Magpie Fortress) near Konch'on Town; (6) Nawang-dae (Silla King's Place) where a pleasure pavilion once stood west of Kyongju. below:*In a small village red peppers dry in late autumn for use in winter* kimchi.

Chapter VII
Historic Sites from Kyongju to the Eastern Coast

1. Nang-san: *Center of the Ancient Silla Capital*
(Historic Site No. 163)

Nang-san (Wolf Mountain) is a small 348 foot hill located in what was once the heart of the capital of Silla. From early times the Buddhists of Silla have regarded Nang-san, shaped as a silkworm cocoon, as holy ground. In August of 413 Shil-song (18th king) saw a towering column of smoke rise from Nang-san and emanating a delightful fragrance. Believing that the heavenly spirits had descended to earth at this place he forbade anyone to cut trees on the slopes of Nang-san. Today the Korean government has designated Nang-san as Historic Site No. 163.

One of the well known tales concerning Wolf Mountain is the story of the legendary Paeg-yol (man with the hundred patches) who

lived on the slopes of Nang-san. He was so poor that his clothing consisted of many patches, thus he received the name of Paeg-yol. However, he was renowned for his ability to play the *komungo*, a type of stringed instrument.

One day as the new year was approaching Paeg-yol and his wife worried about having enough money to prepare *t'ok* (rice cake) for the many visitors that would certainly come on New Year's day. "What will the neighbors think?" chided Paeg-yol's wife.

As the day drew closer Paeg-yol consoled his distraught wife with some encouragement, saying, "Don't worry, we will be away from the house on this day visiting our friends."

"But the neighbors will not hear me making

The Silla people believe that heavenly deities protect the living as well as the departed. Queen Son-dok's tomb on Nang-san was once in the very center of the Silla capital.

t'ok and will know we do not have any because we are so poor,'' she wailed.

Whereupon, Paeg-yol took his beloved *ko-mungo* and played. The sound of the music was as if someone was pounding the flour in preparation for making rice cakes. When the neighbors heard this sound they knew that *t'ok* was being made by Paeg-yol's wife.

Surrounding Nang-san are many historical sites and Buddhist remains, most within easy walking distance of the road. These historic remains include the tomb of Queen Son-dok, cremation site of King Mun-mu, Sondok-sa with Buddhist relief images, Tokso-dang, Hwangbok-sa pagoda and site of Sach'on-wang-sa.

On the west side of Nang-san about a ten minute walk from the road is the small newly established temple called Sondok-sa (name recently changed to Chungsaeng-sa). To the left of this temple about twenty meters away can be found three relief images about three feet high. It is generally believed that they were carved during the Koryo period.

About seventy five meters toward the highway from the temple and on the edge of the fields are the remains of a headless standing Buddha image. This image dates to the Silla era. Also near the temple can be seen the remains of a stone lotus pedestal and several stone pieces from a broken pagoda.

Along the western slope of Nang-san from Sondok-sa is the compound containing two buildings and tablet house called Tokso-dang (Reading Book Pavilion). It can be reached after a ten minute walk. One building is called Haksa-ru (Scholar's Pavilion). It is here that the most famous of Confucian scholars of the latter part of Silla built his study room.

Ch'oe Ch'i-won is one of only two scholars to appear in the Confucian *Book of Records of Noted Men* from the Silla era. It is claimed that

Nungji-t'ap on Nang-san is believed to be the cremation site of King Mun-mu. Reconstruction plans for this pagoda are now underway.

Ch'oe Ch'i-won traveled as far as Persia. When he returned to Korea to give the benefits of his experience he was not accepted and was forced to flee into the mountains. While in hiding he wrote extensively. During the pro-Confucian era of the Yi Dynasty his fame bore fruit.

Koreans of Silla owe him little except the lesson he taught that when a Korean decides to denationalizes himself he can only hope to influence his countrymen slightly. The tablet memorializing Scholar Ch'oe was erected in 1849 by Ch'ol-jong (25th Yi king).

After a five minute walk south of Sondok-sa one can find a large pile of rocks referred to as Nungji-t'ap (Tomb Site Pagoda). Recent excavation has been done and the government is going to reconstruct this pagoda which was built over the cremation site of Mun-mu (30th king). Six feet under this pagoda large stones were found which were still black with soot. Possibly a wooden pagoda was once constructed over this sacred place.

Later a more permanent stone pagoda was constructed. Nine of the twelve zodiac images were found which were used in the pagoda construction. The zodiac stone of the horse was taken to the Kyongju National Museum and is now on display while the other eight are still at the site. These figures are all dressed in military clothing rather than civilian garb. The height of each zodiac image is three feet. The tiger, dragon and snake images are missing from the site of Nungji-t'ap.

Undoubtedly this site was used as a place of worship because of the importance of King Mun-mu who unified Silla. After cremation his ashes were taken to the east coast for burial. Taewang-am (Historic Site No. 158) is the traditional site of King Mun-mu's tomb near Kamun-sa. During excavation over 125 articles were found including a bronze bell and many Buddhist images.

Some of the zodiac relief images can still be observed at Nungji-t'ap. Barley fields surround the area of Nang-san.

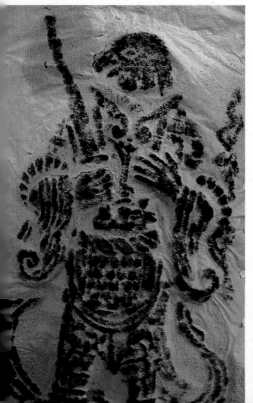

2. Queen Son-dok: *Best Loved of Silla's Three Queens* *(Historic Site No. 182)*

Of the three queens who ruled in Silla, Queen Son-dok (27th ruler) was the most famous and best loved by the people. Chin-p'yong (26th king) had no sons so when he died in 632, the first daughter of the king was selected as ruler. The name *sondok* meaning "sweet virtue" was given. She was probably the first queen of all East Asia to mount the throne by ordinary succession.

Her greatest contributions during her reign were to raise the people's living standards and spread the achievements of China throughout the kingdom. During her reign the greatest temple of Silla, Hwangyong-sa, was completed as well as Ch'omsong-dae.

Her tomb is located among the pines near the summit of Nang-san. There is a two foot retaining wall around a mound which has a 250 foot circumference. Placed at equal intervals into the retaining wall are large uncarved and irregular upright stones. As the stones total twelve they may symbolically represent the twelve zodiac guards. Also it is possible that at one time this tomb contained zodiac images which have since been stolen, while these unhewn stones replaced them to mark the positions.

From this auspicious location one can look over the ancient plains of Silla and ponder as to the size of this capital, the bustling of

foreign trade, commerce of its people, and social life of its royalty. The capital's population hovered around a million people two hundred years later, which is more than ten times Kyongju City's present population. It is even recorded that there were no straw thatch roofs within the capital. This capital of Silla became truly one of the greater cities of the world in the 8th century.

Queen Son-dok was extremely precocious. One story tells that when the Emperor of China sent some flower seeds and a painting of three peony blossoms she remarked that these flowers would have no scent.

When asked the reason for this she replied,

"Because I see no butterflies in the picture and the Emperor must be joking with me for I have no husband." This fact proved to be true when the seeds sprouted. Also the prophecy of the Chinese Emperor was noted as the three flowers without scent represented the three queens of Silla. None of these queens produced an heir for the dynastic throne.

During the fifth year of her reign she again made keen observations which saved the city and cleared the borders of the enemy. During the winter the queen received a report from one of her subjects who heard white frogs croaking near Okmun-ji (Jasper Gate Pond).

The wise queen smiled and directed her

left: Tokso-dang located on the slopes of Nang-san is where the great scholar Ch'oe Ch'i-won studied during late Silla. Nearby the temple of Sondok prepares for Buddha's birthday. right: *Stone carved pedestal and a triad relief are still found with other stone remnants at Chungsaeng-sa.*

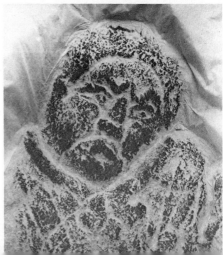

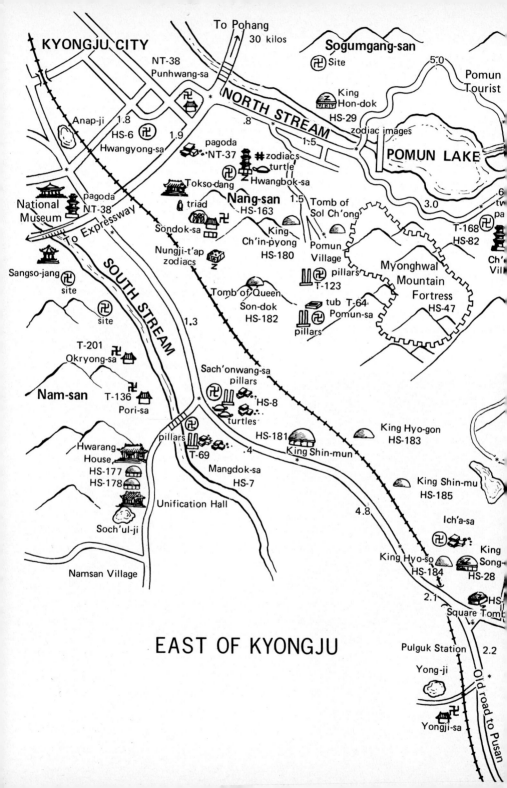

KYONGJU CITY

To Pohang
30 kilos

Sogumgang-san
卍 Site

5.0

Pomun
Tourist

NT-38
Punhwang-sa

卍

NORTH STREAM

King
Hon-dok
HS-29

POMUN LAKE

.8

Anap-ji 1.8
HS-6 卍 1.9
Hwangyong-sa

.8

zodiac images

1.5

pagoda
NT-37

zodiacs
turtle
Hwangbok-sa

3.0

.6
tw
pa

Tokso-dang
triad
Nang-san
HS-163

1.5

Tomb of
Sol Ch'ong

T-168
HS-82

**National
Museum**
pagoda
NT-38

Sondok-sa

King
Ch'in-pyong
HS-180

Pomun
Village

Ch'
Vil

Sangso-jang
site

Nungji-t'ap
zodiacs

pillars
T-123

**Myonghwal
Mountain
Fortress**
HS-47

site

SOUTH STREAM

Tomb of Queen
Son-dok
HS-182

tub T-64
Pomun-sa

1.3

pillars

T-201
Okryong-sa

Sach'onwang-sa
pillars

Nam-san T-136
Pori-sa

HS-8

turtles

King Hyo-gon
HS-183

pillars
T-69

HS-181

King Shin-mun

King Shin-mu
HS-185

**Hwarang
House**
HS-177
HS-178

.4

Mangdok-sa
HS-7

4.8

Ich'a-sa

Unification Hall

King Hyo-so
HS-184

King
Song
HS-28

Soch'ul-ji

2.1

HS
Square Tomb

Namsan Village

Pulguk Station 2.2

EAST OF KYONGJU

Yong-ji

Old road to Pusan

Yongji-sa

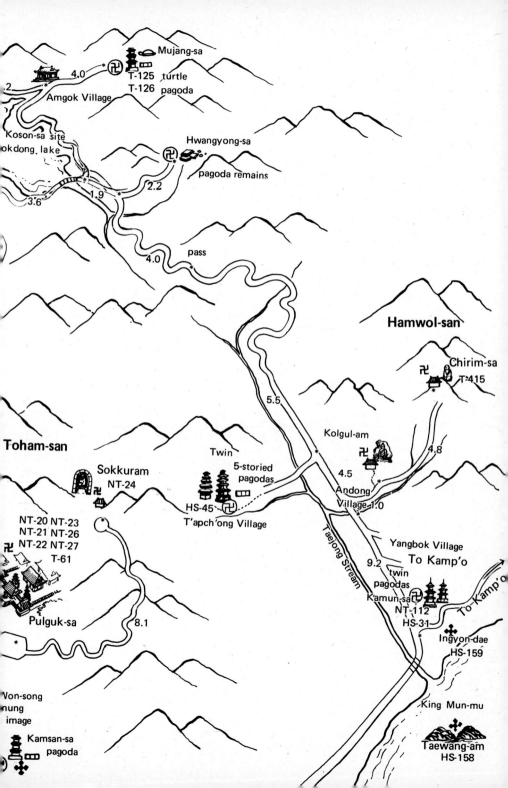

generals to take soldiers to the place called Woman Genitals Valley. In the region between the hill-shaped torso you will find the Paekche soldiers. "Jasper Gate" or *okmun* is the Chinese reference to the genital organs of a woman.

At this very place two thousand Paekche soldiers were found and captured. They had no chance as they had foolishly picked the worst of all possible hiding places. According to the *um-yang* theory any man dominated or hiding behind a woman is destined to fail and die. Today Woman Genitals Valley can be seen west of Kyongju and viewed south of the expressway to Taegu.

In 647 after a fifteen year rule good Queen Son-dok died and was buried on Nang-san. Chin-dok (28th ruler) became Korea's second queen and it seriously looked as if gynecocracy was being established in Silla. Chin-dok was a cousin of Son-dok as she was daughter to a younger brother of Chin-p'yong (26th king).

above: *The pagoda of Hwangbok-sa (NT-37) is one of the most important in the Kyongju area.* below: *One of three relief images are found on Nang-san. The stone pillars of Pomun Village are listed as a treasure.* right: *The tomb of Hon-dok (41st king) has been reconstructed.*

3. Hwangbok-sa Pagoda: *Legends of Priest Ui-sang*
(National Treasure No. 37)

A typical three-storied Silla pagoda was dedicated in 706 by Song-dok (33rd king) at Hwangbok-sa (Imperial Blessing Temple). Located a short distance from Punhwang-sa this picturesque pagoda can be seen on the eastern slope of Nang-san. Though simple and undecorated with a two tiered pedestal, the Hwangbok-sa pagoda is now National Treasure No. 37. Relics of great intrinsic and artistic value were discovered within this pagoda. A bronze relic box was found in the second story and contained the following inscription:

"King Shin-mun died on July 2, the year 692. His son Hyo-so built a hall for meditation, a Buddhist temple and a three-storied pagoda. On June 1, the year 700, the mother of the king died and King Hyo-so died two years later on

July 27, 702. King Song-dok mounted the throne. On May 30, the year 706, Song-dok (33rd king) placed four *sari*, a pure gold Amit'a Buddha and a volume of Sutras in the second story of this pagoda in commemoration of great Shin-mun, (31st king), his father, his mother, and King Hyo-so, his brother.

There were two Buddhist figurines which are masterpieces found within the relic box. In addition there were glass beads, two bracelets, four bronze bowls with stands and a small *sari* box which enclosed a smaller silver box. The two Buddha images are most significant in that they were two of about ten sculptured carvings of Silla that can be dated accurately.

About fifty meters away alongside a field is the remains of a badly damaged turtle base stone. East of the pagoda is a Silla stone well

with an opening about two feet across. Nearby and between the well and pagoda are several large stones which have relief carvings of zodiac figures on them.

About five years ago an excavation was made of the area and these zodiac images were found buried on this site. Scholars are in disagreement as to whether they came from Hwangbok-sa or from a royal tomb which over the years had been destroyed and forgotten. The snake, horse and chicken now remain half buried at the side of the field. They are dressed in civilian attire but did not come from King Hon-dok's tomb nearby. It is generally believed that the zodiacs were brought to this temple site from an unknown Silla tomb.

Hwangbok-sa gained fame through the outstanding scholar Priest Ui-sang who took his vows here. Ui-sang traveled to far China to further his study of Buddhist doctrine. Upon his return he founded the temple of Pusok-sa (Floating Stone Temple) which is located in North Kyongsang Province near Yongju.

Though there are many stories and legends told about Priest Ui-sang, very little is known about his early life. As a young boy in his teens he met and fell in love with a beautiful Silla maiden by the name of Myo-hwa (Delicate Flower).

Ui-sang was the son of an aristocratic family and his future seemed bright but just before his marriage the king's men saw the lovely Myo-hwa and selected her as one of several virgins to be sent as gifts to the royal T'ang court. Young Ui-sang was unconsoled in his grief and vowed that he would never marry. He entered the priesthood and after serious study and preparation took his vows at this temple of Hwangbok-sa.

However, the story does not end here, as Myo-hwa decided that it would be far better to take her own life than become a concubine in the court of T'ang. While traveling along treacherous trails in Mongolia, she deliberately flung herself into the river far below. A poor fisherman saw the girl fall and rescued her. He took her home and adopted her as his own daughter.

Many years passed and one day the girl heard that two priests from Silla were visiting her town. She went to see what news they might

have and one can only imagine her shock and joy when she saw Ui-sang. Priest Ui-sang with his friend Priest Won-hyo were on their way to China to further pursue their studies.

Myo-hwa was still unwed as she also had vowed never to marry. Now she wanted to return to her childhood sweetheart. Though temptation was strong, Ui-sang discouraged the plan by saying that now he could not consider only himself but his obligations to his country and Buddha. He suggested that Myo-hwa become a nun. He left the following day to continue his journey but promised to stop upon his return.

His studies in China took ten years. Upon his return trip the girl was gone so he left a note. When Myo-hwa returned she was disappointed in missing him as she had been weaving a monk's robe and wished to present it. She quickly followed the travelers and arriving on the coast saw their ship in the distance. She decided to put her motives to the test and flung the robe from the cliff.

Instead of falling to the waters below it floated out to Ui-sang's ship. She changed into a dragon and followed the ship back to Korean soil. Myo-hwa in the form of a dragon helped Ui-sang build the temple of Pusok and then later buried herself under the temple altar.

below: *A stone zodiac image lies partially buried on the temple site of Hwangbok-sa.* right: *The tomb of Chin-p'yong is seen across the fields near Po mun Village.*

4. Tomb of Chin- p'yong: *Longest Rule of 53 Years (Historic Site No. 180)*

In a sparse cluster of trees among the fields near Pomun Village and northeast of the site of Pomun-sa is the tomb of Chin-p'yong (26th king) who began his rule of fifty-three years upon the death of his uncle Chin-ji (25th king). The mound circumference is 390 feet and the tomb is designated as Historic Site No. 180.

During the early years of King Chin-p'yong's reign the young king spent most of his time hunting. His faithful defense minister Kim Hu-jik took the king to task warning him that he must give up hunting and tend to matters of state as this was his responsibility. He also reminded his king that to kill animals was prohibited under the tenets of Buddhism.

Tradition says that this faithful minister pleaded continually but it was all in vain. When Kim Hu-jik was about to die he instructed his son to bury him beside the path that the king always used on his way to the hunting fields. After Kim's death it was done.

When the king would pass this area he now heard strange voices. Stopping to listen he thought he heard the voice telling him to give up hunting and spend time on his royal duties. He ordered a servant to find the source of this strange noise immediately. The servant

reported that the voice was coming from the grave of Kim Hu-jik.

Shocked, the youthful king remembered the numerous warnings of his faithful minister and changed his habits from that time on. During the reign of Suk-chong (19th Yi king) in 1701 a tablet was erected for this faithful minister which can still be seen today north of Kyongju at his tomb site.

In 632 King Chin-p'yong died and as he had no son, his first daughter, a woman with an unusually strong personality, ascended the throne to become the first queen ever to rule in Korea. Queen Son-dok ruled for 15 years.

One of the better known folk stories of this period is about the third daughter of King Chin-p'yong named Son-hwa who was the younger sister of Queen Son-dok. This romantic episode tells of the marriage of Son-hwa with King Mu (29th king of Paekche) in the final days of the Paekche Dynasty.

However, there seems to be some historical inconsistency and probably this tale belongs to the reign of So-ji (21st king of Silla) when it was recorded that Tong-song (23rd king of Paekche) asked to marry a Silla princess in 493 and his request was granted. Nevertheless, the *Samguk Yusa* attributes this legend to the period of King Mu.

Mu was conceived when his mother fell in love with a lake dragon. She bore a son who grew up in a majestic manner, worthy to be called the son of a dragon. But the family was so poor that their diet was the wild potatoes they could find, hence the villagers called the boy So-dong (Potato Boy).

So-dong heard that the third daughter of King Chin-p'yong of Silla was unusually beautiful. He decided to visit the capital and became a sweet potato seller. He befriended the small children and soon began to teach them a song he had composed. The words of the ditty went something like this:

"Princess Son-hwa likes the gray sweet

256

potatoes. . .
She married So-dong while men looked the other away;
Every night she slips out to meet her love, and sleeps in his arms giving sweet kisses."

Soon the song became popular in every corner of the capital and was even heard discussed among the polite court ladies of the palace. King Chin-p'yong felt he should exile the princess in order to quiet the apparent scandal. Giving his daughter a large bag of gold he sent her out with a tearful farewell.

As she began her lonely journey into the mountains So-dong approached and offered to serve as her bodyguard and guide. The startled princess did not know him but in her sad plight she welcomed anyone's companionship. "Anyway he was indeed handsome and certainly one with such an honest face could bring no harm," she thought.

For many days the two traveled through the mountainous regions north of the capital and as her friendship and trust grew for him, she discovered that she had fallen in love and at length did in fact sleep in his arms. They were married on their way toward Paekche. One day Son-hwa revealed the contents of her bag. "My dear husband, here is a sack of gold with which we can build a comfortable home," she said. "What is gold?" So-dong laughingly asked. "Don't you know?" exclaimed the surprised princess. "It will make us rich for many years!"

"Since my childhood I have buried rocks like this in the holes from which I dug wild potatoes," So-dong told her.

Princess Son-hwa was amazed. "We must find this place and dig them up." So from many holes the gold nuggets were collected. The two decided to send this gold as a dowry.

So-dong went to Priest Chi-myong at Saja-sa to ask his advice on how to transport the gold to the Silla capital. "Bring the gold to me and I'll send it on the spirit wings" said Priest Chi-myong. Son-hwa then wrote a letter to her father King Chin-p'yong.

The people of Paekche deeply loved the good So-dong and in due time he was raised to the throne and given the name of King Mu. One day while King Mu and his wife were returning from a trip to Saja-sa they passed a small pond. Three images of the Miruk Posal (Bodhisattva of the Future) were seen to rise from the pond's surface. The procession halted to worship the mysterious vision.

"We must build a temple for the Miruk," said Queen Son-hwa. They sought out Priest Chi-myong and again asked him to help. First the old priest moved a mountain and dropped it upside down to cover the pond. Soon a magnificent temple called Miruk-sa was erected. A pagoda was built with the assistance of Silla architects sent by King Chinp'yong.

Today the remains of this temple can be seen 20 kilos from the interchange of Chonju City in North Cholla. The first story of this ancient weather-beaten pagoda of Miruk-sa is 28 feet across and 15 feet high. The roof width is 35 feet.

If the story of King Mu has some validity then this structure is one of the oldest stone pagodas in Korea and apparently patterned after early wooden pagodas which now no longer exist. Six stories remain but scholars speculate that there were seven or possibly nine stories. This 47 foot pagoda has been designated National Treasure No.11. Its height though colossal is only one fifth the height of the nine-storied pagoda of Hwangyong-sa which once stood in the Silla capital.

The Miruk-sa pagoda may be Korea's oldest. (NT-11)

5. Tomb of Scholar Sol Ch'ong: *Son of Priest Won-hyo*

The illicit love affair of Priest Won-hyo and Princess Yo-sok has been the subject of dramas as well as countless books. Though much of the life of Won-hyo is considered legend, the love affair is history for it produced the Confucian scholar Sol Ch'ong. He was to become one of the two Confucian giants of Silla and is enshrined in the central Confucian Hall of Seoul.

The distinction of being the first scholar to be canonized is probably attributed to the fact that it was Sol Ch'ong who invented the *idu,* a form of short connectives and literary phrase endings to be used in the margins of Chinese texts to aid the Korean reader.

Over 600 years, from this period to the close of Koryo, only four Korean scholars are now recognized in the Confucian Hall of Fame: Sol Ch'ong, Ch'oe Ch'i-won, An-yu and Chong Mong-ju. Twelve were selected from the Yi Dynasty. Though this judgment was made during the Yi Dynasty and today's historians may dispute the validity, nevertheless, Sol Ch'ong is ranked as the first of the 16 Korean Confucian scholars. He is responsible for first popularizing Confucian thought and philosophy in Korea.

Introduced through Chinese contacts with the peninsula the philosophies of Confucius had entered Korea long before the lifetime of Sol Ch'ong. It was the aim of Sol Ch'ong, Ch'oe Ch'i-won and other Confucian scholars of Korea to make the teachings of Confucius an indigenous part of the life of the people.

The *idu* invented by Sol Ch'ong, though a clumsy method, served its purpose well until the invention of *hang'ul* in the mid-15th century by Se-jong (4th Yi king). The genius of the scholar Sol Ch'ong lay in the fact that he realized the need for such a system. The *idu* was the first outcry against the difficulty people had when using Chinese characters. Its invention introduced a new era for rapid literary growth.

The most far-reaching result that we have today was the development of the *hyangga* which were lyrical songs often composed by the people who had little formal education. Developed by the use of *idu* the *hyangga* is unique to Korea. Of the many thousands written only 25 remain today and can be found in the *Samguk Yusa* and *Kyonyo-jon,* both written by Buddhist priests.

The *hyangga* was meant to be sung and usually took the form of satire with political overtones. The chant of the Potato Boy for the Princess Son-hwa is a *hyangga.* Others include Ch'o-yong's song of reaction when he discovered the Plague Spirit raping his wife.

In the closing years of the 7th century the wisdom of Sol Ch'ong was known throughout the Eastern world. When Shin-mun (31st king) was on the throne he called his advisors and asked them for their recommendations. As there was no comments from anyone the king looking at Sol Ch'ong said, "As the rainy season is past and the soft gentle breezes of late summer are beginning to blow, surely you can tell us something that would be of interest." Sol Ch'ong nodded and said that he would like to tell a legend he had heard which would be of interest to the court.

"Once there was a Peony King who ruled over the flower garden. Spring came and he opened his court while feeling so proud and treating others with contempt. The common flowers came to give him honor and respect. There also came a maiden flower named Cinnamon Rose, cloaked in green with a red skirt. Her soft tinted cheeks and beguiling sweet smile caused whispering through the court.

"Your humble servant has heard of the many virtues of Your Majesty,' she sweetly said, 'I have come to ask that I might serve you in all your desires.' The Cinnamon Rose was soon sharing the same pillow with the Peony King."

Sol Ch'ong paused in his tale while the faces of the king and many of the courtiers looked flushed. He continued his story. "The ancient Anemone Flower, attired in white, the color of mourning, entered the garden leaning on a cane. He awkwardly bowed before the king saying, 'Outside the palace I heard it said that Your Majesty has possession of many riches yet though you dress in silk you need the common thread as well. Is it not so?'

"The Peony King replied, 'The old man's words are wise yet so rare is perfect beauty that it is hard to sent it away'. 'Remember,' the gnarled Anemone Flower answered, 'It is easy to lose the heart to a pretty face. But a sage ruler who associates with the wise and prudent, it is his kingdom that will flourish.''

"The Peony King nodded, 'Yes, many ancient monarchs have fallen to destruction because of the wiles of a lovely woman and even Mencius was said to have looked in vain for a noble king that he could guide and counsel. I shall mend my ways,' he said.''

The allegory ended and the dignified Sol Ch'ong waited with head bowed. A hush fell over the council room. "Your words are full of thought," spoke Shin-mun, "A tale with wise counsel should be remembered.''

Over the centuries scholars have remembered this allegory and have added prose and poetry to give it more luster, but sad yet true, too many rulers failed to heed Sol Ch'ong's warning and kingdoms continued to fall as a result of the wiles of women. The Cinnamon Rose is still a delightful invitation but also a fearful evil as the latter kings of Silla were to discover. Sol Ch'ong was appointed to a higher office and he continued to guide the rulers of Silla wisely during the remainder of his life.

His tomb is traditionally believed to be found in the village of Pomun east of Chin-p'yong's tomb and a short distance from the main road east of Kyongju on the way to Mun-mu's water tomb. The tomb though simple is well kept.

The temple pillars at Pomun Village have an unusual lotus design. (T-123) below: *The tomb of Sol Ch'ong is nearby.*

6. Myonghwal-san : *Fortress Ruins of Early Silla (Historic Site No. 47)*

Kyongju is surrounded by many mountains which provided a natural defense perimeter. In the center of the ancient capital city rises Nang-san (Wolf Mountain) a hill riddled with legacies and relics, for the people believed this mountain to be sacred.

The rock piles remaining from Myonghwal-san-song (Bright Renewal Mountain Fortress) can be observed on the mountain slope to the right on the road bypassing Pomun Lake. This is the main route to Kamp'o on the east coast.

While Myonghwal-san rises to the east, Sondo-san (Spiritual Peach Mountain) stands at the west. In the south is Nam-san (South Mountain) while to the north is Sogumgang-san (Little Diamond Mountain). Though no fortress was built on Sogumgang-san, this peak was considered one of the four sacred meeting sites used by Silla ministers.

The fortresses of Myonghwal-san, Nam-san and Sondo-san served as Silla's inner line of defenses. Further away from the capital were additional fortifications. Kwanmun-song (Main Gate Fortress), one of the best preserved, is situated southeast of the capital city while Chak-song (Magpie Fortress) and Pu-san (Rich Mountain) Fortress are located further west. Hyong-san (Older Brother Mountain) Fortress was constructed to protect the northern valleys near Pohang.

Myonghwal Mountain Fortress was very probably the earliest Silla fortress. One record claims that a wall was first constructed in 405 during the reign of Shil-song (18th king).

The length of the fortress is about 3,000 feet. This fortress underwent major repairs in 554 during the reign of Chin-hung (24th king) and 593 during the reign of Chin-p'yong (26th king). Myonghwal Fortress served its purpose well in protecting the capital from Japanese pirates as early as the 5th century when a pirate force penetrated up to this area. The fortress was made of dirt with a stone base wall. It has been designated as Historic Site No. 47.

Pomun Lake has been recently developed by the government as Korea's top class tourist resort. Kyongju is Korea's open-air museum and by far the most popular tourist site south of Seoul.

7. Ch'on'gun Village Temple Site and Twin Pagodas
(Treasure No. 168 and Historic Site No. 82)

The twin pagodas are seen about 100 meters to the right of the road at the eastern end of Pomun Lake. There is very little known about these pagodas. They are about medium in size and typical of the Unified Silla period. There are no relief carvings on the surface though it is generally accepted that these pagodas are reconstructed *sari-t'ap.* Four relief pillars appear on each side of the base giving the impression of strengthening supports. Steps appear under the eaves of each roof. These two pagodas have been designated as Treasure No. 168.

Numerous foundation stones are lying about at the edge of the fields. They have been moved by farmers of Ch'on'gun (Thousand Soldiers) Village who were trying to clear the fields. Many of the pottery pieces and roof tiles have been gathered up and piled in several places nearby. Though the temple's name is unknown this site has been designated as Historic Site No. 82, and is always referred to by the name of the village nearby.

left: *The pagoda of Mujang Temple site is most difficult to reach. (T-126)* below: *These twin pagodas are near Pomun Lake Resort. (T-168) (HS-82)*

8. Chirim-sa and Kolgul-am: *The Venerable Forest and Bone Cave (Treasure No. 415)*

To reach Chirim-sa one must take the route to King Mun-mu's tomb on the east coast near Kamp'o travelling over a high mountain pass 29 kilos from Kyongju City to Andong Village. At the river turn left and follow the stream northward about 4 kilos. The temple is located at Hoam Village.

To reach Kolgul-am one must drive about 1.1 kilo upstream from the main road at Andong Village. A foot trail must be taken into the left foothills. After a two minute walk a small reservoir is reached. At a junction behind the lake the left trail is taken. The walking time is about 30 minutes.

Chirim-sa was one of the largest temples near the Silla capital and even today has fourteen buildings which compare in size to Pulguk-sa though not as historically important.

First it was called Imjong-sa (Forest Well Temple) when it was established prior to unification. Queen Son-dok had this temple rebuilt by the famed Priest Won-hyo. The name was changed to Chirim-sa (Venerable Forest Temple) in 643. Won-hyo's family name was Sol and his childhood name was So-dang. He apparently did not study under a tutor yet had considerable knowledge beyond his years.

Won-hyo was a *hwarang* (member of the knighthood) and trained with the elite young men of the kingdom. Later when he became a priest he was still very much of a nonconformist as he often drank and ate meat. The tales of his adventures, his wit and achievements have become a legacy. Though it is difficult to separate fact from fiction, Won-hyo's love affair with the Princess Yo-sok was indeed a reality. The child from this union became the famed scholar, Sol Ch'ong who is one of the two recognized Confucian greats of Silla.

Princess Yo-sok was a youthful widow living in the palace during the reign of Mu-yol (29th king). The story begins one day when

Won-hyo, who observing the bees and butterflies of early spring flitting from flower to flower, was filled with a desire to know a woman. The lonely priest mournfully strolled through the streets of Kyongju singing this ditty: "Who will lend me an axe that has lost its handle as I wish to cut a heaven supporting pole."

The people only laughed at him but the king knew that the wise monk was asking to place his seed in a noble lady. "A son by this monk of distinction would certainly be a worthy subject for the kingdom," the king thought. (In the Confucian Classics there is a poem where the axe handle symbolizes the male's sexual organ so that an axe without a handle would suggest a widow).

The king agreed to act as the go-between for this unconventional monk who wished to compromise his celibacy and the young princess whose husband had died with honor in battle. The rendezvous took place in the palace gardens.

Whether it was a deliberate act or not will never be known but somehow the priest slipped and fell into the lotus pond. Quickly the pretty young princess was on the scene giving aid to the priest who came out dripping. Taking him to her room she helped him change into dry clothes.

Princess Yo-sok, wily in the ways of love, gently took the wet robes from the shivering priest. Her own homespun silk gown parted carelessly and her young breasts like two lotus buds ready to bloom peered shyly from behind the silk. The innocence of her smile and her irresistible beauty were overpowering for the famed priest.

In the Jade Palace the "axe and handle" were joined as Won-hyo, passionate with a spring dream, journeyed through the "jasper gate." At daybreak Priest Won-hyo was gone. But still across the Korean countryside the legends of this unusual priest are whispered from person to person.

At Kolgul-am a priest offers prayer in silence.

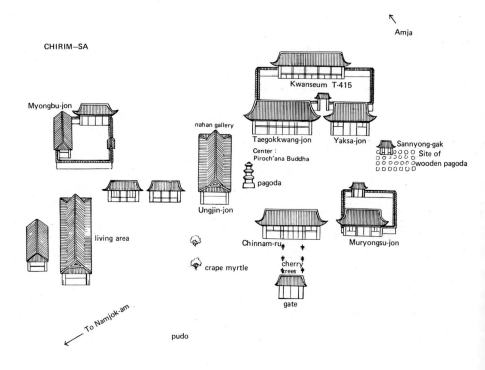

CHIRIM—SA

Amja

Myongbu-jon

Kwanseum T-415

nahan gallery

Taegokkwang-jon   Yaksa-jon

Center :
Piroch'ana Buddha

Sannyong-gak
Site of
wooden pagoda

pagoda

Ungjin-jon

living area

Chinnam-ru

Muryongsu-jon

crape myrtle

cherry
trees

gate

To Namjok-am

pudo

The popular legend of Mun-mu (30th king), who after death became a protective dragon in the Eastern Sea and presented to Silla a magic bamboo flute and jade belt which brought peace and prosperity, is linked with Chirim-sa. His son Shin-mun (31st king) who mounted the throne of Silla in 681 stayed overnight at Chirim-sa while returning to the capital.

As the king was resting beside a small pond behind the temple the crown prince rode up and welcomed his father. He admired the jade belt and exclaimed that every jewel in the belt was a living dragon. "How do you know?" queried the king.

"Throw one of the jewels into this pond and you will see." answered the crown prince. The king did so and immediately a dragon appeared

and flew into the sky. The pool was named *yongyon* (Dragon Pool) and can still be seen behind Chirim-sa.

Near the front gate large gnarled cherry trees line the path to the study hall. Passing between this study hall and buildings where several of the priests reside one enters the main courtyard of the temple. On the right side is a small shrine dedicated to the Sanshin (Mountain Spirit). Using several of sixteen foundation stones it was constructed on the site of a former wooden pagoda. Near this shrine is a large ginkgo tree and stone pagoda. On the other side of the courtyard is a large

The legends of Priest Won-hyo are still whispered throughout the countryside.

building called Ungjin-jon. It contains five hundred small *nahan* (disciples of Buddha) images. Many crape myrtle trees are seen behind the building. Chirim-sa has a wooden carp gong and large drum. The drum surface measures 5.5 feet in diameter and is said to be the largest in the Kyongju vicinity.

Further west of Ungjin-jon is Myongbu-jon (Judgement Hall) and additional residential buildings. On the north side of the main temple courtyard is the Taegokkwan-jon or main hall which houses the large Piroch'ana Buddha and attendants. The floral carved designs on the massive wooden doors are quite unusual.

Adjacent to the main hall is the Yaksa-jon which contains the Yaksa Yorae (Buddha of Medicine). Behind the main hall is the Kwan-seum-jon housing the Mercy Bodhisattva which has been designated by the government as Treasure No. 415. The image is made of wood with a gold lacquered surface. It is claimed to have been made in 1501 during the last Yi Dynasty. In 1786 Chirim-sa was rebuilt. Most of the present buildings date from this period.

Kolgul-am (Bone Cave Hermitage) is located among a cluster of pale white cliffs which gives the impression of bleached bones. The cliff rock is soft and flaky with numerous holes pock-marking the area. The little hermitage is small with only one priest who is a third generation caretaker.

Beyond the hermitage the impressive *ma-aebul* (relief Buddha image) of the Sokkamoni looms above. It is considered one of the finest Silla carvings but unfortunately because of the composition of the cliff much of the image has already fallen away. The face is amazingly clear and well preserved, possibly because over the centuries it has been virtually impossible to climb the cliff to mutilate it.

Flame and cloud designs soar behind the image while lotus petals also radiate from behind the head. There is no historical record concerning Kolgul-am. A legend tells that the unknown sculptor fell to his death before its completion. The right hand is pointed out as being still incomplete.

Some scholars wonder if this was not the cave referred to in the *Samguk Yusa* (Legends of the Three Kingdoms) relating to the death of Priest Won-hyo. It is mentioned that when

Won-hyo died his bones were crushed and pulverized into a life-size image by his son Sol Ch'ong. He went to live in a cottage near a cave where his father once lived.

As there are not many natural caves around Kyongju and since Chirim-sa was frequently visited by Won-hyo, these cave formations of Kolgul-am are strongly suspected as being Won-hyo's residence in his final days and associated with his death. However, scholars are quick to point out that this is purely speculation.

Chirim-sa and Kolgul-am are remote and difficult to find. The remains of a former wooden pagoda indicate the antiquity of the temple dating to the pre-unification of Silla. To spend a day within the temple vicinity and Kolgul-am will be a rewarding experience. The beauty of the countryside during each season provides for the adventurous tourist rare glimpses into the exquisite grandeur of the Korean landscape.

Through the trees the relief image of Kolgul-am is seen high on the cliff wall. below: *A priest is at prayer in the main hall of Chirim-sa.*

9. Twin Pagodas of Changhang-sa Site
(Historic Site No. 45)

The name of this early temple is unknown; however, it is often referred to by the villagers as Changhang-sa as this is the name of the region. The government has designated this unknown temple with twin five-storied pagodas as Historic Site No. 45. These two pagodas and National Treasure No. 39 near Kyongju City are the only five-storied pagodas found within the Kyongju area.

The stones used in construction are quite unusual in that they are light colored and pock-marked. Carved boldly in relief on the surface of the first story are eight ferocious images 3.5

Chirim-sa is one of the larger temples in the Kyongju area. The inwang *image on the five-storied pagoda of T'apch'ong was carved on porous stone.*

feet high. These guards, each holding weapons, are positioned on each side of a relief carved *sari* door. Twin locks on the *sari* door portray scowling faces of the *kuimyon* (devil chasers) with ring handles held in their teeth.

The east pagoda is partially reconstructed. The first story containing the eight relief images is positioned on the ground. The other four stories have disappeared and only the roof stones are tiered one upon the other.

Nearby is an octagonal granite Buddha pedestal. Reconstructed pieces of the broken image are now seen in the gardens of the Kyongju National Museum. The upper portion of the pedestal has a lotus petal design. At the base mythical animal are carved in relief. This pedestal is one of the more unique examples found within the Kyongju area.

From near this temple site one can see the famed Sokkuram high on the ridges of Tohamsan. Possibly this temple was an intermediate stop between Pulguk-sa and Kamun-sa near the water tomb of Mun-mu (30th king).

This side trip to T'apch'ong Village and temple site from the highway will be worth the effort as you travel to the east to view the tomb of King Mun-mu. The hiking time is about 45 minutes.

Two five-storied pagoda remains still stand in the barley fields of T'apch'ong Village temple site. (HS-45) Eight guardian relief figures decorate the sides of the first story.

10. Kamun-sa Twin Pagodas: *Dedicated to the Dragon Spirit of King Mun-mu (National Treasure No. 112 and Historic Site No. 31)*

Kamun-sa (Appreciation and Gratitude Awareness Temple) is one of the most unusual of all Silla temples. On the site are two immense pagodas which are considered the largest three-storied pagodas in Korea. Located near the sea coast this temple site commands a panoramic view of Taewang-am (Great King Rock), the underwater tomb of Mun-mu (30th king). The reign of King Mun-mu which began in 661 marked the beginning of many years of peaceful prosperity following the unification of Silla.

One of the more interesting and unknown tales of King Mun-mu relates to one of his younger half brothers called Ch'a-dok. He was an astute, intelligent young man and his abilities did not go unnoticed. He was soon appointed by King Mun-mu to become Prime Minister.

Ch'a-dok asked that first he might travel incognito in order to observe the true living conditions of the people and the effects of government tax. King Mun-mu admired his wisdom and readily agreed. Carrying a harp and disguised as a vagabond monk, he left the capital.

In the area of Haeyang he met a minor offical named An-gil who suspected that he was not an ordinary begging priest. The haggard Ch'a-dok was invited to his luxurious home for dinner. As night approached An-gil summoned his wives and a concubine to him and asked, "If one of you will be willing to share your beauty with our lonely guest I will promise to keep you in my household for life."

The two wives indignantly objected and loyally exclaimed that they would never even consider sleeping with another man for a night. However, the concubine who was far more attractive realized the sincerity of her husband's request and boldly answered that she would obey if he promised never to cast her out even in her old age. With downcast eyes the young concubine entered the room of the surprised

vagabond. As she was fresh and fair the night passed all too swiftly for Ch'a-dok.

The following morning the departing guest told his host that his home stood between Hwangyong-sa and Hwangsong-sa. "If ever you have the occasion to visit the capital please come and see me," Ch'a-dok cordially invited.

Several years later the official An-gil and his family moved to Kyongju. An-gil tried to find the home of the vagabond priest and discovered that the royal palace was located where the directions were given. He went and spoke to one of the palace guards.

Soon the Prime Minister himself came out and invited his former host into the palace. When the tale of his brother's country romance reached the ears of King Mun-mu, he laughed heartily and ordered a large tract of land be presented to An-gil.

The construction of Kamun-sa was begun by King Mun-mu but was completed by his son Shin-mun (31st king) and is considered so unique that few temples of this kind have been found in the Eastern world. Instead of placing single foundation stones for each pillar, three stones were placed one upon the other so that an open chamber was created beneath the floor. This permitted the dragon spirit of former King Mun-mu to enter with the inflowing tide.

Kamun-sa was built in an attempt to secure divine aid from Buddha in repelling Japanese pirates along the coastal regions of Silla. But the great king died in 681. Prior to his death he said, "When I am gone from this world, I would like to become a guardian dragon to protect Silla from the eastern enemies."

He did not want public money wasted on a costly tomb. In his will he instructed that his body be cremated and buried in the East Sea as in the manner of the people from the West. This concept may have come from Arab or Indian traders who had contact with Silla during this early period of commercial expansion.

The good king's wish was respected and

Mun-mu's ashes were taken to a small island off the east coast near Kamun-sa. Mun-mu's son Shin-mun completed this temple two years later and called it "Appreciation and Gratitude" in honor of his father.

Soon after completion in 683 an official came to King Shin-mun to report his recent observation of a small island floating offshore near Kamun-sa. The king quickly summoned his court astrologers to ask the meaning.

"Your majesty," they replied, "Your honored father, the sea dragon spirit in the Eastern Sea, has arrived with the spirit of the late General Kim Yu-shin. These two deities wish to present you with holy treasures."

On May seventh King Shin-mun climbed the knoll called Igyon-dae (Viewing Prophecy Hill) and observed the floating island with great amazement. The hill, shaped like a turtle, had two bamboo stalks growing side by side.

Legends relate that the earth shook with thunder while rain and darkness prevailed for seven days. Finally on the eighth day the storm subsided. The king boarded a small boat and soon landed on the floating island where an enormous dragon presented him with a belt

Two of Korea's largest three-storied pagodas still are seen at Kamun-sa site near the east coast and Mun-mu's underwater tomb. (NT-112 and HS-31)

of black jade.

A piece of the bamboo was cut and then the king after presenting gifts to the spirits of Mun-mu and Kim Yu-shin returned to shore. The island vanished in the rising mist. A flute was made from the bamboo and preserved in a vault at Panwol-song (Half Moon Fortress). It was called the "Calming Ten Thousand Waves Flute" and was prized as one of Silla's national treasures.

Except for some foundation stones and tiles found about the site all that is left at Kamun-sa are the twin three-storied pagodas.

Kamun-sa has been designated as Historic Site No. 31 while the pagodas are National Treasure No. 112. Their style is the prototype of Silla pagodas following the unification period and they emerged as true masterpieces of Korean architecture.

Stair step effects are seen under the eaves of the roof while the roof line has a gentle slope and is comparatively broad-brimmed. In a later period Buddhist images and designs appeared on the surface of pagodas and after the 9th century pagodas degenerated to ornamental objects rather than simple monuments to honor

The rocky island tomb for King Mun-mu appears as a dragon floating on the Eastern Sea near the fishing village of Kamp'o.

272

Buddha.

The base structure is five feet high and 16 feet square. The first story dimensions are nine feet square while the total height is 47 feet. The carved relief *sari* doors on these pagodas are conspicuously absent. However, the *sari* doors are seen on the pagoda (National Treasure No. 38) of Koson-sa which is about the same size and was constructed in the same era. The Koson-sa pagoda was moved in 1977 to the Kyongju National Museum.

In 1959 while the west pagoda was being repaired several treasures were found which are now on display in Seoul's National Museum. The discovery included four *sach'onwang* bronze images attached to a bronze box. In this box was an elaborate *sari* case with four bronze images holding musical instruments.

In the middle of the case is a stupa-like cap covering a small crystal bottle which once contained *sari* (calcified remains of a priest). These are all designated as Treasure No. 366.

Another legend of Kamun-sa reveals that once a large bronze bell was kept at this temple. One story alludes to the idea that Japanese pirates came ashore and stole the bell, but in attempting to set sail foundered at Taewang-am. This bell falling into the sea was never recovered.

The villagers now claim that on a windy day one can hear the resonating throb of this bronze Silla bell somewhere beneath the waves. The stream flowing by Kamun-sa still bears the name Taejong Ch'on (Great Bell Stream) to remind us of the legacy beneath the sea.

Along the rugged eastern coast near Kamp'o many rocks appear as islands where fishermen grow kelp for sale in the cities.

11. Taewang-am: *Underwater Tomb of King Mun-mu*
(Historic Site No. 158)

Taewang-am (Great King Rock), an island representing King Mun-mu's tomb, is located about one hundred meters off the coast near the twin pagodas of Kamun-sa. The rocky island is easily viewed as the road reaches the sea. A small fishing village is located less than one mile north of the stream's mouth. One may rent a small boat to make the round trip to the island. It is worth the effort and recommended when the sea is calm.

The question is often raised, were King Mun-mu's remains actually buried under the oval rock in the center pool? Scholars believed that he was cremated at a known site on the slopes of Nang-san in Kyongju and his ashes were brought to this place by the sea, while possibly other remains were once enshrined at Kamun-sa. In the center of the island is a calm pool of sea water.

In the center of the pool a large rock, approximately twelve feet in length, marks the burial site. At low tide the top of this oval rock

The underwater tomb for King Mun-mu is called Taewang-am. (HS-158) In the center of the pool a large oval rock marks the burial site.

is almost visible above the pool's surface. One wonders how this rock was brought to this site. Along the side of this boulder a crack is seen which might indicate that two stones were once joined together. There is some speculation that this rock is actually a stone coffin though most scholars do not think so.

Historical records reveal that Mun-mu (30th king) was buried in the Eastern Sea along the coast as he requested. He wished to have his body burned and buried at sea. King Mun-mu was quoted as saying that the tombs of ancient rulers are but names and today many are not even known.

The heroes of the past have now turned to handfuls of dust in an eternal home where goat herders blow their pipes and foxes make their holes. Thus the greatest of the Silla kings was memorialized at sea, the home of the dragon spirit, where seawater enters the eastern passage at high tide and flows through the western passage at low tide.

The historic site called Igyon-dae (Viewing Prophecy Hill) is where Shin-mun (31st king) first saw the floating island which transported the dragon spirit of his father. It is now a fenced area to the right of the road several hundred meters from the stream which passes Kamun-sa. The cliff drops away to the sea and through the trees along the brink one may obtain an excellent view of the rock tomb island of King Mun-mu floating on the waves like a giant dragon. Igyon-dae has been designated as Historic Site No. 159.

The view from Igyon-dae to the underwater tomb of Mun-mu reminds visitors of the dragon legend of Silla's most famous ruler. (HS-159)

12. Other Historic Sites from Kyongju to the East Coast:

Pomun Village (Treasures No. 64 and No. 123):

West of Chin-p'yong's tomb and village of Pomun are two designated treasures, one a set of temple banner pillars and the other a stone tub. Closer to the village are the 5'6'' pillars with 8 petal lotus blossoms (1'6''dia.) carved on the outside top of each pillar. The girth of each pillar is 5'10'' while the space between is 2'4''. There is a notch at the top of both pillars. These pillars are now designated as Treasure No. 123.

Several hundred meters further west is the site of Pomun-sa (Wide Gate Temple). Here a taller pair of supporting pillars are seen. Numerous tile and foundation stones are seen about the temple site. Nearby is a large stone cistern (3'6'' × 8') carved from a single piece of granite. This tub has been designated as Treasure No. 64.

Koson-sa Site:

One of Silla's most important temple sites, where Korea's largest three storied pagoda was once located, is now underwater due to the Tok dong Lake Development Project sponsored by the government. This gigantic pagoda was moved to the Kyongju National Museum along with a turtle base stone and lotus lantern base stone. The pagoda is listed as National Treasure No. 38. The base is 17 feet square and seven feet high. The *sari* door size is 3'6''×5' , while the first story is 9'6'' square and six feet high. The total estimated height is 30 feet.

In 1915 a fragment of the memorial tablet for Priest Won-hyo was found and brought to

(1) Stone tub on the temple site of Pomun-sa (T-64); (2) Koson-sa, site before the pagoda was moved to the Kyongju National Museum (NT-38); (3) Portion of Priest Won-hyo's tablet found at Koson-sa site and now in the Kyongbok Palace of Seoul;

276

Seoul. It is now in the corridor of the main audience hall of Kyongbok Palace. In 1966 another portion of this tablet was found and is now in the Dongguk University Museum in Seoul. With a lake now covering this entire site other chances for discovery of any additional pieces of this historic tablet are gone.

Pagoda and Tablet Remains of Mujang-sa Site (Treasures No. 125 and No. 126):

A few kilos from Kyongju a road may be taken to Amgok Village north of Pomun Lake. The site is most remote and difficult to find. Following the unification of Silla, arms were stored here; thus the name of *mujang* means "hidden arms." The temple was built at the end of the 8th century. On the site stands a three storied pagoda rebuilt in 1964 and designated as Treasure No. 126. The base is 7'7" square and 3'7" high. The total height is 17 feet. In front is a stone lantern base stone three feet in circumference.

On the top terrace where the massive main hall dedicated to the Amit'abul once stood is another lantern base stone and broken pillar. Nearby is a turtle base and a piece of the dragon sculptured cap stone for this historic tablet. The remains have been designated as Treasure No. 125. The body of the turtle is five feet across with two necks (both heads are missing). In 1915 portions of the tablet with calligraphy were discovered and taken to Seoul. They can be seen in the corridors of the main audience hall of Kyongbok Palace.

The tablet told the origin of the Mit'a-jon, a colossal hall which stood for centuries, a masterpiece of Buddhist architecture. The calligraphy collected and used on this tablet was taken from the writings of the famous Chinese scholar Wang Hui-ji. Referred to as a "collecting tablet" there are few extant today. This particular one at Mujang-sa is the oldest in Korea and possibly the oldest in the world.

So-song (39th king) who died after ruling one year in 800 left behind a grief-stricken queen who had this gigantic hall built for her husband's departed soul. The building crumbled and was forgotten until the discovery of the tablet, broken and shattered.

Pagoda Remains of Hwangyong-sa Site:

Another small temple site bearing the name of the famous central temple of Silla located on the outskirts of Kyongju City is found in a remote valley 15 kilos east toward the east coast. Only the Chinese character of *hwang* is different. This temple called "Yellow Dragon" rather than "Imperial Dragon" has the remains of a three-storied stone pagoda. The temple site is above the village and in a field.

(4) Pagoda of Mujang-sa site (T-126); (5) Turtle tablet base at Mujang-sa (T-125); (6) Pagoda remains of Hwangyong-sa. next page: *Alone in the woods a priest has time for meditation.*

Chapter VIII
Places of Interest North of Kyongju

1. King Hon-dok: *Tomb of a Scheming Uncle*
(*Historic Site No. 29*)

This tomb, traditionally belonging to Hon-dok (41st king), is located across the North Stream, upriver several hundred meters from Punhwang-sa. One can walk from the road in less than ten minutes. The tomb mound can be found in a grove of large pines surrounded by rice fields. King Hon-dok began his seventeen-year rule in 809.

Most of the tombs of later kings of the dynasty were located on hills while pre-unification kings tended to select their tomb sites in valleys. Hon-dok's tomb apparently is an exception as the location is in the lowland. Because of its close proximity to the stream it is some wonder that the tomb has not long since washed away.

When So-sang (39th king) died in 800 his son who was under age mounted the throne as Ae-jong (40th king). His uncle, younger brother to King So-sang, became regent for the boy. When Ae-jong became king in his own right this uncle was selected as defense minister. He later plotted to have Ae-jong commit suicide. After King Hon-dok's death a third brother became Hung-dok (42nd king) in 826.

The mound is 268 feet in circumference and 100 feet across. This royal tomb contains the zodiac images; however, some are missing. There are now only five (north to east): the pig, rat, cow, tiger, and rabbit. The images dressed in civilian attire, are three feet high and 1.5 feet wide.

The tomb recently has been reconstructed and has a five foot support wall. This wall consists of four-foot stone slabs alternating with two-foot slabs. Zodiac images were once carved on every other small slab. Pillars were placed around the mound to form a stone fence.

The rabbit figure of the zodiac is found on the traditional tomb of Hon-dok. This is the only royal tomb where the zodiac figures appear dressed in civilian attire. (HS-29)

The fence circumference is 308 feet.

Though the political strength of the dynasty was waning during the 9th century, Buddhism continued to prosper. One of greatest priests of the 9th century was wise Nang-hye who was growing up as a boy during the reign of King Hon-dok.

Nang-hye was later to become the tutor of two Silla rulers and a religious saint in the eyes of all. It was said that when he died at the age of 87 the people of Silla lost their eyesight and could no longer see the living Buddha.

While the prince (later King Hon-dok) was serving as regent for his nephew, Ae-gong, the famed temple of Haein-sa was established in the remote mountains of Kaya. Today it is considered one of the greatest temples of Korea and certainly the scenery of this region is difficult to equal anywhere in the country.

Now the *Tripitaka* wood blocks (National Treasure No. 32) made during the Koryo Dynasty and considered the oldest set in the world are preserved at Haein-sa. Still many great priests with their religious piety coupled with literary achievement continued to meander the pages of Silla history, though the dynasty was in decline with ineffective and morally corrupt leaders.

left: *The patterns of tile have a tradition of beauty and character at P'yo-am.* right: *legends of Sok T'al-hae tell of his appearance off the eastern coast. He became Silla's fourth king.*

2. Tomb of T'al-hae: *First Ruler of the Sok Family*
(Historic Site No. 174)

Sǫk T'al-hae, a man of mythological origin, married into the royal family and to this day provides for Korea some of the most cherished legends and traditions of early Silla. He was to become the fourth king of Silla upon the death of Yu-ri (3rd king) who had no heir. T'al-hae was the first of the Sok family and was one of the great leaders of this period 2000 years ago.

Legends claim that he came from an island kingdom north of Japan. However, Korean scholars look to Cheju Island. This mystic kingdom was ruled by 28 dragon kings supposedly born from the wombs of only two prolific women and each boy ascended the throne at the age of six.

The father of T'al-hae was King Ham-dal-p'a, though for many years the queen bore no sons. After the seventh year she became pregnant; however, at the end of only seven months she brought forth from her womb a large egg. The shocked royalty believing this to be a bad omen decided to destroy the egg.

But the mother secretly wrapped the egg in silk and placing it on a ship set it adrift. Two servants were placed aboard to care for this precious cargo. As the ship drifted out to sea a red dragon appeared and gently nudged the ship along. During the long journey the egg hatched and a small boy stepped forth.

According to one legend the ship landed first on the shores near Kimhae but the frightened people pushed it out to sea again. (This might further validate the Cheju Island origin theory.) Eventually it drifted to the shores of Silla where an old woman saw the boat foundering and surrounded by a flock of noisy magpies.

Calling the villagers to help she pulled the craft ashore and taking the boy raised him as her own son. He grew almost seven feet tall (some records state nine feet) and became more handsome and wiser than his peers.

The boy had no name but the villagers remembering the day of his arrival with the noisy magpies called him *sok*. According to the *Samguk Yusa* historically the first radical for the Chinese character of magpie was *sok*. Today the Chinese character for the Korean family name of Sok is rare and has no meaning.

The boy was taken from a box which once contained the egg so he also received the name of *t'al-hae*. The character *t'al* means "to put off" which refers to his separation from the egg while *hae* means "to open" as the sea chest was opened and T'al-hae was taken out.

Sok T'al-hae's fame soared like a comet through the skies and King Nam-hae entrusted to him a great portion of the affairs of state. His position was firmly secured when King Nam-hae offered his daughter in marriage.

In 24 AD King Nam-hae died but before his death he willed that T'al-hae, his son-in-law, succeed him rather than his own son. But Sok T'al-hae refused and insisted that the young son of Nam-hae succeed his father. To break the impasse a compromise was suggested by T'al-hae.

"A virtuous man has more teeth than a rogue," he declared. Each man bit into a rice cake and it was discovered that the prince had more teeth than T'al-hae. In this manner the prince ascended the throne to become Yu-ri (3rd king) with the title of *nijilgum* (tooth game). This title was also used for succeeding monarchs of Silla. The present Korean word of *imgum* (king) was probably a derivation or corruption of this Silla title.

King Yu-ri ruled for 33 years and upon his death the reins of government fell to the aged statesman T'al-hae who was now 62. He ruled as fourth monarch for 23 years and died at the age of 85.

Another legend, one of the most famous of all Silla myths, took place in the eighth year of Sok T'al-hae's reign. History dates this event to the fourth day of the eighth month in the year 65 AD.

A gold box emanating a strange eerie light was found dangling from a tree branch in a wood near the palace. Perched nearby was a regal white cock. When the box was opened a baby boy was found inside whom the king called Al-chi which means "infant child."

King T'al-hae chose an auspicious day and formally adopted Al-chi as his son. He was given the family name of Kim which is written with the same Chinese character of *kum* (金) meaning gold because he had been found in a gold box.

After 180 years and seven generations Kim Mi-ch'u (13th king) became the first of Kim Al-chi's descendants to mount the Silla throne. Of the entire spectrum of 56 Silla kings 38 belonged to the Kim Clan. The Sok family provided eight rulers and the Pak family ten kings.

Silla was known as a peaceful nation where the industrious spirit of a people and their early rulers successfully laid the foundation for a dynasty which permitted Korea to develop a high level of culture, art and intellect. How many other kingdoms of the world can boast of a millennium of existence? Though the myths are difficult to believe, they do typify the aspirations of people who were enjoying a relatively quiet existence with minimal outer interference from other more warlike nations.

In 80 AD King T'al-hae died and was buried in a remarkable way. Court officials preserved him in a plaster cast to be kept at the palace. Later his remains were buried on the eastern hill.

The traditional tomb site of T'al-hae is listed as Historic Site No. 174 and is located in a beautiful grove of aged and gnarled pines. The tomb locations of the other kings of the Sok family are unknown. The tomb mound is quite small as it is only 150 feet in circumference. The site is less than 50 meters from the new highway bypassing Kyongju City for Pohang along the western slopes of Sogumgang-san.

3. P'yo-am: *Shrine for the Kyongju Yi Ancestral Family*

Situated high on a rocky bluff near the tomb of Sok T'al-hae (4th king) is the shrine of P'yo-am dedicated to the Kyongju Yi ancestral family. This family clan is not to be confused with the royal family of the Yi Dynasty which came originally from Chonju in North Cholla Province.

Kyongju Yi was one of the six village elders who helped in the selection of the first king of Silla, Pak Hyok-ko-se. This present shrine was reconstructed in 1925. During the reign of Sun-jo (23rd Yi king) in 1803 the stone tablet was dedicated.

The Silla people believed that when the rocks of this cliff would begin to crumble the decline of Silla was imminent. During the dynasty period grass was planted to help prevent the cliffs from crumbling. From this legend comes the name of P'yo-am, which mean grass shrine. When the fall of Silla did come in 936 it is not known if these rocks did in fact fall. The cliff even now appears to be staunchly holding up.

Yi P'yo-gong was the first of the Yi family clan. Here at this cliff site he planted the first

left: *A guard is stationed in the judgement hall of Paegyul-sa.* below: *The shrine gate of P'yo-am illustrates the Confucian symbolism of the universal forces of nature.*

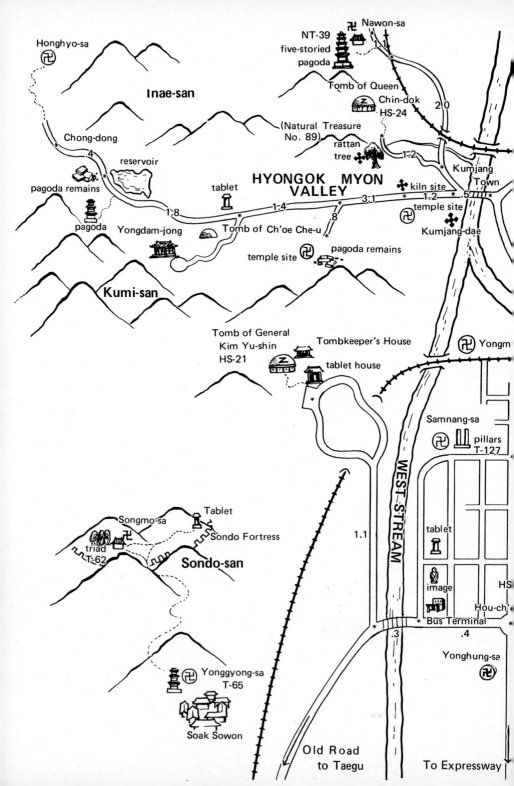

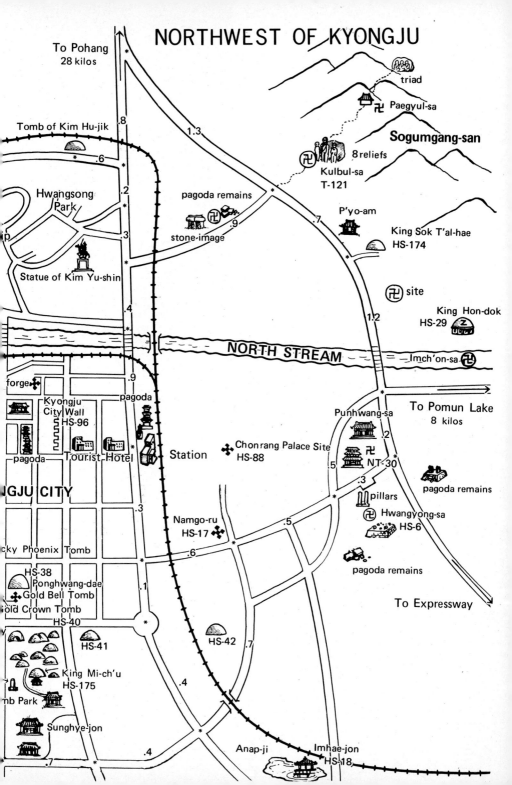

NORTHWEST OF KYONGJU

To Pohang
28 kilos

triad

Paegyul-sa

1.3

Sogumgang-san

8 reliefs

Kulbul-sa
T-121

Tomb of Kim Hu-jik

.8

.6

.2

Hwangsong
Park

.3

pagoda remains

stone-image

.9

.7

P'yo-am

King Sok T'al-hae
HS-174

Statue of Kim Yu-shin

.4

site

King Hon-dok
HS-29

1.2

NORTH STREAM

Imch'on-sa

forge

.9

pagoda

Kyongju
City Wall
HS-96

To Pomun Lake
8 kilos

Punhwang-sa

.2

pagoda

Tourist Hotel

Station

Chonrang Palace Site
HS-88

.5

NT-30

pagoda remains

GJU CITY

.3

.3

pillars

Hwangyong-sa
HS-6

Namgo-ru
HS-17

.5

.6

cky Phoenix Tomb

pagoda remains

HS-38
Ponghwang-dae
Gold Bell Tomb
old Crown Tomb
HS-40

.1

To Expressway

HS-41

HS-42

.7

King Mi-ch'u
HS-175

mb Park

.4

Sunghye-jon

.7

.4

Anap-ji

Imhae-jon
HS-18

gourd seed. As one of the six village elders P'yo-gong helped Pak Hyok-ko-se, Silla's first king and served as ambassador to Mahan. The king of Mahan told Yi P'yo-gong that Silla was small and weak; therefore, tribute should be sent to Mahan.

Yi P'yo-gong only smiled before the king of Mahan and replied, "Our king of Silla was sent from heaven so if you attack we are not worried because we know that heaven will help us. Our king is loved by his people because he rules the country well."

Yi P'yo-gong continued by saying, "Our king is respected by all others and has always been polite to you. That is why I am here yet you have not returned this courtesy. Actually no one in Silla is afraid of you or your country."

Upon hearing these words the king's wrath became so great that he tried to kill Yi P'yo-gong but was prevented by court attendants. The king learned to respect the integrity of P'yo-gong, and upon his return to Silla many rich gifts were sent to King Hyok-ko-se and the two countries lived in harmony.

above: *At Kulbul-sa site a four-sided stone is covered with Buddhist images. On the north side is a standing Bodhisattva.* below left: *Facing west is the Amit'a Buddha and two attendants.* below right: *On the east side is the Yaksa Yorae image.* next page: *A student group receives a lecture at Kulbul-sa site.* (T-121)

4. Mystifying Buddha Images of Kulbul-sa Site
(*Treasure No. 121*)

Called *samyon-sokbul* (four-sided stone Buddha) these unusual carvings sculptured on a twelve foot square-shaped rock are located on the way to Paegyul-sa. Legends are told that one day Kyong-dok (35th king) was on his way to Paegyul-sa when he heard strange voices coming from the ground. For him it sounded like a priest chanting a Buddhist sutra.

He immediately ordered his servants to dig and soon they unearthed a large stone with Buddha images carved on four sides. Excited over this discovery King Kyong-dok ordered Kulbul-sa (Excavated Buddha Temple) to be built on this auspicious site. Though the temple has long since disappeared the four-sided rock with Buddha images still remains. The government has designated this stone as Treasure No. 121.

The arrangement of the various figures is unusual and deserves further explanation. In the center facing west is the main twelve-foot image of the Amit'abul (Buddha of Western Paradise). The body portion is in relief while the head rises over the top of the natural stone. The two attendants were carved from separate pieces of granite.

Usually the Kwanseum Posal (Bodhisattva of Mercy) is on the Buddha's right side but in this case both attendants appear to be the Kwanseum Posal. It is believed by most scholars that these images were added in a later period. In a 1920 photograph it was observed that the head on the left Kwanseum was intact, but today this head is missing as well as other major portions of the body.

Directly behind is the relief carving of a six-foot sitting Yaksa Yorae (Buddha of Medicine). On the north wall are two relief images over five feet high. The right standing Bodhisattva is carved in bold relief. Its garments fall in loose folds about the body. The other figure which is sitting is barely discernible.

On the southern side of the rock are two deeply carved five-foot *ma-aebul* images.

Apparently Bodhisattvas, both figures are standing. The head of the left figure is missing while the right image is holding a container in the left hand next to the thigh.

These two figures are more feminine in form. The waist is tighter with pleasing swelling of the hips while the face under a crown is rounder and more fleshy. The gowns cling to well proportioned bodies giving a beautiful yet dignified appearance.

The *samyon-sokbul* and the meaning of the four directional images has held a strange baffling fascination for present day scholars. The origin of the *sabul* (Four Buddhas) likely comes from the early period of Chin-p'yong (26th king) when in 586 it is recorded that during an earthquake a huge rock, ten feet square, fell to the valley floor wrapped in red silk.

Upon taking away the silk the people saw Buddhist images carved on four sides. When King Chin-p'yong heard of this he journeyed to the site and prostrated himself before the *sabul*. The mountain is now called Sabul-san and is located in North Kyongsan Province.

In the Kyongju area the two most famous *sabul* images are to be found at Ch'ilbul-am and here at this site of Kubul-sa. Another small *sabul* is found at Kumgok-sa site near Angang Town. The accurate identity of the images continue to baffle Buddhist scholars. Also at Horyu-ji, a Japanese temple near the city of Nara, a similar square rock is kept with four images of Korean origin.

The west and east images are most certainly the Amit'abul and Yaksa Yorae; however, the north and south images pose problems. Some scholars say that the image on the north is the Sokkamoni while the south wall contains the Miruk (Future) Buddha, yet in the case of Kulbul-sa there are two images. These scholars point to Horyu-ji to justify their arguments.

In the Hwaom, one of the basic scriptures (sutra) of Korean Buddhism, there is a brief mention of the four directional *yorae* (Buddha) and their positions. The Amit'abul is positioned in the west while the Yaksa Yorae faces east. The Posungjang Yorae (Widely Victorious and Magnificent Buddha) faces south while the Pudongjon Yorae (Immoveable Buddha) is positioned in the north. These two Buddhas are not commonly known now and only appear in the Hwaom Sutra. In addition to the Hwaom Sutra there are other scriptures which also give positions of the Buddha at the four cardinal points of the compass. In total there are seven different opinions on this matter.

Near the square stone treasure are several pillar foundation stones which were probably used for an early temple structure.

Climbing the long steps to Paegyul-sa a priest returns.

5. Paegyul-sa: *Overlooking Kyongju from Sogumgang Mountain*

In a well-wooded slope of pines, chestnuts and elms a small temple called Paegyul-sa (Chestnut Curd Temple) is seen overlooking the city of Kyongju. A short fifteen minute hike from the road at the foot of the mountain will take the visitor past the famous cultural attraction of Kulbul-sa (Excavated Buddha Temple) site.

The peak behind is historically significant It was traditionally on Sogumgang-san (Little Diamond Mountain) that the head of the Buddhist martyr Yi Ch'a-don fell after being severed from his body. This historic event took place in 524 during the reign of Pob-hung (23rd king) and as the legend elaborates the martyr's blood ran white rather than red as he prophesied.

This miracle made it possible for Buddhism to become the officially recognized religion of the people. Paegyul-sa is the only temple in this vicinity. The founding date of Paegyul-sa is unknown but it is recorded that Shin-mun (31st king) first ordered the temple to be constructed.

Formerly located in the Taeung-jon was a standing gilt bronze image of the Yaksa Yorae (Buddha of Medicine) which was moved in 1930 to the Kyongju National Museum and designated as National Treasure No. 28. This 5' 9'' image along with the sitting Amit'a Buddha and Piroch'ana Buddha at Pulguk-sa are now the three classic examples of gilt-bronze sculpturing of the Silla period. The two hands of the Yaksa Yorae are later additions as they were once broken and lost.

It is legendary that the artist who painted the portrait of the eleven-faced Kwanseum Posal (Bodhisattva of Mercy) of Chungsaeng-sa also sculptured the Yaksa Yorae of Paegyul-sa. He was a master artist from T'ang China who fled due to a narrow escape from death.

He had been commissioned by the Emperor to paint the portrait of the beautiful court favorite. So dazzling was her exquisite beauty that upon accomplishing the finishing touches his trembling brush slipped, making a small blemish just below the girl's navel. As it was so slight he was certain no one would notice. The artist then presented his portrait to the Emperor.

"How could you have known that she had a small mole under her navel unless you had taken liberties with her?'' the ruler screamed. The poor artist was thrown into prison but before the execution the Prime Minister came to his defense.

Finally agreeing to give him one more chance, the Emperor made a bargain with the artist. "Your life for another painting of the woman I dreamed about last night.'' he said. The grateful artist then painted the graceful figure of the eleven-faced Kwanseum much to the amazement of the court.

The Emperor was astonished but had to reluctantly give him his freedom. After this narrow escape the artist fled to Silla where he again painted the image of the Kwanseum and sculptured the image of the Yaksa Yorae of Paegyul-sa.

The temple is reached by a flight of stone steps. In the courtyard lie numerous stone remains of another temple. Pillar base stones and broken remnants of lanterns and pagodas are evident. A relief pagoda eight feet high and four feet wide can be seen on the cliff wall directly in front of the main hall.

This particular relief is typical of Silla stone pagodas, and not similar to the two pagoda reliefs found in T'ap Valley of Nam-san, south of Kyongju. The sloping roofs and stair-step effect under the eaves can be noted.

Also in the courtyard is a small rectangular stone with pagoda reliefs on four sides. This is one of three fragments of a pillar pagoda which was found near the triad relief images above Paegyul-sa fifty meters from the summit on the east slope of Sogumgang-san. The other fragments are located in the Kyongju National

Museum and the Dongguk University Museum
of Seoul. These fragments were discovered in
1958.

An eight-sided tablet memorializing the
Buddhist martyr Yi Ch'a-don was also found
near Paegyul-sa but was moved to the Kyongju
National Museum. Traditionally this martyr
was buried somewhere near the summit of this
peak but his tomb site is unknown.

In the Taeung-jon is a large gold image of the
Sokkamoni Buddha with two attendants of
equal size, Munsu Posal and Pohyon Posal.
The murals on the walls are new and gaudy.
The main beams are shaped like dragons with
long whiskered snouts facing toward the temple
entrance rather than at each other as is typical
for most temples. The yellow dragon on the
left is the male while the blue dragon on the
right is the female. There are sixteen white
nahan (disciples) positioned along a side wall.
This Taeung-jon is the main hall where once
stood the famed Yaksa Yorae which can now be
seen in the Kyongju National Museum.

*Paegyul-sa is located on the slopes of Sogum-
gang Mountain and is one of the major temples
near Kyongju. The standing Yaksa Yorae
bronze image, now in the Kyongju National
Museum, came from Paegyul-sa. (NT-28)*

6. Chin-dok: *Traditional Tomb of a Silla Queen (Historic Site No. 24)*

The tomb is located 6 kilos from Kyongju. Cross the West Stream to Kumjang Village and follow the left fork at the school. Near another small stream is a grove of rattan trees that are designated as Natural Treasure No. 89. If the visitor walks from here it is about twenty minutes to the tomb site on the side of a hill.

Queen Chin-dok (28th ruler) began her seven year rule in 647 following the death of her cousin Queen Son-dok (27th ruler). Records indicate that Queen Chin-dok sent an embroidered silk brocade to the T'ang ruler with a short poem that she had composed called the "Song of a Peaceful Reign." There are few people who do not thrive on praise and the Emperor of China was no exception as the queen lauded his wisdom and virtue.

Of the six royal tombs in the Kyongju area which portray the zodiac images this tomb traditionally belonging to Queen Chin-dok is the earliest. The relief images are smaller (2' × 1'6") and the sculpturing is somewhat inferior to the others. The circumference of the tomb mound is 147 feet. There is no other stonework near the tomb.

Many of the tombs belonging to Silla rulers are in serious dispute by scholars with the most prominent example being this tomb. As Queen Chin-dok ruled before unification and her achievements are less than Mu-yol (29th king) many may wonder how it is that her tomb is far more elaborate with sculptural reliefs than that of King Mu-yol's.

The use of protective zodiacs at royal tombs was developed in China during an earlier period and then used by royalty in Silla sometime around unification. This dispute of tomb identity still continues and may not be confirmed until the tomb is excavated and even then proof may not be conclusive.

The Korean government has designated 36 tombs in the vicinity of Kyongju as historic sites. These tombs all traditionally belong to designated kings of Silla. Of this total number

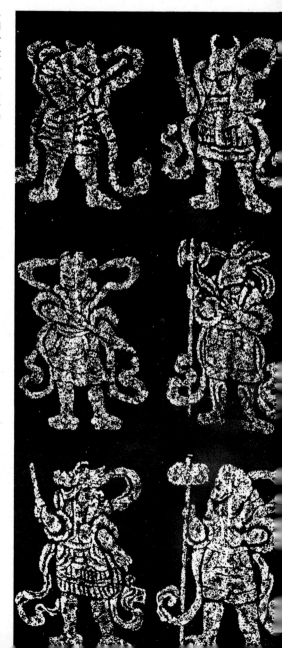

less than five can be claimed with any certainty as belonging to a particular Silla ruler.

The tomb location of twenty Silla monarchs is completely unknown with very little chance of being accidently discovered unless massive excavation is done among the hundreds of large tomb mounds surrounding Kyongju.

The reign of Queen Chin-dok also marked the end of a particular society structure. Silla had developed a unique class system called *kolp'um* (bone rank) where social status was determined by heredity but strongly influenced by kin and marriage. At the peak of society were two classes called *songgol* (sacred bone) and *chin'gol* (true bone).

Before unification of Silla the *songgol* class predominated as rulers. Usually kings of the Kim Clan married women of the Pak Clan. As is demonstrated by King Mu-yol who married a Kim daughter (sister of Kim Yu-shin) this connection with the Pak Clan ceased and the royal prince had a wider choice of marriage partners. The descendants of these later marriages made up the *chin'gol* class.

During the early years of Queen Chin-dok's reign there were some high officials who were becoming discontented as it appeared that gynecocracy was being established. The rebel forces gathered near the capital and prepared to lay siege. One night as the two armies were facing each other a falling star appeared to drop into the loyalist camp causing consternation. When the rebels saw this omen there was great rejoicing for they took this as a sign that victory was imminent.

But General Kim Yu-shin hastened to console the queen promising that he would personally reverse the ill omen. That night he prepared a great kite and fastened a torch to its tail. He exhorted his soldiers to be of good cheer and sacrificed a white horse. General Kim Yu-shin then flew the giant kite.

When the rebels saw the star rise from the loyalist camp they trembled with fear believing the omen had been reversed. When the queen's troops made their attack the hearts of the rebels turned to water and they fled into the hills.

Zodiacs at Queen Chin-dok's tomb include: Rat. Cow, Tiger, Rabbit, Dragon, Snake, Horse, Sheep, Monkey, Chicken, Dog and Pig.

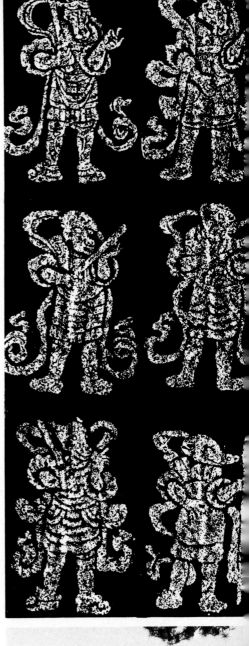

7. Pagoda Development: *Five-Storied Pagoda of Nawon Village (National Treasure No. 39)*

The five-storied stone pagoda located at an unknown temple site near Nawon Village is one of three 5-storied pagodas near Kyongju. The other twin pagodas though smaller and broken are located at Changhang-sa site near T'apch'ong Village on the way to Kamp'o and Kamun-sa.

This particular five-storied pagoda is an excellent prototype of the more simplified earlier Silla pagodas. The first story is 8.5 feet square and the total height of the pagoda is over 32 feet. There are no decorative carvings on the side. This monument ranks among the giant pagodas of Korea and is listed as National Treasure No. 39. Some foundation stones are seen in the fields while other stones were used in the foundation of the present temple building.

Korean pagodas can be grouped into three categories according to the building material used: wood, brick or stone. Now the stone pagoda is most prevalent in Korea because of the abundance of rock. In comparison China found brick to be more popular while in Japan because of the abundance of wood rather than stone we can find many wooden pagodas.

The term for pagoda in Korean is *t'ap*. This word originated from the Indian Sanskrit word *stupa* which means "tomb." The word *stupa* referred to the monument where the cremated remains and *sari* of Buddha were enshrined after his death. The Chinese borrowed the phonetic sounds of the Sanskrit word *stupa* and called it *sol-t'ap-pa*. When the term arrived in Korea the *sol* was omitted. Today the pagoda is sometimes called *t'ap-pa* in scholarly circles though the common term is simply *t'ap*.

Originally the *stupa* was erected for the enshrinement of the *sari* of Buddha. According to legends there were over eight million *sari* found in Buddha's ashes after cremation. The *sari* are small calcified jewels inexplicably

found after the cremation of a Buddhist disciple or priest. Also these *stupa* were later used to enshrine sacred Buddhist treasures, images or portions of Buddhist scripture.

In the seventh century the famed Priest Cha-jang returned from China with many sacred relics including a bone from Buddha's head which is now enshrined in the Sokka Sari-t'ap at Tongdo-sa near Pusan. However, this *stupa* is more bell-shaped. Eventually the most famous of priests whose cremated remains produced *sari* were also honored by taking the *sari* and enshrining them in a monument referred to in Korean as *pudo*.

The *pudo* have the general characteristics of a bell-shaped monument. Occasionally

A woman worships at the five-storied pagoda of Nawon. (NT-39)

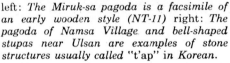

left: *The Miruk-sa pagoda is a facsimile of an early wooden style (NT-11)* right: *The pagoda of Namsa Village and bell-shaped stupas near Ulsan are examples of stone structures usually called "t'ap" in Korean.*

they are roofed and the *pudo* can also be lantern-shaped or a single-storied octagonal structure. The term *pudo* came from the word Buddha and can be considered another term for the pagoda or *t'ap*. Occasionally the term *t'ap* and *pudo* are used interchangeably for these bell-shaped monuments though the word *pudo* is never used for the multi-storied pagoda structure.

At the larger temples there is usually a special compound provided for the many *pudo*. Both Pokyong-sa and Oo-sa near Pohang provide excellent examples. There are five *pudo* scattered about the grounds of Pulguk-sa. The *sari-pudo* listed as Treasure No. 61 and shaped like a lantern can be found on the grounds of Pulguk-sa.

The chronological course of early pagoda construction in Korea is difficult to determine. The oldest of Korean pagodas that exist today are stone pagodas built to imitate wooden structures. The partial pagoda of Miruk-sa (National Treasure No. 11) near Chonju is the prime example from Paekche and probably

the oldest pagoda in Korea.

The oldest datable pagoda of early Silla was built during the reign of Queen Son-dok (27th ruler). Now located on the temple grounds of Punhwang-sa in Kyongju City it gives further evidence that wooden pagodas were built first. This pagoda of Punhwang-sa (National Treasure No. 30) has the unique distinction of imitating brick construction as well as copying the earlier wooden style. All the stones used were cut to the size of bricks.

Wooden pagodas were more easily destroyed but several wooden pagoda sites can still be seen. The largest pagoda ever constructed in Korea was the nine-storied wooden pagoda of Hwangyong-sa located several hundred meters from Punhwang-sa. Hwangyong-sa's massive pagoda had a base 78 feet square and rose to the astounding height of 224 feet. This giant wooden structure burned five times and finally succumbed in 1238 during the Mongol invasion.

Other wooden pagodas were constructed at the temple sites of Sach'onwang-sa and Mang-dok-sa. Also a wooden pagoda site can be seen at Chirim-sa. Today at Popchu-sa in the Songni Mountains is Korea's only wooden pagoda which was built in 1607.

Stone pagodas imitating the brick style are to be found at Namsan Village and on the slopes of Sondo-san near Kyongju. The fact that the brick pagoda shows elements of the wooden pagoda while the stone pagoda shows characteristics of both wood and brick leads one to believe that a possible course of development was from wood through brick and imitation brick to stone.

There are a few true brick pagodas left in Korea today. Some are located in the Andong vicinity. Though the brick pagoda did not flourish it seems that the artisan's infatuation with brick continued throughout the years.

A unique style of stone pagodas emerged after Silla unification which was to become the prototype of all Korean stone pagodas. Typical of this type is the five-storied pagoda of Nawon Village, the three-storied pagodas located at Kamun-sa site and Koson-sa pagoda relocated to the Kyongju National Museum. These early pagodas are characterized by simplicity and beauty of form.

The first general characteristic is that the pagoda was built on a double platform with the lower platform wider.

The second characteristic is that corner and center pillars were often depicted in relief on both the double platforms and story blocks.

The brick pagoda of Andong City (NT-56) and imitation brick pagoda near Uisong (T-327) illustrate various architectural styles.

Sandwiched between each pillar is a solid stone slab. The use of stone in this manner probably was derived from the architectural style of the wooden pagodas of an earlier period.

The third and fourth characteristics are that the roofing stone of each story depicts a staircase effect of five steps under each eave, while each section of the pagoda was built with different stones. In smaller pagodas the roof was carved separately from the body stone while on the larger pagodas the roof as well as pillars and wall slabs were cut from separate stones. The angle of the roof slope is gentle.

The last characteristic is that no decorative figures or patterns were carved into the body of the pagoda or pedestal. The five-storied pagoda of Nawon Village maintains the five prototype characteristics of the early post-unification period.

During the latter half of the eighth century simplicity began to lose favor as decorative elements appeared on the surface of the pagoda while their overall height was reduced.

From the ninth century Buddhist images appeared on the surface of the base and story blocks of the pagoda as it degenerated into an ornament of the temple rather than a sacred object of reverence and devotion.

The pagoda became so embellished with decoration that it seemingly lost its value as a remembrance of faith and a commemorative monument. Many figures appeared including images of the Buddha, Bodhisattva, *sach'on-wang* (Four Heavenly Kings), *p'albujung* (Eight Congregated Devas), *inwang* guards and the twelve zodiac figures. Flying devas, lotus flowers, *puloch'o* (grass of eternal life), heavenly clouds and many other Buddhist patterns appeared on the pagodas of Koryo in contrast to the simplicity of 7th century Silla.

The best examples of 9th century pagodas which portray many figures are found at the temple sites of Wonwon-sa, Namsan Village and Changrim-sa. From *stupa* to *t'ap* or *pudo* we can witness one of the most fascinating aspects of Buddhist art development. The countryside of Korea still abounds with many of these monuments in a variety of types.

During the eighth century the population of the capital of Silla was slowly rising to a

Pagodas of Nam-san characterize the imitation brick and post unification style. (T-124)

million inhabitants. Many artisans flocked from all over the known world as Buddhism held sway and distinctive art sculpturing was created from simple stone. These were the golden days of famed builders whose names are forgotten but whose skills have left indelible prints in the fields surrounding Kyongju City. A simple roof stone, a square granite block or lotus design pedestal stone may be all that remains of a once flourishing temple.

The remains of many pagodas are more in abundance in the Kyongju area than is realized. Not considering those moved to the National Museum over sixty reconstructed pagodas and remains are still to be found in the immediate countryside near Kyongju.

As you walk about the hillsides you meet the mysteries of a noble civilization. Many temple sites have no names or recorded history and occasionally an inscription reaches the surface which brings to light the life of a great scholar or Buddhist priest who can cast only a shadow across a history dimmed by age. Through the Silla remains in Kyongju only glimpses of a glorious heritage and profound culture can be witnessed.

8. Yang-dong: *Traditional Yangban Village*
(Treasures No. 411, No. 412 and No. 442)

The village of Yang-dong is near the road to Pohang, 17.5 kilos from Kyongju City. At the junction to Angang Town the road crosses a bridge. A small lane leads to the right, under the railroad track and directly to the village of Yang-dong.

In this village of Yang-dong traditions from the early Yi Dynasty still remain strong and unchanged. However, during the past years many of the younger generation have left Yang-dong so now the population is shrinking.

Many century-old homes can still be seen in this quaint scenic hamlet hidden from the main stream of progress. At the turn of the century there were over 300 traditional homes but now

In the town of Yang-dong customs and tradition are still evident. Architectural styles have not changed over the last 300 years.

A scholar in study or a farmer in the field; women at work, ironing or preparing a meal, are all part of each day in Yang-dong Village, Building designs denote traditional class now seldom seen in Korea.

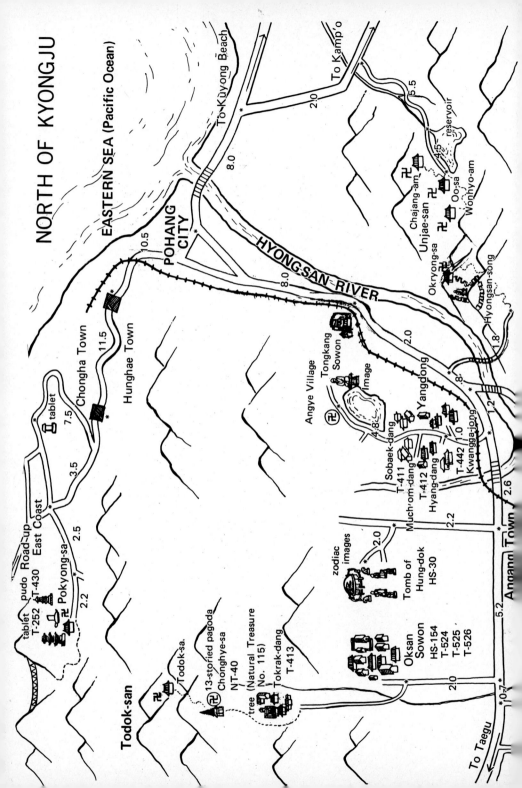

NORTH OF KYONGJU

EASTERN SEA (Pacific Ocean)

To Kŭyong Beach

To Kamp'o

reservoir

5.5

4.5

卍 Chajang-am
Unjae-san
卍 Oo-sa
Wŏnhyo-am

8.0

卍 Okryong-sa

Hyongsan-song

POHANG CITY

HYONGSAN RIVER

10.5

8.0

1.8

Chongha Town

11.5

7.5

Hunghae Town

卍 tablet tablet

Tongkang
Sowon

Image

2.0

0.8

Angye Village

Yangdong

1.2

3.5

4.8

卍

Sobaek-dang

Muchŏm-dang

Hyang-dang

T-411

T-412

T-442

Kwangga-jong

1.0

East Coast

2.5

Pokyong-sa

2.7

2.2

2.2

zodiac images

2.0

Tomb of Hung-dok

HS-30

Angang Town

2.6

tablet pudo Road-up

T-252 T-430

卍

Todok-san

Todok-sa.

13-storied pagoda
Chŏnghye-sa
NT-40

tree (Natural Treasure No. 115)

Tokrak-dang

T-413

Oksan Sowon

HS-154
T-524
T-525
T-526

5.2

2.0

0.7

To Taegu

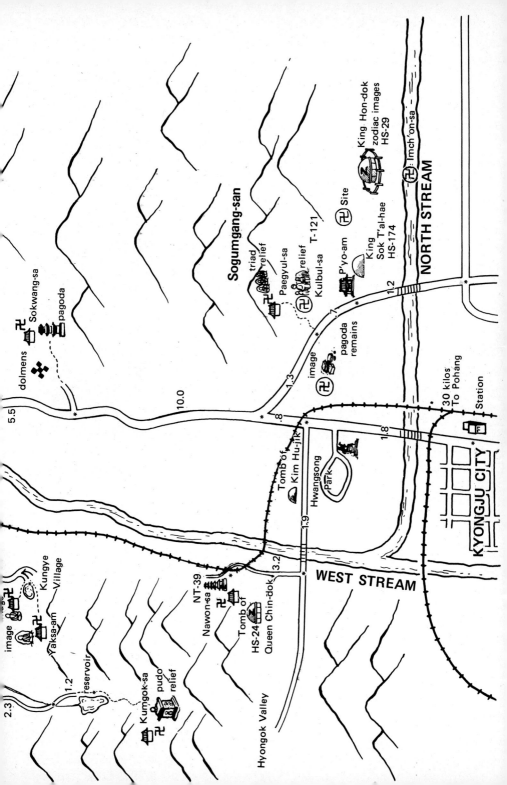

less than 50 remain. Three of these larger villas have been designated by the government as Listed Treasures (*pomul*).

Most of these traditional homes belong to the Yi or Son families. Yi On-jok, whose penname was Hoe-jae, was born here in 1491. He became one of the truely great Confucian scholars of the Yi Dynasty period.

In the hills west of Angang Town the governor of Kyongju in 1572 built Oksan So-won (Historic Site No. 154) in memory of Yi On-jok. It is now the second largest *sowon* (Confucian Study Hall) in Korea.

Back from the main road of this village near the church the villa called Much'om-dang is seen on the right side of the hill. This building is designated as Treasure No. 411 and was built by the father of Yi On-jok. Though he was not born here, nevertheless, the famed scholar grew up as a boy in Much'om-dang. Crape myrtle and cedar trees are growing in the courtyard. Behind the home is a small ancestral shrine containing the spirit tablet of Yi On-jok.

By the main road near the town church is another villa called Hyang-dang (Treasure No. 412) which was formerly a ninety-nine *kan* house. This was the largest size home building permitted by the king during the Yi Dynasty. When Yi On-jok became governor of Kyong-sang Province he had this home built for a younger brother.

It was partly destroyed in 1592. In 1950 during the Korean conflict Hyang-dang was again partly destroyed. A sixteenth generation descendant lives in Hyang-dang. The 450-year-old structure was renovated in 1976 and

The village life of Yang-dong with people at work and children at play illustrates the folk culture and tradition seldom observed in a modern Korea. Almost fifty buildings are over two centuries old.

completely rebuilt as a historic monument.

Kwangga-jong listed as Treasure No. 442 overlooks the river and is first noted when entering this village near the school. Kwangga-jong is situated on a conspicuous promontory with several large ginkgo trees at the entrance. The pastoral view from this pleasure pavilion is beyond comparison.

Gnarled cedars landscape the front yard. In spring a wide variety of flowering shrubs and trees still decorate the gardens of Kwangga-jong reminding one of the pleasures of the leisured nobility who must have come frequently

over the years to enjoy the blissfulness of nature.

Kwangga-jong was built by Son U-jae, a noted scholar descendant of the Son family. From this family came the mother of Yi On-jok. Son U-jae was an uncle to the scholar On-jok.

Located between Hyang-dang and Kwangga-jong is a memorial tablet. It was erected to honor General Son Chong-no who fought in the wars during the Manchu invasion of the 17th century. He lost his life in the seige of Namhan-san-song near Seoul. The king after a forty-five day struggle finally capitulated to the enemy.

Away from the main road in the second valley on the left is found the ancestral home of the Son family. This villa has been owned by the eldest son over many generations. At present there is a twenty-fourth generation descendant of the Son family living in this house.

Called Sobaek-dang (Hundredth Letter House) it has been designated recently by the government as Folk Cultural Treasure No. 23. The house was built in 1450 and forty years later the scholar Yi On-jok was born in this house as the mother returned to her ancestral home to have her baby.

The birth room can still be pointed out to the right of the porch after entering the courtyard. Initially when the house was constructed in the 15th century the local geomancer predicted that three great men were destined to be born in this house. The first two were Son U-jae and Yi On-jok. The third great person is yet to be born. Every effort is being made now to limit this prophecy to the Son family as only daughter-in-laws are permitted to use the birthroom for having their child. Also they are permitted to use this room on the first night following the wedding.

Recently an exception was made which ended tragically. A Kim who had married a daughter of the Son family requested that they be given permission to have their first child in the birthroom of On-jok. It was a bad omen and the baby died at childbirth. As a result of this incident the respect for tradition was more firmly embedded and only daughter-in-laws will be permitted to use this room.

At this ancestral home is also found a family shrine which memorializes the grandfather of Yi On-jok on his mother's side. A large cedar tree planted when the house was first built is still growing in the front courtyard. Though Sobaek-dang is not as large as other houses it is certainly one of the more charming villas of this village.

Kyongsan Sodang is seen across the valley from Sobaek-dang. Though not as large it has a unique attraction with roofs and walls amid the flowering shrubbery of spring. Also within the village are four small *sodang* (study halls) dedicated to the four grandsons of Yi On-jok. This great scholar had no sons so adopted a boy to become his son. These shrines are known by the four names of the grandsons, Tong-ho, Yang-jol, Yang-gu, and Sol-ch'on.

9. King Hung-dok: *Elaborate Tomb Architecture*
(Historic Site No. 30)

This royal tomb is near the town of Angang 21 kilos from Kyongju City in the direction of Pohang. The road is followed for over 16 kilos, then a left junction is taken over the river. After taking the northern road out of Angang Town 2.2 kilos a left lane is followed into the foothills for another 2.2 kilos. The tomb is located in a grove of pines and is difficult to see until one actually reaches the immediate area. This tomb is one of the few positive examples where the king and queen were known to be buried together.

Hung-dok (42nd king) reigned for ten years from 826. He followed the rule of his nephew and two elder brothers. This was the period of Silla decline. King Hung-dok had no heir so upon his death a cousin once removed became Hui-gang (43rd king) who later was forced to kill himself.

On April 18, 1957 a piece of the original tomb tablet was discovered. The inscription written on the stone confirmed that this tomb belonged to King Hung-dok. The turtle base stone which once held this tablet is seen near the tomb site. It is one of the largest stone turtles known as it measures 12'8'' long and 10 feet wide.

Many scholars point to King Hung-dok's tomb as the most typical of Silla tomb architecture. The tombkeeper indicated that there was also another tablet portion found during the Japanese occupation but buried by the authorities. Several years ago an effort was made to relocate this lost buried tablet piece; however, the search was futile.

The mound itself has a circumference of 213 feet. The retaining wall which consists of 36 perpendicular rectangular stones is four feet high. The zodiac figures are carved on every third stone. (2'7'' × 1'7'') Hung-dok's tomb is the last of six tombs belonging to kings where the twelve zodiac figures are found.

In winter during school vacation the teeter-totter sport among children is still popular.

Though the site is the furthest from Kyongju it is, nevertheless, considered one of the finest examples. The horse image faces due south while the rat faces due north similar to the other royal tombs (Chin-dok, Song-dok, Kyong-dok, Won-song and Hon-dok).

A six-foot stone apron protrudes from the retaining wall of the mound. Once there were over 40 pillars used for supporting a stone fence about the mound; however, now only six still remain while two are broken. These pillars are 4'6'' in girth and six feet high.

The tomb faces south. At the entrance are two *mangjusok* (Yearning Pillar Stone) which appear as stylized rock candles. Their origin is shamanistic and their purpose is not known, but strangely enough their function has lasted throughout the centuries. They are still seen at the sites of today's graves. During the Yi Dynasty the *mangjusok* stone took on other characteristics with small reptile-like animals crawling up and down the pillars.

Also on either side of the 54 foot passageway to the tomb, stone military and civil officials stand over nine feet tall. The military officials appear truly formidable with one hand clutching the hilt of their unsheathed swords while the other hand is raised in a clenched fist. A forehead strap is used rather than a helmet to hold the hair away from the face.

The civil officials are holding their hands together as the sleeves flow to their knees. As in life the desire for peace rather than war is greater so the civil guards are always positioned nearer to the king in death as well as life. The civil servant is always available while the military is only called upon in time of war.

On four sides of the tomb are positioned four stone lions. The lion is often represented as a symbol of protection both at temples and tomb sites. Though not a native to Korea, the lion image concept arrived with the influence of Buddhism. In the Buddhist world the lion is symbolized as the king of all animals and the

power he possesses is comparable with the power that the Buddhist Law has over the people.

Traditionally a lion is positioned under the table used for preaching and expounding the Buddhist law. The Tabo-t'ap at Pulguk-sa and the oldest pagoda in Korea at Punhwang-sa are examples of Silla's use of the protective lion in Buddhist architecture and design.

Lions at tomb sites have the same appearance as the temple dogs of Japan. These dogs which are referred to even today in Japan as *koma-inu* or Korean dog were believed to originally come from Korea. Though this theory is held by some, it is doubtful that there is a correlation between the protective lion guards of Korean Buddhism and the Japanese immigrant Korean dog. These lions are four and a half feet high and compared to other tomb sites are by far the most handsome in terms of sculpturing.

Recently several attempts were made by grave robbers to enter this mound. These few attempts were at night during winter months as the dark hours were longer. On each attempt a chamber wall was reached which could not be pierced. Within the mound a large stone room was made which held the remains of the royal pair.

The elaborate tomb of King Hung-dok is still relatively unknown. Stone officials, zodiacs, and lions are evident. (HS-30) right: Silla's largest turtle tablet base is seen at the site.

10. Oksan Sowon: *A Period of Confucian Leadership*
(Historic Site No. 154)

Oksan Sowon is one of the two most important known Confucian schools in Korea today. The other well-known school called Tosan Sowon was founded by Yi T'oe-gye and is located near Andong. Oksan Sowon was established in 1572 to honor the Confucian scholar Yi On-jok whose penname was Hoe-jae. Yi On-jok was born in 1491 about the period that Columbus was sailing the Atlantic in search of the New World.

Korea was being ruled by a nonconformist king called Yonsan-gun. This tenth king of the Yi Dynasty brought utter chaos to the country, and Confucianism which was being strongly promoted by previous kings suddenly came to a standstill. His first act on becoming king in 1491 was to behead his former tutor. Confucian shrines and schools were converted into halls of entertainment and. housed dancing girls. In 1506 the king was overthrown.

A younger brother came to the throne called Chung-jong (11th Yi king) and the country took a violent swing back to conformity. Thus began what is now referred to as the "Golden Age" of Confucianism. The Yi kings lost their supremacy over the Confucian scholarly force and were not to regain it again until several centuries later.

Though a "Golden Age" in one respect, historians also refer to this period as one of division and rivalry among the scholar classes.

Politically and socially the scholars were supreme, effectively controlling the entire country's economy and politics. Scholars were able to place themselves out of reach of common law. If they committed a crime they were tried by the Confucian College and not by the state.

Born to the family of Yi from Yoju, On-jok grew up in an atmosphere of prospering Confucianism. On-jok's mother was from the Son family and the ancestral family still owns many homes in Yang-dong on the east side of Angang Town. The home is called Sobaek-dang where this famous scholar was born. Nearby is another old fifteenth century home called Much'om-dang (Treasure No. 411) where Yi On-jok grew up as a boy.

By 1514 Yi On-jok passed the civil service exam and was appointed governor of Andong City and later Miryang. Somehow he was able to survive the scholar purge of 1519 and became third-grade advisor to the king in 1530. But his good fortune in freedom from political entanglement ran out during this same year and he was exiled. Seven years later he was recalled to serve King Chung-jong again as governor of Chonju. He rose to become Education Minister and later governor of Kyongsang Province.

In 1544 Yi On-jok continued to serve the government under the reign of In-jong (12th Yi king). However, In-jong soon died and there were rumors that he had been poisoned. When Myong-jong (13th Yi king and half brother of In-jong) mounted the throne under the watchful eye of the dowager Queen Yun, intrigue again stalked the courts. Thousands of lives were snuffed out before this family feud ended. Yi On-jok was pulled into the whirlpool of political affairs and was exiled again to Kanggye in far northern Korea where he died in 1533 at the age of 63. He is now buried north of Pohang.

When Son-jo became king in 1567 he raised

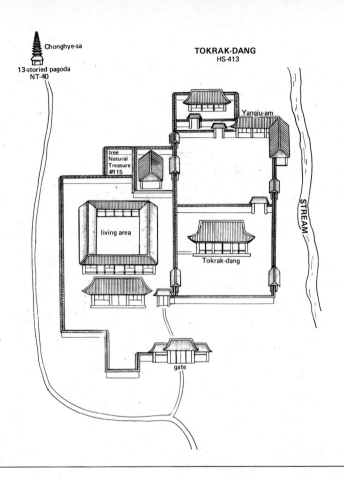

Chonghye-sa

13-storied pagoda
NT-40

TOKRAK-DANG
HS-413

Yangju-am

tree
Natural
Treasure
#115

STREAM

living area

Tokrak-dang

gate

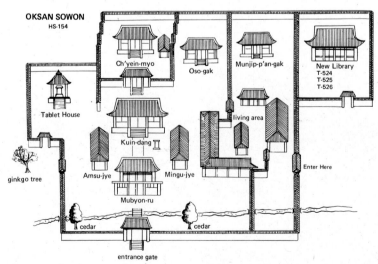

OKSAN SOWON
HS-154

Ch'yein-myo

Oso-gak

Munjip-p'an-gak

New Library
T-524
T-525
T-526

Tablet House

living area

Kuin-dang

Enter Here

ginkgo tree

Amsu-jye

Mingu-jye

Mubyon-ru

cedar

cedar

entrance gate

Yi On-jok posthumously to the highest rank under the king and in 1610 Kwanghae-gun (15th Yi king) highly praised On-jok calling him the most famous of the Songni scholars. Yi T'oe-gye (Yi Hwang) the most highly esteemed philosopher of the sixteenth century calls Yi On-jok one of the four wisest men of Asia.

In 1772 during Son-jo's (14th Yi king) reign the governor of Kyongju had Oksan Sowon built. In the 1860's the Taewon-gun (father of King Ko-jong) had most of Korea's *sowon* destroyed or closed because he regarded them as centers for rising anti-government activity. Fortunately Oksan Sowon survived this purge and now remains as second largest *sowon* in Korea. Seventy years ago a fire accidently burned some of the buildings and now only fourteen structures remain.

During this period the scholars were divided into two groups, the legal and educational. The former were more involved in government positions, giving little concern for the welfare of the people, while the latter who did not study for public office filled the educational

positions and usually lived in the country. As they were more often removed from political uncertainty their learning was often broader. They created in 1541 the institution called the *sowon* (literary school) the first of which was built in Kyongsang Province. Their numbers rapidly reached thousands.

The *sowon* became the center of cultural dispersal and learning for the rural regions. Today the art historian considers the *sowon* important because often these literary schools were the centers for production of much of the calligraphy and paintings of Korea during the dynasty's last three centuries.

This vicinity is truly one of the most delightful places to visit any time of year. The stream is usually full of water, rushing over rocks in front of the buildings. Below the rapids are placid pools which offer peaceful solitude to any weary traveler, an ideal place for study and concentration. Many shade trees including flowering cherry bring a glint to the eye of any artist looking for subjects of pastoral beauty.

As one wanders through the grounds among the numerous buildings, pausing to read the

Oksan Sowon is Korea's second largest Confucian school. It was dedicated to the scholar Yi On-jok (Hoe-jae) in 1572. (HS-154; T-524; T-525; T-526 and Natural Treasure No. 115)

above: *The Yi Dynasty architectural style of buildings and walls at Oksan Sowon permeate the atmosphere with Confucian tradition.* below: *Hoe-jae lived at Tokrak-dang. (HS-413)* next page: *Near Oksan Sowon is the site of Chonghye-sa and a 13-storied pagoda. (NT-40)*

inscriptions, one can almost hear the echo of the students chanting in rhythm to the beat of the teacher's stick.

The main gate is a two-storied pavilion with picturesque charm. Behind the first courtyard is another gate which enters the last compound containing the main shrine of Ch'yein-myo where the *wip'ae* (spirit tablet) of the famed scholar is enshrined. Normally the gate to this last courtyard is locked. To the west is a pavilion with a tablet memorializing Yi On-jok. Oso-gak and Munjipp'an-gak are located to the east. Recently a new library building was constructed which holds the 2,200 volumes of books on 230 different subjects which are preserved here. Oksan Sowon has now been designated by the government as Historic Site No. 154.

Also at Oksan Sowon and in the town of Oksan are three listed Treasures, all designated by the government in 1970. The "List of Successful Candidates for State Civil Service Examination" (Treasure No. 524) and nine volumes of the *Samguk Sagi* (Treasure No. 525) are kept here under lock and key. The *Sam-guk-Sagi* (History of the Three Kingdoms) is one of the oldest historical accounts of early Korean history. The famous calligraphy of Kim Saeng is kept in a private collection of the

family and listed as Treasure No. 526.

After a ten minute walk behind Oksan Sowon a residence of its founder Yi On-jok can be seen. Tokrak-dang was used by Yi On-jok while he was living here. Yangju-am, a small shrine on the compound, was built over the stream and is truly a place of charm and beauty. Poetry plaques written by Yi On-jok and descendants of the scholar are hanging from the walls of this pavilion. On one side is a flowering quince from China which has been designated as Natural Treasure No. 115, Tokrak-dang has been designated as Treasure No. 413.

11. Thirteen- Storied Pagoda of Chonghye- sa Site

(National Treasure No. 40)

This unusual pagoda behind Tokrak-dang is the only one of its type in Korea. It is almost impossible to trace the origin of this pagoda yet scholars are fairly certain that it dates to the Silla post unification period. This pagoda is not typical of the mainstream of Korean style stone pagodas. On a pedestal stands the first 6.5 foot story within which an image was possibly enshrined. The use of the Buddha niche (1'2"×2'6") in pagodas was developed during the construction of earlier wooden type pagodas prior to the popularity of stone. From the second story the space between roof stones is gradually reduced until the top stories seem to blend together. The crown had the usual ball-plate sequence.

This twenty-one foot pagoda is located several hundred yards behind Tokrak-dang on the temple site of Chonghye-sa (Pure Grace Temple). Chonghye-sa prospered until 1592 at which time it was destroyed.

Fields surround this historic relic. A few feet away is a farmhouse with people toiling over their daily chores paying little heed to this unusual National Treasure No. 40. From here over an hour walk up Todok-san the small temple of Todok-sa is reached. This temple was recently built and consists of five buildings.

Fishing is now a popular sport in Korea. The new lake of Tokdong near Kyongju is part of the Pomun Lake Development Project.

12. Other Historic Sites North of Kyongju

Imch'on-sa Site:

Directly south of King Hon-dok's tomb in the stream bed is the temple site of Imch'on (Forest Stream). Only foundation pillar stones remain and can be seen.

Stone Block with Four Buddhist Images:

Located in the field less than half a kilometer from the entrance to Paekyul-sa is a three-foot-square stone with four interesting Buddhist images carved in relief. The roof is shaped like a lotus petal. Some scholars wonder if this might be the site of Howon-sa (Tiger Respect Temple) famous for the tale of Kim Hyon who fell in love with a tiger lady. About 200 meters away are pagoda remains. The largest roof stone is five feet across.

Relief Triad Behind Paegyul-sa:

After reaching the peak of Sokumgang-san behind Paegyul-sa one can climb down the other side about fifty meters and find three Buddhist carved relief images. The center sitting image is 7'6'' high. The hand positions are not clear. The two attendants face inward to the center image. The right attendant's face has disappeared; however, the mandala and crown are clear. Two square holes above the images once were used for a roof structure. (Twenty minute hike from Paegyul-sa)

Grave of Kim Hu-jik:

About 100 meters north of Hwangsong Park is the grave called Kanshin-myo (Advice Giving Grave) which belongs to Kim Hu-jik, a former defense minister. He received the rank of *kanshin* and thus was responsible for giving advice to Chin-p'yong (26th king). This he continued to do even after death. The six foot tablet was erected in 1701 by the Kyongju mayor Nam Chi-hun. The grave circumference is 270 feet while the distance across the mound is 100 feet.

Temple Site Near Hyongok Primary School:

Less than three kilometers from the West Stream and Kumjang Town is the Hyongok Primary School. Opposite this school is a temple site where several stone fragments of a Silla pagoda were found and later moved to the front of the Education Building in Kyongju City. The temple site is about 300 meters west.

Silla Kiln Excavation Site:

Located at the entrance of Hyongok Valley 1.7 kilos from the bridge on the north side of the road are 64,000 square meters of land excavated in 1978. This was the largest known Silla kiln used primarily for roof tile. It was here that a clay image of a bear's head was discovered (see story of Ungsu-sa).

Koch'on Village Temple Site:

After traveling 1.5 kilometers beyond the Hyongok Primary School into Hyongok Valley a small road to the left leads to Koch'on (Old River) Village (less than one kilometer). In the center of the village is a small shrine which honors the Suh Family. Thirty-five years ago six zodiac images were discovered by Ch'oe Nam-ju and are now in the Kyongju National Museum. Stones which came from a three-storied pagoda are seen on the shrine grounds. The temple's name is unknown.

Yongdam-jong (Birthplace of the Tonghak Movement):

About five kilometers from the West Stream is the small village where Ch'oe Che-u, founder of the Tonghak movement, was born in 1824. His grave is nearby. The pavilion of Yongdam-jong (Dragon Pool) was recently reconstructed in a picturesque valley a short drive from the road. It was here that the Tonghak (Eastern Learning) movement germinated.

This indigenous faith, comprised of some characteristics from Confucianism, Buddhism,

and Christianity was highly nationalistic. Fifteen of the 33 signers of the 1919 Independence effort belonged to this movement which came to be known as Ch'ondokyo (from 1905).

A memorial tablet was erected several years ago by the government with the title written by President Park Chung-hee. Dr. Lee Seun-keun, the former President of Dongguk University, composed the inscription which was written by Choi Duk-shin, former Minister of Foreign Affairs and leader of Ch'ondokyo.

Pagoda Remains of Namsa Village:

Beyond the reservoir and in the village of Namsa are a few stone remains of a pagoda. Parts were taken to the Kyongju Police Station and used in the reconstructed pagoda in front of the building.

Three-storied Stone Pagoda Near Namsa Village:

After a twenty minute walk behind Namsa Village an unusually picturesque three-storied Silla pagoda is seen on the upper terraced fields. The left valley trail which passes a small pond should be taken. The total height is 13 feet. The name of the temple is unknown.

Kiln Sites Near Namsa Village

About 200 meters left and behind the village are found several ancient kiln sites from Silla and Koryo periods. Many small pieces of pottery can still be found.

Honghyo Temple Site:

The site is reached after. a thirty-minute hike from Chong-dong (Bell Village) at the end of the road. Honghyo-sa (Great Filial Piety Temple) refers to an interesting legend in which a father was going to sacrifice the life of his son for his mother's life because of poverty.

(1) Four images on a stone block; (2) Site near Paegyul-sa ; (3) Triad relief behind Paegyul-sa; (4) Grave of Kim Hu-jik; (5–6) Entrance gate and shrine of Yongdan-jong (birthplace of Tonghak); (7) Pagoda near Namsa Village; (8) Pagoda remains of Namsa Village; (9) Koch'on Village temple site; (10) Four-sided Buddha rock of Kumgok-sa site

While digging the grave they discovered a bell which brought them good luck. Hung-dok (42nd king) heard of the case and rewarded the man. The temple site is located beyond the last terraced field. Only the remains of a stone wall and a few foundation stones can be seen.

Sokwang-sa Imitation Brick Pagoda:

At Oya Village 12 kilometers from Kyongju City on the main road to Pohang, the temple can be reached after a twenty-minue walk east from the highway. There are only five imitation brick pagodas known to exist in the Kyongju area. Many years ago the Shin family destroyed this pagoda to obtain a better view for a grave site. Recently this pagoda was reconstructed with the remaining stones that could be found. The third story stone is still missing. The largest roof span is 5'3'' across. There is a niche on the side where a Buddhist image was once placed (1'1'' X 1'3''). Nearby is a stone piece of a Silla lantern roof. Several large dolmens can be seen in the fields below.

A Sitting Stone Buddha Image of Angye Village:

One must travel through the village of Yang-dong off the route to Pohang to reach Angye Village. On the opposite side of the reservoir (4.8 kilometers from Yang-dong) a five-foot image can be seen beside the road. The temple site is nearby. The face of the image is badly damaged. The folds of the robe across the back are perfectly sculptured. A lantern roof was placed on the head to give the Buddha the appearance of a Miruk. The left hand is in the lap while the right hand is over the right knee. The right foot is over the left crosslegged. The image is partially hollow inside.

Under the image is a lotus carved pedestal 4'6'' in diameter. Under the pedestal is a stone rectangular block (2' X 3' X 21''). Two deva images are carved in relief in the front. Squatting lions are carved on each end of the stone while on the back side is a carved *nahan* (disciple) image holding a censer and a small pagoda relief. This interesting three-storied pagoda relief is 15 inches high and nine inches wide. Near the image is a roof-cap stone coming from a stone pagoda.

Two Stone Images of Kungye Village:

Kungye Village is located about three kilometers south of Angang Town just off the route to Pohang. The hermitage of Yaksa-am is reached after a fifteen minute walk. The 5'8" Silla stone image has been placed in a small building making it difficult to study. It is set in cement just below the knees as the feet were previously broken and lost. The head of the image was also lost so a new cement head was created, causing grotesque proportions. The capsul in the hand of the Yaksa Yorae is also broken and missing.

The mandala is 7'8" high. On the back side of the mandala is a superb 6'4" three-storied pagoda relief, one of five to be found in the Kyongju area. In the center of the first story is a 13-inch sitting Buddha. The *kamshil* (niche) with a Buddha makes this pagoda relief unique.

Nearby on the other side of the lake is another image housed in a small building. The name of the temple site behind is unknown. This seven-foot sitting image is entirely covered with plaster giving it an unusual appearance. It is unknown how much of the stone is broken under the plaster. The lotus design pedestal is six feet in diameter.

A rectangular rock (1'8" × 4'8") is used to support the pedestal. It contains several fine relief carvings. A deva face and shoulders of a second image are seen on one side while a 15-inch sitting Buddha image is depicted on the other side. On the rear side are two 14-inch relief devas facing each other. Both are kneeling on one knee while one elbow is resting on the other knee which is raised. One hand holds a censer toward the center where a flaming flower-like object is carved.

Four-sided Buddha of Kumgok-sa Site:

One must take the route to Angang Town (21 kilometers from Kyongju). On the road to Taegu travel five kilometers further. At the first small road left before reaching the reservoir drive 3.5 kilometers up this narrow valley. From another reservoir near the end of the road the hiking time is about one hour. The valley is narrow and steep. The stone remains are believed by some scholars to belong to the *sari* pagoda for Priest Won-gwang, one of

(11) Sokwang-sa imitation brick pagoda; (12) Stone image covered with plaster at Kungye Village; (13) Deva carved into pedestal of Kungye Village image; (14) Yaksa Yorae image of Kungye Village; (15) Sitting image of Angye Village; (16–17) Kiln excavation site of 1978 in Hyongok Valley

Silla's earliest and most famous monks.

Several roof stones and other fragments are seen but the cube stone of real importance is a three-foot block carved with four deep Buddha relief images 16 inches high. All four images are sitting with different hand positions. There are few examples of square stone Buddha sculpturing in Korea though the four directional Buddhas are mentioned in the Hwaom Sutra. Though their true identity is not certain one theory is that West is the Amit'a, East is the Yaksa Yorae, North is the Sokkamoni and South is the Miruk Buddha.

Hyong-san Fortress:

This fortress is located on the peak of Hyong-san (Older Brother Mountain) east of the highway to Pohang. After passing the intersection to Angang Town one kilometer a road

to the right leads to Kukdang-san Village (1.8 kilos further). Here a trail leads to Okryon-sa (Jade Lotus Temple) which can be reached after a 40 minute hike. Near the temple are the fortress remains. A wide three meter road used by horses to quickly reach different sections of the inner fortress can still be observed.

Some of the tombs within the fortress may date to the Silla period. A natural spring and a pond at the peak are interestingly shaped to form, the map of Korea though rock wall remains have crumbled all around. The site of a fire tower, used for sending signals from peak to peak to warn of an approaching enemy, is seen near this pond. Constructed in 673 during the reign of Mun-mu (30th king) this Older Brother Mountain Fortress was the central point of defense north of the Silla capital.

Okryon-sa (Jade Lotus Temple) or Hyongsan-sa:

The original temple was evidently dedicated to the last 56th king of Silla, Kyong-sun. A bronze image of Kyong-sun was maintained here even during the Yi Dynasty. However, the wealthy Yu family also used this area for their ancestral tombs. One Yu member threw the bronze image into the Hyongsan River nearby and soon ill fortune struck. About one hundred years ago a wooden image was erected and placed in a mud hut in an attempt to reverse the Yu family calamity. This wooden pillar image can still be seen in the main hall. The red-faced wooden image next to Kyong-sun's image is his son-in-law who became a general. The mural behind represents the four directional sea dragons with King Kyong-sun in the middle. This temple is maintained by the married sect.

An interesting legend tells of a wager King Kyong-sun had with his son-in-law over a flood control project for the capital. (This was probably King Kyong-jong, grandson of Wang-gon, who became 5th king of Koryo in 975. It is recorded that after Silla's surrender Kyong-sun gave his daughter in marriage to this grandson of the 1st Koryo king.) The loser would offer his head as payment. Kyong-sun lost the wager but the son-in-law refused to take his reward by saying, "How can I kill my father? I will only give some small mark as a sign.'' Thus he cut the king across the nose with his sword leaving a gash. This mark is seen on the image in the main hall of this temple.

Tongkang Sowon:

Tongkang Sowon (East River Study Hall) consists of a cluster of buildings overlooking the Hyongsan River. This Yi Dynasty school was built and dedicated to the mother of Yi On-jok (Hoe-jae). Hoe-jae became one of the Yi Dynasty's greatest scholars. He was born in 1491 in the village of Yang-dong a few kilometers south from Tongkang Sowon. The mother's ancestral home (Son family) is still seen in Yang-dong and is called Sobaek-dang (Hundredth Letter House). Further to the west Oksan Sowon was built to honor Hoe-jae in the mid-sixteenth century. Tongkang Sowon is seen near the highway to Pohang a few kilometers beyond the intersection to Angang Town. The railroad runs directly below the buildings yet the view is still magnificent.

(18) At Hyong-san Fortress overlooking Hyong-san River; (19–20) Images of King Kyong-sun (white-faced) and his son-in-law (red-faced) at Okryon-sa; next page Okryon-sa.

Chapter IX
Further Beyond the Silla Capital

1. Pokyong-sa: *Koryo Priest Won-jin Kuksa*
(Treasures No. 252 and No. 430)

Pokyong-sa (Treasured Mirror Temple) may have been founded during the reign of Chinp'yong (26th king) prior to Silla unification. Stone relics do exist from the Koryo period which include several pagodas, a stone memorial tablet and *pudo* (priest's tomb) monument. Both the tablet and *pudo* erected for Priest Won-jin have been designated as Treasures No. 252 and No. 430.

Another legend is recorded that during the reign of Song-dok (33rd king) two priests brought copies of Buddhist sutras with twelve-sided mirrors from India. They gave the mirrors to Priest Il-cho, instructing him to proceed to the east coast and bury them. He was to build a temple calling it "Treasured Mirror."

Pokyong-sa consists of thirteen buildings. The large main gate called Ch'onwang-mun (Heavenly Kings Gate) is reached first. Inside the main gate is a five-storied stone pagoda. In front of the pagoda is a three-foot lotus base stone probably once used for a lantern.

Situated behind the pagoda is Chokkwang-jon (Quiet Light Hall) housing the Piroch'ana Buddha. On the left is a study hall where the four customary instruments found at all temples are kept, the bell, drum, brass gong and wooden carp gong. The long wooden boat which pilgrims traditionally use on their journey to paradise is also depicted in this building.

Directly behind the Chokkwang-jon is the main hall called Taeung-jon which houses the Sokkamoni. On the left is Illohyang-gak in which the 19th Yi Dynasty king Suk-ch'ong used when visiting Pokyong-sa in the late 17th century. Still treasured at this temple are large wood blocks containing carved poetry written by King Suk-ch'ong.

Though the kings of the Yi Dynasty were avid Confucianists there were several rulers who favored Buddhism and Suk-ch'ong was one of them. As he had many concubines his reign was noted for frequent squabbling

between his wives. The most notorious case was the power struggle between Chang Hui-bin and Ch'oe Suk-bin. Concubine Chang's deceit and conniving eventually brought about her own death by poison.

During this period of palace intrigues King Suk-ch'ong often left the capital for the peace of a mountain temple. He came to Pokyong-sa in the spring we are told and as he watched the blossoms he was filled with dreamy thoughts. Poetry began to flow from his brush and was then recorded on wood. Eight of these wood blocks remain with two large characters on each side.

"While taking a spring nap
  I'm unaware of time.
I hear the trill of many birds around.
But when the night falls,
  I also hear the wind and rain,
And viewing the falling blossoms,
  I know of passing years."

King Suk-ch'ong was only 24 in the year 1684 when he wrote these poetic words. Having reigned for ten years he had lost his first queen in childbirth four years earlier. Min, his second queen, could not give him a child. Soon his infatuation for the concubine Chang grew until five years later Queen Min was banished in favor of Chang Hui-bin. One senses in this poem the strain of life bearing down and giving a premonition of more strife to come.

Directly behind the Taeung-jon are several smaller buildings. The structure on the far left is the Palsang-jon (Eight Scenes Hall). Large murals of the eight events during the life of the Buddha are depicted. A smaller building houses the shamanistic spirit trio of Sanshin, Toksong, and Ch'ilsong.

The Wonjin-gak houses the portraits of the temple's renowned priests. Koryo Priest Won-jin Kuksa and the two Yi Dynasty priests, Sa-myong Taesa and his teacher So-san Taesa hold positions of honor. Sa-myong was a

POKYONG-SA

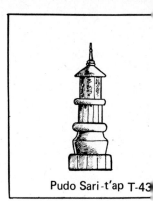

Pudo Sari-t'ap T-43

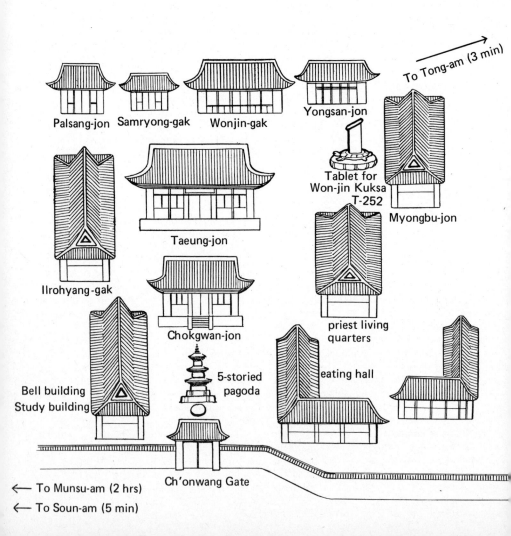

To Tong-am (3 min)

Palsang-jon   Samryong-gak   Wonjin-gak   Yongsan-jon

Tablet for
Won-jin Kuksa
T-252

Myongbu-jon

Ilrohyang-gak

Taeung-jon

priest living
quarters

Chokgwan-jon

Bell building
Study building

5-storied
pagoda

eating hall

Ch'onwang Gate

← To Munsu-am (2 hrs)
← To Soun-am (5 min)

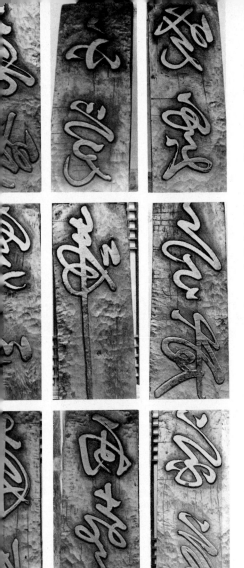

noted militant Buddhist priest who fought valiantly against the Japanese invaders at the end of the 16th century.

Sa-myong was born into the Im Family in 544 in South Kyongsang Province near Miryang but was orphaned at an early age. He traveled to Korea's Diamond Mountains to study under the great Priest So-san who is also pictured in Wonjin-gak on the right.

Sa-myong studied the martial arts under Priest So-san, until eventually his own fame became so great that now he is considered the greatest of Korea's militant monks as well as statesman. Sa-myong and So-san trained the priesthood to defend Korea against the invading Japanese armies. Following the war years Sa-myong became the chief emissary in a mission to Japan in 1604. He completed a peace treaty and returned home with over 3000 released prisoners. In 1610 he died at Haein-sa at the age of 66.

In the center position of the Wonjin-gak hangs the portrait of Won-jin Kuksa who served as head priest of this temple and was tutor to the king's son during the early 13th century. His cremated body was later enshrined at Pokyong-sa.

To the right of the Wonjin-gak is the Yong-san-jon which houses the Sokkamoni Buddha and sixteen *nahan* (disciples of Buddha). The last building located behind the tablet is the Myongbu-jon (Judgment Hall).

The turtle tablet (Treasure No. 252) located before the Myongbu-jon was constructed by order of Ko-jong (23rd Koryo king) after the death of Priest Won-jin in 1221. The head is grotesque while its open mouth is holding a small *kusul*. Turtles sculptured during the Koryo era are usually dragon-like in appearance, rich in design and quite stylized.

After a five minute climb behind this temple a tall fifteen-foot *sari-pudo* (Treasure No. 430) is found on a knoll. This monument is believed to belong to Priest Won-jin. Tall and slender, with an elegant double lotus petal base stone and elaborately designed roof, this six-sided monument towers impressively.

The twelve wood blocks preserved at Pokyong-sa depict the calligraphy of Suk-ch ong, 19th king of the Yi Dynasty.

above left: *In the Wonjin-gak at Pokyong-sa hang the portraits of* (left to right) *Sa-myong, Won-jin and So-san.* below left:*The entrance gate holds the traditional guardian deities.* below center: *The* sari-pudo *is the tomb for Won-jin Kuksa.* *(T-430)* below right: *A memorial tablet on the grounds of Pokyong-sa honors Priest Won-jin.* *(T-252)* above right: *A devil-chasing face adorns the temple door.*

Near the temple is Chongryon-am (Blue Lotus Hermitage) while deeper in the valley from Pokyong-sa are two additional hermitages called Munsu-am (two-hour walk) and Soun-am (five-minute walk). Near Soun-am is a compound with eleven additional impressive *pudo.*

Priest Won-jin was born in 1171, the same year that Ui-jong (18th Koryo king) was banished to Chin-do an island southwest of Korea. Buddhist corruption in the courts had reached a new height. The king, who had an insatiable desire for drink and fair women, spent his time at the temples behaving in such a way that the entire nation was scandalized. No sound counsel could make him mend his ways. The king gave high positions to many uneducated priests who used these positions to further their own gain. Eventually General Chong Chung-bu led a successful uprising and placed the king's uncle Myong-jong (19th Koryo king) on the throne.

Hearing that the banished King Ui-jong had returned as far as Kyongju, General Chong sent General Yi Ui-min with a band of assassins. After members of the king's guards were killed the ex-king was dragged to a nearby temple. General Yi, who was an immense giant of a man, crushed the king in his arms. Stuffing his broken body into two iron kettles placed mouth to mouth, he threw the dead king unceremoniously into the temple's pond. Later the shocked priests raised the king's body and gave it a decent burial.

Shortly after this cruel event the seven-year-old Won-jin entered the temple of Unmun (Cloud Gate). Six years later Won-jin took his vows and became a priest at Pongam-sa (Phoenix Rock Temple) in North Kyongsang Province. This temple has five registered treasures. Later in 1185 when offered another high position Won-jin refused the honor and instead traveled to Kangwon Province.

Again the political scales tipped and Ch'oe Ch'ung-hon killed the court favorite, General Yi Ui-min, to take full control of the throne. In 1198 he deposed the old king and placed a younger brother on the throne called Shin-jong (20th Koryo king). However, Ch'oe ruled the country with an iron fist while the king had little power.

A few years later in 1214 Ko-jong (23rd Koryo king) mounted the throne. His rule was the longest during a period of political turmoil between the Ch'oe family and the Mongols which eventually forced the royalty to take refuge on Kanghwa Island.

In 1215 Won-jin received the rank of *taeson-sa* and became the chief priest of Pokyong-sa. Five years later he became the private tutor of King Ko-jong's fourth son but unfortunately this great priest died the following year at Yongbul-am (Shadow Buddha Hermitage) near Tonghwa-sa (Taegu).

King Ko-jong granted him the title of *kuksa* (National Priest) and built a memorial tablet for him at Pokyong-sa. Pokyong-sa is one of the larger temples in the Kyongju vicinity and is located about 30 kilos north of Pohang City. The two towns of Hunghae and Chongha are passed on the main road north from Pohang along the coast. The temple is five kilometers inland from this main road.

Along the coastline near Pohang diving girls are trained to farm the ocean floor. Called haenyo *they are known for their stamina and ability to stay long periods underwater.*

2. Oo-sa: *The Legend of My Fish Temple*

Oo-sa is literally translated as "My Fish Temple." Its very name draws a curious smile as one wonders how any temple could posses such an undignified title. This temple was built during the reign of Chin-p'yong (26th king) in the early seventh century and was originally called Hangsa-sa (Perpetually Sandy Temple). When Silla rulers came to this valley they always found clean white sand.

Before reaching the temple grounds seven *pudo* (relic container for priest) are seen near the road. Four brightly colored *inwang* guards were elaborately painted on the entrance gates overlooking the lake. The temple grounds have been carefully landscaped with persimmon, crape myrtle, elm, chestnut, maple and pine. Groves of bamboo are seen behind the temple and below the cliffs which tower to the sky.

Oo-sa has eight buildings with the main hall containing the Sokkamoni. Behind the Taeung-jon is the Nahan-jon which was rebuilt recently following a fire. The Ch'ilsong-gak contains the spirits of Toksong and the Dragon King. Also there is a small shrine for the Mountain Spirit. The Taeung-jon appears quite old. The rafters are massive and crudely carved. The floor is formed of thick square blocks. The ornate altar containing the Buddha also appears worn.

Ferocious guards are painted on the main gate to Oo-sa.

Carved and mounted against the ceiling is a flying crane. A legend which originated in China tells why the crane is symbolized as a good luck bird in the Orient.

In ancient times an acclaimed artist was commissioned to sculpture a dragon for the Imperial Temple. The Emperor after gazing upon this masterpiece was first shocked and then furious, for it appeared that the artist had forgotten to paint in the dragon's eyes. The artist was summoned to explain his apparent insulting oversight. He bragged that his work was so authentic that if he painted in the eyes the dragon would escape to heaven.

The Emperor not believeing this braggart's word threatened to have the artist killed. Another artist was summoned to paint in the dragon's eyes. Wishing to please his ruler, he

told him that there was nothing to worry about but even before the paint dried on the eyes, the dragon gave a mighty lurch and flew to paradise taking the entire temple on its back.

The people who watched this event claimed that the dragon flew in the manner of a giant crane. Now the image of a crane is sometimes seen in the Taeung-jon to remind worshippers of this incident. On the rafters of this building are two dragons (with eyes) fighting for the possession of a flaming *kusul* (jewel) hanging in the middle.

The eminent Priest Hye-gong visited this temple at which time the name was changed from Hangsa-sa to Oo-sa. He was known to have the power of healing, But Hye-gong's behavior was consistently strange. He drank excessively and was frequently seen with a basket thrown over his shoulder. Thus the people called him the "basket-carrying" monk. Hye-gong often went into the temple well to meditate and though he was sitting in water his robe never was wet.

In many ways this unconventional monk was very similar to great Priest Won-hyo and

left: *The portrait of Cha-jang is seen at Chajang-am near Os-sa.* center: *The buildings of Oo-sa are nestled in the peaks south of Pohang and portray an aura of serenity.* right: *Wonhyo-am near Oo-sa is named for Korea's most famous monk.*

apparently the two priests were friends. On one occasion when Priest Won-hyo was residing at Oo-sa while compiling a Buddhist commentary he was visited by Hye-gong. Won-hyo asked many difficult questions which often had no answer; however, Hye-gong always answered them in a jesting manner.

One day the two priests went fishing. Again the unconventional habits of these two monks are noted for normally priests do not eat flesh. However, the catch was good and they caught several fish which they ate by the side of the stream. Following their fish meal both priests needed to defecate. After relieving themselves in the stream they noticed that from the feces swam two fish.

One swam upstream into the current while the other floated downstream. Won-hyo pointed to the stronger fish and exclaimed "That's my fish!" Hye-gong of course claimed that the stronger fish belonged to him. This humorus situation of which fish was whose, argued by the two priests, so impressed the inhabitants that they soon called the temple "My Fish Temple" in memory of this peculiar incident.

The small hermitage of Chajang-am named to honor Priest Cha-jang can be reached after a twenty-minute walk up the steep slope behind Oo-sa. A portrait of this priest can be seen. Behind a glass case is the image of the Kwanseum Posal (Bodhisattva of Mercy). In an annex building can be seen the Sanshin (Mountain Spirit) and Ch'ilsong (Seven Star Spirit). Behind the Sanshin is a strangely shaped rock called *chishin* (earth spirit). In the folk culture of Korea the *chishin* is a most important spirit which must be placated when a family moves into a new home.

It is unusual to find the *chishin* depicted in this manner at a temple. The natural rock closely resembles a face. The building was constructed over this large boulder. Nearby the cliff wall plummets hundreds of feet below to the streambed. Perched like an eagle's nest, it is a small miracle that this hermitage has not tumbled over the precipice.

Unlike Hye-gong, Priest Cha-jang, whose family name was Kim, came from the ranks of the nobility. His parents at first had no children.

His father prayed with the promise that if he could have a son he would make him a bridge to eternal paradise. His wife dreamed that a falling star entered her womb. She conceived and in due time gave birth to a son on Buddha's birthday.

He was orphaned early in life and later as a young man deserted his wife and children. He sold his estate to have a temple built and led the life of a hermit priest. Because of his noble birth he repeatedly was asked by the king to take a responsible position in court. Cha-jang adamantly refused until the king issued an ultimatum saying, "If you do not accept, I will have your head severed for disobedience to the king."

"I would rather die keeping the commandments of Buddha for one day than live for a hundred years while breaking them." he retorted.

Seeing the wisdom in his classic reply the king bowed to the will of Cha-jang. He became one of Silla's greatest priests.

Numerous other tales are told about this honored priest and the many miracles he performed. Priest Cha-jang founded more than a dozen temples throughout the kingdom. Probably the most important is the present temple of Tongdo-sa near Pusan which is now the largest in Korea. Personal belongings of Priest Cha-jang are treasures at Tongdo-sa. Also other relics were brought back from China by Priest Cha-jang and enshrined at Tongdo-sa in 647. According to records these relics included a piece of the skull and a tooth of Buddha.

Priest Cha-jang suggested the use of the T'ang court dress because of its elegance and dignity. The style was accepted and worn by the people of Silla. The T'ang calendar was also adopted and events were recorded by the reign of the Chinese emperors both in official and unofficial records. He lived his final days quietly in the T'aebaek Mountains.

Besides Chajang-am there is one other hermitage called Wonhyo-am located in the narrow gorge to the west about a 25-minute walk from Oo-sa. Wonhyo-am is dedicated to the Kwanseum Posal. Of special interest is the signboard in the shape of a large fish over the main worship room. Named for one of the greatest priests of Silla, and probably all Korea, this humble hermitage is beautifully landscaped with shrubbery and flowers. Several large persimmon trees are on the grounds. Nearby is a rocky bluff called Tong-dae-am. The view from here to the Eastern Sea is truly spectacular. Oo-sa and the adjacent lake can be seen far below. This could well be one view without parallel for this vicinity.

Oo-sa with its unique name is located about nineteen kilos south of Pohang City. Take the route past the steel refinary. At Yongdok Town (10 kilos from Pohang) a right turn is taken. The left side of the stream is followed for an additional five kilos until the stream is crossed by a bridge. After 3.2 kilos of poor road a reservoir is reached. A road on the right side will soon reach Oo-sa a few minutes from the dam.

3. Manghae- sa: *The Legend of Ch'o-yong* *(Treasures No. 173 and No. 382)*

The present buildings of Manghae (Viewing Sea) Temple were constructed in 1828. This valley has been used as a temple site since the days of Silla when Hon-gang (49th king) wished to honor the Dragon Spirit of the East Sea and had a temple built. Of the many roof tiles that have been found some have a blue glaze typical of the Koryo period. Walls of earlier temple construction are noted nearby.

Behind the present buildings on the former site are twin *sari-pudo* (relic monuments for the cremated priests' remains) which were reconstructed by the Japanese and have been designated as Treasure No. 173. They were probably erected during the Koryo period. These octagonal lantern-shaped *pudo* stand about ten feet high and are twenty feet in circumference.

Some stones that were missing were newly cut during reconstruction to complete these monuments fully. Portions of the roof stones are broken; however, the slope of the roof remains regal and elegant.

Upon the death of his father King Hon-gang ascended the throne in 875. Hon-gang ruled for eleven years. On one occasion King Hon-gang and his attendants went to the beaches near Ulsan to enjoy a few days of leisure. As he was preparing to return a dense fog suddenly enveloped the entire countryside.

The royal geomancer was summoned. He said that the Sea Dragon was at play nearby and due respect must be given. The king then decreed that a suitable place be found to honor this dragon. Shortly after, a scenic spot was selected which had a view over the Eastern Sea. A temple was erected and named "Viewing the Sea Temple."

One of the dragon's seven sons returned with the king to Kyongju to become his faithful subject. The king named him Ch o-yong. He was a bright and eager lad who learned rapidly. When he came of age he was offered the most beautiful maiden in the kingdom as his wife.

Her beauty drew such attention that the Plague Spirit fell in love with her. He visited many nights while Ch'o-yong was away. On one occasion Ch'o-yong returned unexpectedly and was surprised to see four feet protruding from beneath the blankets. He chuckled over the humor of the situation and composed a song which he sang as he danced before the two caught in adultery.

The Plague Spirit rose from the bed and fell on his knees before Ch'o-yong saying, "I was captivated by the ravishing beauty of your wife and could not control my passion.

"I know that my actions can never be forgiven but this I can do to repay you. Hereafter, whenever I see your portrait on any doorway I will not enter the house."

The Plague Spirit then suddenly disappeared leaving Ch'o-yong amazed. For many centuries the Korean people would hang the picture of Ch'o-yong on their gates as protection against the evil spirits which bring disease.

It has been speculated that if this legend refers to an actual person, Ch'o-yong might well have been a foreigner. The fact that he did not become angry when his wife was seduced is given as a reason. No Korean would be able to contain his temper under circumstances similar to this.

This particular story of Ch'o-yong leads one to ponder about the morality differences of Silla compared to the rigid codes existing during the Confucian period of the Yi Dynasty. There appeared to be a greater sexual freedom, liberality and willingness to condone deviant morality and even joke about it.

Peppers dry before the portrait of Priest Cha-jang at Chajang-am, a hermitage above Oo-sa. A fish plaque at Wonhyo-am is a reminder of the unusual legend of Oo-sa. A row of pudo are noted at the entrance of Oo-sa.

The author priest of the *Samguk Yusa* was celibate yet many of his stories describe illicit affairs in an earthy manner. These stories and many others give the *Samguk Yusa* a spicy eroticism which may well have existed in early Silla and continued during the Koryo period. Apparently Buddhism did not keep aloof and remote from occasional erotic behavior among the people and these stories have come to us among many of the favorite legends of Silla.

To reach Manghae-sa the expressway to Onyang and Ulsan must be taken. The distance is 48 kilos from Kyongju. After exiting at the Ulsan tollgate take the right road at the first junction. After traveling 3.8 kilometers from this rotary a small road to the right leads to Manghae-sa. Near Manghae-sa is the temple site of Yongch'u-sa where the remains of two three-storied pagodas are seen. Beyond the temple site is Munsu-am (2 hrs). Further up the highway in another valley (about a 45-minute walk) is the village of Ch'onsong where a three-storied pagoda (Treasure No. 382) punctuates the village landscape. An eleborate *pudo* assemblage is also evident in this vicinity.

A typical three-storied pagoda is located in a small village near Manghae-sa. (T-382) The two sari-pudo *located at Manghae-sa site were erected during the Koryo period. (T-173)*

4. Soknam-sa: *Beauty and Tranquility in the Kaji Mountains* (*Treasure No. 369*)

Though the temple of Soknam (Southern Rock) has few legends it is today one of the larger temples of the area and located in a valley of unparalleled beauty. It is possible to drive to the temple. From the Kyongju tollgate it is a short drive to Onyang (29.3 km). The road from Onyang Town westward on the backroad to Miryang is unpaved. From the tollgate of Onyang it is about 12.3 kilometers to the temple parking lot.

Soknam-sa was founded in 825 during the final years of Hon-dok's (41st king) reign. In the reign of the previous Silla ruler his nephew Ae-jang, Hon-dok and younger brother Hung-dok conspired to force Ae-jang to commit suicide in 809. Hon-dok had served as regent for young Ae-jang and also become defense minister.

Great Priest To-ui established Soknam-sa and his tomb monument is located behind the temple. This 12-foot *sari-pudo* has been shaped with a 12-foot circumference. Two guardian figures (possibly the *sach'onwang*) are seen carved on the body of this monument. The other two images were destroyed. Also reliefs of the *sari* door can be seen. The base has four lions crouching amid cloud designs. Lotus petals round out the base support in typical Silla style. The roof stone has a tile design while the cap is a stone lotus bud.

At present there are 80 nuns living at Soknam-sa. This temple became a nunnery after the Korean war. During the Yi Dynasty the temple housed one thousand priests and had many buildings. This temple extended all the way to the parking lot. At the entrance is a grindstone (4'6'' in dia.) used during the Yi Dynasty period. Within the temple is a stone

The entrance gate of Soknam-su has ferocious guards painted on the wooden doors The pagoda was reconstructed in 1973 in the main courtyard of the temple.

cistern (9'6" X 4') dating from the Silla period and still in use.

Before the Japanese wars of 1592 Soknam boasted of having the tallest pagoda in Korea. This 15-storied structure was pulled down by the Japanese soldiers. In 1973 with a few of the remaining stone blocks of this pagoda the temple reconstructed a three-storied pagoda in the main courtyard of the temple. The present pagoda is 36 feet high and 15 feet wide. It is called the Sokka-t'ap to honor the Sokkamoni (Historic Buddha) as a *sari* of the Buddha was brought from abroad to be enshrined in this pagoda.

Another three-storied pagoda may date to the late Silla period but is probably early Koryo. It is located near the Chosa-dang and has been designated as a Provincial Treasure No. 22.

Kaji Mountain provides a natural backdrop to the scenic surroundings of Soknam-sa, a large nunnery south of Kyongju. below: Earthenware pots are kept in the temple court-yard to be used for preserving winter foods for the nuns.

SOKNAM-SA

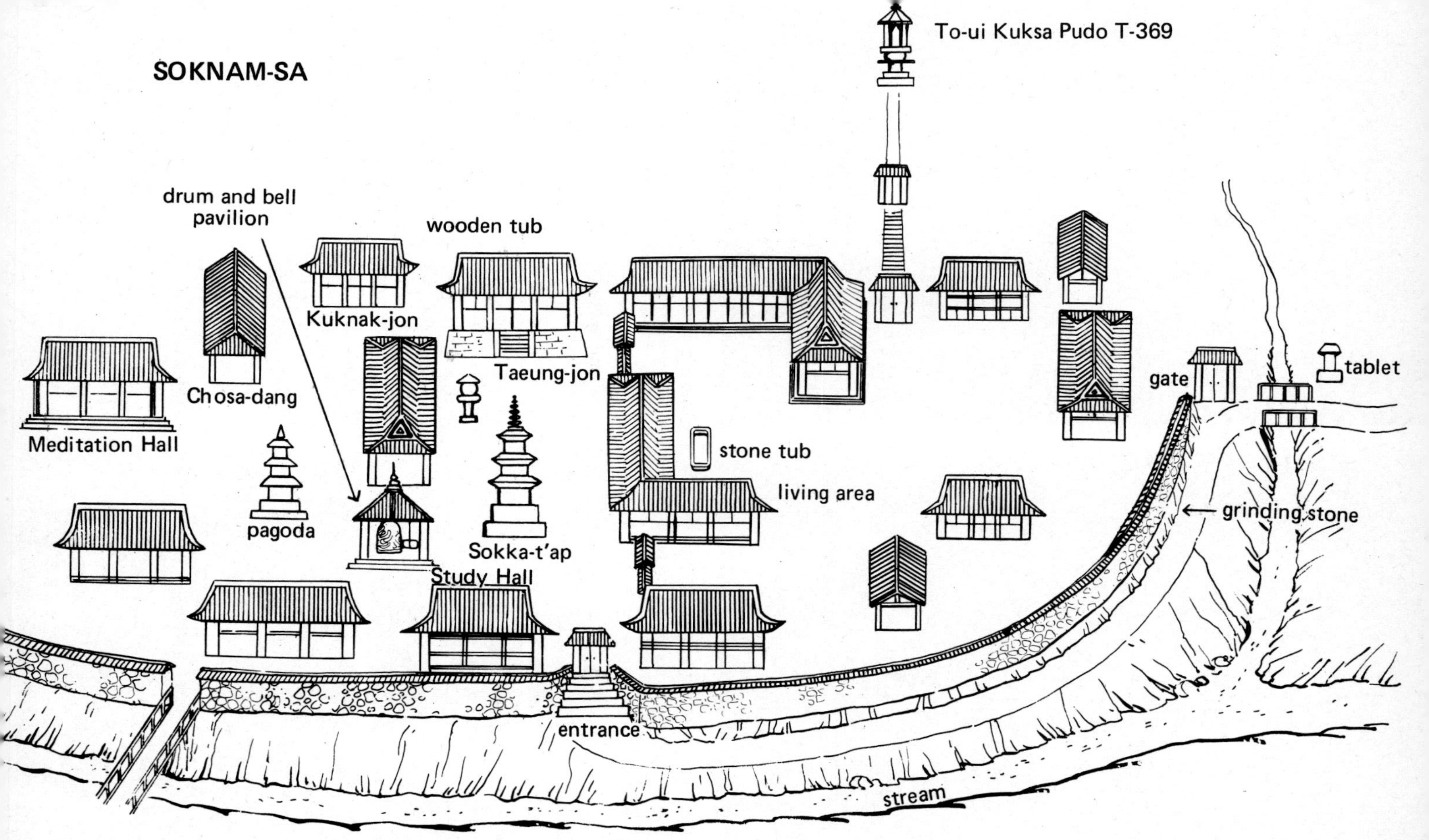

To-ui Kuksa Pudo T-369

tablet

grinding stone

gate

stream

stone tub

living area

entrance

Taeung-jon

Sokka-t'ap

Study Hall

wooden tub

Kuknak-jon

drum and bell
pavilion

Chosa-dang

pagoda

Meditation Hall

above: *The* sach'onwang *(Four Heavenly Kings) images are often portrayed as guards at temple entrances.* below: *The* pudo *or tomb monument for Priest To-ui is located behind Soknam-sa. (T-369)*

A turbulent stream tumbles over rocks into lazy pools in front of Soknam-sa making the entrance walkway delightful for those who enjoy outdoor sights and sounds. The large elms and maples in this valley groan with age and exhibit gnarled beauty.

The main entrance is next to the study hall. The nuns' living quarters are on the right. The Taeung-jon is the center hall and houses the Sokkamoni Buddha. Behind this hall is a large boat-shaped wooden dugout. A bell and drum pavilion are located next to the study hall. Toward the rear of the temple grounds is the Kuknak-jon, housing the Amit'a Buddha of Western Paradise.

Nearby is the Chosa-dang which is often kept locked. This building houses the portraits of many noted priests who were associated with Soknam-sa. If a key is obtained to the center room the portrait of To-ui may be seen in a special place of honor. A new large meditation hall further west was recently constructed.

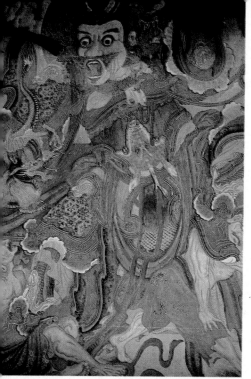

The sach'onwang *guards are usually found at larger temples. They are often depicted crushing demons beneath their feet. Representing the four cardinal directions they hold swords, dragons, pagodas and stringed instruments.*

Though the valley below is often used as a resort for the local inhabitants the nuns discourage any loud talking, eating or smoking on the temple premises. Proper respect must be maintained by everyone at all times while within the temple compound. As is typical of all nunneries the temple grounds are immaculately clean and care is taken to keep the buildings in good repair.

After the temple was destroyed during the Japanese Wars of 1592 it lay in ruin for many years. In 1841 during the reign of Hon-jong (24th Yi king) a small temple was rebuilt by two priests, T'ag-nyong and Sol-ch'ol. Only two buildings date to this reconstruction. The mountains behind Soknam-sa have the name of Kaji-san. The word *kaji* refers to one of the nine sects of Korean Zen (Hwaom) established by Priest To-ui during the latter part of Silla.

right : *The portrait of Soknam-sa's founder is enshrined in the Chosa-dang.*

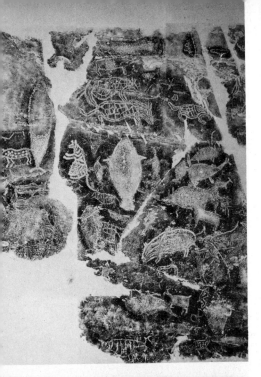

Pangu-dae (Flat Turtle Place)

Recently discovered in the last decade and acclaimed as a rare treasure is the wall inscription with animal and fish figures located at Pangu-dae about seven kilometers from Onyang. The road from Onyang north should be taken on the west side of the expressway past the school. A small road to the right leads over the expressway and down to Pangu-dae Valley. A picturesque lake with a 300-year-old pavilion honoring the scholar Chong Mong-ju decorates the landscape. Considered one of Korea's earliest inscriptions, a large ink rubbing has been made and is on display in Seoul's National Museum.

left: *Pangu-dae pictorial inscriptions was discovered recently.* below: *Musical instruments such as the gong and drum call the priests to worship.* next page: *While at worship the shoes are left outside the sanctuary.*

Chapter X
Appendix and Index

ANCESTRY OF SILLA KINGS AND TOMB INFORMATION

1. *HYOK-KO-SE* (赫居世) 57 BC–4 AD (60-year rule) Map: p. 60–61

Ancestry: (Pak family: reign title, *Ko-so-gan*) As the first ruler of the Pak Clan he was found according to a legend in 69 BC in an egg-like gourd herald by a shining light and kneeling white horse at Na-jong near Nam-san(South Mountain). The word gourd in Korean is *pak-a-ji* which may have given the family name to this clan. He was selected king at age 12 by six village elders (Yi, Ch'ong, Son, Ch'oe, Pae and Sol) who witnessed his dramatic appearance in the country called Sorabol. At age 16 Hyok-ko-se married A-ryong. His queen was born from the rib of a dragon according to a legend in the well behind Sungdok-jon. She had a chicken's beak which soon fell off after bathing in a stream near Half Moon Fortress. In 37 BC Hyok-ko-se built Kum-song (Gold Fortress) on the slopes of Toham-san for his palace. He and his queen traveled throughout the six villages teaching farming methods and the silk culture industry. Upon his death his son Nam-hae ascended the throne.

Tomb: Historic Site No. 172 (O-nung, Five Tombs)

    Circumference: (a) 380 feet (b) 262 feet (c) 188 feet (d) 150 feet (e) 297 feet

    Distance Across: (a) 130 feet (b) 85 feet (c) 50 feet (d) 53 feet (e) oblong: 124 feet by 65 feet

    Altar: 8' × 4'10"; Ht. 4'6"

2. *NAM-HAE* (南解) 4 AD–24 AD (20-year rule) Map: p. 60–61

Ancestry: (Pak family: reign title, *Ch'a-ch'a-ung*) Nam-hae was the only known son of Hyok-ko-se. He took the royal title meaning sorcerer and was considered the chief of shamans. His eldest son by Queen Un-je succeeded him. His second son Nae-no had no heir. Nam-hae's eldest daughter A-hyo was married to Sok T'al-hae in 6 AD. T'al-hae became prime minister in 10 AD and 4th king in 57 AD.

Tomb: Historic Site No. 172 (O-nung, Five Tombs)

3. *YU-RI* (儒理) 24 AD–57 AD (33-year rule) Map: p. 60–61

Ancestry: (Pak family; reign title, *Ni-gil-gum*) Yu-ri was first son of Nam-hae. He had two sons by Queen Sa-yo who later became 5th and 7th rulers of Silla. When Nam-hae died court elders and Yu-ri tried to convince T'al-hae to take the throne; however, he refused, saying that the kingdom should go to the man with the most teeth. The reign title of "many teeth" for the king lasted for 18 rulers. After the death of his brother-in-law, T'al-hae of the Sok Clan became ruler. In 28 AD the first *hangga* was written and in 32 AD seventeen civil positions were established by the government.

Tomb: Historic Site No. 172 (O-nung, Five Tombs)

4. *T'AL-HAE* (脫解) 57 AD–80 AD (23-year rule) Map: p. 284–285

Ancestry: (Sok family: reign title. none) T'al-hae was the first of the Sok Clan to sit on a Silla throne. Legends tell that he was hatched from an egg and later discovered in a box on a ship drifting offshore on the east coast. King Nam-hae married T'al-hae to his first daughter, A-hyo. T'al-hae was born in 4 BC and died at the age of 85. Legends tell that he was seven feet tall. He made his home at Panwol-song which later became the palace of Silla rulers until the fall of the dynasty. In 65 AD Kim Al-chi the first of the Kim Clan was found in a gold box at Kyerim (Chicken Forest) announced by a crowing rooster. T'al-hae adopted Kim Al-chi as a son. Because of the origin of Silla's three clan kings the people became known to the outside world as the "chicken people." King T'al-hae's grandson became 9th king of Silla. Seven other members of the Sok Clan sat on the throne of Silla until 356. After the death of T'al-hae the second son of King Yu-ri became King P'a-sa. T'al-hae's body was first buried in a well but later was reburied on an eastern hill in a plaster cast.

Tomb: Historic Site No. 174

    Circumference: 150 feet; Distance Across: 54 feet; Altar: 4'6" × 2'9"; Ht. 2'8"

5. *P'A-SA* (婆娑) 80 AD–112 (32-year rule) Map: p. 60–61

Ancestry: (Pak family; reign title, none) P'a-sa was second son of King Yu-ri by Queen Sa-yo. Though King T'al-hae had a son called Ku-ch'u the kingdom went back to the PakClan after T'al-hae's death. P'a-sa had a son by Queen Sa-ch'o who became 6th ruler in 112. It is thought that the first son of King Yu-ri was not immediately selected because of low intelligence; however, he became 7th king.

Tomb: Historic Site No. 172 (O-nung, Five Tombs)

6. *CHI-MA* (祇摩) 112–134 (22-year rule) Map: p. 186–187

Ancestry: (Pak family; reign title, none) Chi-ma was the only recorded son by King P'a-sa by the concubine Sa-sung. Chi-ma had no heir by Queen Ae-rye so upon his death his uncle, the elder brother of his father, became 7th king. This uncle must have been over eighty when he ascended the throne.

Tomb: Historic Site No. 221
Circumference: 130 feet; Distance Across: 45 feet; Altar: 3'9" × 2'8"; Ht. 2'0"

7. *IL-SONG* (逸聖) 134–154 (20-year rule) Map: p. 186–187

Ancestry: (Pak family; reign title, none) Il-song was the eldest son of Yu-ri (3rd king). As a younger brother and nephew ruled before him it is strange that Il-song did not reign sooner. He must have lived over 100 years. His only son A-dal-la was born to Queen Nae-rae, a daughter of King Chi-ma.

Tomb: Historic Site No. 173
Circumference: 153 feet; Distance Across: 56 feet; Altar: 4'0" × 2'8"; Ht. 2'0"

8. *A-DAL-LA* (阿達羅) 154–184 (30-year rule) Map: p. 186–187

Ancestry: (Pak family; reign title, none) A-dal-la was the first son of King Il-song. A-dal-la had no heir so the throne went to a grandson of Sok T'al-hae. A-dal-la was the last of the Pak Clan to rule until 913 in the final days of the dynasty.

Tomb: Historic Site No. 219 (Sam-nung)
Circumference: 193 feet; Distance Across: 69 feet; Altar: 3'9" × 2'8"; Ht. 2'0"

9. *POL-HYU* (伐休) 184–196 (12-year rule)

Ancestry: (Sok family; reign title, none) Pol-hyu was son of Ku-ch'u and grandson of King T'al-hae. Pol-hyu had two sons, Kol-jong and Im-ae, neither one of whom became kings. However, three of Pol-hyu's grandsons became 10th, 11th and 12th rulers. Pol-hyu had the reputation of being an excellent fortune teller and was often referred to as a holy man.

Tomb: Unknown

10. *NAE-HAE* (奈解) 196–230 (34-year rule)

Ancestry: (Sok family; reign title, none) Nae-hae was the son of Prince Im-ae and grandson of King Pol-hyu. Nae-hae had two sons, U-no and I-um, neither of whom became rulers. However, in 310 a grandson of Nae-hae and son of U-no became 16th and last king of the Sok Clan. According to the king's will when he died a cousin became the 11th ruler. It appears that he was also Nae-hae's son-in-law.

Tomb: Unknown

11. *CHO-BUN* (助賁) 230–247 (17-year rule)

Ancestry: (Sok family; reign title, none) Cho-bun was the eldest son of Kol-jong and grandson of King Pol-hyu, 9th ruler of Silla. Cho-bun, cousin of King Nae-hae, had two sons, Yu-rye and Kol-suk. The eldest son Yu-rye became 14th ruler. Cho-bun's daughter Kwang-myong married Mi-ch'u who later became 13th ruler and first of the KimClan to reign. Upon the death of Cho-bun a younger brother became next ruler.

Tomb: Unknown

12. CHOM-HAE (沾解) 247–262 (15-year rule)
Ancestry: (Sok family; reign title, none) Chom-hae was the second son of Kol-jong and grandson of King Pol-hyu, 9th ruler of Silla. As Chom-hae had no heir. Mi-ch'u, a nephew by marriage, became the first of the Kim Clan to reign in 262. Mi-ch'u was a 7th generation descendant of Kim Al-chi who was discovered in a gold box in Kyerim (Chicken Forest) during the reign of T'al-hae (4th king). Diplomatic relations were first established with Koguryo during Chom-hae's reign.
Tomb: Unknown

13. MI-CH'U (味鄒) 262–284 (22-year rule) Map: p. 60–61
Ancestry: (Kim family; reign title, none) Mi-ch'u was first of the Kim Clan to reign and 7th generation descendant of Kim Al-chi. Lineage was: Al-chi, Se-han, A-do, Su-ryu, Yuk-p'o, Ku-do and Mi-ch'u. Kim Al-chi was found in Kyerim in March 65 AD. The mother of Mi-ch'u was Princess Sul-lye of the Pak Clan while his queen was Kwang-myong, a member of the Sok family and daughter of Cho-bun (11th king). From Mi-ch'u 38 descendants of rulers came from the Kim Clan. Mi-ch'u had no heir but the son of younger brother Mal-gu became 17th king. After the death of Mi-ch'u an older brother of his queen and son of the late King Cho-bun became 14th king. During the reign of Mi-ch'u the name of Kyerim (Chicken Forest) was given to the country and the kingdom became known as the "Land of the Chicken People." According to legend the tomb of Mi-ch'u is called the "Bamboo Tomb" because of a strange army wearing bamboo leaves that disappeared in front of this tomb after helping Silla win a major battle.
Tomb: Historic Site No. 175
    Circumference: 520 feet; Distance Across: 210 feet; Altar: 5'6" × 3'6" Ht. 3'0"

14. YU-RYE (儒禮) 284–298 (14-year rule)
Ancestry: (Sok family; reign title, none) Yu-rye was the eldest son of Cho-bun (7th king). His mother was from the Pak Clan. As Yu-rye had no heir upon his death a nephew, son of younger brother Kol-suk, became 15th king. Legends tell that Yu-rye's mother was struck by a falling star resulting in pregnancy and the birth of Yu-rye. The palace of Panwol-song was reconstructed. Coastal attacks by Japanese were frequent and the king wished to build a navy for protection. Contacts with Paekche were frequent.
Tomb: Unknown

15. KI-RIM (基臨) 298–310 (12-year rule)
Ancestry: (Sok family: reign title, none) Ki-rim was the only known son of Kol-suk who was a younger brother of Yu-rye(14th king). Ki-rim had no heir and after his death the throne went to a 3rd generation cousin, Hul-hae, whose common ancestry was the great-great-grandfather Pol-hyu (9th king) of Silla. Some sources indicate that in 307 the name of Silla was formally used though other sources place the name in the reign of Chi-jung or Pob-hung. Silla means "New Embrace" implying a unity of the people to follow the virtuous kings.
Tomb: Unknown

16. HUL-HAE (訖解) 310–356 (46-year rule)
Ancestry: (Sok family; reign title, none) Hul-hae was the last of the Sok Clan to rule in Silla. He was son of U-no and grandson of Nae-hae (10th king). Hul-hae had no heir so upon his death the kingdom went to the Kim Clan where it remained for 557 years. Nae-mul was nephew of Mi-ch'u. During Hul-hae's reign Paekche armies invaded Silla for the first time.
Tomb: Unknown

17. NAE-MUL (奈勿) 356–402 (46-year rule) Map: p. 60–61.
Ancestry: (Kim family; reign title, none) Nae-mul was the first of 36 rulers from the Kim Clan who held the throne of Silla in succession until 913. Descendant of Kim Al-chi he was son of Mal-gu, a

younger brother of Mi-ch'u (13th king). Nae-mul had four sons by Queen Po-ban who was cousin and daughter of his uncle Mi-ch'u. His eldest son became Nul-chi (19th king). However, when Nae-mul died a distant relative, an uncle by marriage, became 18th king. The reign of Nae-mul marks the beginning point of the Silla Dynasty as previously the leadership rotated among three clan members. Chinese culture and literature came into vogue and Nae-mul's name was the first of a Silla ruler to appear in historical Chinese records.

Tomb: Historic Site No. 188
　　　　Circumference: 226 feet; Distance Across: 80 feet; Altar: 4'0 × 3'0" Ht. 2'0"

18. *SHIL-SONG* (實聖) 402–417 (15-year rule)
Ancestry: (Kim family; reign title, none) Shil-song was son of Tae-so-ji who was a 6th generation descendant of Kim Al-chi. His mother was member of the Sok Clan. Shil-song's queen was daughter of King Mi-ch'u and he married his own daughter to Nul-chi. He had no male heir by Queen A-ryu. Before his reign Shil-song had been a captive of Koguryo for 9 years. In 402 he sent Mi-sa-hun, a son of Nae-mul, to Japan as a hostage and guarantee of a treaty. In 412 Shil-song sent another son of Nae-mul as a guarantee hostage to Koguryo. In 417 the king plotted to kill Nul-chi, eldest son of Nae-mul, who had recently returned as an emissary to Koguryo. The plot failed and Shil-song was killed instead. Nul-chi claimed the crown.
Tomb: Unknown

19. *NUL-CHI* (訥祇) 417–458 (41-year rule)
Ancestry: (Kim family; reign title, *Ma-rip-kan*) Nul-chi born in 386 was eldest son of Nae-mul (17th king). His queen was daughter of King Shil-song whom he killed to take the throne. At the time of his father's death Nul-chi was considered too young to rule and his uncle by marriage had more political power; thus this uncle Shil-song became king. Of Nul-chi's three younger brothers the first, Mi-sa-hun, was sent to Japan at the age of ten while Pok-ho was sent to Koguryo in 412. Pak Chae-sang, Korea's first true patriot, was able to rescue both the king's younger brothers but was martyred by the Japanese. Mi-sa-hun married a daughter of Pak Chae-sang. Third brother of Nul-chi married his son Sup-po to Cho-saeng, daughter of Nul-chi. Marriages of cousins were common in Silla. Buddhism first arrived in Silla through the efforts of Priest A-do or Priest Muk-ho-ja though the religion did not flourish until 100 years later during the reign of Pob-hung (23rd king). The title of "many teeth ruler" previously used by earlier kings was replaced by the title "great chief."
Tomb: Unknown

20. *CHA-BI* (慈悲) 458–479 (21-year rule)
Ancestry: (Kim family: reign title, none) Cha-bi was the eldest son of King Nul-chi by Queen A-ro. Upon his death his third son became So-ji (21st king). Cha-bi's sister married a cousin whose offspring became Chi-jung (22nd king). In 479 Japan was defeated in an invasion attempt. Myonghwalsan-song was built to protect the eastern boundaries.
Tomb: Unknown

21. *SO-JI* (炤知) 479–500 (21-year rule)
Ancestry: (Kim family; reign title, none) So-ji (sometimes called Pi-ch'o) was third son of Cha-bi and his mother was the daughter of Mi-sa-hun, younger brother of King Nul-chi. So-ji was great-grandson of Pak Che-sang. So-ji had no heir and in 489 killed his queen due to an illicit love affair she was having with a Buddhist priest. Upon his death a cousin became king.
Tomb: Unknown

22. *CHI-JUNG* (智證) 500–514 (14-year rule)
Ancestry: (Kim family; reign title, none) Chi-jung's father was Sup-po who married Princess Cho-saeng, a daughter of Nul-chi. Sup-po was also a nephew of Nul-chi and cousin of his wife. Chi–jung

had two sons by Queen Yon-je with the eldest becoming Pob-hung (23rd king). The younger brother Ip-chong became the father of Chin-hung (24th king) of Silla. The custom of burying servants alive for the departed king was terminated. The name Silla was now definitely being used as the official name for the kingdom.

Tomb: Unknown

23. *POB-HUNG* (法興) 514–540 (26-year rule) Map: p 214–215

Ancestry: (Kim family; reign title, *Kon-won*) Pob-hung was the first ruler to take the Chinese title of "wang" for ruler and be given a posthumous title. Pob-hung was the eldest son of King Chi-jung. Buddhism became so influential that the king neglected his duties and became a priest at Aegong-sa while Queen P'o-do became a nun at Yonghung-sa. Yi Ch'a-don was martyred in 527 and gave Buddhism its strongest impetus since the period of Priest A-do. As Pob-hung had no heir the crown was passed to a nephew, son of younger brother Ip-chong. In 522 two sisters were sent to Kaya for royal marriages. The king promulgated laws that prohibited killing animals on certain days. Pob-hung's posthumous name was Won-jong. (1st Silla king to use)

Tomb: Historic Site No. 176

Circumference: 141 feet; Distance Across: 50 feet; Altar: None

24. *CHIN-HUNG* (眞興) 540–576 (36-year rule) Map: p. 214–215

Ancestry: (Kim family; reign title, *Kae-guk*) Chin-hung was born in 533 and became king at age 7. His mother, a member of the Pak Clan, ruled as regent. Silla was a rapidly expanding as a powerful nation. Four tablets designating the boundaries of Silla still remain today and have been listed as National Treasures. The *hwarang* movement emerged during this period. Buddhism continued to prosper and Chin-hung also became a priest. The Kaya Kingdom in the south fell to Silla. The *kaya-gum*, a musical instrument, was first introduced from Kaya and has since found its way into the hearts of the Korean people. Chin-hung's second son became Chin-ji (25th king). Tong-nyun, Chin-hung's eldest son, did not rule; however, his offspring became Chin-p'yong (26th king). During Chin-hung's reign the first history of Silla was written. Hwangyong-sa, Silla's largest temple, was constructed during this period. Chin-hung's posthumous name was Sam-maeg-jong.

Tomb: Historic Site No. 177

Circumference: 198 feet; Distance Across: 77 feet; Altar: None

25. *CHIN-JI* (眞智) 576–579 (3-year rule) Map: p. 214–215

Ancestry: (Kim family; reign title, none) Chin-ji was second son of King Chin-hung. Queen Chi-do was of the Pak Clan. Chin-ji died early in his reign and was succeeded by his nephew Chin-p'yong. Grandson of Chin-ji was later to become the famous Mu-yol (29th king) who began unification of Silla. Chin-ji's posthumous name was Sa-ryun.

Tomb: Historic Site No. 178 (same tomb for King Mun-song)

Circumference: 208 feet; Distance Across: 78 feet; Altar: None

26. *CHIN-P'YONG* (眞平) 579–632 (53-year rule) Map: p. 250–251

Ancestry: (Kim family; reign title, *Kon-bok*) In the Kim Clan Chin-p'yong ruled longer than any other king. He was eldest son of Prince Tong-nyun and grandson of Chin-hung (24th king). Chin-p'yong's mother Princess Man-ho was also a great aunt as she was a younger sister of King Chin-hung. The second brother of Chin-p'yong was the father of Queen Chin-dok (28th ruler) of Silla. Chin-p'yong had two queens, Ma-ya of the Kim Clan and Sung-man of the Son Clan, yet he had no male heir so he placed his eldest daughter by his first marriage on the throne to become the 1st female ruler of Korea, Queen Son-dok. Chin-p'yong's second daughter Ch'on-myong became the mother of Mu-yol (29th king), thus making Mu-yol the nephew of Queen Son-dok. Chin-p'yong's posthumous name was Paek-chong.

Tomb: Historic Site No. 180

Circumference: 390 feet; Distance Across: 136 feet; Altar: None

27. *SON-DOK* (善德) 632–647 (15-year rule) Map: p. 250–251

Ancestry: (Kim family: reign title, *In-p'yong*) Son-dok was to become the first woman ruler of any kingdom in Korea. Her mother was Ma-ya, first queen of Chin-p'yong. Her prince consort was Um-kal-mun. Queen Son-dok was by far the wisest of the three women rulers of Silla. Though failing in military objectives she achieved merit in substantially introducing Chinese T'ang culture to Silla. Buddhism continued to flourish with the construction of Hwangyong-sa's gigantic nine-storied wooden pagoda. Ch'omsong-dae and pagoda of Punhwang-sa were erected during her reign. Her posthumous name was Tok-man.

Tomb: Historic Site No. 182

Circumference: 250 feet; Distance Across: 100 feet; Altar: 3'9" × 2'6" Ht. 2'0"

Other Remains: The mound has a low two-foot retaining wall consisting of two tiers of roughly hewed stones. Placed in upright positions at almost equal intervals are 12 larger irregular uncut stones with a natural flat surface facing outward. These 12 stones may be the early representation of zodiac guardians which appear on tombs of later Silla rulers.

28. *CHIN-DOK* (眞德) 647–654 (7-year rule) Map: p. 284–285

Ancestry: (Kim family; reign title, *Tae-hwa*) Chin-dok was a cousin of Queen Son-dok (27th ruler) and daughter of the 3rd son of Chin-p'yong (26th king). In 752 Kim In-mun, younger brother of Mun-mu (30th king), was sent as ambassador to China. Before the reign of Queen Chin-dok Silla had developed a unique social system called "bone rank" where social class was determined by heredity and marriage. At the top of society were the classes called *songgol* (sacred bone) which ended with Queen Chin-dok and *chin'gol* (true bone) which began with King Mu-yol. These two classes were exclusively the ranking royal family. Upon Chin-dok's death the crown went to Mu-yol, grandson of Chin-ji (25th king). Her posthumous name was Sung-man.

Tomb: Historic Site No. 24

Circumference: 147 feet; Distance Across: 58 feet; Altar: None

Other Remains: There is substantial doubt as to whether this tomb actually belongs to Queen Chin-dok. This is the earliest tomb depicting the zodiac guardians. The relief images are smaller and inferior in technique to others (2' × 1'4"). The retaining wall is 3'6" high and constructed with 24 small upright panel stones (2' × 2'6") and 24 larger panel stones (4' × 2'6") which alternate. On every other small panel stone a zodiac relief image has been carved wearing military attire. The images are depicted with human male bodies with animal heads. The rat is first in order facing due north (rear of tomb). The correct order proceeds clockwise. Eleven are missing and thirteen remain of the larger panel stones. Only five of the 24 edging stones still remain (6' long). No other tomb images are at the tomb.

29. *MU-YOL* (武烈) 654–661 (7-year rule) Map: p. 214–215

Ancestry: (Kim family; reign title, *Tae-jong*) Mu-yol was grandson of Chin-ji (25th king). His father was Prince Yong-ch'un and his mother Princess Ch'on-myong, the daughter of Chin-p'yong and younger sister of Queen Son-dok (27th ruler) of Silla. Mu-yol married Mun-hui (Queen Hun-jae), second sister of General Kim Yu-shin thus fulfilling a dream which was sold from the 1st to 2nd sister. Their eldest son Mun-mu, who later became 30th king, was conceived out of wedlock. Mu-yol had a total of 7 sons by Queen Hun-jae. A daughter of Mu-yol was later married to Kim Yu-shin when the general was 40. Kim Yu-shin had 5 sons and 4 daughters by this wife and one son by another wife. Unification of Silla began and was completed during Mun-mu's reign. Diplomacy with T'ang earned recognition as the Chinese decided to help Silla defeat Paekche and Koguryo. Paekche fell in 660. The Golden Age of Silla began. After his death he received the posthumous reign title of *Tae-jong* which means "Great Ancestor" and is customarily awarded to the 2nd ruler of a dynasty. This was an exceptional honor. His posthumous name was Ch'un-ch'u.

Tomb: Historic Site No. 20

Circumference: 380 feet; Distance Across: 124 feet; Altar: 9'10" × 7'10" (ground level)

Other Remains: Though the tomb does not have a retaining wall there are 9 large stones buried in the mound surface. The turtle base and cap (tablet of stele is missing) which identify this tomb as belonging to Mu-yol are located in a pavilion near the entrance of the tomb grounds. This stone tablet is considered one of the most important historic relics in the Kyongju vicinity. It is designated as National Treasure No. 25. Nearby is the stone turtle base for the tablet of Kim In-mun (Treasure No. 70).

30. *MUN-MU* (文武) 661–681 (20-year rule) Map: p. 250–251

Ancestry: (Kim family; reign title, none) Mun-mu is considered to be the greatest of all Silla rulers. He was the eldest of 7 sons of Mu-yol and Queen Hun-jae. Second son was Kim In-mun, a scholar and diplomat, living most of his life in China. During the reign of Mun-mu with the help of General Kim Yu-shin the unification of Silla was achieved. Mun-mu requested that upon his death his body be cremated and buried in the Eastern Sea (near Kamun-sa site). His spirit would become a dragon to protect Silla from Japanese pirates. His request was carried out by his son who became King Shin-mun. This site recently discovered in 1967 is called Taewang-am. General Kim Yu-shin died in 673 during the 12th year of King Mun-mu's reign. Koguryo was defeated by Silla in 668. His posthumous name was Pob-min.

Tomb: Historic Site No. 158 (Taewang-am)

31. *SHIN-MUN* (神文) 681–692 (11-year rule) Map: p. 138–139

Ancestry: (Kim family; reign title, none) Shin-mun was the eldest son of Mun-mu and Queen Cha-ui. The kingdom continued to prosper during this period. Shin-mun had two sons by Queen Shin-mok both of whom became rulers in 692 and 702. Also two of Shin-mun's grandsons became rulers in 737 and 742. During the first years of his reign his father-in-law Kim Hum-dol who was prime minister attempted an unsuccessful rebellion. Shin-mun then divorced his queen and in 683 married a daughter of Kim Hun-won. Relations with T'ang China were still good. Sol Ch'ong, the first great Confucian scholar and son of Priest Won-hyo, lived during this period. The *idu*, a form of literary phrase endings to be used with Chinese to aid the Korean reader, was invented by Sol Ch'ong. Shin-mun's posthumous name was Chong-myong or Il-so.

Tomb: Historic Site No. 181

Circumference: 303 feet; Distance Across: 117 feet; Altar 13'0 × 9'6" Ht. 3'0"

Other Remains: The altar is composed of ten stones pieced together. The retaining wall is 4'6" high consisting of five tiers of cut rectangular stones averaging 1'6" in length. The retaining wall is supported by 44 triangular buttress stones (width 1'10"; length 5'). Only at two other tombs (Song-dok and Min-ae) are buttress stones still found in tomb construction. This is the largest Silla tomb with a retaining wall.

32. *HYO-SO* (孝昭) 692–702 (10-year rule) Map: p. 138–139

Ancestry: (Kim family; reign title. none) Hyo-so was the eldest son of Shin-mun, 31st king. As Hyo-so had no heir, upon his death in 702 his younger brother became Song-dok, 33rd ruler. In 692 medicine was introduced to the people. In 694 Kim In-mun, younger brother of King Mun-mu, died on his return from T'ang China and was buried near his father Mu-yol's tomb. Hyo-so's posthumous name was Ig-ong.

Tomb: Historic Site No. 184

Circumference: 206 feet; Distance Across: 70 feet; Altar: None

Other Remains: There are several large stones protruding from the surface of the tomb mound.

33. *SONG-DOK* (聖德) 702–737 (35-year rule) Map: p. 138–139

Ancestry: (Kim family; reign title, none) Song-dok was the younger brother of Hyo-so and second son of Shin-mun (31st king). His two sons, Hyo-song and Kyong-dok, by his second Queen So-dok both became rulers in 737 and 742. Song-dok's first queen was Om-jong. His eldest son died at an early age. A daughter of Song-dok, Princess Sa-so married Hyo-bang, a 9th generation descendant of 17th

King Nae-mul and their son was to become Son-dok (37th king) in 780. In 718 a water clock was made for the first time. In 725 the bell now housed at Sangwon-sa in Kangwon Province was cast. This bell remains the oldest existing Korean bell and is listed as National Treasure No. 36. Cultural exchanges with T'ang China became more frequent. Song-dok's posthumous name was Hung-gwang.
Tomb: Historic Site No. 28
　　Circumference: 150 feet; Distance Across: 62 feet; Altar: 7'11 × 4'2''; Ht. 3'8''
Other Remains: The four-foot retaining wall was built with large panel stones. Long molding stones along the crest of the retaining wall protrude several inches. Now 30 triangular stone buttresses are positioned around the mound while a stone apron flares 6'6'' from the retaining wall. This stone apron has an outside circumference of 190 feet. Between the buttresses are fragments of zodiac images. (The only tomb where they are not depicted in relief.) The best preserved monkey image was taken to the Kyongju National Museum. The best preserved image at the tomb site is the chicken. The other ten zodiac images are all broken beyond recognition. The height of the images was approximately 3'6''. With animal heads and human bodies the images are attired in military uniform. A stone fence surrounds the tomb. Eight new pillars were recently added to 25 remaining pillar stones. (Also four partially broken pillars were repaired.) The pillar's height is 5'6'' and girth is 3'10'' while new cross stones were placed paralleled to each other between pillars. At the entrance of the tomb is a standing civil official (7'8'' high) and also a fragment remains of a civil official's head and shoulders. The military officials are gone. Three guardian lions remain, one in front and two behind the mound, (length: 3'; width: 2'2''; and height: 3'6''). Fifty meters in front of the tomb is a large turtle base (9'9''x9'0'') which once held a memorial tablet. The head is missing.

34. HYO-SONG (孝成) 737–742 (5-year rule)

Ancestry: (Kim family; reign title, none) Hyo-song was the second son of Song-dok and his second Queen So-dok. Hyo-song had no heir by Queen Hye-myong so upon his death a younger brother also born to Queen So-dok became Kyong-dok (35th king). According to his last wishes he was cremated and his ashes were spread on the waters of the Eastern Sea. The site of the cremation is believed to be south of Pobnyu-sa. During his reign he fell in love with a daughter of Yong-jong and took her as a second wife. Queen Hye-myong tried to kill her. Yong-jong revolted against the king but was unsuccessful and all were killed. Hyo-song's posthumous name was Sung-gyong.
Tomb: Unknown

35. KYONG-DOK (景德) 742–765 (23-year rule) Map: p. 186–187

Ancestry: (Kim family; reign title, none) Kyong-dok was the third son of Song-dok by Queen So-dok. He came to the throne upon the death of his older brother Hyo-song. His reign was considered the peak of Silla prosperity. Buddhism and T'ang Chinese culture flourished. The giant bell of Hwang-yong-sa was cast in 754 and according to records was four times the size of the Emillie Bell. Kyong-dok also commissioned artisans to cast the famous Emillie Bell to honor his father Song-dok (33rd king). Kyong-dok died before the bell's completion. It was finally completed in 770 and placed in Pongdok-sa. Pulguk-sa and the Sokkuram were completed during Kyong-dok's reign by Kim Tae-song to honor his parents according to tradition. Kyong-dok's reign achieved the peak of a brilliant "golden age" of art throughout Silla. His first queen could bear no children and was exiled. The second Queen Man-wol had one son by the king who became the next ruler. Kyong-dok's posthumous name was Hon-yong.
Tomb: Historic Site No. 23
　　Circumference: 215 feet; Distance Across: 85 feet; Altar: 8'0'' × 4'0''; Ht. 3'8''
Other Remains: The retaining wall is four feet high. Thirty-six small panel stones (2' × 3') are alternated with 36 larger stones. Each zodiac image in military uniform on every third small panel is 2'6'' high and 1'6'' wide. Each larger panel is slightly recessed. The molding stones at the crest of the retaining wall protrude several inches. The zodiac images are in a good state of preservation and appear cheerful. A stone apron flares out from the retaining wall six feet while 40 stone pillars

are positioned encircling the mound. The outer circumference of the apron is 250 feet. It is five feet between each pillar which is 5'9" high and 4'9" in girth. Though most parallel stone cross pieces are missing, one stone cross piece between the pillars is still in place. There are no other remains at Kyong-dok's tomb.

36. HYE-GONG (惠恭) 765–780 (15-year rule)

Ancestry: (Kim family; reign title, none) Hye-gong came to the throne at the age of six while his mother, Queen Man-wol, second wife of Kyong-dok, served as regent. Hye-gong was weak and had an effeminate character thus bringing to realization the prophecy received by Kyong-dok before the boy's birth. At age 21 both he and his queen were murdered in a court conspiracy. His first queen was Shin-bo and his second daughter of Kim Chang. Without an heir a 10th generation descendant of Nae-mul (17th king) became 37th ruler called Son-dok (not to be confused with Queen Son-dok). The Emillie Bell was completed in 770 and placed in Pongdok-sa. Now in the Kyongju National Museum it is listed as National Treasure No. 29 and considered the finest ancient bell in the world today. Hye-gong's posthumous name was Kon-un.
Tomb: Unknown

37. SON-DOK (宣德) 780–785 (5-year rule)

Ancestry: (Kim family; reign title, none) Son-dok was the son of Prince Hyo-bang who was ninth generation descendant of Nae-mul (17th king). Son-dok's mother was Princess Sa-so, a daughter of Song-dok (33rd king). His queen was Ku-jok. After death his body was cremated and his ashes enshrined in the Eastern Sea. As Son-dok had no heir his cousin became 38th ruler of Silla. Son-dok served as prime minister during the reign of Hye-gong and assisted in suppressing a rebellion led by Tae-gong. Though this might appear to be a meritorious act he then turned about and killing both king and queen, elevated himself to the throne. The prophecy of Priest P'yo-hun concerning the decline of Silla came true. Son-dok's posthumous name was Yang-sang.
Tomb: Unknown

38. WON-SONG (元聖) 785–799 (14-year rule) Map. p. 138–139

Ancestry: (Kim family; reign title, none) Won-song was a cousin of Son-dok (37th king). Won-song's father was Prince Hyo-yang, a younger brother of Prince Hyo-bang who was Son-dok's father. Won-song had three sons by Queen Suk-jong though none became rulers. He also had two daughters. Upon Won-song's death his grandson, eldest son of Prince In-gyom, became 39th ruler. In-gyom, eldest son of Won-song, was the father of three future kings. Prince Ye-yong, third son of Won-song, was the grandfather of three additional future kings. Won-song's body after death was cremated and his ashes were buried near Sungbok-sa and Kamsan-sa according to his will. Won-song's posthumous name was Kyong-shin.
Tomb: Historic Site No. 26
      Circumference: 229 feet; Distance Across: 93 feet; Altar: 8'0 × 4'2"; Ht. 4'0"
Other Remains: This tomb is called Kwoe-nung meaning suspended tomb and was once thought to belong to Mun-mu (30th king). It is the largest of all the tombs which contain the zodiac images. After the discovery of Taewang-am on the east coast Kwoe-nung was designated as traditionally belonging to Won-song. The retaining wall in 4'6" high and consists of 36 small panel stones alternating with 36 larger panel stones. A zodiac image is carved in relief on every third small panel stone (2'6" × 1'6"). Each larger panel is slightly recessed by several inches. The molding stones at the crest of the retaining wall protrude several inches. The zodiac animals are positioned in the same direction as at all other tombs. With animal heads and human bodies the figures are attired in military uniform. Proceeding clockwise the animals are as follows: rat (north), ox, tiger, rabbit (east), dragon, snake, horse(south), sheep, monkey, chicken (west), dog and pig. A stone apron flares out from the retaining wall 5'6" giving an outer circumference of 260 feet. Now 42 pillars 5'10" high are positioned encircling the mound (girth: 4'6"). At the entrance are 9-foot pillars (*mang jusok*) placed 73 feet apart.

Stone officials are positioned on either side of the tomb entrance. Here at this tomb and the tomb for Hung-dok (42nd king) the officials at the entrance are the most complete. About 17 feet from the *mangjusok* on each side of the entrance are large 8'6" military officials. Their swords are unsheathed and pointed toward the ground. The free hand of each official is closed in a clenched fist with a ferocious scowl on the face. The feet of the stone officials appear to have been broken. Stone civil officials are located 23 feet distant from the military officials. With hands folded under long flowing robes these two civil officials are 9'9" high. Northward 27 feet from the civil officials are positioned two of the four guardian lions. Two stone lions are situated 28 feet apart on each side of the aisle(length:2'10"; width: 2'1"; height: 3'10"). Two lions face straight forward (inside left and outside right) while one faces the tomb (inside right) and the fourth faces away from the tomb (outside left). Legends say that Kwoe-nung was originally built over water or a pond.

39. *SO-SONG* (昭聖) 799–800 (1-year rule)

Ancestry: (Kim family; reign title, none) So-song was the eldest grandson of Won-song (38th king) and eldest son of Prince In-gyom. He adopted a son who later became 40th ruler upon his death in 800. It is believed that So-song was an invalid. His wife was Queen Kye-hwa. He did not receive a posthumous name.

Tomb: Unknown

40. *AE-JANG* (哀莊) 800–809 (9-year rule)

Ancestry: (Kim family; reign title, none) Ae-jang was the adopted son of So-song (39th king) and according to records committed suicide after ruling nine years. As he had no heir a younger brother of So-song (39th king) became the 41st ruler. It is claimed that his two uncles (Hon-dok and Hung-dok) in a conspiracy forced the boy to kill himself (July 19, 809). Haein-sa where the world's oldest set of *Tripitaka* is kept was constructed in 803 by order of Ae-jang in expression of gratitude for the miraculous healing of his queen by a hermit priest living in the Kaya Mountains. However, history also records that there was a repression of Buddhism during this period. Ae-jang's posthumous name was Chung-myung.

Tomb: Unknown

41. *HON-DOK* (憲德) 809–826 (17-year rule) Map: p. 284–285

Ancestry: (Kim family; reign title, none) Hon-dok was So-song's (39th king) younger brother and grandson of Won-song (38th king). Some sources indicate that he was an uncle of So-song rather than brother. Hon-dok had no heir by his Queen Kwui-sung. As uncle of King Ae-jang he became defense minister and traveled to T'ang China in 805. He served as regent for young Ae-jang and later with others plotted to have his nephew killed. Upon Hon-dok's death a younger brother became next ruler. Hon-dok's posthumous name was On-sung.

Tomb: Historic Site No. 29

　　　　Circumference: 220 feet; Distance Across: 90 feet; Altar: None

Other Remains: The four-foot retaining wall of this tomb was recently repaired. Five of the twelve zodiac images are left in their respective directional positions. The most unique feature is that the zodiac figures are attired in civilian dress rather than military as at other tombs of royalty. These include the pig, rat, ox, tiger and rabbit. The images are 2'6" high and 1'6" wide. The molding stones along the top are six feet in length. Four-foot stone panels alternate with two-foot stone panels. A zodiac image is carved on every fourth two-foot panel. A new stone fence was reconstructed around the tomb. There is no other statuary.

42. *HUNG-DOK* (興德) 826–836 (10-year rule) Map: p. 300–301

Ancestry: (Kim family; reign title, none) Hung-dok was the 3rd son of Prince In-gyom who was the eldest son of Won-song (38th king). Two older brothers and a nephew were rulers before him. He conspired with Hon-dok (an older brother) to have his nephew Ae-jang (40th king) killed by forcing him to commit suicide in 809. He had no heir by his Queen Ch'ang-hwa who was daughter of So-song (39th king) and niece. After Hung-dok's death the son of his cousin Prince Hon-jong became 43rd ruler. Prince Hon-jong was the second son of Prince Ye-yong, a younger brother of Hung-dok's own father. Records taken from a tomb tablet revealed that Hung-dok's queen was also buried within the same tomb mound. Hung-dok's posthumous name was Kyong-hwi.

Tomb: Historic Site No. 30

Circumference: 213 feet; Distance Across: 85 feet; Altar: portions remain

Other Remains: Because of the complete regalia this tomb is one of the two best examples of royal tombs of Silla rulers. The other tomb is Kwoe-nung. The retaining wall is four feet high and consists of 36 small panel stones alternating with 36 larger panel stones. The zodiac images which are carved in relief on every third small stone panel are 2'7" high and 1'7" wide. With animal heads and human bodies the figures are dressed in military attire while holding weapons. Molding stones at the top of the retaining wall protrude several inches. A stone apron flares out from the retaining wall 6'2". There are six remaining six-foot stone pillars (girth: 4'4") and two broken pillars. However, there are positional holes for 41 pillars. These pillars are the remains of a stone fence encircling the mound. At the entrance are two broken pillars (*mangjusok*) positioned 52 feet apart. Next across the aisle are two 8'11" military officials with swords unsheathed and pointed toward the ground. Nearer the tomb are two 9'8" high civil officials standing with hands folded under long robes. There are four superbly carved stone lions positioned at the four corners of the tomb (length:3'3";width:2'2"; height:4'5"). Near the entrance to the tomb are the stone remains of a huge turtle base which once held a memorial tablet. This example is found at only two other tombs (King Song-dok and Mu-yol). Though the head is not completely broken off it has been badly mutilated. As its size is 12'8" × 10' it is the largest turtle base stone found in the Kyongju area. Pieces of the tablet were found but have since been lost again.

43. HUI-GANG (僖康) 836–838 (2-year rule) Map: p. 214–215

Ancestry: (Kim family; reign title, none) Hui-gang was son of Hon-jong who was a cousin of Hung-dok (42nd king). After the death of Hung-dok a younger brother, Prince Ch'ung-gyong, and the cousin Hon-jong fought for political control. Min-ae who later became 44th king killed his own father Prince Ch'ung-gyong to help place his cousin Hui-gang on the throne. He then became prime minister to Hui-gang. In another rebellion in 838 Hui-gang was forced to commit suicide. Min-ae, a nephew of Hung-dok (42nd king), became the next ruler. Hui-gang's posthumous name was Che-hang.

Tomb: Historic Site No. 220

Circumference: 150 feet; Distance Across: 45 feet; Altar: None

44. MIN-AE (閔哀) 838–839 (1-year rule) Map: p. 214–215

Ancestry: (Kim family; reign title, none) Court intrigue was rampant in the capital. Min-ae, a nephew of Hung-dok, killed his own father Prince Ch'ung-gyong to help his cousin gain the throne. He served as prime minister under Hui-gang (43rd king) but in another conspiracy joined the rebellion to force the king to kill himself and then he took the crown. Min-ae's rule was shortened when he in turn was murdered by Shin-mu (45th king). Shin-mu was a second cousin of Min-ae and it is claimed that Min-ae had murdered Shin-mu's father, Prince Kyun-jong, in a previous revolt. Min-ae's queen was Yun-yong. Min-ae's posthumous name was Myong.

Tomb: Historic Site No. 190

Circumference: 136 feet; Distance Across: 50 feet; Altar: None

Other Remains: The retaining wall is 2'6" high consisting of three tiers of rectangular cut stones. The wall at the rear of the tomb is buried in the hillside. There are now 11 buttress stones remaining in position leaning against the retaining wall. Buttress stones are also found at the tombs of Song-dok (33rd king) and Shin-mun (31st king). Uniquely different, these buttress stones are five-sided with the "V" shaped side facing outward. The girth of the buttress stone is 3'7". There are no other stone remains.

45. *SHIN-MU* (神武) 839–839 (four-month rule) Map: p. 138–139
Ancestry: (Kim family; reign title, none) Shin-mu was son of Prince Kyun-jong who was a grandson of Won-song (38th king). Shin-mu was first cousin of Hui-gang (43rd king) as their fathers were brothers. Shin-mu plotted with General Kung-p'a to have Min-ae murdered with the promise that the general would have the king's daughter in marriage. When Shin-mu became king he did not keep the promise and General Kung-p'a rebelled. His rule of only four months was the shortest of any Silla king. He died in July and his son Mun-song by Queen Chin-jong became Silla's 46th ruler. Shin-mu's posthumous name was U-jing.
Tomb: Historic Site No. 185
  Circumference: 160 feet; Distance Across: 78 feet; Altar: None

46. *MUN-SONG* (文聖) 839–857 (18-year rule) Map: p. 214–215
Ancestry: (Kim family; reign title, none) Mun-song was the son of Shin-mu (45 king) and Queen Chin-jong. His wife was Queen So-myong. Mun-song's reign was riddled by many revolts. Upon his death the crown went to his uncle, a younger brother of his father who became Hon-an (47th king). A sixth generation descendant of Mun-song's was Kyong-sun (56th king) who became the last ruler of Silla when he abdicated to Koryo in 936. In 857 the foremost scholar of Silla, Ch'oe Ch'i-won, was born. He is considered the father of Korean literature. Mun-song's posthumous name was Kyong-ung.
Tomb: Historic Site No. 178 (same tomb for King Chin-ji)
  Circumference: 208 feet; Distance Across; 78 feet; Altar: None

47. *HON-AN* (憲安) 857–861 (4-year rule) Map: p. 214–215
Ancestry: (Kim family; reign title, none) Hon-an was a half brother to Shin-mu (45th king). His father Prince Kyun-jong was killed by Min-ae (44th king). His mother was Princess Cho-yong whereas Shin-mu's mother was Princess Chin-gyo. Hon-an had no heir so upon his death a son-in-law became the next ruler. This was Kyong-mun who was grandson of Hui-gang (43rd king), who in 838 was forced to take his life in a conspiracy. Hon-an's posthumous name was Ui-jong.
Tomb: Historic Site no. 179
  Circumference: 156 feet; Distance Across: 57 feet; Altar : None

48. *KYONG-MUN* (景文) 861–875 (14-year rule)
Ancestry: (Kim family; reign title, none) As a young *hwarang* and prince he was given the choice of the king's two daughters in marriage. Though the youngest was the most beautiful he chose the eldest. Kyong-mun was the grandson of Hui-gang (43rd king) and son of Prince Kye-myong and Princess Kwang-hwa who was the daughter of Shin-mu (45th king). Thus Kyong-mun's mother and wife were first cousins. According to legends Kyong-mun is called the ruler with "donkey-like" ears. In 875 Ch'oe Ch'i-won, the man who was to become Silla's most famous Confucian scholar, passed the civil exams in China at the age of 18. In this same year Kyong-mun died. King Kyong-mun's posthumous name was Ung-myon.
Tomb: Unknown

49. *HON-GANG* (憲康) 875–886 (11-year rule) Map: p. 168–169
Ancestry: (Kim family; reign title, none) Hon-gang was the eldest son of Kyong-mun and Quee· Mun-ja. His rule was one of the better periods during this era of Silla decline. During his reign history records that tile roofs could be seen as far as the eye could see while the capital of Silla rose to over one million inhabitants. The famous story of Ch'o-yong comes from this period. Also three notorious rebel generals were born during Hon-gang's reign, Kyun-hwun, Kun-gye and Wang-gon. Kyun-hwun was the legendary son of an earthworm who fed on tiger's milk and rose to power to eventually kill Kyong-ae (55th king) during his merry-making at Posok-jong in 927. Kun-gye was the one-eyed illegitimate son of Hon-gang's concubine who was ordered killed but saved by a maid. Wang-gon was later to become the first ruler of Koryo in 936. Upon Hon-gang's death a younger brother became

Chong-gang (50th king), followed one year later by a sister, Queen Chin-song (51st ruler). Hon-gang's posthumous name was Chong.

Tomb: Historic Site No. 187
Circumference: 157 feet; Distance Across:65 feet; Altar: small stone placed at ground level. *Other Remains*: The retaining wall is 3'10" high consisting of four tiers of rectangular cut stones. The average length of each stone is over three feet.

50. CHONG-GANG (定康) 886–887 (1-year rule) Map: p. 168–169
Ancestry: (Kim family; reign title, none) Chong-gang was a younger brother of Hon-gang (49th king) and had no heir. After ruling one year he died suddenly. His desire was that his sister become the next ruler of Silla. She was Chin-song, the third ruling queen of the kingdom. King Chong-gang's posthumous name was Hwang.

Tomb: Historic Site No. 186
Circumference: 161 feet; Distance Across:63 feet; Altar: small stone placed at ground level. *Other Remains*: The retaining wall is two feet high consisting of two tiers of rectangular cut stones which average over three feet in length. The tomb size is similar to the brother's tomb nearby.

51. CHIN-SONG (眞聖) 887–897 (10-year rule)
Ancestry: (Kim family; reign title, none) Chin-song was a sister of both Hon-gang (49th king) and Chong-gang (50th king). She came to power as Chong-gang had no heir and it was his wish that she succeed him. Morality dropped to new depths as the queen kept several court favorites in the palace to satisfy her own sexual desires. In her youth she took the husband of her nurse Lady Pu-ho as her lover and later when she mounted the throne he became her official spouse Prince Wi-hong (posthumously titled Hye-song Tae-wang). The kingdom was on the brink of collapse. Chin-song adopted the illegitimate son of Hon-gang (49th king) who was her nephew and abdicated in favor of this boy who became Hyo-gong (52nd king). She died soon after. Her posthumous name was Man.

Tomb: Unknown

52. HYO-GONG (孝恭) 897–913 (16-year rule) Map: p. 138–139
Ancestry: (Kim family; reign title, *Mu-dae*) With the reign of Hyo-gong the historic unbroken record of the Kim Clan rule came to an end. Mi-ch'u (13th king) was the first of the Kim family in 262 to reign. From Nae-mul's (17th king) reign in 356 to Hyo-gong there were 36 rulers of the Kim Clan reigning continuously for 557 years. Hyo-gong's father was Hon-gang (49th king) and his mother may have been Queen Mun-ja yet some sources indicate that Hyo-gong was an illegitimate son. Traditions tell that mysterious signs appeared which foretold the collapse of Silla. Hyo-gong was the nephew of Queen Chin-song but was adopted as her own son. Upon his death the crown passed to a son-in-law and member of the Pak family who was married to the king's daughter, Princess Ui-song. Hyo-gong's posthumous name was Yo.

Tomb: Historic Site No. 183
Circumference: 232 feet; Distance Across: 82 feet; Altar: None

53. SHIN-DOK (神德) 913–917 (4-year rule) Map: p. 186–187
Ancestry: (Pak family; reign title, none) Shin-dok was the first of the Pak Clan to reign in Silla since the rule of A-dal-la (8th king) in 184 A.D. He married Hyo-gong's daughter Princess Cha-song and was popular among the people to be king as Hyo-gong had no heir. Three Pak Clan kings ruled for 14 years and in 927 the Silla throne was given back to Kyong-sun, a member of the Kim family. Upon Shin-dok's death his son by Queen Cha-song became Kyong-myong (54th king) and later a second son became Kyong-ae (55th king). Shin-dok's posthumous name was Kyong-hwi.

Tomb: Historic Site No. 219 (Sam-nung)
Circumference: 207 feet; Distance Across: 78 feet; Altar: Front of A-dal-la's tomb.

54. KYONG-MYONG (景明) 917–924 (7-year rule) Map: p. 186–187

Ancestry: (Pak family; reign title, none) Kyong-myong was the eldest son of Shin-dok (53rd king) and Queen Cha-song. Internal problems and revolts constantly plagued the nation. The Koryo kingdom was founded in 920 under the leadership of General Wang-gon with the capital established in Songdo (Kaesong). Many signs and omens predicting the fall of Silla continued. Upon Kyong-myong's death a younger brother became king. Kyong-myong's posthumous name was Sung-yong.

Tomb: Historic Site No. 219 (Sam-nung)
    Circumference: 168 feet; Distance Across: 60 feet; Altar: Front of A-dal-la's tomb.

55. KYONG-AE (景哀) 924–927 (3-year rule) Map: p. 186–187

Ancestry: (Pak family; reign title, none) Kyong-ae, a younger brother to Kyong-myong (54th king) and son of Shin-dok (53rd king) was the last of the PakClan to reign (total of ten PakClan rulers during the Silla Dynasty period). While he was revelling at the pleasure pavilion of Posok-jong the capital was invaded by General Kyun-hwun, the tiger-spirited leader who called himself the King of Later Paekche. He advanced within the courts of Silla to become the general of Queen Chin-song's (51st ruler) personal guards. He revolted because of the queen's misrule and immorality. Sweeping down upon the capital in August 927 he took the royalty by surprise at Posok-jong. He forced King Kyong-ae to fall on his own sword and violated the queen and royal princesses while his soldiers raped the city. General Kyun-hwun appointed Kyong-sun, a member of the Kim family and 6th genera-tion descendant of Mun-song (46th king), to rule. Taking the city's wealth he departed with many prisoners. By now Silla had lost most of its vast territory. Kyong-ae's posthumous name was Wi-ung.

Tomb: Historic Site No. 222 (Tok-nung)
    Circumference: 138 feet; Distance Across: 47 feet; Altar 3'9" × 2'8"; Ht. 2'0"

56. KYONG-SUN (敬順) 927–936 (9-year rule)

Ancestry: (Kim family; reign title, none) Kyong-sun was the last Silla king to rule. (Kim Clan rulers: 38; Pak Clan rulers: 10; and Sok Clan rulers: 8) Kyong-sun was son of Prince Hyo-jong who was a 5th generation descendant of Mun-song (46th king). His mother was Princess Kye-a, daughter of Hon-gang(49th king). Kyong-sun was placed as a puppet king on the throne by General Kyun-hwun who had murdered Kyong-ae (55th king) at Posok-jong. The end of Silla had come after 993 years. In 936 Kyong-sun abdicated to Wang-gon and journeyed to Songdo the new Koryo capital. The Crown Prince Ma-ui fled to the Diamond Mountains while a younger prince fled to Haein-sa and became a Buddhist priest. King Wang-gon gave his eldest daughter to the retiring king in marriage while Kyong-sun gave a beautiful daughter of an uncle in marriage to Wang-gon. The old capital of Silla was given the name of Kyongju. Kyong-sun died in 978. It is believed that he was buried near the Koryo capital. Kyong-sun's posthumous name was Pu.

Tomb: Unknown

INDEX OF NATIONAL TREASURES IN KYONGJU VICINITY
Kukbo

Note: Grotto reliefs of Shinson-sa have recently been designated as a National Treasure (Dec. 1978).

INDEX OF TREASURES IN KYONGJU CITY AND VICINITY
Pomul

INDEX OF HISTORIC SITES IN KYONGJU CITY AND VICINITY
Sajok

SILLA RULERS (57BC-936AD)

Designated Tombs of Rulers (36)
(Numbered as Historic Site)

1.	Hyok-ko-se	(赫居世)	No. 172 (O-nung)
2.	Nam-hae	(南　解)	No. 172 (O-nung)
3.	Yu-ri	(儒　理)	No. 172 (O-nung)
4.	T'al-hae	(脫　解)	No. 174
5.	P'a-sa	(婆　娑)	No. 172 (O-nung)
6.	Chi-ma	(祇　摩)	No. 221
7.	Il-song	(逸　聖)	No. 173
8.	A-dal-la	(阿達羅)	No. 219 (Sam-nung)
13.	Mi-ch'u	(味　鄒)	No. 175
17.	Nae-mul	(奈　勿)	No. 188
23.	Pob-hung	(法　興)	No. 176
24.	Chin-hung	(眞　興)	No. 177
25.	Chin-ji	(眞　智)	No. 178 (Same as Mun-song)
26.	Chin-p'yong	(眞　平)	No. 180
27.	Son-dok(Queen)	(善　德)	No. 182
28.	Chin-dok(Queen)	(眞　德)	No. 24　(zodiac)
29.	Mu-yol	(武　烈)	No. 20
30.	Mun-mu	(文　武)	No. 158 (Taewang-am)
31.	Shin-mun	(神　文)	No. 181
32.	Hyo-so	(孝　昭)	No. 184
33.	Song-dok	(聖　德)	No. 28　(zodiac)
35.	Kyong-dok	(景　德)	No. 23　(zodiac)
38.	Won-song	(元　聖)	No. 26　(Kwoe-nung: zodiac)
41.	Hon-dok	(憲　德)	No. 29　(zodiac)
42.	Hung-dok	(興　德)	No. 30　(zodiac)
43.	Hui-gang	(僖　康)	No. 220
44.	Min-ae	(閔　哀)	No. 190
45.	Shin-mu	(神　武)	No. 185
46.	Mun-song	(文　聖)	No. 178 (same as Chin-ji)
47.	Hon-an	(憲　安)	No. 179
49.	Hon-gang	(憲　康)	No. 187
50.	Chong-gang	(定　康)	No. 186
52.	Hyo-gong	(孝　恭)	No. 183
53.	Shin-dok	(神　德)	No. 219 (Sam-nung)
54.	Kyong-myong	(景　明)	No. 219 (Sam-nung)
55.	Kyong-ae	(景　哀)	No. 222 (Tok-nung)

Rulers Whose Tombs are Unknown (20)

9.	Pol-hyu	(伐　休)
10.	Nae-hae	(奈　解)
11.	Cho-bun	(助　賁)
12.	Chom-hae	(沾　解)
14.	Yu-rye	(儒　禮)
15.	Ki-rim	(基　臨)
16.	Hul-hae	(訖　解)
18.	Shil-song	(實　聖)
19.	Nul-ji	(訥　祇)
20.	Cha-bi	(慈　悲)
21.	So-ji	(炤　知)
22.	Chi-jung	(智　證)
34.	Hyo-song	(孝　成)
36.	Hye-gong	(惠　恭)
37.	Son-dok	(宣　德)
39.	So-song	(昭　聖)
40.	Ae-jang	(哀　莊)
48.	Kyong-mun	(景　文)
51.	Chin-song(Queen)	(眞　聖)
56.	Kyong-sun	(敬　順)

PAK AND SOK ANCESTRAL DESCENDANTS OF SILLA KINGS

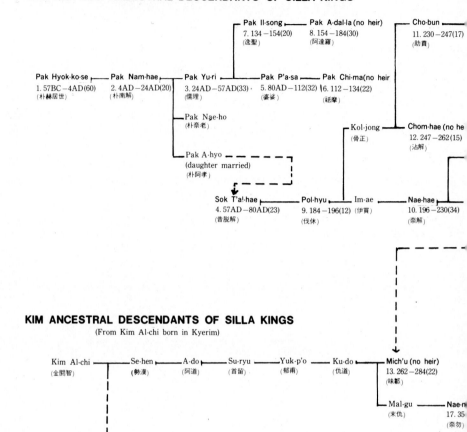

KIM ANCESTRAL DESCENDANTS OF SILLA KINGS
(From Kim Al-chi born in Kyerim)

* Shil-song (18th king) was murdered.
  Shil-song's daughter was married to Nul-ji
  and later Nul-ji killed Shil-song.
* Both Hye-gong (36th king) and his Queen were
  murdered in a conspiracy led by Son-dok (37th king).
* Ae-jang's (40th king) two uncles Hon-dok (41st king) and
  Hung-dok (42nd king) in a conspiracy forced him to
  kill himself on July 19, 809.
* Min-ae (44th king) who had murdered his own father
  was in turn killed by Shin-mu (45th king), a second
  cousin. It is believed that Min-ae also murdered
  Shin-mu's father.

* Hui-gang (43rd king) was forced to kill himself in
  a conspiracy led by Min-ae (44th king).
* Kyong-ae (55th king) and his queen were killed at
  Posok-jong in August 927 by General Kyun-hwun w
  then placed Kyong-sun (56th king), 6th generation
  descendant of Mun-song (46th king) on the throne.
* The Crown Prince Ma-ui rather than surrendering
  to the Diamond Mountains of northern Korea whe
  abdicated to Koryo in 936.

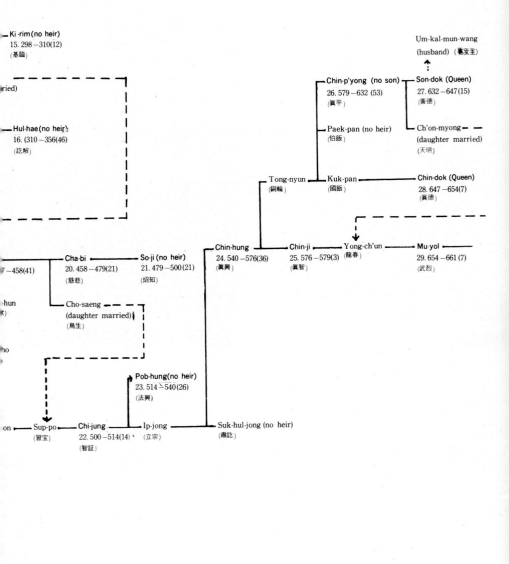

Ki-rim (no heir)
15. 298 — 310(12)
(基臨)

ried)

Hul-hae (no heir)
16. (310 — 356(46)
(訖解)

Um-kal-mun-wang
(husband) (嚴葛文王)

Chin-p'yong (no son)
26. 579 — 632 (53)
(眞平)

Son-dok (Queen)
27. 632 — 647(15)
(善德)

Paek-pan (no heir)
(伯飯)

Ch'on-myong
(daughter married)
(天明)

Tong-nyun
(銅輪)

Kuk-pan
(國飯)

Chin-dok (Queen)
28. 647 — 654(7)
(眞德)

Chin-hung
24. 540 — 576(36)
(眞興)

Chin-ji
25. 576 — 579(3)
(眞智)

Yong-ch'un
(龍春)

Mu-yol
29. 654 — 661 (7)
(武烈)

Cha-bi
20. 458 — 479(21)
(慈悲)

So-ji (no heir)
21. 479 — 500(21)
(炤知)

7 — 458(41)

hun
)

Cho-saeng
(daughter married)
(鳥生)

ho

Pob-hung (no heir)
23. 514 — 540(26)
(法興)

on

Sup-po
(習宝)

Chi-jung
22. 500 — 514(14)
(智証)

Ip-jong
(立宗)

Suk-hul-jong (no heir)
(肅訖宗)

9th generation descendant

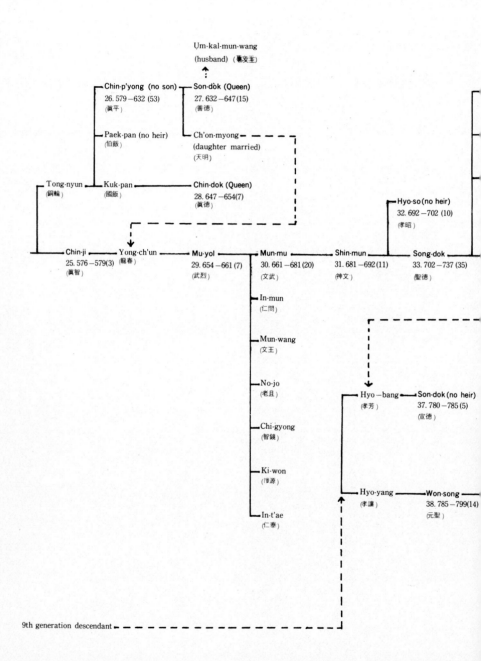

Um-kal-mun-wang
(husband) (嚳文王)

Chin-p'yong (no son)　　Son-dòk (Queen)
26. 579 −632 (53)　　　27. 632 −647 (15)
(眞平)　　　　　　　　(善德)

Paek-pan (no heir)　　Ch'on-myong
(伯飯)　　　　　　　(daughter married)
　　　　　　　　　　(天明)

Tong-nyun　　Kuk-pan　　　Chin-dok (Queen)
(銅輪)　　　(國飯)　　　　28. 647 −654(7)
　　　　　　　　　　　　　(眞德)

Hyo-so(no heir)
32. 692 −702 (10)
(孝昭)

Chin-ji　　　Yong-ch'un　　Mu-yol　　Mun-mu　　　Shin-mun　　Song-dok
25. 576 −579(3)　(龍春)　　29. 654 −661 (7)　30. 661 −681 (20)　31. 681 −692(11)　33. 702 −737 (35)
(眞智)　　　　　　　　　(武烈)　　　(文武)　　　　(神文)　　　(聖德)

In-mun
(仁問)

Mun-wang
(文王)

No-jo
(老且)

Hyo −bang　　Son-dok (no heir)
(孝芳)　　　　37. 780 −785 (5)
　　　　　　　(宣德)

Chi-gyong
(智鏡)

Ki-won
(愷源)

Hyo-yang　　　Won-song
(孝讓)　　　　38. 785 −799(14)
　　　　　　　(元聖)

In-t'ae
(仁泰)

9th generation descendant

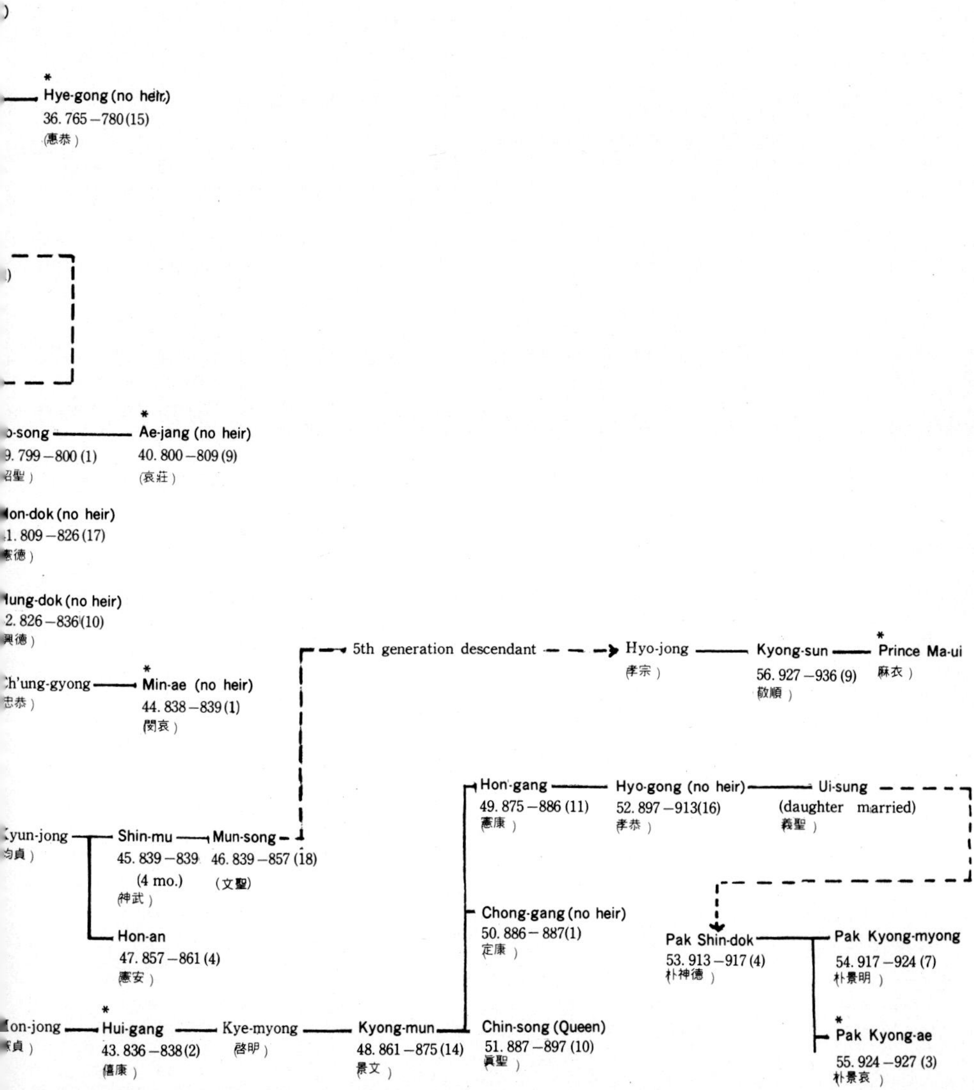

)

*
├─ Hye-gong (no heir)
   36. 765—780 (15)
   (惠恭)

)

:o-song ────── * Ae-jang (no heir)
9. 799—800 (1)   40. 800—809 (9)
召聖)   (哀莊)

Mon-dok (no heir)
1. 809—826 (17)
惠德)

Mung-dok (no heir)
2. 826—836 (10)
興德)

:h'ung-gyong ──┬─ * Min-ae (no heir)
志恭)   44. 838—839 (1)
                  (閔哀)

                              ┌─── 5th generation descendant ──→ Hyo-jong ──── Kyong-sun ──── * Prince Ma-ui
                              ┆   孝宗)   56. 927—936 (9)   麻衣)
                              ┆   敬順)

                                        ┌─ Hon-gang ──────── Hyo-gong (no heir) ───┐ Ui-sung
                                        │ 49. 875—886 (11)   52. 897—913 (16)   (daughter married)
                                        │ 憲康)   孝恭)   義聖)

Kyun-jong ──── Shin-mu ──┬─ Mun-song ──┘
勻貞)   45. 839—839 46. 839—857 (18)
             (4 mo.)   (文聖)
             神武)
             └─ Hon-an   ┌─ Chong-gang (no heir)   Pak Shin-dok ─────┬──── Pak Kyong-myong
                47. 857—861 (4) │ 50. 886—887 (1)   53. 913—917 (4)   │   54. 917—924 (7)
                憲安)   │ 定康)   朴神德)   │   朴景明)

Mon-jong ──┬─ Hui-gang ──── Kye-myong ──── Kyong-mun ──┬─ Chin-song (Queen)   * Pak Kyong-ae
裒貞)   43. 836—838 (2) 啓明)   48. 861—875 (14)   51. 887—897 (10)   55. 924—927 (3)
             僖康)   景文)   眞聖)   朴景哀)

HOW TO GET TO KOREA

Airlines:

There are over 200 flights weekly by international airlines connecting Korea with Japan, Taiwan, Hong Kong, the Philippines, Thailand, Singapore and other world destinations. Only 1½ hours from Tokyo, Korea can be visited at no extra cost to your airfare enroute to other Asian countries.

Ferry:

Three times weekly Pukwan (Pusan-Shimonoseki) Ferry provides service between Korea and Japan. Having a capacity of 950 passengers the ferry is comfortable and pleasant.

ENTRY FORMALITIES

A tourist can easily enter Korea. Travelers are required to present a current passport and valid vaccination certificates when applying for visa. Tourist visas may be granted for thirty days which can be renewed for an additional thirty days at the Ministry of Justice in Seoul. Tourists in transit may visit Korea for five days without visa, but must have proof of confirmed air reservation on to the next destination. Custom laws permit a visitor to bring in practically anything which is for personal use and not for resale. Upon leaving the country all imported effects must be taken from the country.

Taxis are available from the air terminal and charges are made according to meter. The taxi fare to a downtown location in Seoul is approximately $5.00. Tipping is not customary unless extra services are rendered by the driver. KAL also has bus service from the airport to downtown Seoul.

TRANSPORTATION INFORMATION

Taxis: Taxi fares are registered on meters. The basic fare is ₩600 up to two kilometers and

₩40 added for every 400 meters. It is not necessary to tip but it is often done when taxi drivers help with additional baggage Often it is hard to hail a taxi in downtown·Seoul. There are regular taxi pickup points throughout the larger cities and many of them are covered to protect passengers waiting during inclement weather. Many taxi drivers speak some English.

Domestic Air Flights: Korean' Air Lines (KAL) is the only airline that operates within the country. They do provide flights to all major cities. For information on schedules and time call Tel. 778-8221. With the opening of the Pomun Lake Resort in Kyongju air service there will be available.

Railway Service: A well organized network of railroads connects the entire country. Fast express trains run between Seoul and Pusan as well as Seoul to Kwangju. At present there is no direct train to Kyongju from Seoul but a transfer can be made in Taegu.

Highway Express Bus: The main trunk roads in Korea have been converted into several networks of well paved modern expressways. Comfortable high speed express buses busily transport passengers to and from major areas of the country including principal cities and resorts. Often no reservations are needed and departure times are frequent. Tourist agencies and hotel staff can assist you in travel plans. Seoul's central bus terminal is located in Yongdong directly across the Chamsu Bridge on the south side of the Han River. It takes about 15 minutes by taxi from the downtown hotels. The Chunil, Kwangju and Hanil bus lines go directly to Kyongju from Seoul.

Suburban Buses: Seoul as well as all major cities have city buses. They come frequently and are often quite crowded especially during certain periods of the day. Routes are constantly changing with new routes always being added. The fare is only ₩120 (15¢) and a token system is being used. Payment should be made to the bus girl as passenger disembarks. The token coins can be purchased near most bus stops. You may stay on the bus as long as you wish. There are no maps available showing the entire bus routes in Seoul. There is no transfer system to another bus once passenger disembarks.

Subway: An excellent subway system is now in use going as far as Chongnyangni Station in eastern Seoul through the downtown area and as far south as Suwon and west to Inchon. In downtown Seoul it passes the South Gate and Toksu Palace to turn east on Chongno. Following under Chongno the subway passes East Gate to terminate at Chongnyangni Station. A second subway is under construction which will loop through Songdong, Chamshil, Yongdong, Pan po, Yongdungpo, Yoido and return to Seoul. Completion date for this project is 1980. The fare is determined by distance. The subway system is a clean and pleasant way to travel about the city.

Car Rentals: Some car rentals are available but they are expensive as this is not really fully developed in Korea. Information can be obtained at the air terminal or through the major hotels or travel agencies.

Ferries: An economical and comfortable way to travel is by ferry. The Pukwan Ferry links Pusan with Japan's western port of Shimonoseki three times weekly. For reservations call Seoul 22-9716; Pusan 44-1471/5. (Tokyo office: (03) 567-0974; Osaka Office: (06) 345-2245; Shimonoseki Office: (0832) 66-8211; Car ferries connect Pusan with Cheju Island three times weekly. (Seoul: 23-5538; Pusan: 44-0606) Hydrofoils ply the scenic waters of the Hallyo Waterway linking Pusan with Yosu via the resorts of Chungmu and Namhae. (Pusan: 44-3851)

COMMUNICATION

For information on overseas calls and cables dial 117. Operators speak reasonably good English. Hotel operators can assist you. No long distance calls can be made through public pay phones. Public city pay phones are red or green and two ten won coin is needed to make a call. The connection automatically breaks off after three minutes.

KOREAN CURRENCY

The unit of Korean currency is called WON (₩) and coins are used for 1, 5, 10, 50 and 100 won. Notes come in 500, 1,000, 5,000 and 10,000 denominations. Bank drafts can be obtained for larger amounts. Exchange rate for one US dollar is about ₩780 as of the date of this publication. (There are small day by day variations.) This exchange rate has been in effect for several years.

DEPARTURE FROM KOREA

The airport departure tax for all passengers is ₩3,000 per person. No Korean cultural properties should be carried out of Korea that date back to 1910 or earlier without permits which can be obtained from the Ministry of Culture and Information in advance. For further information call Tel: 725-3053. In regard to ginseng, up to three kilograms of both the white and red ginseng can be taken from Korea without permits; however, sale slips must be shown. Up to 20 boxes of powdered ginseng are allowed to be taken from Korea.

A downtown Seoul Airport Terminal is available for passengers near the Great South Gate. Baggage must be checked three hours or earlier prior to departure. Time schedules for the bus shuttle can be verified by calling Tel. 444-8211. Walker Hill buses are used and the fee is ₩500 per person.

CLIMATE OF KOREA

The meaning of the word Korea (or Koryo) means high and clear, symbolic of the country's craggy and towering mountains. The clear blue skies and rushing streams have earned the nation the nickname of "Switzerland of Asia." The nation's climate is temperate. Moderately cold dry winters and hot humid summers are characteristic of Korea's climate. July is usually the wettest month of the year with July and August the hottest as temperatures reach the low 90's. Spring and autumn are very pleasant with crisp weather and many days of sunshine. The winters of Korea are said to be characterized by three consecutive cold days followed by four warmer days. If you can chose the season, spring and autumn are the best times to visit Korea.

HOW TO REACH KYONGJU

Kyongju City, the ancient Silla capital, is located on the Seoul-Pusan Expressway in the southeastern portion of the Korean peninsula. Kyongju is 68 kilometers (43 miles) from Pusan and 359 kilometers (223 miles) from Seoul. The distance from Taegu to Kyongju is 54 kilometers (34 miles).

ROUTE FROM SEOUL:

Express Bus: This is the easiest and surest way. Comfortable buses go directly to Kyongju from 7:00 am to 6:00 pm every hour and a half daily. The travel time is about 4½ hours. Though reservations can be made, often they are not necessary except during Korean holiday seasons. Kwangju, Chunil and Hanil bus lines go direct from Seoul to Kyongju. Other lines require transfer at Taegu. The travel time is about five hours.

Train: There is no direct train to Kyongju. One can take a deluxe "Saemaul-ho" sightseeing coach to Taegu in three hours. There are normally three departures during the day (10:00 am, 1:00 pm and 5:00 pm). Other semi-express trains leave Seoul hourly for Taegu during the day. The Bus Terminal in Taegu is a short walking distance from the railway station. Time schedules are changeable so it is best to check with tourist agencies and information centers at the hotels.

ROUTE FROM PUSAN:

Express Bus: Buses leave every 20 minutes from 6:00 am to 7:30 pm. All lines leave from one central Pusan Bus Terminal. The local train is not recommended.

HOTELS

Though there are many Western style hotels located in Korea only a few of the first class hotels which cater exclusively to foreign travelers will be listed. These hotels are rated as superior (designated by the Five Roses of Sharon) and provide truly deluxe accommodations.

Reservations should be made well in advance especially in the spring and fall which are the peak of the tourist season. These hotels have brochures which can be requested through the tourist agencies. Prices range from $30 — $60.00 for a double. The hotels that have advertised in this guide represent the finest of Korea's accommodations for foreign tourists. These hotels are:

CHOSUN HOTELS
(Located in Seoul, Pusan and Kyongju)

The Westin Hotels have expanded during the last several years from the Chosun Hotel in Seoul to include the Chosun Beach Hotel at Haeundae near Pusan and the Chosun Kyongju Hotel at Bomun Lake Resort. The Chosun Kyongju Hotel located near the lake shore has over 300 rooms. It is one of Korea's growing first class hotels outside the capital city of Seoul offering high international standards in accommodations. The Chosun in Seoul has long been the center of the foreign social life where one can enjoy the blend of the Continental and the Asian. In the lower lobby of the Chosun of Seoul one can find Korea's most complete shopping center of forty-five exclusive shops for gifts and services. When dining out consider the authentic Italian cuisine at Ristorante Opera located at the Seoul Sejong Cultural Center and managed by the Chosun Hotel.

Room Prices: Single $48.00 ;

Double $52.00 ; Suite $120.00-$400.00

KOLON HOTEL
(Located in Kyongju)

As Kyongju has developed into Korea principal tourist attraction the Kolon Hotel met the need to become Kyongju's first 5-star deluxe hotel for international clientele. With a choice of 240 air-conditioned, centrally-heated rooms and suites the Kolon Hotel decor has accomplished the pleasing blend of Korean tradition with modern conveniences. Located on 59 acres of rolling hills the hotel is situated within easy walking distance of Kyongju's main attraction, the Pulguk Temple. With Korean, Japanese and Western dining available the Kolon Hotel also has a 500 seat theater restaurant, casino and night club. An 18 hole golf course is adjacent to the hotel. Other available sports include tennis, fishing and swimming.

Room Prices:
Twin or Double $35.00-$45.00;
Suite $55.00-$300.00

KYONGJU TOKYU HOTEL
(Located in Seoul and Kyongju)

This new 5-star deluxe hotel for international clientele is beautifully situated along the shores of picturesque Pomun Lake, Kyongju. Located only 6 kilometers from downtown Kyongju and also the famous Pulguk Temple, the Kyongju Tokyu Hotel offers 300 air-conditioned/centrally heated rooms and suites with a selection of Western, Korean and Japanese cuisine and a variety of entertainment such as tennis, golf, swimming, fishing and sailing. A night club featuring entertainment from Seoul with game room and a casino are also available. Tours to the scenic historic sites near Kyongju can be arranged by the friendly and well informed tourist center. Kyongju Tokyu Hotel is a member of the Pan Pacific Hotels and reservations can be made internationally or through the Seoul Tokyu Hotel.

Room Prices:
Twin or Double $40.00; Suite $90.00

FESTIVALS AND CEREMONIES HELD IN KYONGJU

Memorial Ceremony at the Confucian School: (Feb. 5 and Aug. 5) Held twice a year this traditional Confucian ritual honors Confucius and is held at Hyang-gyo near Panwol-song. Other famous Chinese and Korean Confucian scholars are also honored.

Samjon Hyang-sa, Three Shrine Ceremony: (spring and autumn equinox) Held twice a year this ceremony is conducted at the three major shrines of the city, Sungdok-jon, Sungshin-jon and Sunghye-jon. Sungdok-jon is a shrine honoring the first king and queen of the Silla dynasty at O-nung. The other two shrines are located near the tomb of Mi-ch'u and honor Kim Al-chi, first Kim Clan member and kings Mi-ch'u, Mun-mu and Kyong-sun.

Kumsan Ceremony: (March 25 and Sept. 25) A memorial ceremony is held to honor General Kim, Yu-shin, the unification leader, at the tombkeeper's house (*chesil*) near the tomb site. This traditional Confucian ceremony is held twice a year.

Memorial Ceremony for Priest Won-hyo: (March 29) Won-hyo was probably the greatest Korean priest that ever lived. His portrait is enshrined at Punhwang-sa where a yearly Buddhist ceremony is conducted.

Buddha's Birthday: (April 8) This day is a National Holiday and all temples around the countryside honor this event. Pilgrims visit the temples during the entire day and an evening lantern parade is usually held in the streets. The larger temples near Kyongju should be visited, however, this event can be witnessed throughout the entire country.

Memorial Ceremony for Yi Ch'a-don: (Aug. 5) Yi Ch'a-don is the Buddhist martyr who offered his life in the sixth century so that Buddhism might flourish. A Buddhist ceremony is held to honor Yi Ch'a-don at Hungnyun-sa, the site of Silla's earliest temple very near O-nung. A small nunnery has been recently established nearby.

Ceremony for the Six Village Elders: (Aug. 17) At a small shrine near Na-jong a memorial ceremony is conducted honoring the six village chiefs who witnessed the strange appearance of Pak Hyok-ko-se. He was selected to become Silla's first ruler in the 1st century BC.

Sam-nung (Three Tomb) Ceremony: (Aug. 21) Located on the western slopes of Nam-san are three tombs traditionally belonging to kings of the Pak Clan. A ceremony is held once a year to honor these rulers.

Ceremony at Yulsan Sowon: (Oct 3, Solar Date) At Tamun-dong Kyongsan-gun (near Taegu) this traditional Confucian rite is held at the newly built Yulsan Sowon. The ceremony honors Milsung Taegun and five other descendants of Pak Hyok-ko-se (1st king of Silla).

Memorial Ceremony for Paeg-yol: (Oct. 28) This rite is held at Hyang-gyo (Confucian School near Panwol-song) for Paeg-yol, a poor man whose only talent was playing the *komungo*. He and his wife lived on the slopes of Nang-san.

Silla Festival: (Oct. 15 - three days) This festival is by far the largest held during the year and one of the most impressive for the entire country. Many of the photographs in Kyongju Guide were taken of the Silla Festival. A gigantic parade with floats portraying the folk stories of Silla wends through the streets. Games of skill and folk dances are noticed everywhere. The population of Kyongju almost doubles during these three days of festivities.

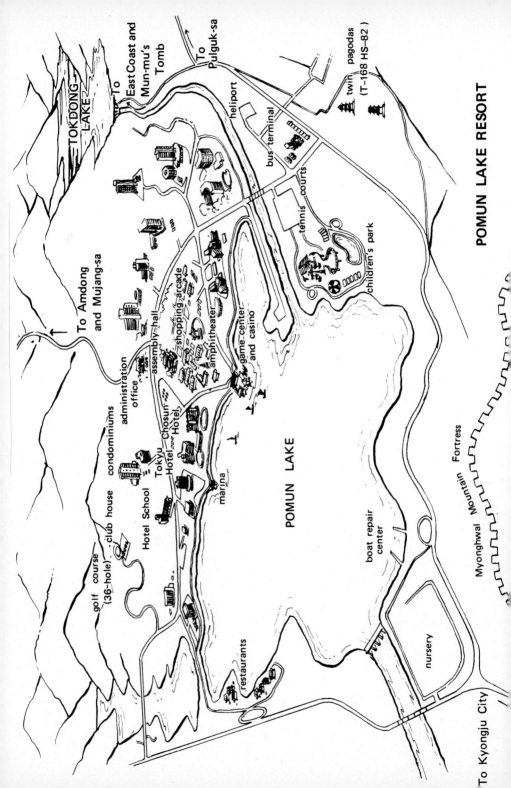

POMUN LAKE RESORT

POMUN LAKE RESORT

Only six kilometers on the eastern outskirts of Kyongju City the Korean government is developing what will be one of Asia's first class international tourist resorts. Work began in 1974 under the Kyongju Tourism Development Plan as two large lakes (reservoirs) were developed in picturesque valleys surrounded by wooded mountain scenery.

The entire 2570 acre area has a leisurely atmosphere of peace and tranquility, suitable for large scale conferences, exhibitions and other business gatherings. The lake site is not only ideally located in southern Korea but it is also near the rich historic relics from the "golden age" of Korea's past. Many of the larger industrial sites such as Pohang, Ulsan, Pusan and Masan are easily reached from Kyongju.

Beside the capital city of Seoul, Kyongju is already the most popular tourist attraction. It is estimated that over one million foreign tourists will be visiting the Kyongju vicinity yearly by 1980. Also over three million Korean tourists will come yearly to this historic capital of the Silla Dynasty.

One major factor which caused the rapid rise of tourism has been the phenomenal growth of the Korean economy. As economic standards increase, the attraction of Korea's tourist and vacation destinations have more appeal. Korea's economic progress over the last ten years has been the most impressive throughout the world.

The Kyongju Tourism Agency (KTA), a wholly owned subsidiary of the Korea National Tourism Corporation (KNTC), is state owned and invested with the responsibility of developing and promoting tourism in Korea. KTA will manage the Pomun Lake Resort complex. The total cost of this project is $60 million while the International Bank for Reconstruction and Development is lending $25 million to the Korean government.

By 1981 the following tourist facilities will be in operation:
* 1600 hotel guest rooms available in three major hotels.
* Amenity Core including 120 store shopping arcade, 900 seat convention hall, 1000 seat open air theater, administration offices and health clinic.
* Traditional Korean restaurants grouped near one end of the lake.
* Game center and casino located on the lake

Guests enter a restaurant on the shores of Pomun Lake .

The Pomun Lake Hotel School is sponsored by KNTC.

Wild chrysanthemums blow above Pomun Lake valley.

shore and sponsored by the Chosun Kyongju Hotel.

*Marina and club house to provide assistance in all water sports is sponsored by the Tokyu Kyongju Hotel with restaurant.

*18 hole golf course with club house designed to attract international tournaments (Note: With the later development of an additional 18 holes,this will make the course the largest in Korea). Parking space for golf course club house will accommodate 300 cars.

*Other recreational facilities such as tennis courts with proshop, horseback riding,archery, and a children's park will be available to visitors.

*Transportation terminal and heliport to facilitate the arrival and departure of resort guests.

*Hotel School designed to train hotel employees for the resort area.

By spring 1979 and the PATA conference 640 hotel rooms will be ready for occupancy. The Kyongju Tokyu Hotel and the Kyongju Chosun Hotel will provide for tourists, deluxe accommodations which meet high international standards. Hotel facilities will include swimming pools, night clubs, banquet halls, conference rooms and restaurants.

Six kilometers from Pomun Lake near Pulguk-sa is the Kolon Hotel in full operation with 240 air-conditioned and centrally heated rooms. (see hotel listing for further information and ad pages).

Part of the Pomun Lake community will be developed into private villas, condominiums and apartments for residents and individual investors interested in a vacation home in the lake resort vicinity. A hotel school was established in 1976 by KNTC to properly train hotel employees for the projected sixteen hotels to be built in the resort. It is expected that by 1987 the total sixteen deluxe hotels will be completed along the lake shores. Connected to the Hotel School is the Pomun Lake Hotel which serves as a practice hotel for students.

TOKDONG LAKE

Above Pomun Lake is a larger 490 acre artificial lake developed for water skiing and fishing. The water from Tokdong Lake provides a reserve supply to Pomun Lake during drought periods. The hillsides will remain wooded with picturesque natural beauty. Roads lead from Pomun Lake to scenic points around Tokdong Lake.

Index

Seoul International Tourist Publishing Co. is proud to present other books on Korea.

KOREA GUIDE
Size: 15cm x 21cm, 404 pages,
Published: 1983 (fourth edition)
Price: US16.00

Korea Guide is an exciting pictorial guide book to scenic and cultural Korea. The legacy of traditional Korea is vividly portrayed. Over 290 color prints attractively illustrate the life of the Korean people. Compact and easy to carry, this handy guide book will be a newcomer's constant companion.

PALACES OF SEOUL
Size: 15cm x 21cm, 218 pages
Published: 1982 (second edition)
Price: U$10.00

Palaces of Seoul portrays the existing palaces within Seoul. It was within these palace walls that history was made during the 500 years of Yi Dynasty rule. Over 120 color prints were used. Palaces' maps and index will help the newcomers explore the palaces by themselves.

ART TREASURES OF SEOUL
Size: 23cm x 27.5cm, 172 pages
Published: 1982 (second edition)
Price: U$20.00

This book is unique in its correlating emphasis on the classic as well as the folk art. In viewing Korea's vast repository it is clear that an indigenous art style did develop which is down to earth, humorous, animated, satirical as well as sentimental and recurrently original over the years.

THROUGH GATES OF SEOUL, VOL. I & II
Size: 19.5cm x 26.5cm, 800 pages
Published: 1977 (second edition)
Price: U$22.00

Beautifully bound with gold seal on the cover and golden phoenix on the jacket, this two volume set explore history, art and religion around Seoul. With 210 color and B&W pictures, numerous maps and charts with index, these 2 volumes will be a treasure book for the study of Korean history.

KOREAN WITH CHINESE CHARACTERS
Korean used with Chinese characters is a uniquely illustrated book of derivation and origin of Chinese characters as they relate to the Korean language.

KOREAN TRADITIONS
Size: 26cm x 25cm, 115 pages
Published: 1983 (second edition)
Price: U$14.00

The pictorial classic, of black and white photographs with stark contrasts, superbly portray the sample collection of 84 monochromatic prints taken by the author over the last ten years.

KOREAN CHESTS
Size: 15cm x 21cm, 94 pages
Published: 1980 (third edition)
Price: U$5.00

The various styles of Korean chests are well illustrated with photos. For those interested in Korean antique furniture, its authenticity and function, this book is a valuable asset.

KOREAN FOLKS STORIES FOR CHILDREN
— **Blindman's Daughter**
— **Two Brothers and Their Magic Gourds**
— **Herdboy and Weaver**
— **Korean Cinderella**
— **Woodcutter and Nymph**
Size: 19cm x 26.5cm, 32 pages
Published: 1981
Price: U$5.00 each

Though in the past many Korean folk stories have been written on an adult level, this is the first English series of Korean folk stories written for children to read and enjoy. Each page is beautifully illustrated with pictorials that render a true image of "Old Korea" and its cultural past. Costumes are faithfully reproduced for children's pleasure and understanding of Korea's heritage.

COLORING BOOK
Size: 26cm x 34cm, 42 pages
Published: 1983
Price: U$3.50

This is a 42 pages coloring book for children which portrays various aspects of Korean culture and tradition through the eyes of children.